PORTABLE C
SOFTWARE

Mark R. Horton

AT&T Bell Laboratories
Columbus, Ohio

PRENTICE HALL
Englewood Cliffs, New Jersey 07632

Library of Congress Cataloging-in-Publication Data

Horton, Mark.
    Portable C software / Mark Horton.
        p.   cm.
    Includes bibliographical references.
    ISBN 0-13-868050-7
    1. C (Computer program language) 2. Software compatibility.
    I. Title.
    QA76.73.C15H67 1990
    005.13'3--dc20   89-25578
                                                               CIP

Editorial/production supervision: **Brendan M. Stewart**
Cover design: **Lundgren Graphics Ltd.**
Cover photo: **Slide Graphics of New England**
Manufacturing buyer: **Ray Sintel**

© 1990 by AT&T Bell Laboratories

 Published by Prentice-Hall, Inc.
A Division of Simon & Schuster
Englewood Cliffs, NJ 07632

Printed in the United States of America
10 9 8 7 6 5 4 3 2

ISBN 0-13-868050-7

Prentice-Hall International (UK) Limited, *London*
Prentice-Hall of Australia Pty. Limited, *Sydney*
Prentice-Hall Canada Inc., *Toronto*
Prentice-Hall Hispanoamericana, S.A., *Mexico*
Prentice-Hall of India Private Limited, *New Delhi*
Prentice-Hall of Japan, Inc., *Tokyo*
Simon & Schuster Asia Pte. Ltd., *Singapore*
Editora Prentice-Hall do Brasil, Ltda., *Rio de Janeiro*

CONTENTS

PREFACE

The C language has become one of the most popular programming languages in use today. Many programs are written in C for the UNIX system, or for the MS DOS system, using only the distributed manuals as a guide.

I've come across an amazing variety of nonportable software. Often the software's author had no idea that the program wasn't portable, or even that portability was an issue. It's quite common, for example, to see a useful program posted to Usenet's `comp.sources.unix` newsgroup claimed to run "on the UNIX system." Someone else tries to compile it and finds out it doesn't work on their system. I have seen many statements along the lines of "This program is junk, because I tried to compile it and it said `getopt` was undefined." What has really happened is that the softwae's author was on UNIX System V, and the user has a Berkeley UNIX system with slightly different C libraries. There are just as many problems going in the other direction; for example, a program tries to call `select` and finds it undefined on System V.

The real cause of the problem is that the programmers are unaware that there are different versions of UNIX systems. Even if they are aware of different versions, they have no way to tell which features are present in every version and which features are specific to the system they have. The typical user's manual describes all features on an equal basis; unportable system extensions like Berkeley's symbolic links, or System V's `a641`, are documented exactly the same as portable features like `fopen`. Users have no way to tell whether they are using an unportable feature, so they assume everything is portable.

In recent years, it has become apparent that software written in C need not be confined to UNIX systems. A good deal of software written originally for the UNIX system has been ported to machines running the MS DOS system, and many C libraries for other machines have become complete enough to support many programs. I have written programs that ran on several operating systems. It's really not hard to design a program to be this portable.

It's much harder, on the other hand, to port a program that was written specifically for one machine, especially if it's badly written code with many hardware assumptions and bugs that were undetected on the original machine. (Programs that expect NULL pointers to point at a location containing a zero are quite common, and tend to work perfectly on some systems that put a zero in location zero. These programs abort on other systems.)

This book will make programmers aware of exactly which features are and are not portable. They can use this information when deciding which features to use. Sometimes a nonportable feature can be easily replaced with a portable one. Sometimes the nonportable feature can be used conditionally only if it is present. Sometimes the program can choose one of several possible ways to do the same thing, based on which one is supported. Sometimes the feature is absolutely required for the program, or the cost would be to great to duplicate the feature; in these cases the feature must be used, but the program can still be written modularly to allow a similar feature to be used at a later date.

This book addresses portability of programs written in the C language. This is not the same thing as portability of programs written for the UNIX system, although there is considerable overlap. I view the various standards as layers of an onion; the most general ''least common denominator'' standard is ANSI standard C, with POSIX (the IEEE P1003.1 Portable Operating System Interface Standard) being specific to UNIX and UNIX-like systems, and the SVID being specific to System V. (Reality is that ANSI C and POSIX will take years to catch on, and K&R C, UNIX System V, and 4.2BSD are more likely to be found as system bases in the meantime.)

The book will be useful to those concerned about portability within System V implementations, and to those writing portable code for POSIX systems, as well as those writing very portable code that runs on the UNIX system, MS DOS system, and other operating systems.

The emphasis is on avoiding duplication of development effort through source code portability. Issues such as binary machine language compatibility, documentation, and the format of binary files are usually less important, and are not addressed here.

This book concentrates on language features, rather than on specific versions of the UNIX system or C compilers. Many examples are taken from the V7, 4.2BSD, System V releases 2 and 3 UNIX systems, as well as Microsoft C and Lattice C for MS DOS. While future releases will add new features and blur the distinctions between the systems (System V release 4, for example, adds the Berkeley symbolic link feature) the intent is to keep the book from becoming dated by concentrating on the features, not the systems.

This book is intended both for professional programmers and for upper-division or graduate students to use as a textbook or supplementary text. It it not an introductory programming or introductory C language book; it assumes the reader already knows how to program in C. One semester of C programming may be sufficient background. More experienced programmers will find the book even more useful.

Several chapters of this book highlight issues about the design process, to ensure that a program can be written portably. The porting of existing, less portable programs is addressed. Many common problems are discussed, with different solutions and their advantages and disadvantages considered.

Each feature of the C environment is addressed, and its portability is rated. Widely implemented functions from the C library are discussed. System calls are also rated. External variables and macros are covered. User commands are discussed from the point of view of the C programmer, who must make use of compilation tools, makefiles, and shell scripts to compile and install each application, and may call commands from inside the C program.

This book is divided into four parts. Part I consists of introductory chapters. Part II contains four chapters giving advice about the correct way to write portable software, ''what to do.'' Part III is made up of four chapters describing many of the more common mistakes, ''what not to do.''

Part IV is a detailed reference examining several aspects of the C environment, and evaluating their portability. Chapter 11 lists the most widely available subroutines available in C libraries (traditionally, Section 3 of the UNIX system manual), rating their portability, describing the situations when each subroutine might or might not be available, and making suggestions about dealing with its absence. Chapter 12 examines operating system calls (traditionally, Section 2) in the same way. Chapter 13 covers header include files. Chapter 14 covers predefined variables in the C library. Chapter 15 rates UNIX system shell commands.

A number of appendices are also provided. The ANSI C standard lists a large number of potential portability problems, and their list is described and explained in Appendix A. Appendices B and C describe POSIX. and the AT&T System V Interface Definition (SVID), respectively. Appendices D ane E give advice for porting to MS DOS systems and 32-bit home computers such as the Apple Macintosh, Commodore Amiga, and Atari ST. Appendix F lists the source code for the public domain AT&T getopt function, so that programmers can feel free to incorporate its user interface into their applications without worrying about whether their system supports getopt. Appendix G is a table of functions, showing which of several representative systems support each function, and therefore how portable the function is. Appendix H is a similar table for shell commands.

I would like to thank the many people who have helped make this book a reality. Andy Duff encouraged me to go ahead with the original idea. The reviewers and editors have given me valuable feedback, although many of them have remained anonymous. I would especially like to thank John Blair, Clayton Elwell, Nancy Firestone, Chris Fox, Jeff Furrow, Steve Johnson, David Korn, Dwight Marshall, Elizabeth Marshburn, P. J. McCormac, J. Reilly, Dennis Ritchie, Clayton Rose, Eric Rosenthal, Chris Seiwald, Gary Sitzmann, Steve Sommars, Henry Spencer, Brendan Stewart, John Wait, J. Whiteside, and Thomas Williams.

PART I
INTRODUCTION

CHAPTER 1: **WHY WRITE PORTABLE SOFTWARE?**

You will soon embark upon an enormous task. You must develop a program with product-quality code. The initial target machine has been selected, based on careful market studies. Getting the product running on the target machine is the top priority right now, and a lot of work will go into the finished system. But there are long-term plans to support the product on other systems. It would be nice to be able to get the program running on another machine with little effort. If the program is written portably in the first place, this work can be easily done with little extra development work on the initial system.

As with any software development effort, there is a huge amount of work to be done. It may take one or two years to develop. You don't know yet what processors will be available when the product is sent to the users. There are many different computer systems available, each with many users that represent potential customers. Each of these has very different hardware. This hardware is controlled by different operating systems. Some run the MS DOS system. Some run UNIX System V. Some run other AT&T releases of the UNIX system. Still others run operating systems derived from an AT&T UNIX system release, such as Berkeley's 4.2BSD.

In the future, the situation may be entirely different. New, bigger, and better machines will be available for less money. There may be customers who want the product ported to their existing hardware and are willing to pay a premium price for it. Processors difficult to imagine today may be available at an attractive price. The latest versions of popular operating systems may be very different from today's versions.

If you write code that assumes one particular processor running one specific release of the UNIX system, you may find yourself in five years with a large body of software that only runs on such a processor. The computing field moves very rapidly. Five years is a reasonable lifetime for a product, and the most successful programs are around much longer. Even though vendors make strong efforts to ensure that each release is upward compatible with the previous release, the environment can change considerably over a program's lifetime. Even if the older environment is still supported 5 or 10 years later, new features will almost certainly be available that users will want with their programs.

Suppose your project had made a commitment years ago to a locally enhanced derivative of an old release of the UNIX system and the 16-bit processor on which it ran. A few years later, you might have been struggling to port your code to a distributed environment of 32-bit processors running a later UNIX system release. The target system hardware and software would be obsolete in a few years. Another upgrade would be years off, because the pain of the port would be remembered.

A much smarter alternative would be to design your products to be portable in the first place. By expending a small amount of effort now, you can save yourself and your successors a lot of future work.

Portable code is also reusable code. Reusable code is valuable code. When a program is first written, the author usually has a particular combination of hardware, software, application, and user in mind. In a year or two, you may find a customer with a similar application requiring changes only to the user interface, or only to the hardware. Your code can be easily adapted if you avoid making unnecessary assumptions.

If you ensure that your program is portable while in the early stages of development, it is usually easier than a large-scale port at a later date. While the program is first being developed, it is fresh in your mind, and hence easier to change. Six months later, you will have forgotten the details of some coding trick, or why you made a particular decision. Sometimes even well-written comments are not enough to explain to you why a particular section of code is written in a way that may look strange.

It is important to do a port early in the development process to ensure that you won't make unportable assumptions that pervade the rest of your program. When you do your first port, you'll probably discover something you did that you thought was portable, but that turns out to be specific to one system. If you find this out early, you won't perpetuate unportable code and programming practices.

What Is Portability?

Some people believe that a portable program is one that can be carried to a new environment, compiled, and run, with no changes at all. More pragmatic is a definition from Steve Johnson. *A program is portable to the extent that it can be easily moved to a new computing environment with much less effort than would be required to write it afresh.* [1]

There are degrees of portability. A totally portable C program is one that plugs into any C environment and works without any changes. Such programs tend to be small. Many filters fit into this category. (A filter is a program that copies from standard input to standard output, making some transformation. For example, a program that translates from upper-case to lower-case could be a filter.)

Some programs are unportable. A program written entirely in assembly language is generally not useful on a different machine. A program with some machine-specific assumption scattered throughout the code is extremely unportable. An example might be a program containing many calls to `printf` with device-specific command sequences like

```
printf("\033EYear\033H (Amount");
```

These are one terminal vendor's commands to clear the screen, print `Year`, address the cursor to row 0, column 8, and print `Amount`.

---

[1] S. C. Johnson and D. M. Ritchie, Portability of C Programs and the UNIX System, *Bell System Technical Journal*, Vol 57, No. 6, July—August 1978, page 2021. Definition originally from W. S. Brown.

Most programs fall somewhere in between. They may require some work to port, but do not need to be rewritten. A well-written program[2] can be ported by someone other than the original author. The porter should not have to understand more of the program than the part being changed.

Portability can be measured in many ways. One way is the amount of work necessary to port the program to a new environment. Another is the number of systems on which the program will run unchanged. (This may mean the number of systems to which the program has already been ported.) A third is the amount of system-specific code present in the program, for example, the number of #ifdefs (see Section 3.3); portable programs should require fewer sections of conditionally compiled code, and these sections should be concentrated in one source file.

A portable program should have only one master copy. If separate copies are maintained for each system, improvements to one copy are not automatically made to the other copies. If another person or group ports the program to another environment, or makes other enhancements, it is often useful if the original author (or other owner of the master copy) can "buy them back" by incorporating them into the master copy. This ensures that future versions of the program will port easily to the other environment.

A portable program is ported frequently. Before any major release of source code, the program is carried to each alternate environment and tested. Often this process turns up new bugs or unportable constructions that have been recently introduced.

Overall, a portable program is one that requires very little effort to keep running in different environments. The more effort necessary to keep it running on different systems, or the more effort spent by others because the program has not been ported to another environment, the less portable the program.

But Won't It Be a Lot of Work?

Perhaps you fear that writing the code portably will result in a lot of extra work. The extra effort, however, is usually quite small. Indeed, if it makes it too hard for you to write a program portably, it may not be worth it. Usually, no superhuman efforts are necessary; a little awareness of the issues, combined with experience and common sense, will do nicely. Even when significant extra effort is needed, it is often worthwhile in order to keep one version of the program that will run in different environments.

The most important part of portable programming is knowing which features can be safely used and which ones are specific to the particular implementation you are using. Unfortunately, most programmer's manuals give no clue; they imply that their implementation is the only one in the world, and that all features are equally portable.

A few manuals will include a footnote that indicates when a function is experimental, obsolete, or otherwise not recommended. Very few will tell you which features are their

---

[2] A *well-written program* is one that is modular, portable, easily modified, readable, efficient, meets the original requirements, and that the users are happy with.

own inventions. This makes it very difficult to write portable software using just one manual.

How Portable is Portable?

There are different degrees of portability. One program might run only on UNIX System V release 3 on a 3B2 processor. Another program might run on any UNIX System V on any 3B processor. Another might run on several versions of the UNIX system. A very portable program might run on the UNIX, MS DOS, and QNX systems. An extremely portable program might also run on systems with significantly different user-interface models, such as the Apple Macintosh, IBM OS/MVS, and Honeywell GCOS. (See Chapter 11 for definitions of degrees of portability used here.)

There are different sorts of features provided by operating systems. One system might support a windowing environment and a mouse. Another might provide only an ASCII terminal. A third might only have a half-duplex terminal or a card reader and printer. A mouse-oriented graphics application doesn't make sense on a card reader and printer.

This book uses certain precise terms to define degrees of portability. An *unportable* feature is specific to one particular system. A feature may be *portable among UNIX systems*, meaning that it is generally present on UNIX systems, but should not be expected to work on other operating systems. A *fairly portable* feature is present on many systems, but is missing from many others. A *very portable* feature is present on most, but not all, C implementations. An *extremely portable* feature is supported essentially everywhere.

Rating portability of programs is different than rating portability of features used by programs. One measure of a program's portability is the amount of effort needed to port it to another system. This will depend on the number and degree of unportable and somewhat portable features it uses. Another measure is more "turnkey" in nature: a program is as portable as the least portable feature it depends on without modifications to the source code.

A portable program should have only one master copy. If separate copies are maintained for each system, improvements to one copy are not automatically made to the other copies. If another person or group ports the program to another environment, or makes other enhancements, it is often useful if they are "bought back" by incorporating them into the master copy. This ensures that future versions of the program will port easily to the other environment.

It's important to decide how portable your application needs to be. Some features, such as a CRT screen or a network, may be absolutely required. Other features, such as a mouse or a special keyboard, may make your application more powerful, but the program is still useful on systems without them. Some decisions must be made about which features are critical; and about which features should be used only if present, and simulated or avoided otherwise.

Some environments, such as 8-bit home computers, may not offer a lot of functionality, but have a huge installed base. This may make it worthwhile to support a version of your program for the environment anyway. A program might make good use of the UNIX system and a large hard disk, but if you can make it run in 256K of RAM on a floppy-disk-based MS DOS environment, you've opened up a large market. A very large base of 8-bit machines exists in homes and schools, but many of these machines have only 48K or less of RAM. There are millions of home computers, but many of them don't even have a floppy disk drive. Some computers may have only a cassette drive, or a cartridge slot.

The proper way to make the decision is not to ask *"How much machine is needed to run my application?"* Instead, ask yourself, *"Can a stripped down version of my application run on this machine?"*

In the early days of screen oriented editors, it was generally felt that you needed a 9600-bits-per-second (BPS) hardwired connection, and an intelligent terminal with certain keys (such as arrow keys) to make a screen editor useful. Bill Joy, the original author of the UNIX system's `vi` screen editor, found himself with a 300-BPS modem and a "dumb" terminal at home, and wanted to use a screen editor. Rather than giving up, he found a way to make the `vi` editor useful at 300 BPS on such a terminal. The decision made was *given that I'm stuck with 300 BPS, would I rather use a line-oriented editor such as* `ed`, *or a modified* `vi`? Innovative features came from this challenge, such as cursor-motion optimization, repainting only the bottom 8 lines of the screen, and not updating the screen fully until the user gives a command to clean up the display. Within a few months, the `vi` editor was quite usable at 300 BPS on a "dumb" terminal.

By thinking creatively, it is often possible to stretch a program to work in an environment that was never originally thought possible. As a result of such thinking, `vi` is very popular on dialup lines today. Similar thinking made it possible to run `vi` on a printing terminal! Of course, you must temper the decision with other considerations, such as the resources you have for development. But plan to keep your options open in the future.

In order to understand the different versions of C, it's important to understand their history. The language is closely tied to the UNIX system, so some understanding of UNIX system versions is also helpful. Most implementations are derived from or inspired by another implementation. Knowing how these all fit together makes it easier to keep track of which features are in which implementation.

The C language was initially designed in 1972 by Dennis Ritchie. It was inspired by a typeless, interpretive language called B, which in turn came from a systems programming language called BCPL (Basic Combined Programming Language), which itself has been fairly successful.

The first version of C was a high-level system-implementation language. When the UNIX operating system was rewritten from assembly language into C, the new language got its first major use. Many of the features of the C language and libraries are motivated by practical concerns found in the implementation of the UNIX system. As a result, C is far from an ivory tower academic language; it spits on its hands and goes right to work.

The earliest widely used C compiler came with the sixth edition of the UNIX System (V6) distribution for the PDP-11 computer. Many features taken for granted today were not present in V6. These include the concept of system-provided include files in /usr/include, unsigned and long integers, union data types, typedef, structure assignment, void, enum, bit-fields, and standard I/O. The compiler had originally been written as a replacement for the assembler, so it was very lenient about accepting programming constructs that were better suited for assembly language, such as this:

```
/* Example of very unportable code. */
struct {
        char hibyte, char lobyte;
};
int sbuf[3];
char erasechar;
...
gtty(0, sbuf);
erasechar = sbuf[1].hibyte;
```

The `gtty` system call is the same as the V7 `TIOCGETP ioctl`, and similar to the System V `TCGETA ioctl`. It is defined to return the following structure:

```
struct sgttyb {
        char    sg_ispeed;
        char    sg_ospeed;
        char    sg_erase;
        char    sg_kill;
        short   sg_flags;
};
```

This program sample asks the operating system for the user's current erase character, and is highly unportable. Note the assumptions that an `int` is 2 bytes long, that the structure passed to `gtty` is 3 integers long, and that the unnamed structure with two members can be used to get the high and low bytes of an arbitrary integer.

While C has been enhanced considerably from the earliest replacements for the assembler, much of the flavor of the language remains. C provides high-level control and data structures, making it easier to write software without so many of the usual coding errors found in languages that depend heavily on **goto** constructions, yet it doesn't get in the way if you really want to get at the hardware. C has evolved to give the programmer considerable help in catching errors, yet the code generated by the compiler remains nearly as good as the assembly code it replaced. (If the generated code were poor, the UNIX system could not have been rewritten in C.)

The philosophy of C is simple: a source program may be compiled only once, but the object code may be run thousands or millions of times. C gives the programmer some help at compile time, but at run time, anything that might cause overhead is avoided if at all possible. A type mismatch will be caught quickly by the compiler, where possible, but an array subscript overrun is usually not checked. (A few C implementations do make such run time checks.)

For many years, C was the only UNIX system programming language, and was not used anywhere else. Other languages have traditionally not been as well supported in the UNIX system environment, so most applications for the UNIX system are also written in C. As a result, support was required for application-level code. Tools like `lint`, which examines a program and points out possible portability problems, and `sdb`, a symbolic debugger that can match source code with generated code, make it easier to debug C applications on the UNIX system.

The change from V6 C to V7 C was a major step in the evolution of the language. In 1978, the UNIX system was ported to two other systems, the Interdata 8/32 and Digital's new 32-bit machine, the VAX 11/780. Steve Johnson wrote a portable C compiler, that was used for systems other than the PDP-11 in the mid-1970s. The presence of a second compiler helped establish the language definition. The V7 dialect of C was far less dependent on the underlying hardware and made equally good sense on both 16- and 32-bit processors. A flood of UNIX system ports appeared for inexpensive machines based on chips such as the Zilog Z8000 and Motorola 68000. The V6 dialect can be safely ignored, but is discussed in this book to give a more complete historical picture.

The UNIX system community gained experience porting Johnson's compiler and began to consider C as an implementation language in other environments. Compilers for ports of the UNIX system to the Intel 8086 were already available, and these compilers could also generate code for other 8086 operating systems, such as the MS DOS and CPM/86 systems. C turned out to be an excellent implementation language for other operating systems, even though it grew up on the UNIX system. Even some of the assumptions specific to the UNIX system in the C library (such as the `system` and `stat` functions) turned out to be possible to emulate on other operating systems.

The C Programming Language, by Brian Kernighan and Dennis Ritchie (K&R), was published in 1978. (This book was updated in 1988 to reflect the new ANSI C standard. References herein to K&R refer to the 1978 version.) This book, and the original Ritchie compiler, served as the definition of the C language until 1987, when ANSI C started to appear in products. The C language grew somewhat after K&R was released. Since V7 was distributed shortly after K&R, four features were present in V7 C that were not in K&R: enumerated types, structure assignment, structures passed by value as function parameters, and structures returned by value as function results.

In the years following the release of V7, only a few features were added to the language. These include the `void` type, for subroutines that do not return a value; unique structure names, i.e., structure members are associated with their containing structure; and the flexnames extension, ensuring that variables with names longer than seven or eight characters would be unique within the program, even when all characters are considered.

The C language is built around a byte-oriented architecture. Copying a section of memory is done by figuring out the size, in bytes, of the memory, and copying the bytes. This doesn't work well on machines that pack five characters of 7 bits each into a 36-bit word, leaving 1 bit unused (and hence uncopied). (There have been successful implementations for 36-bit processors packing four 9-bit characters into each word, so it is unwise to assume that bytes have exactly 8 bits.) Fortunately, the microprocessor world adopted the 8-bit byte as a de-facto standard at about the same time the C language caught on, and new computers have generally been designed to be byte-oriented. This has permitted C to become a very popular implementation language on most microcomputers.

C compilers have been written for some very different environments, such as word-oriented machines. Implementations on word-oriented machines sometimes stretch the language. For example, a character pointer must reference part of a word, so it may be larger than an integer pointer. This is allowed by the language, but many unportable programs exist with assumptions about pointer sizes built into them.

In recent years, C has become popular as an implementation language for many microcomputer operating systems. C has become the preferred software implementation language for MS DOS systems. Many new operating systems have been written in C for portability. C compilers exist for most widely used 16- and 32-bit microprocessors.

Subsets exist for 8-bit processors, although these machines are so limited that features such as bit-fields and floating-point numbers are often left out.

Support for the C language has become so widespread that it is now possible to write a program in C that can be easily ported to almost any microcomputer system. It was once true that the most portable way to write a program was to use FORTRAN 66, and this approach was used for many popular packages. Unfortunately, such applications must work even in an environment using a card reader and line printer for input and output, and this model limits their functionality.

Interactive, screen-oriented applications were usually written in an unportable local language. Today, the language of choice for a portable application is almost certainly C. Other good languages exist, such as Pascal, Modula II, and PL/1. These languages have their own advantages and useful features, but are not as widely implemented and supported as C.

In the mid-1980s, the ANSI X3J11 committee developed an ANSI standard for the C language and library. This standard added several major new features, and made official many of the enhancements made to the UNIX system compilers since the K&R C book was written in 1978. Until then, K&R was taken as the official definition of C by authors of C compilers for other systems, and some features taken for granted on the UNIX system were not supported. The evolution from V7 C to ANSI C is as important a step as the move from V6 to V7. By 1989, ANSI C was beginning to be considered the official definition of the C language on MS DOS systems. It took a few years longer to become widespread on UNIX systems.

In the mid-1980s, an enhanced dialect of the C language, called C++, was developed. While retaining most of the underlying flavor of C, C++ adds the concept of *classes* originally found in the SIMULA language. Classes are an extension of structures, allowing object-oriented programming by sending messages to structures, attaching functions to them, and protecting their contents from unstructured external access. C++ is not entirely upward compatible with K&R C. Both languages have prospered separately.

2.1 UNIX System History

The following figure shows some of the most influential versions of the UNIX system and their heritage. Five columns show the organizations that created each release. The AT&T USG (UNIX Support Group) released the internal systems, such as UNIX 3.0. The USG was later renamed the USDL (UNIX System Development Laboratory), and released external versions as shown in the leftmost column, such as System V. (The USDL has since been renamed a number of times, and continues to develop System V releases.)

Until 1979, the UNIX system came from AT&T Bell Laboratories Research in Murray Hill, NJ. The latest release from Thompson and Ritchie was considered the "official version." The sixth and seventh editions, commonly called V6 and V7, respectively, were widely used outside Bell Labs. V6 was released in 1976 and supported the DEC PDP-11 only. V7 came out in 1978 for the PDP-11, and parallel development for other

The UNIX System Family Tree

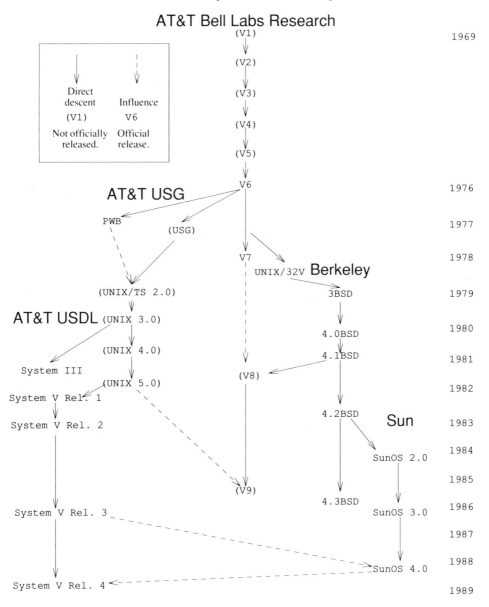

machines had helped the system grow to a point where it no longer contained many assumptions about the PDP-11 architecture.

One of the most exciting machines available in 1978 was the VAX 11/780, which had paging hardware, a 32-bit addressing space, and a modest price tag. Universities wanted to use the VAX product, and to use the UNIX system on it. The UNIX/32V system was essentially V7 for the VAX architecture. (It branched off shortly before V7 was frozen, resulting in a few minor differences. The biggest difference was that the `strcmpn`, `strcpyn`, and `strcatn` subroutines were renamed `strncmp`, `strncpy`, and `strncat`, respectively, in V7 after 32V branched off, but shortly before V7 was released. 32V supported both names, but the 32V documentation mentioned only the older names.) Unfortunately, the 32V release was, like all versions of the UNIX system at the time, a swapping operating system.

Ozalp Babaoglu and Bill Joy at the University of California at Berkeley added paging in 1979 as a research project and along with many others made many enhancements to the system. The academic community was interested in this version of the UNIX system, and Berkeley made it available as the Third Berkeley Software Distribution (3BSD.) (The two previous distributions had been add-on features for the AT&T PDP-11 UNIX system distributions.) The Berkeley UNIX system gathered a large following in the academic community and attracted support from DARPA (the U. S. Defense Advanced Research Projects Agency) for the ARPANET version of the UNIX system for the VAX architecture. Under DARPA support, Berkeley added many more features, including a user-friendly terminal driver, job control, TCP/IP networking, enhanced mail facilities, and implementations of other programming languages such as Pascal and Lisp.

UNIX system development and support continued within AT&T Bell Laboratories for internal projects. The version used inside AT&T had diverged from the V7/Berkeley branch in 1977. An AT&T group called the UNIX Support Group (USG, later called the UNIX System Development Laboratory, USDL, and then the UNIX Software Organization, USO) was formed to support an internal version of the UNIX system. Another group created the Programmers Workbench (PWB), adding enhancements such as SCCS (Source Code Control System) and RJE (Remote Job Entry); this version was released outside AT&T as PWB 1.0 in 1977. The USG and PWB groups merged their versions into an internal distribution called the UNIX/TS system, version 2.0 (''UNIX/TS 2.0''), in 1979. (The ''TS'' stood for ''timesharing,'' and contrasted with the UNIX/RT system, the ''real time'' version also known as MERT.) The UNIX/TS system was similar to V7, but with the PWB enhancements, and missing certain V7 features.[1]

---

[1] V7 features missing in UNIX/TS 2.0 included `learn`, `dbm`, the `CBREAK` and `TIOCSETN` `ioctl` in the terminal driver, and the `ftime` system call.

The USG released the UNIX system version 3.0 ("UNIX 3.0") for internal use in 1980. 3.0 was similar to 2.0, but with a completely rewritten terminal driver. Provisions were made for compatibility with the 2.0 terminal driver, but since 2.0's driver did not support V7's heavily used CBREAK mode, and since the compatibility calls cleared the popular ECHOE bit, the compatibility mode was not very widely used.

In 1982, AT&T released 3.0 to the world as UNIX System III. Because of constraints on AT&T due to government regulation, releases through System III were shipped outside AT&T up to 18 months after they were in use internally, and AT&T did not offer support. Later releases, starting with UNIX 5.0, became UNIX System V. System V was released simultaneously internally and externally, and had full AT&T support. The internal naming scheme changed when AT&T standardized on the UNIX System V name, so that what would have been 6.0 became System V release 2, both internally and externally.

The researchers at Murray Hill who originated the UNIX system continued to evolve their own version, avoiding much of the complexity demanded by the users of Berkeley's version and System V. Since they wanted a virtual-memory implementation for a 32-bit machine, they started with 4.1BSD and created a separate branch from there. The result was called the Eighth Edition (V8) and was not generally available outside Bell Laboratories. In 1986, V8 was frozen and work toward the V9 system began.

Microsoft developed a version of the UNIX system, called Xenix, for microcomputers. The original Xenix system was based on V7, with enhancements developed at Microsoft, and considerable updating from System III and System V. Xenix is very widely used on 68000-based machines, such as those from Altos and Tandy, and on 80x86 machines, such as the IBM PC and compatibles. In 1987, an agreement between AT&T and Microsoft was reached to merge Xenix and UNIX System V release 3, with the result to be sold under the "UNIX" trademark.

Later that same year, AT&T and Sun Microsystems, a major vendor of 4.2BSD-based UNIX Systems, agreed to merge their systems. AT&T included the major features from Sun's system that were not present in System V, in addition to internally developed features and features that were improvements over both systems, such as POSIX P1003.1 compliance. The resulting merged system became System V release 4 in 1989, and became the core of both AT&T and Sun UNIX products.

In addition, there are many UNIX systems in the marketplace that run derivatives of one of these major versions. The UNIX system is very popular, and is supported by most computer vendors. These derivative UNIX system versions tend to be based on, and compatible with, one or more of the AT&T or Berkeley releases. Often they add some extensions to the C library, or, occasionally, the language itself. Such extensions often help get the job done on a particular system, but can contribute greatly to lack of portability in a program.

The various versions of the UNIX system were all derived from V6, and are all largely upward compatible with V7. This means they all have a large core of features that work on all UNIX systems as well as many other systems. Many of the extensions made since V7, such as flexnames, can be found on most UNIX system implementations as well. Some recent developments, such as networking and bitmapped workstations, are not yet very standardized, and are difficult to use portably.

The proliferation of these versions of the UNIX system in the marketplace began to lead to an image of the UNIX system as a nonstandard entity. Each vendor had to add features to the hardware, software, or price to gain market differentiation from their competitors. In reality, the UNIX system has always offered far more portability among different vendor's systems than other operating systems, but 100% compatibility is not possible due to private enhancements.

Some application developers wrote software for one version of the UNIX system, assuming that whatever ran on their system would run anywhere. They did not realize that there were other versions of the UNIX system. These people were surprised when told that their program, written for ''the UNIX system,'' wouldn't run on a different UNIX system. Had these programmers followed the advice in this book, chances are their programs would have been more portable.

UNIX System Standards

Although the UNIX system was originally thought of as a portable environment (where software written for one system automatically runs on another system running the same environment), divergence between versions tended to cause incompatibilities between systems. This, in turn, caused unportable software to be written. Because of incompatibilities between versions, several UNIX system-related standards have been prepared. As these standards become more widely supported, it will become easier to write portable programs for the UNIX system.

The IEEE P1003.1 (POSIX) standard is derived largely from UNIX System III, and it seems likely that most products advertised as being compatible with the UNIX system will eventually conform to the POSIX specification. P1003.1 was approved in 1988. Systems released in 1989 or later are likely to conform to POSIX P1003.1. Within a few years, it will be safe to assume POSIX compatibility for many operating systems, not just those related to UNIX systems.

Other related standards are the American National Standards Institute's ANSI C standard (ANSI C), the AT&T System V Interface Definition (SVID), and the European X/OPEN portability guide. These standards can be viewed roughly as layers of an onion, as shown in the figure below. K&R C is at the outermost layer, because it includes nearly all systems supporting the C language. ANSI C is next, POSIX is inside that, X/OPEN is next, and the SVID is the most specific standard. Other bodies vying to standardize their version of the UNIX system include UNIX International (standardizing on System V release 4) and the Open Software Foundation (standardizing on IBM's AIX system). An implementation that conforms to the SVID can be viewed as inside the SVID layer, at the

core of the onion. Other implementations may fall somewhere else in or near the onion.
In addition, most standards change over time. It is important to note to which version of
any given standard a particular implementation conforms. For example, some systems
claiming SVID conformance may actually conform to an outdated issue of the SVID.

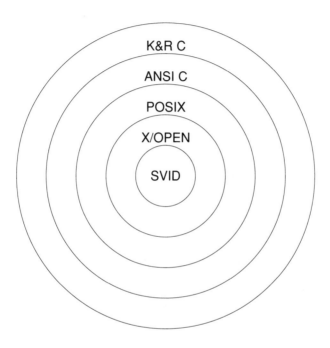

PART II
WRITING PORTABLE SOFTWARE

CHAPTER 3: **HOW TO DESIGN A PORTABLE PROGRAM**

The key to writing portable software is in the initial design. Although this book devotes much space to specific features of the C language and to pitfalls to avoid, portable design should not be confused with avoiding traps. A well-written program is likely to be portable, but a poorly written program is not. Writing portable software and easily maintained software go hand in hand.

It is possible for a poorly written program to be portable if it manages to avoid the use of unportable features or more than the simplest assumptions about the environment. However, if the program is poorly thought out in the first place, chances are that it won't work on more than one system. In this case, when it comes time to port it, significant changes will be needed, and these changes will not be easily made.

A well-written program is easy to change. At the highest level, few assumptions about the environment are made, and those assumptions that are made are fundamental to the nature of the program. The program is modular, with each low-level detail restricted to one module. When porting a program to a new system, chances are that some feature used by the program will have to be used differently. By hiding knowledge of the feature in one place, only one place must be changed to the new system's method.

For example, a program may use color text messages in many places throughout the program. If the program is full of code such as

```
/* print "ERROR" in red at top right. */
panic()
{
        printf("\033[1;71H\033[31mERROR\033[0m");
}
```

it will be very difficult to port the program to an environment that has different conventions for color, or one without color. (Such code is also extremely difficult to read!) Every such line of code must be located and changed to use the new method. Usually, these changes must be made by hand, a very time-consuming process. Once the changes are made, the new program cannot be easily used in the old environment (the #ifdef construction must be overused) and the usual result is that the two versions diverge.

The modular approach hides the details about color usage (and cursor positioning) in one subroutine. This way, in a new environment, only the set_color subroutine must be changed. This example makes the same assumptions as before, but with a modular design. Note that a real program would contain many subroutines such as panic, but only one instance of the support subroutines such as set_color.

21

```
#include "appscreen.h"

/* Print "ERROR" in red at top right. */
panic()
{
      pos_cursor(TOPLINE, COLUMNS-10);
      set_color(C_RED);
      printf("ERROR");
      set_color(C_NORMAL);
}
```

The support subroutines would typically be stored in separate files.

```
/* This is header file in appscreen.h */
#define TOPLINE 0
#define COLUMNS 80

#define C_BLUE 1
#define C_GREEN 2
#define C_CYAN 3
#define C_RED 4
#define C_MAGENTA 5
#define C_YELLOW 6
#define C_WHITE 7

#define C_NORMAL C_WHITE
/* This is source file screen_support.c */

#define ESC 033
#define FG_BASE_COLOR 30

/* Set the current foreground color */
set_color(color)
int color;
{
      printf("%c[%dm", ESC, FG_BASE_COLOR+color);
}

/*
 * Position the cursor to (line,col),
 * with (0,0) at the upper left corner.
 */
pos_cursor(line, col)
int line, col;
{
      printf("%c[%d,%dH", ESC, line+1, col+1);
}
```

3.1 Choosing a Paradigm

When designing a program, you must decide what overall paradigms will be used. That is, decide what models or assumptions exist about the compilation and execution environment. A program may be a filter, copying standard input to standard output. It may run interactively in scroll mode, accepting input from the keyboard and writing text, a line at a time, to the display or printer. It may assume a CRT screen. It may require graphics and a pointing device.

The fewer assumptions made, the more portable a program will be. The most portable C programs are filters, since C implementations generally support standard input and output. A less portable program might require color graphics and a specific pointing device. If your program really requires color graphics, then you should make that assumption and rule out any environment without color graphics. But if your program makes sense in an environment with, say, monochrome graphics, or with only a text-based display, you may be able to run it on a wider variety of systems.

It's important to give some hard thought to just what sort of environment a program really needs to be useful. If the program requires a complex set of disk files as a database, those databases may be required on the software distribution. This usually implies a system with a hard disk. If the program needs to have options specified on the command line, it can only run in environments with a command-line interface; this might rule out icon-based environments like the Macintosh.

This section lists many questions you should ask yourself about your application. They should help you become aware of some of the assumptions you may be taking for granted. For many questions, the best answer is "the program can use the feature if present, but will function in a degraded mode otherwise." Another good answer is "the program makes no use of that feature." If the answer is "the program cannot run without the feature," you've found a potential cause of unportability. In the end, you must decide what the appropriate answers are for your application.

If a program catches on, it is likely that someone will want to port it to an environment the author originally decided against. Even the original author may later reconsider if some computer that was originally rejected or unavailable gains a large installed base. The more care taken to keep assumptions from spreading throughout the entire program, the easier such a port will be.

You should ask yourself, *who is the user of the program?* Is it a secretary? A factory worker? A scientist? A computer guru? Some combination of the above? Different users expect different things of their software. A sophisticated user may want a terse, command-oriented interface that doesn't get in the way. A novice may want a chatty, menu-based interface. Most novices become good with programs they use often, but many users will use a program only once every several months. Some interactive applications may want to support both interface styles.

You should also ask yourself, *what are the performance requirements?* Does it need real-time response? A screen response within a second or two? How much CPU time can it use? Special applications such as communications software and disk utilities may have other performance requirements.

Sometimes performance and portability are in direct conflict. The portable solution will also be the slow solution. Some special hardware feature exists that can make the program run faster, but won't be there on other systems. Making the performance/portability trade-off can be one of the most important decisions to be made.

In many cases, there is a small part of the program that makes most of the performance difference: some inner loop, or some key subroutine that is called hundreds or thousands of times. In such loops, sometimes performance enhancements at the expense of portability are justified.

In the remaining 90% of the program, the performance often will not matter. If an initialization routine is called once, and the portable way takes a tenth of a second, compared to a hundredth for an unportable way, it would seem that the portable method is preferable.

In some cases, there is no choice; the only way to get acceptable performance is to use an unportable feature. (Even so, the portable method can be conditionally compiled in for other configurations.)

The remainder of this section lists some questions you should ask yourself about your application. The answers to these questions will tell you which special features may be required, which you would like to use if available, and which aren't needed at all. Using this information, you can get an idea of the sort of system to which the application can be reasonably ported. Be sure to document your assumptions!

If you find yourself deciding you need a particular feature, make sure you really need it. Requiring the feature may make your program difficult or impossible to port to a large class of machines. If possible, localize code containing unportable assumptions.

Memory Requirements

Does the application always require a large amount of RAM for a work space? Alternatively, can it make use of as much RAM as the system can make available? Can it fit in the 64K limit found on early 16-bit machines? Does it need shared memory? Does it require a special read-only data segment, or more than one data segment? Do the stack or data segments need to grow using some mechanism other than the standard function call mechanism or `malloc` function?

Floating Point

Does the application make heavy use of floating-point operations, or can it run in an environment with interpreted floating point emulation, or one with no floating-point support? Floating-point requirements are often related to performance. What are the performance requirements? If floating point is used moderately, interpreted floating point may suffice. This will open the application to wider markets.

Special Hardware

Does the program need special hardware, such as a special device that controls external equipment, or a speaker for sound, or a speech synthesizer? If it needs special hardware, would the application be useful on a machine without that hardware?

What about special display hardware? Does the application need bitmapped graphics? Does the screen have to be a particular size? (24 by 80 and 25 by 80 are no longer universal industry standards; processors that can display on ordinary TV sets and windowing environments make small screens a real possibility.) Does it require color? How many colors does it need? Do the particular colors matter? Can other forms of highlighting, such as underline, boldface, blinking, or a different font, substitute for color on a monochrome display?

Printing

Does the program require the ability to generate hard copy? If so, does it need graphics, or will text do? Must graphics be in color, or will monochrome do? If the application can display in color, can it produce monochrome hard copy if no color printer is available? What resolution is needed for monochrome graphics? Is 50 dots per inch, typical of low-cost printers, sufficient, or does it require the 300 dots per inch of a laser printer? Does it need a particular feature of a particular printer, or can the program be structured to use any one of several different printers? Laser printers supporting Postscript are nice, but there is a large market of less expensive laser printers and impact printers that your application might also support.

Keyboard

How will the user convey input to the program? Should the input be prepared in advance, on a tape or in a disk file? Must the input and output be interactive, or can the program run unattended using input prepared in advance? Does it require a keyboard with certain special keys, such as arrow keys, general-purpose function keys, or extra keys such as *delete line* or *page down*? Or can the program be run on a keyboard with only the ASCII character set available?

Pointing Device

Does the application require a mouse? Can another sort of pointing device, such as a trackball, joystick, or light pen, be used instead? Must the pointing device have buttons? How many buttons are required? Must button motions up and down be detected separately, or are button clicks sufficient? Must the motion of the pointing device be detected separately, or is knowing the location of the cursor when a button is clicked all that's necessary? If no pointing device is available, can arrow keys be used instead?

Operating System

Does the application require a particular operating system? Does it require features that only some operating systems provide? Are files stored on disk? Are the files text, graphics, or binary data? Does it need a hierarchical file system, or will a flat namespace do? Does it require a hard disk? Does it require removable media, such as a floppy disk? Does the program require separate upper-case and lower-case character sets, or will it work well on operating systems that fold the case on command-line arguments or encourage users to keep their CAPS LOCK key on?

Multitasking

Does the application need a multitasking capability? Must a single program monitor more than one possible source of input, and respond to the first source producing data without becoming hung up waiting for another source? Is a multiuser system required, or is a single user system required? Is communication among different active users at different terminals needed? Can a critical but expensive resource, such as a printer or disk, be shared? Does it need a particular version of the operating system, such as UNIX System V?

Networking

Does the application require access to a network? What features must the network have? What assumptions are made about how other computers are named or addressed? What is assumed about the particular library calls used to communicate with the network? Will the program make sense if it runs on a host not on a network?

Libraries

Is a special subroutine package or library, such as a screen manager or database manager, needed? If so, the program is only as portable as the library it uses. Is the library itself portably written? Do you have access to the source code of the library so you can port it as needed? If you don't have the source, does the vendor intend to make it available for the systems you want to support? If it isn't portably written, does the *interface* between the program and the library make sense in other environments, or does it contain assumptions about the hardware or operating system?

3.2 Information Hiding

Information hiding is a technique where each function is isolated in a single module or subroutine. Modules communicate through well-defined interfaces, usually procedure parameters. Use of global variables is discouraged. This allows implementation details to be hidden away in a few subroutines that really need to know about them. This programming technique is taught in most programming classes, and is very important for writing high-quality code. A few modern programming languages such as Modula, Ada, and C++ have features to *force* the programmer to communicate through defined interfaces and prevent direct access to information internal to another module. C doesn't have features to enforce modular programming, but it does not get in the way of a programmer who wishes to write modular code.

In addition to being good programming practice, modular programming also tends to make programs more portable. The basic idea is that each part of the program should be implemented separately from the other parts. Each part worries about only one task and is (at least in theory) not concerned about how any other part of the program works. Then, if one section of the program turns out to be unportable, or some convention needs to be changed, only that one section must be rewritten. Otherwise, you must hunt throughout the program, looking for places where the old convention was assumed.

Let's look at an example. Suppose we need to determine the user's erase character. (This is the keystroke sent when the user wishes to backspace over a typing mistake.) Many programmers of screen-oriented applications prefer to do erase processing themselves, because they have to get commands without waiting for the return or enter key to be pressed. There are many ways to determine the erase character. Some of these methods are more portable than others.

Although it is possible to use an I/O control (`ioctl`), suitably protected by `#ifdef`, to determine these values, suppose the screen-handling package has already done the appropriate call and has put the results, for internal use, in a global variable called `tty`. This variable is declared in a library header file so that it can be used by macros in the header file. Programmers discover that it is convenient to directly use the field in the global structure:

```
c = getch();
if (c == tty.sg_erase)
        . . .
```

This program fragment is written to use the V7 terminal driver interface. Now, what happens when such an application is ported to System V? The library itself must be ported, but this turns out to be straightforward; only a few changes to the terminal driver are needed in the library itself. These changes include using a `struct termio` for the `tty` variable instead of the V7 `struct sgtty`. Since the `termio` structure has a different structure, there is no `sg_erase` field to use. This means that a programmer, when porting such an application between V7 and System V, must find all such references and change (or `#ifdef`) them.

The problem here was that the *interface* between the library and the application had an operating system dependency in it. When the interface isn't portable, the applications using it can't be. Also, this particular interface was not formally documented, but was instead handed from programmer to programmer as part of the folklore of the package.

One solution to this problem is to add a function to the interface to determine the erase character. The application can then query the package:

```
char erase, erasechar();        /* User's erase character */

    ...
/* Initialize erase at startup */
erase = erasechar();
    ...
c = getch();
if (c == erase)
        ...
```

The implementation of the two routines can use #ifdef, hiding all the system-dependent code in one, easily changed place:

```
erasechar()
{
        char ret;

        ret = '\b'; /* default */
#ifdef SYSV
        ret = tty.c_cc[ERASE];
#endif
#ifdef BSD
        ret = tty.sg_erase;
#endif
        return ret;
}
```

When porting the package to additional operating systems, it's easy to add more cases to the #ifdef chain. For example, on MS DOS systems, the erase character cannot be changed, and the following code is added after the BSD case:

```
#ifdef MSDOS
        ret = '\b';
#endif
```

This segment is now portable. The same operation is done on several different kinds of systems, and it is obvious how to extend the technique for additional systems. However, this does require the identification of the target system, and it will be necessary to modify the code for some ports.

Note that, as a *defensive programming* technique, the value \b (backspace) is returned if none of the known operating system types is defined. While this should never happen, you should never allow an undefined value to be returned by falling out the end of the function.

Another alternative is to create a deliberate syntax error at the end of the function, compiled only if none of the other cases is defined. This draws the programmer's attention to the appropriate code at compile time instead of allowing an obscure error that only appears at run time.

This method is not recommended. While it works well, it produces code that is harder to read, and harder to maintain. The programmer discovering the deliberate error may not know what to make of it.

```
erasechar()
{
#undef OSDEF
#ifdef SYSV
# define OSDEF
        return tty.c_cc[ERASE];
#endif
#ifdef BSD
# define OSDEF
        return tty.sg_erase;
#endif
#ifndef OSDEF
        /* deliberate syntax error */
        Operating_System undefined;
#endif
#undef OSDEF
}
```

We can improve the erase example even further. At some point, we should ask the question: *Why are all these programs doing erase processing in the first place?* What is really desired is to get a line of input from the user, and pass that line back to the calling routine. How the user and the program interact to get the line of input may vary from system to system.[1]

Some systems support extra control characters, for example, 4.2BSD has a "word-delete" character that deletes the last word typed by the user. MS DOS systems have keys such as INSERT and DELETE and arrow keys to be used in line editing. Mouse-based systems may allow pointing with a mouse or menu operations. Why should each application reinvent erase processing, allowing the simple notion of erase to propagate to other systems where other facilities may be appropriate?

A better interface is for the application to provide a routine that just gets one line of input from the user, doing any appropriate editing. A routine such as `getstr` can be provided, which will obey local operating system conventions. The application may provide different implementations for each system to copy local conventions.

On operating systems that allow the system line editing routine to be called from an application, without messing up the rest of the screen, the system routine can be called directly. This ensures that the user interface will be identical to the interface provided by the system, even when the application is run on a subsequent release of the operating system that offers new features.

---

[1] It is fair to ask why the programs don't just call `fgets` and let the terminal driver do all this. The reason is that a screen-oriented program must ensure that the rest of the screen isn't damaged. The screen package must keep track of what's on the screen. Because of the possibility of erase processing involving one or more lines of the screen, additional support from the library or application is usually needed.

3.3 Using the Preprocessor

It's common to use conditional compilation (the `#ifdef` and `#if` constructions) to enable a program to run in more than one environment. It is possible to get into trouble by misusing conditional compilation. As a rule, it is best to use conditional compilation sparingly, avoiding it completely if possible. If you must use it, isolate the uses in separate modules with portable external interfaces.

An extremely portable program won't use conditional compilation at all, and will still run everywhere. Such programs are restricted to only the most portable library functions (those rated ***** in Chapter 11), and assume nothing about their environment. For example, many UNIX system filters, such as `sed` and `tr`, are extremely portable.

Unfortunately, there are severe limits to the functionality possible in an extremely portable program. It is not possible to make use of screen-oriented or graphics-oriented hardware. Many operating system features can't be used. Many recently added features can't be used. Most real programs have to use unportable features.

There are several widely used methods about conditional compilation. The first is a machine-architecture-specific method:

```
#ifdef u3b2
        /* do things the 3B2 way */
#endif
#ifdef vax
        /* do things the vax way */
#endif
```

A second variation is an operating-system-specific method:

```
#ifdef SYSV
        /* do things the System V way */
#endif
#ifdef BSD
        /* do things the Berkeley way */
#endif
```

The third method is feature-specific, using macros defined by the programmer:

```
#ifdef LITTLE_ENDIAN
        /* do things the little endian way */
#else
        /* do things the big endian way */
#endif
```

A fourth method is to key on built-in macros. For example, suppose the application needs to determine whether the user has already pressed a key in order to avoid needlessly redrawing the CRT screen. Some systems provide the `FIONREAD` I/O control, which returns the number of pending unread characters. `FIONREAD` is defined in the system header file with the other I/O control definitions, if the system supports it.

```
        check_typeahead(fd)
        int fd;
        {
        #ifdef FIONREAD
                n = ioctl(fd, FIONREAD, 0);
                if (n > 0) return 1;
                else return 0;
        #else
                /* Guess there must be input waiting */
                return 1;
        #endif
        }
```

This example uses the FIONREAD ioctl to determine if there is input waiting to be read on the file descriptor. If any input is waiting, it returns the value 1. If FIONREAD is not available, the program must make a pessimistic guess that input might be waiting.

Any of these methods can get the job done quickly. The difference is that when it comes time to port the program to another environment, the first two methods will be harder to port. Keys based on machine names, or even on operating system names, become out of date as new systems appear. Each #ifdef must be examined, and often an additional case must be added, or an additional option added to a #if line.

Another problem with machine or operating system names is that some operating systems are hybrids. For example, an operating system might be derived from 4.2BSD, but also contain enhancements to support System V compatibility. A program that must decide at compilation time which variant it has may become confused, especially since some emulations are incomplete. Keying on a machine name can also cause problems. A future release of the operating system might add compatibility for another implementation.

When using conditional compilation keying on feature names, the program can be manually or automatically configured without having to reexamine every case. Sometimes a configuration file must be edited to determine whether to define such macros as LITTLE_ENDIAN. In many cases, the program can key directly from a built-in macro such as FIONREAD and manual configuration can be eliminated. Another possibility is to write a small program that detects the appropriate facets of the environment (byte order, word size, operating system, etc.) and produces the appropriate compile time macros so that your application will compile appropriately without manual configuration.

Code based on a machine name, such as u3b2 or vax, is especially troublesome. The set of machine names is not well standardized, and is growing rapidly. ANSI C forbids such predefined names unless they begin with an underscore, and existing convention does not use underscores. Generally, what is really needed to key on is some property of the hardware or implementation, such as the byte order. If you must key on a machine name, do it only for a machine-specific optimization, such as inline assembly language, or to program around a machine-specific bug. Be sure to provide a portable version in a #else clause.

3.4 Redesigning an Unportable Program

There's no doubt that it's much easier to do it right the first time than to try to generalize a program later. Nonetheless, the real world has many constraints and many surprises, and it's not uncommon to find yourself in a position where you'd really like to offer a version of your program on a system that doesn't meet the program's assumptions.

Suppose a program, such as a text editor, is written for a keyboard and CRT screen. It runs nicely on the UNIX and MS DOS systems. Then you consider a port to the Apple Macintosh, running the standard Macintosh Operating System. The market is large, but programming for a mouse in an event-driven environment is nothing like a keyboard/screen environment. There's more to running on a Macintosh than just making sure the program passes inspection by lint.

If the program contains assumptions that aren't valid, there are three basic approaches: make the program fit the environment, make the environment fit the program, or emulate a standard environment.

Making the program fit the environment basically means rewriting all parts of the program that contain assumptions that don't fit. For example, if there is a main loop getting characters from a keyboard, you might replace it with a main loop getting events and processing them. This approach usually produces the cleanest code, since inappropriate code is rewritten. If the original program is very well written, this may be practical. If the character-based command assumption is scattered throughout the program, however, rewriting may involve too much effort.

A second approach is to find a way to represent the new environment in terms of things the program knows about. This may mean fitting the new features into the paradigm the program uses, for example, encoding mouse motions as sequences of keystrokes. This allows new functionality to be added without major rewriting. In practice, making the environment fit the program is often the most practical approach.

The third approach is to ignore the new features, but to instead emulate a "standard environment." In this case, the "standard environment" may be a CRT screen and a keyboard with no mouse or windows. The necessary steps are taken to provide keyboard input at a low level and to update the screen. This is the sort of environment, for example, that curses provides. (Curses is a screen-management package, and is described further in Chapter 5.) Although this allows a program to run in another system, the resulting application may not be properly integrated into the new environment, and may be dissatisfied.

Another, even more primitive, standard environment is a line-oriented terminal. The user types keystrokes, which the program receives a line at a time, typically with fgets or getchar. Output is printed on standard output, with no escape sequences or control characters other than newline. (Sometimes tab, backspace, and return are also used.) The output scrolls by a line at a time. This kind of environment is the one around which the C language is built, and any C implementation will support at least this much. A program that needs only such a line-oriented environment can be extremely portable.

One type of program that is both highly portable and very useful is the filter. Filters read standard input, modify their input in some way, and produce a modified version on the standard output. A filter written to allow other filters and UNIX pipelines on both standard input and output can be very portable. Filters can range from simple, such as translation from ASCII to EBCDIC, to complex, such as translation from C source code to a particular assembly language.

3.5 Example–Mouse Input

Most programs are structured to be able to deal with certain kinds of things, such as alphanumeric screens and keystrokes from the keyboard. Adding a mouse can be accomplished by arranging for the mouse to transmit characters (representing position changes and key clicks) to the application as though they were typed at the keyboard.

For some mice, mouse motion generates the same keystrokes as arrow keys. Clicking a mouse button is the same as a preselected function key. This seriously limits the usefulness of the mouse as a pointing device because the mouse can only point at whole characters. There is no way to detect when a mouse button is pressed and held. Finally, the program itself must process all the arrow key motions.

Even if your mouse doesn't work this way, you might choose to emulate a mouse that does. Mouse motions can be processed in an interrupt routine or keyboard handler. The mouse driver determines how far the mouse moved since the last known position and sends the corresponding number of arrow keys to the application.

This is a very simple approach that may work adequately for many applications on many types of computer. It does assume that arrow keys make sense, which in turn assumes that the display uses a fixed-width font. On a Macintosh with variable-width fonts, you may have to stretch things a bit to make this work. Either arrange for the application to use a fixed-width font, or somehow compensate for the variable width when generating arrow keys.

A somewhat fancier approach is to turn mouse motions into escape sequences and merge them into the keyboard data stream. For example, if the operating system tells the application, ''the mouse is now at location 150, 400, and buttons 1 and 3 are down,'' this can be encoded as ESC m \1 \026 \3 \020 \5, where the ESC m means that a mouse command follows, the next two bytes encode the number 150 (one times 128 plus 26_8), the next two bytes encode 400 (3 times 128 plus 20_8), and the last byte encodes the buttons (4 for button 1 plus 1 for button 3, if a three button mouse is being used). This can now be passed transparently through the main keyboard command loop (assuming there is a provision for pushing keystrokes into a read-ahead buffer) and treated like any other command.

Chances are there are already commands for the arrow keys and other special keys that send multiple bytes when they are pressed. If you know the sequences (this means the program only works on one particular keyboard), it's easy to add the mouse in as just another special key, one that sends a few extra bytes of information that the command can read. If you are using something like curses to translate escape sequences into single keystroke values, you can generate KEY_MOUSE (a new value you make up) instead of ESC m. (Newer versions of curses have mouse support.)

A variation is to save the mouse values in a set of global variables and have the command look directly at those variables instead of encoding them as keystrokes. If you use globals, be careful of mouse-ahead; it's possible that mouse input will come in faster than the program can deal with it, and it may lose some of the values. Depending on the application, mouse-ahead may or may not matter; if mouse positions are absolute rather than relative, and the routine only has to track the cursor, it can catch up easily. But if it loses button presses, there may be a problem. Fortunately, people can only press a button so fast, and for many applications, they tend to wait for a response before continuing. Expert users often type rapidly, however, and do not wait for a response when performing a common sequence of operations.

In the case of the Macintosh, there is much more to do than simply tracking the mouse. A typical Macintosh program is supposed to be *event-driven*, which means that the command loop looks for events such as keystrokes, mouse input, an interrupt, or the insertion of a floppy disk.

If you can't rewrite the parts of the program that assume keyboard input, you can arrange that the keyboard input routine checks for all kinds of events and encodes events other than keystrokes as escape sequences. A floppy disk insertion, for example, might become ESC f.

An interrupt routine is another story. Most operating systems will handle interrupts and only call a user-provided interrupt routine when you want to handle it yourself. C provides the signal function for this. On the Macintosh, the programmer handles many details such as this. In such an environment, if the application must repeatedly check for interrupts, the code to check can go anywhere, as long as it is called "often enough." The keyboard input routine may be a good place to do this. If the next event is an interrupt, call the appropriate interrupt routine and then go back for another keystroke to return to the caller.

Exercises

Exercise 3-1. Modify the modular error message example to use enumerated types instead of integers for the color values. Which method do you prefer, and why?

Exercise 3-2. Modify the example to use terminfo or termcap to position the cursor.

Exercise 3-3. The examples at the beginning of the chapter set the color to white when finished, no matter what the setting was previously. Make necessary modifications to the modular example to restore it to the old value. How would you make this modification to the unmodular example?

CHAPTER 4: **PORTING EXISTING PROGRAMS**

Most of this book is intended to help you write new code portably. This chapter, however, discusses techniques for dealing with programs that have already been written. It is sometimes useful to evaluate the portability of an existing program. Sometimes an existing program, of unknown portability, must be ported to another environment. In addition to the actual porting work, it is necessary to physically copy the program to the other system. This chapter discusses these topics.

4.1 Portability Testing Techniques

When you have written a program, and you believe it to be fairly portable, what comes next? One possibility is to just assume it's portable and distribute it in source form to users with different environments. No matter how good a programmer you are, chances are fairly good that somebody running your program in a different environment will run into some problem that you didn't encounter. This is why testing is so important.

How much testing should you do? That depends on what your goals are and how much time you have to put into testing. It may also depend on the testing resources you have available; it may be hard to test for portability to System V if your system only supports MS DOS.

When the portability goal is to offer a product in binary form, on one immediate machine with no networking, and to eventually support versions of it on some other systems, some developers feel there is no immediate need for serious testing beyond the primary environment. Sometimes they run `lint` on it (as described below.) This attitude is dangerous. Porting should occur during development. The author still understands the code, and unportable assumptions do not have a chance to become widespread throughout the program.

If you are developing in one environment but the initial market will be in another environment, then you'll want to port it back and forth often. This situation is fairly common: many people develop a program using a UNIX system, since it is so friendly to developers, but sell it for PCs running the MS DOS system, since it represents such a large turnkey market. You'll want to get the program working first on the UNIX system, but try it out on a PC periodically just to keep yourself honest. Eventually, there will be a phase of serious MS DOS development, but you'll want to port it back to the UNIX system to make sure it still works there.

If your intention is to distribute your program in source form to be used in a variety of environments, you need to work harder. It's important to have access to as many

35

representative machines as possible, and to test the program in all of them. Since you'll have to make special changes for many of the systems, you should use the preprocessor to conditionally compile the proper code. (Sometimes it's appropriate to do the test at run time, but this is rarely true in C.)

Write the program initially for the first environment. Create a set of regression tests and use them to test the program. When it works satisfactorily there, copy it over and try it in a different sort of environment. (For example, if it was originally written on System V, a good second system would be 4.3BSD.) After doing the port, copy the new version back and make sure it still runs. If you find new problems in the original setting, fix them so that you have one version that runs on both systems. This version becomes your new master copy, to be kept on your main system. Add to the regression tests as appropriate and carry them along with the program for testing on each system.

This new master copy can then be used as the base for a port to a third system. Choose a third system (possibly different hardware) and do the same thing. When you're done, you should have a version that runs on all three systems, although as a formality you should test it again on the second system.

As each port progresses, your program has become more portable. You'll probably find that after the first one or two ports, additional ports become pretty routine. You may have to modify the makefile, and possibly fix up a configuration header file, but the program itself is likely to compile and run the first time. Sometimes it's useful to keep different versions of the makefile in the master directory so you can copy the proper file into place as the first step in installing the program.

When it comes time to port the program to a completely different operating system, such as from the UNIX system to the Macintosh, you'll probably find you're in for a bit more work. You may discover your assumptions have crept into the program. Even if the program is very portable, the user interface may not be appropriate for the new operating system. It may be necessary to add support for windows, mice, or alternate forms of command-line invocation, such as from a menu.

In general, you'd like to take as much advantage as possible of the special features of the hardware and software and yet keep the program portable. There are no easy answers here; just use your common sense and appropriate #ifdefs.

If you add a wonderful feature that uses something machine-dependent, such as a mouse or a special key, try to also provide a way to get the same feature using an ordinary sequence of keystrokes. Even if it's less convenient to draw a picture with arrow keys than with a mouse, users with no mouse can still draw pictures.

One of the most important tools available on the UNIX system is lint. The lint program not only helps find bugs, but it helps point out potentially unportable code. You should always lint your programs before you distribute them.

To run lint, call it just like you would the C compiler:

```
lint -Ddefines filea.c fileb.c filec.c
```

You can pass it command-line options, such as -D and -I, just like the compiler.

Be sure to lint all your source files together, so `lint` can check for inconsistencies between different modules. (The C compiler, in the interests of efficiency, only looks at the file currently being compiled, so it won't notice if a different file declares a variable or function differently. The linker is also unlikely to notice an inconsistency. ANSI C, with its function prototype feature, offers hope for a solution to this problem.)

One problem with `lint` is that it will complain about *every little detail* it doesn't like about your program. For example, if you haven't been careful about casting your calls to `sprintf` as `(void) sprintf`, `lint` will object that `sprintf` returns a value that you are ignoring. Lint has no way of knowing that it is unlikely that you will care what value `sprintf` returned.

You may find that the number of picky error messages such as this hide the real errors that `lint` finds. If you hunt through the list, ignoring the burst of repeated complaints that don't really indicate a bug, you may find several real problems that `lint` has found. Typical problems include failing to return a value from a function that should be returning one, using an uninitialized automatic variable, or assigning a variable to a value of a different type that might not be the same size on some machines. Lint is a big help in fixing such problems.

Lint also will miss many errors. It will ignore some problems masked by improper use of casts. It does not know about generic functions like `malloc`. It does not know how to check the arguments and formats of functions like `printf`. ANSI C cannot check these sorts of problems either.

In order to avoid having to hunt through a long list every time you want to run `lint`, it's worthwhile to "lint clean" your program. If you "pick off the pieces of lint" from your program, you'll be left with a nice clean program, so that any output from `lint` will indicate a real problem. This makes it practical to run `lint` more often, and your code will tend to be cleaner.

To "lint clean" your program, you need to address each error message much as you would handle errors and warnings from the compiler. Typically, you can add a `(void)` cast in front of functions whose values you wish to ignore, and use some other form of cast when you are mixing types but know what you are doing. (Beware that "knowing what you are doing" may not extend to other processors with different sizes of data types, for example.)

In most cases, you can fix up your program so that `lint` doesn't find anything to complain about; it will silently return another prompt. In some cases, however, you may find that nothing you can do will make `lint` happy. The solution here is a bit drastic, but if you're sure your code is safe, you can use the preprocessor to present a different program to `lint` than it presents to the C compiler. For example, if you have a static variable called `sccsid` in each of several source files, `lint` may complain about the apparent name conflict. This can be solved by typing

```
#ifndef lint
static char *sccsid = "main.c %G%";
#endif
```

In this case, a better solution is to give the variable a unique name in each file:

```
static char *main_sccsid = "main.c %G%";
```

This technique can also be used to provide `lint` with *more* information than the compiler has available. For example, if you call a function that varies depending on a parameter, you can insert an example function so that `lint` will check the arguments:

```
subr(p)
int (*p)();
{
#ifndef lint
        (*p)(1, "string");
#else
        myfunc(1, "string");
#endif
}
```

4.2 Porting Techniques

Porting a program from one system to another is fairly straightforward, as long as the original author didn't make any system-dependent assumptions. Even if some assumptions crept in, often they are easy to fix. Sometimes, however, the program is written in such a way as to make it nearly impossible to port. For example, a program with hundreds of `printf` calls that contain escape sequences for a particular terminal would be very difficult to port to some other terminal. Such a program is badly written, since it could easily have been structured to hide all the terminal-dependent sequences in a few isolated routines.

In some cases, it is impractical to port a program. A program that depends on the graphics capabilities of a particular color monitor, or that fundamentally requires shared memory, isn't going to be very portable. It usually doesn't take very long to find such problems. Solving them can require great creativity, if a solution is even possible.

Once you have the program copied to the target machine, you may have to do some local configuration. If you have a local configuration section to edit in a makefile or a header file, look it over and make any appropriate changes. Once it's configured, try to compile it. Hopefully you've used a makefile, and you can just type ``make''. Otherwise, you'll have to invoke the C compiler directly.

When you run into a problem, take a look at it, and figure out what went wrong. It helps a lot to know the system to which you are porting, or to have a manual handy. This book can serve as a guide to the differences between the source and target system, but as an official definition of what can be expected to work, you will need your target machine's current manual. Copies of standards documents, such as ANSI C, P1003, and the SVID, are also very useful as references.

When you find out what went wrong, there are two possible ways to fix it. One is to change the program to something that will work on the target system. Another action is to modify the program so it will work on *both* systems by replacing unportable code with portable code. If both fixes are possible, make the portable fix, unless there is some significant performance or functionality advantage to using the system-dependent code.

If it is impossible, or undesirable, to use a single portable construct, you can use the preprocessor to insert the appropriate code.

```
#ifdef unix
        /* UNIX system dependent code */
#else
        /* MS DOS system dependent code */
#endif
```

If there are more than two possibilities, use separate ifdefs.

```
#ifdef unix
        /* UNIX system dependent code */
#endif
#ifdef msdos
        /* MS DOS system dependent code */
#endif
#ifdef mac
        /* Macintosh dependent code */
#endif
```

Use built-in symbols, like ''unix'', if possible. If there are no built-in symbols (for example, System V vs. BSD), you must define them in a header file or in the makefile.

Another approach is to emulate a missing feature. For example, if a handy subroutine, such as `strspn`, is provided in System V but not on 4BSD, you can write `strspn` and include it as a subroutine in your program. You can either ifdef the routine so it is only compiled when needed, or always include it. It's probably better to ifdef it, since a shared library might cause a linker conflict, and you might miss out on an assembly-coded version present in the C library. If you have to create a special ifdef just for the routine, however, using ifdef is generally not worth it; always include the routine. The extra effort to edit makefiles every time you port the program is probably more than you'll gain with extra efficiency.

Keep compiling the program and fixing problems until it compiles and links. Then run the program to see if it works. Most problems are usually found at compile time, but sometimes a run time problem will appear. It's also quite common for the program to appear to run at first glance, but to contain a subtle bug. Be sure to test the program thoroughly on the new system. If you have a test suite, run it. If possible, stress test the program on the target machine; more problems may turn up.

4.3   Copying Files

The first step in porting a program is to copy the source to the target machine. (If you are using a cross-compiler, you may need to copy it to the machine containing the cross-compiler. Even if it's the same machine as the master, make a fresh copy in another directory so you can scribble on it without worrying about destroying your original, and so you can diff the two versions to see what you changed. Version control systems such as SCCS make this easy.)

Copying may turn out to be the hardest step of all. Not all machines are on local area networks, nor are floppy disk media always compatible. (In writing this book, I've used MS DOS machines with 3½-inch disks, with 5¼-inch disks, and UNIX machines with only hard disks. Copying between them has been somewhat inconvenient.)

LAN Copy

If you have a local area network (LAN), copying is easy. Just use a remote copy command such as `rcp` or `ftp` and copy the entire directory. For example, if the destination machine is called `target`, type a command such as

```
rsh target mkdir myprog
rcp * target:myprog
```

If your program is complex enough that the source code occupies a directory hierarchy, you may prefer to encapsulate it into a tar or cpio disk image:

```
find . -print | cpio -ocv > /tmp/myprog.cpio
rcp /tmp/myprog.cpio target:/tmp
rsh target "mkdir myprog; \
     cd myprog; \
     cpio -ivcd < /tmp/myprog.cpio; \
     rm /tmp/myprog.cpio"
rm /tmp/myprog.cpio
```

or

```
tar cvf /tmp/myprog.tar .
rcp /tmp/myprog.tar target:/tmp
rsh target "mkdir myprog; \
     cd myprog; \
     tar xvfo /tmp/myprog.tar; \
     rm /tmp/myprog.tar"
rm /tmp/myprog.tar
```

If you have a tightly coupled LAN where everything is working well, a simpler form will do just as well:

```
tar cvf - . | rsh target "mkdir newprog ; cd newprog ; tar xvfo -"
```

An even simpler method is possible. Suppose the current directory is called `newprog`:

```
cd .. ; tar cvf - newprog | target tar xvfo -
```

Other forms are possible. One possibility (which is supposed to work, but some implementations don't work in practice) is

```
rcp -r . target:myprog
```

If you have a remote filesystem linking the source and target machines, it's even easier. You just make a local copy. On 4BSD, you can use

```
mkdir /target/usr/me/myprog
cp -r . /target/usr/me/myprog
```

On System V, you can use

```
mkdir /target/usr/me/myprog
find . -print | cpio -pdm /target/usr/me/myprog
```

UUCP

If your systems are connected by UUCP, it's a little harder, but not much. Package your program into a tar, cpio, or shell archive (shar) image.

The choice of packaging depends on the tools available on the local and target machines; tar is nearly universal; cpio generates smaller images, but is only available on System V, and you must be careful to use the -c option to get a portable image; shar works with any UNIX target but is best suited to flat directories, and requires a nonstandard but simple encoding program presented here:

```
: shar: shell archiver
t=$1
shift
for i
do
        echo r $i
        echo "echo x $i" >> $t
        echo "cat > $i << 'EoF'" >> $t
        cat $i >> $t
        echo EoF >> $t
done
```

This depends on the UNIX shell (and nothing else) on the target machine.

To package using tar, type

```
tar cvf /tmp/myprog.tar .
```

To use cpio, type

```
find . -print | cpio -ocv > /tmp/myprog.cpio
```

To use shar, type

```
shar /tmp/myprog.shar *
```

Once your program is packaged, send it over with uucp.

```
uucp /tmp/myprog.tar target!~/
```

This will (eventually) deposit the program on the target machine in the ~uucp directory (normally, /usr/spool/uucppublic.) You'll get a prompt back after a few seconds, but this just means the file is queued to go to the remote machine. By watching files under /usr/spool/uucp, you can monitor its progress. In general, however, you should plan to go do something else for a few hours and then check ~uucp on the target machine to see if your file is there. (Depending on system load and the size of the file, it may take anywhere from a few minutes to several hours to get the file transferred. If there is a problem with the UUCP configuration, a dialer, or a telephone line, it might never make it, at least until the system administrator can fix the problem.) If it doesn't make it over in a reasonable amount of time, ask your system administrator for help with UUCP.

Once the file shows up on the target machine, cd to your target directory there and extract the directory structure. To extract the tar image, type

```
cd myprog
tar xvfo ~uucp/myprog.tar
rm ~uucp/myprog.tar
```

(If ``~uucp'' doesn't work, you can expand it to ``/usr/spool/uucppublic''.) To extract a cpio image, type

```
cd myprog
cpio -icdv < ~uucp/myprog.cpio
rm ~uucp/myprog.cpio
```

To extract a shell archive image, type

```
cd myprog
sh ~uucp/myprog.shar
rm ~uucp/myprog.shar
```

If you don't have a UUCP connection, but your source and target machines have compatible media, such as 5¼-inch 360K floppy disks or 9-track tapes, you can make an appropriate media image and physically carry it to the target machine. You must first make sure there is compatible software on the source and target machines. For example, if both machines run the UNIX system and have 9-track tape drives capable of writing 1600 BPI tapes, you can use tar or cpio to create a tape image, and carry the tape. Although the names for the tape drives may vary from one UNIX version to another, a typical use on the source machine is

```
tar cvf /dev/rmt8 .
```

with a corresponding use on the object machine

```
tar xvfo /dev/rmt8
```

The equivalent cpio commands would be

```
find . -print | cpio -ocvB . > /dev/rmt8
```

with a corresponding use on the object machine

```
cpio -icvdB < /dev/rmt8
```

UNIX to MS DOS Systems

If your compatible media is an MS DOS formatted floppy-disk drive, it's not much more complicated. Suppose that your source machine is an IBM PC or AT class machine, running Xenix, and the target machine is a PC running DOS. You can use Xenix's doscp command to create the floppy disk. After inserting a formatted floppy disk into the A drive, cd into the source directory, and type

```
doscp * A:
```

When the copy finishes, insert the floppy into the target machine and copy the files onto the local target disk.

```
mkdir myprog
cd myprog
copy a:*.* c:.
```

If the source development machine is a larger UNIX host, and the target is an MS DOS PC, another possibility is to use a PC-class machine capable of running the UNIX system, such as the AT&T 6386, as an intermediate. UUCP the files to the PC, and from there create the MS DOS floppy. If the PC target machine runs both the UNIX and MS DOS systems, it's even easier. UUCP the files to the PC, and copy the files to a location from which they can be accessed from DOS. Using a DOS-under-UNIX emulation, such as Simul-Task, the files can be copied directly. Using the Xenix system, the following commands can be used:

```
tar xvf ~uucp/myprog.tar
dosmkdir C:myprog
doscp * C:myprog
```

Kermit/Xmodem/Crosstalk

If you don't have compatible media, you can usually still copy the files between machines using a serial RS232 port. If the machines are right next to each other, you can connect the ports using a null modem cable. If they are further apart, you can use a pair of modems and a phone call to connect them.

Once the cables are in place, you generally run a terminal emulation program on the smaller system. Crosstalk and Kermit are examples of such programs. This causes the smaller system to act like a terminal connected to the larger system. If modems are involved, you'll have to tell it the phone number of the larger system and have it place the call. Once connected, the larger system should prompt you to log in. You log into it and get a command-level prompt. Move to the directory containing your files, if you're copying from the larger system, or to the directory to contain your files, if you're copying to the larger system. Now you're ready to copy files.

There are two ways to copy files via RS232 and terminal emulation. One method uses a *data-link protocol* such as Kermit or Xmodem. The other method is sometimes called SAP/RAS (send and pray, or receive and swear.) With SAP, you tell the target machine to expect a file to be typed in by hand from the terminal, and tell the source machine to send the file down the wire.

The details of these two steps will vary from system to system. Often, the target machine has a command such as

```
COPY TTY: MYPROG.C
```

to copy from the serial port to the named file. After sending the file, an end-of-file character, such as Control-Z, can be typed. If no copy operation is available, it may be possible to enter a text editor, put the editor into the text input mode, and then send the file.

While this requires no special software on either machine, there is plenty that can go wrong in the transmission. Any noise on the line can cause garbage to appear in the file in place of your program. If the receiving system can't keep up with the sending system, and if flow control isn't working perfectly and agreed to by both sending and receiving systems, large pieces of the file may be missing from the file when it arrives on the target's disk.

Data-link protocols handle these problems. The sending machine sends more than just your file; it also sends some extra information that tells the receiver what the file was supposed to look like. For example, it may send the file a *packet* (a line or so) at a time, each packet being preceded by the length of the packet, and followed by a *checksum* to verify that the packet arrived looking just like it did when it left the sender. The receiver will acknowledge each packet, and if anything goes wrong, the sender will retransmit a packet that didn't arrive properly. These acknowledgments also keep the sender from getting ahead of the receiver, and ensure that all packets are received in order. The result is that the file will arrive intact, even in the presence of a noisy line.

If you have support for a data-link protocol on both machines, by all means use it. If you don't, you have may have little choice but to use SAP or RAS. If you must use an unsafe file transfer method such as SAP, I recommend that you keep the speed down to about 1200 BPS. Most machines can keep up at that speed. Also, be sure to check your files after they arrive to be sure they don't have any garbage in them. Checking their lengths to be sure they are about the same size is a good first step. (Due to differences in newline representations, and possible extra characters at the ends that count in file name lengths, it's not unusual for intact files to have slightly different lengths. For example, a 500 line file may be 500 bytes longer on DOS than on the UNIX system, due to the extra CR character stored at the end of each line.)

CHAPTER 5: **THE USER INTERFACE**

One of the key parts of many programs is the user interface. Some packages are meant to be called by other programs, but most must somehow interact with the user. Since there is such a wide variety of terminal equipment available, with little standardization, it is easy to write a program that only works with a particular kind of terminal, or a with a particular bitmapped screen.

Many partial solutions to the user interface portability problem have been offered. Official standards for text-oriented terminals and graphics have been created. De facto standards for interfaces have affected the marketplace. Software packages that isolate the programmer from hardware dependencies have been created.

This chapter discusses problems that a programmer may run into when making assumptions about particular hardware, and explores ways to avoid becoming too dependent on the hardware.

The first section deals with the different control sequences needed to control different terminals, as well as other terminal-specific properties. The modem section describes the differences among modems. The printer section describes differences among graphics printers. The graphics section considers graphics and bitmapped CRT screens. The next section explores different sorts of pointing devices and their common features, differences, and interfaces. The final section deals with the specific operating system conventions for invoking a program and specifying options to it.

5.1 Terminals

The recent advent of personal computers and workstations has decreased the use of ordinary terminals. It is common to use a PC running a terminal emulator instead of a terminal. Since a PC generally has a standard keyboard and screen, one might wonder if writing a program to work with many different terminals is still worthwhile.

The answer is a resounding *yes*! The character-stream user interface is widespread, and even though direct access to the PC screen is sometimes possible, there are many uses of computers that do not have such direct access. These include the use of modems and terminal-emulation programs to dial into other computers, and the use of networks to remotely run programs on other computers. Even in a PC, the methods used to access the screen are not very standard, and there are severe performance vs. portability trade-offs.

Input/Output Models

There are three commonly used models for interfacing with programs. The first, and most portable, is the *standard input, standard output* model, which treats the input and output as a stream of characters, possibly attached to a file, possibly to a user. Programs that use this model are portable across the entire range of C implementations. Simple filters, such as a program to add line numbers to a file, fit into this class. Programs that take no input and produce a status report on the output are also this portable. Finally, simple, interactive programs, such as the UNIX line editor ed, fit into this category.

Such programs can take input from a keyboard, from a file, from a tape or floppy disk, from the output of another similar program in a pipeline, or even a network connection. They can send output to the screen, a file, a device, another program, a network connection, or the UNIX /dev/null "throw away" device. Although filters are very flexible, only a limited class of applications are suitable for implementation as filters, and they are more often used by experienced users than by novices. The UNIX system makes heavy use of filters, but many other systems, and even applications built on top of the UNIX system, provide their own complete user interface.

Another model assumes that programs are attached to a terminal. The terminal is assumed to have a keyboard and either a screen or a printer. (Often a screen is assumed.) A terminal driver, with the capability of handling or disabling features such as backspace (erase), line delete (kill), echoing, and interrupting on input and output, is often assumed to be present. The terminal can be connected to the program by a serial RS232C port, by a program that makes a personal computer console behave like a terminal, or by a "remote login" network connection, used to log in to one computer over a network.

This class of program also communicates with the program via the standard input and output, but treats these channels as a keyboard and display rather than a file of characters. Properties of these "interactive terminal" applications include prompting, special keys on the keyboard, correction of typing errors by a human user, and possibly output to the display in a "screen-oriented" manner rather than in the "scroll mode." (In the scroll mode, the cursor is normally at the bottom line, and once a line of text has been printed and ended with newline, it scrolls up the screen until it disappears at the top. A screen-oriented program moves the cursor around to update any part of the screen.)

A third class of programs assumes direct hardware access. A screen might be updated by direct writes to memory. A keyboard could be accessed at a low level to detect when keys are depressed or released. A mouse may send its position on the screen directly via a special hardware interface.

The developer of a portable program will recognize that all three situations are popular, and try to write a program that will work in as many different environments as possible. An interactive program that does not need screen-oriented output, such as a line-oriented editor or debugger, can include an option to suppress the prompt, allowing it to be run with standard input redirected from a script file. Facilities for remote access to a workstation exist, allowing another workstation on a network to run a graphics, mouse-oriented application. It is sometimes possible to store graphics output in a file, allowing it to be sent to a printer or to another system. Proper layering of subroutine calls can make it possible to easily port a program between a workstation and a terminal environment, or even for the same program to run in both environments.

Available Features

Until around 1970, most computers were accessed with decks of cards and printed results on line printers. Card reader/printer programs usually used the standard input/output model, and advanced programs accessed magtapes or disk files. Some mainframe systems in use today are built around this "batch job submission" model, even though the available technology is quite different. Some electronic computer-communications networks communicate by punching virtual decks of cards on virtual punches, sending the result over a high-speed communications line, reading it into a virtual card reader, queueing the job for execution, and finally running it. It is possible to accomplish a great deal with this model, although there are penalties in performance, functionality, and conformance to standards.

In the 1960s and early 1970s, the new, innovative "time-sharing" systems were used with printing terminals such as the Teletype model ASR 33. Not only could several users use the same computer at the same time, but this use was interactive. This allowed improved, "user-friendly" interfaces, such as prompting, and made it practical to write computer games. Such programs were usually terminal-oriented, although since there were no CRT screens, the programs were also line-oriented.

In the late 1970s, CRT terminals became widely available. At first they were just used as replacements for printing terminals, operating in a scroll mode. Some special control characters allowed screen-oriented programs to be written. For example, form feed (control L) might clear the screen. This is an adaptation of the printer convention that form feed ejects to the beginning of the next page.

Additional features such as arrow keys, insert/delete line, and dim/bold display made very sophisticated software possible. Forms packages allowed forms to be filled out on the screen. Screen-oriented text editors were found to boost user productivity over line-oriented editors. Screen-oriented games, although usually limited to alphanumerics, were also very popular.

Due to a lack of standardization and a proliferation of terminals with incompatible commands, a typical application ran on only one kind of terminal. This was acceptable for turnkey systems where the terminals were supplied by the system vendor, but universities often had many different kinds of terminals attached to the same computer system. A method of running the same screen-oriented program on different terminals was needed.

In 1981, ANSI standard X3.64 defined a standard set of escape sequences in an effort to eliminate the inconsistency in the marketplace. While nearly all terminals designed since that date conform to this standard, the problem is not completely solved. The once pervasive 24×80 character screen size has become a thing of the past, with 25-line personal computers, 16×40 character displays on ordinary TV sets, and windowing environments using windows with variable sizes.

There is no minimum subset of X3.64 required, and a few widely used implementations are missing features that are supported by nearly every other implementation, such as clear to end of screen. Some applications use extra functionality that is not part of the standard, but is supported by a few terminals, such as a status line, function key programming, screen-labeled keys (SLKs,) and special-purpose keys. Many older terminals, and emulators for them, are still in widespread use. (It's rare for anyone to throw a terminal away if it still works; it's usually just passed along to another user who would otherwise have no terminal.)

There are many approaches for the programmer to deal with this diversity of terminal types. The remainder of this section discusses several different approaches.

5.1.1 Universal Subset

An early approach was to limit the application to the capabilities that all, or nearly all, terminals had in common. The ASCII characters CR, LF, BEL, FF, and BS were commonly implemented, although many very early terminals had no BS capability, and some terminals used an escape sequence rather than a form feed to clear the screen. Simple applications could update the bottom line using these characters, with the use of ordinary characters to replace text, and blanks to clear areas of the line.

This method requires no knowledge of specific terminal capabilities, although it does make the assumption that the user is not on a printing terminal, and that the line speed is fast enough that the user won't mind redrawing an entire line to update a single character. This method was used in early UNIX editors such as hed[1] and ex to create a one-line "open" mode for simple screen editing of single lines, and is used today in the UNIX Korn shell to avoid adding much additional complexity to the shell. This method is best suited to applications that only want to update the bottom line, not to full-screen applications.

This subroutine shows how to position the cursor to any column on the current line, without making any special assumptions about the terminal. It requires that the rest of the program keep track of the current contents of the current line in the array curline.

---

[1] hed was an extended version of the ed editor, similar in concept to ex, but with a simpler implementation.

```
/* MAXCOLS should be at least 80 and probably 256. */
extern char curline[MAXCOLS]; /* Contents of current line */
extern int curcol;            /* Column cursor is in now */

void poscursor(col)
int col;
{
      /* Maybe we're already there - common case. */
      if (col == curcol)
            return;
      /* Output CR if we want to go a long way to the left */
      if (col < curcol / 2) {
            putchar('\r');
            curcol = 0;
      }

      /* Move left if necessary */
      while (col < curcol) {
            putchar('\b');
            curcol--;
      }

      /* Move right if necessary */
      while (col > curcol) {
            putchar(curline[curcol]);
            curcol++;
      }
}
```

5.1.2 Terminal Drivers

A somewhat more powerful method is the concept of a *terminal driver*.[2] The application defines the set of functions it requires from the terminal; for example, a simple screen editor might require *clear screen*, *address cursor*, *set/clear highlighting*, *insert line*, and *delete line*.

The programmer codes the application to call a subroutine for each operation. For each terminal to be supported, a separate subroutine is written for each function. This set of subroutines is packaged into a terminal driver. The program can be compiled with any one driver, resulting in a separate executable program for each terminal type.

Since separate copies of a program consume more disk space and memory than a single copy, a provision was usually made to configure all the drivers into a single executable. The subroutines were given unique names, often by prefixing them with the terminal name, and configured into an array. At run time, the user selected the appropriate

---

[2] This is not to be confused with the part of the operating system that controls character input and output, called the tty driver, or sometimes the terminal driver.

terminal type, and the program called that particular set of subroutines.

For example, consider clearing the screen. Let's assume the sequence \033C is used in our virtual-terminal definition as a *clear-screen* sequence. (The code \033 is the ASCII ESC character, commonly used to begin terminal-control sequences. It is unfortunate that the C language does not support \E directly, as terminfo does.) The application simply sends this sequence, regardless of the actual terminal type.

```
clear_screen()
{
        printf("\033C");
}
```

We assume a low-level routine, called transmit, that will send the given string to the terminal. The transmit routine might call write for a user application. The terminal driver for an ANSI X3.64 terminal might look like this:

```
ansi_clear()
{
        transmit("\033[H\033[J");
}
```

For a Hewlett-Packard terminal, the driver might look slightly different:

```
hp_clear()
{
        transmit("\033E");
}
```

Now we need a mechanism to arrange that the proper version of the clear routine is called when \033C is printed. The exact mechanism will vary; it might involve trapping calls to printf or putchar. It might require a pipe, with a filter reading the standard output from the application.

Let's assume that our application uses a variation on printf, called myprintf, sending all its characters through outchar, so we can trap the output at a low level.

```
outchar(c)
register char c;
{
        static enum {norm, esc} state = norm;
        extern int (*t_clear)();

        switch (state) {
        case norm:
            if (c == ESC)
                    state = esc;
            else
                    transmit(c);
            break;
```

```
        case esc:
                switch (c) {
                case 'C':    /* clear screen */
                        (*t_clear)();
                        state = norm;
                        break;
                default:     /* pass through */
                        transmit(ESC);
                        transmit(c);
                        state = norm;
                        break;
                }
        }
}
```

Now we need to somehow arrange that the function pointer t_clear is properly initialized when the program is started. Normally, there will be several such pointers to be
initialized at the same time.

```
extern int hp_clear();
extern int ansi_clear();

int (*t_clear)();
t_init(termtype)
char *termtype;
{
        if (strcmp(termtype, "hp") == 0) {
                /* Hewlett-Packard terminals */
                t_clear = hp_clear;
                /* etc */
        }
        else if (strcmp(termtype, "ansi") == 0) {
                /* ANSI X3.64 compatible terminals */
                t_clear = ansi_clear;
                /* etc */
        }
        else {
                /* Probably should not just give up. */
                transmit("Unknown terminal type: ");
                transmit(termtype);
                transmit(".\n");
                exit(1);
        }
}
```

Somehow t_init must be called once, when the program starts. One way to do this
is to have the application call it explicitly. A more transparent method is to modify
outchar by adding the following check:

```
static int init_done = 0;
extern char *term;

if (!init_done) {
        term = getenv("TERM");
        if (term == NULL) {
                fprintf(stderr, "No TERM defined\n");
                exit(1);
        }
        t_init(term);
        init_done = 1;
}
```

More complex programs usually also include terminal-dependent operations such as *initialize* to be called at the start (to send any special sequences needed to put the terminal into a screen-oriented mode); *restore* to be called before the program exits (to undo the effects of *initialize*); *output text*, rather than just writing text directly, to take any special properties of the terminal into account; *insert text* to use the terminal's insert mode or insert character function; and *clear to end of line* and *clear to end of screen* to increase performance.

Determining the Terminal Type

The method used to determine the terminal type has also varied over the years. Early programs assumed a particular kind of terminal was being used. Later, they asked the user to specify the terminal type, but it quickly became unwieldy to have to ask the same question every time a program is entered. Some programs used an integer index into an array of terminal types, with the index stored in a disk file such as .term in the user's home directory. Others put a code, to be looked up in a file, in a disk file such as /etc/ttytype, indexed by the terminal port. Some programs use a command-line argument such as −T to set the terminal type, although this usage is currently rare. Some applications try to deduce the terminal type by sending it popular escape sequences asking it to identify itself, then examining any responses from the terminal.

When the environment became a standard part of the UNIX system in V7, the terminal name was, by convention, placed in the environment variable TERM. In cases where a name is used, the driver software must include the terminal name as one of the elements in the configuration table. On other operating systems, some equivalent convention must be made to determine the terminal type. On a PC, very often this will involve an assumption that the program is running on the console screen and keyboard. In some cases, the TERM convention has been found useful for PC software.

5.1.3 Virtual Terminals

The driver approach has been used in many editors and in the tty drivers of several operating systems. When it is placed into the tty driver, the operating system becomes the program with the drivers, and all applications must communicate with the tty driver using some standard control sequences. This approach is called a *virtual terminal.*

When a virtual terminal method is used, it affects all applications running on or through the computer system, not just a single application. In such an environment, portability is not usually a concern, because the implementation is specific to the system. However, applications may use virtual terminals to increase their portability to additional terminals.

The virtual terminal approach is a simple, elegant, and powerful approach. Unfortunately, there are difficulties in handling real terminals.

Terminal drivers and virtual terminals must define a standard set of capabilities. Some terminals may be missing a capability from the standard set. Since the applications assume the capability exists, the driver must emulate the capability using capabilities the terminal does have. For example, if the terminal supports local cursor motions but does not support absolute cursor addressing, the driver can keep track of the cursor position and emulate cursor positioning using local motions.

If the terminal does not have the insert-line capability, but does have a scrolling-region capability, the driver might emulate insert line by setting the scrolling region to the area below the line to be inserted, and then reset the scrolling region. If scrolling regions are also not supported, it may be necessary to keep a copy of the entire screen image in the driver, and redraw the part of the screen below the line in question.

Some terminals have additional capabilities that are not part of the standard set. For example, there may be a capability to configure soft labels on the screen. One way to handle this is to extend the standard set of capabilities. This requires extending all the other drivers, and emulating or ignoring the capability on terminals that do not support it.

Another solution is to handle such extensions outside the scope of the virtual-terminal drivers. For example, if the sequences start with the ESC character, the virtual-terminal driver can be designed so that doubling the ESC will cause a single ESC to be passed through to the terminal. Then the application must be modified to check for the particular terminal, or to use a database such as terminfo. It must also be modified to double the ESC.

A variation is to use nontraditional commands in the virtual-terminal driver. Since terminal commands traditionally begin with ESC, the virtual commands might begin with another control character, such as DLE (Data Link Escape, or Control-P.) No doubling is necessary with this method, but the other considerations apply.

A major problem is the size of the screen. The traditional virtual-terminal implementation makes a 24 × 80 screen part of the standard. All terminals are then assumed to have the standard size. In the 1970s, this was a very reasonable assumption. By the 1980s, many other popular sizes had emerged. The PC class of screens is 25 × 80, which is sometimes passed through to the user as a 25-line screen, or sometimes used to emulate a 24-line screen with a status line. Windowing environments make smaller sizes quite common. Ordinary TV sets usually support only 40 columns.

In order to handle different screen sizes, it is necessary to extend the virtual-terminal concept to make it interactive. The application program must be able to query the operating system to find out the number of rows and columns available.

Existing applications must be modified to make this query, usually at run time. Simply substituting a different number is often not enough, because form layouts are often made for a 24 × 80 screen. Sometimes it is necessary to design the program or the form to work on a smaller screen. Often, the application does not make sense on a small screen, and will be restricted to only work on a full-size terminal or window.

Once the query capability has been added, other queries become useful. Unusual operations that are not part of the base set, such as screen labels, might be supported, and the application can query the operating system about the existence of the capability. Once availability of the capability has been verified, the application can assume a standard interface, and let the driver deal with the terminal-specific details.

Queries are also useful to check for missing standard features. Insert and delete line and character functions can be expensive to emulate on terminals missing these functions, and the application might decide to use an alternate strategy that does not depend on the expensive emulation.

Queries are also useful for other purposes. Finding out the line speed of the terminal (e.g., 300 bits per second, 1200 BPS, 9600 BPS, or the like) can be useful in deciding how much screen updating to do. Repainting a 24 × 80 screen (often half full) can take 30 seconds or more at 300 BPS, but only about one second at 9600 BPS. The UNIX screen editor `vi` only updates an 8-line window at 300 BPS, a 16-line window at 1200 BPS, and uses the full screen at higher speeds to make the editor more responsive in different environments. (9600 BPS may be too slow for some graphics applications, however.) At 2400 BPS or higher, speed concerns can often be ignored by the programmer, since most text operations, other than full-screen repainting, tend to be acceptably fast.,

It is also sometimes useful to be able to query to determine the user's editing characters, such as the *erase* and *kill* characters, in order to do interactive line editing. In the UNIX system, the erase character serves as a backspace, deleting the previous character typed, and the kill character deletes the entire current line. Other operating systems often have similar editing characters, although they do not always use the same ASCII characters.

When designing a virtual-terminal system to run over a network, if queries are to be made, there must be a provision in the network protocol to pass the queries and their responses over the net.

5.1.4 Capability Databases

Another approach is to define the characteristics of the terminal in an external database, and use a generic program driven by the database. An example of this method is the UNIX System V *terminfo* database. Although the specifics of the terminfo database are described here, the methods used are applicable to other databases. Terminfo is fairly complex because it has grown to handle many needs over many years. Simpler systems can be used for simpler needs.

The original database from Berkeley was called *ttycap*. It contained information such as the mode bits to set and clear with an `stty` call, and did not specify how cursor addressing worked. A `switch` in the `vi` program handled cursor addressing for each supported terminal.

Ttycap was soon replaced with *termcap*, which was far less specific to the `vi` editor. Eventually, the database outgrew the structure of termcap, and it was rewritten by AT&T and called terminfo. Terminfo has more general parameter and padding mechanisms, and is not restricted to two-letter-capability names.

Termcap is an interpreted database, but terminfo is compiled. This makes terminfo preferable for most production applications, but termcap can be useful for applications that need to dynamically create a terminal description and export it into the environment. If the only capabilities to be dynamically changed are the screen size (as for a window manager), terminfo can export these values in the environment variables `LINES` and `COLUMNS`, or use unportable `ioctl` calls to set the window size for the particular window system. For a more complex variation, such as the selective inclusion or exclusion of capabilities, termcap may be preferable.

In practice, the choice of database may be determined by the particular system you use: older systems and Berkeley systems use termcap, newer and System V releases use terminfo. It is even better if you write your application to use a portable interface, such as curses. If you require a low-level interface, the terminfo curses package is upward compatible with termcap. This makes it possible, if inconvenient, to write a program to use termcap and have it work on both systems.

Terminfo Capabilities

In terminfo, generic capabilities are defined, such as `cup` to position the cursor, and `clear` to clear the screen. In many ways, these are similar to the capabilities of X3.64, but not all X3.64 capabilities are appropriate to screen handling. Also, terminfo has many extensions, and new capabilities can be easily added.

These capabilities are defined in a description file, such as this one for the Microterm ACT 4:

```
microterm|act4|microterm act iv,
        cr=^M, cud1=^J, ind=^J, bel=^G, am,
        cub1=^H, ed=^_, el=^^, clear=^L,
        cup=^T%p1%c%p2%c, cols#80, lines#24,
        cuf1=^X, cuu1=^Z, home=^],
```

This file describes a terminal using Control-M for *carriage return* (`cr`), using Control-J for *cursor down one position* (`cud1`), having the *automatic margin* property (`am`), having 80 columns and 24 lines, and so on.

The file is translated from this text format into a fast binary format by a *terminfo compiler* called `tic`. The binary format is read in with a routine called `setupterm`, after which a set of global terminfo variables are made available to the C program.

These global variables have names chosen for readability, and defined by the terminfo standard. For example, `cr` is called `carriage_return`, `cud1` is called `cursor_down`, `am` is called `auto_right_margin`, `lines` is called `lines`, and `cols` is called `columns`.

For example, here is a program that displays a message centered on the first line of the screen. The message is given as a single argument, in quotes, on the command line.

```
#include <term.h>

main(argc, argv)
int argc;
char *argv[];
{
        int startcol;
        char *message;

        if (argc != 2) {
                printf("Usage: %s 'message'\n", argv[0]);
                exit(1);
        }
        /* required terminfo initialization */
        setupterm(0, 1, 0);

        message = argv[1];
        startcol = (columns - strlen(message)) / 2;

        putp(clear_screen);
        for (i=0; i<startcol; i++)
                putchar(' ');
        printf("%s", message);
        putchar('\n');
        exit(0);
}
```

The variables `clear_screen` and `columns` are defined by `<term.h>` and contain the sequence to clear the screen and to find the number of columns the terminal has, respectively. The routine `putp` is similar to `fputs` in that it writes the string on the standard output. It is important, however, to call `putp` to send control sequences, rather than simply using `printf` or `write`, because of the possibility of a sequence containing a special code, such as padding information, discussed below.

Keyboard Input

Capabilities also exist to define keys that are present on the keyboard and the sequences they transmit. For example, a typical ANSI X3.64 conforming terminal has arrow keys transmitting the same codes as their motion would require; thus, a down-arrow key might be defined with `kcud1=\E[B`, indicating that the arrow key transmits

ESC, [, B. Programs can use these capabilities to examine characters received from the keyboard and determine whether the user has pressed a special key.

Care must be taken if the program uses the ESC key, because an incoming ESC might have been generated by the ESC key or by a special key transmitting a sequence beginning with ESC. In general, other ambiguities are possible; for example, there is usually no way to distinguish between the BACKSPACE key and Control-H.

One solution to the ESC problem is to examine the time between the ESC and the next character. A terminal will usually transmit the following characters within 1/10 second, but a human will usually take longer to press another key. It is possible, using alarm, to check for such time delays by setting a 1-second timeout (using the alarm system call) and assuming that after one second with no input, the key was ESC. Such a check is fairly portable among UNIX systems. Unfortunately, 1 second is so long that many users will have time to press another key. A smaller timeout is preferable, although there is no portable way to specify such a timeout. Possible unportable methods involve poll in System V release 3 with the TLI networking extension, the VTIME field in the System V release 2 terminal driver, select in 4.2BSD, and busy-waiting solutions involving ftime in the MS DOS and 4.2BSD systems or times in System V.

In general, no matter what precautions you take, it is still possible for users to press another key within 1/10 second, or for network delays and buffering to hide any timing present in the original keystrokes. It is also necessary for the application programmer to check the incoming characters to determine if they are part of a possible keystroke generated by that terminal. If not, they should be returned as individual characters. All this complexity is not needed if ESC is not used as a single keystroke in the application, so new applications are advised to avoid it if any other special non-ASCII keys are used.

Special Keys

A capability database such as terminfo will describe special function keys such as *right arrow*, *clear*, and *F1*. Many terminals do not have such keys, and applications should be prepared to deal with the case when the terminal does not have the desired key. For example, the vi editor uses ASCII characters h, j, k, and l as substitutes for arrow keys, and the ASCII character Control-L to clear and redraw the screen. The command set should make sense on terminals with no special keys at all.

Function keys (F1, etc.) are a bit harder to support portably. Users do not necessarily have universal uses for these keys, but applications often allow for function keys to be programmed. Some terminals have function keys that always transmit a known string, and these strings are described by terminfo. Other programmable terminals allow the keys to be programmed with arbitrary strings. (Some programmable terminals initialize the keys to a known string, and others initialize them with the null string.) You can't be sure if the user has reprogrammed these keys to transmit an unknown value.

One approach to dealing with the possibility of missing function keys is to provide an equivalent syntax using ASCII characters. For example, vi uses the syntax #*i* for function key number *i*. Since # is a printing character, a keyboard-mapping application might be better off using a control character. For example, Control-F followed by a digit *i* might be equivalent to pressing function key `i`.

Flow Control

Many terminals cannot accept characters and process them as fast as computers can generate them. This is especially true of bit-mapped screens, which must copy large portions of the screen to scroll, and of PC-class computers running terminal emulators, but it also applies to many terminals, particularly when high line speeds are used.

If no special provisions are made, a terminal that cannot keep up will lose characters. A typical terminal may have a buffer to hold incoming characters while it carries out some time-consuming operation, but the buffer will eventually overflow if continuous high-speed data is sent at a rate faster than the terminal can process. In order to keep the amount of data generated down to a rate that the terminal can handle, the terminal must be able to *flow control* the sender, that is, to send it a signal to stop while it catches up, and then send another signal to start it back up.

Some older terminals do not have buffering or flow control. When the connection is over a network, flow control can be done *out of band,* meaning that no characters visible to the application are used. When the connection is over an RS232C serial port, several methods of flow control are possible.

RS232C flow control methods include *hardware flow control* using *RTS/CTS,* which is an out-of-band method involving dedicated signals on the RS232C connector. Another is *ENQ/ACK*, an in-band method where the ASCII ENQ character (Control-E) is sent to ask if the terminal is ready, and the terminal waits until its buffer has enough room and sends ACK (Control-F) to indicate that it is. The most widely used, and a current industry de facto standard, is XON/XOFF. With this method, the terminal sends an XOFF (Control-S) when its buffer is nearly full, and the sender stops. When the buffer has enough room, the terminal sends an XON (Control-Q) and the sender resumes.

Robust terminal packages deal with older terminals that do not support the XON/XOFF convention. Terminfo does this by allowing *padding* to be specified in capability strings. Padding codes such as `$<5>` indicate that 5 milliseconds of delay should be inserted at this point. Terminfo calculates the number of characters equivalent to the resulting delay and transmits the appropriate number of padding characters. For example, at 9600 BPS (960 characters per second), a character takes about 1 millisecond, and a 5-millisecond delay requires 5 pad characters. The ASCII NUL (Control-@) character is used, unless another padding character is specified, because most terminals will discard null characters without placing them into the buffer.

Even for terminals supporting flow control, padding information can be useful as an estimate of the cost of a particular function. An optimizing screen management package, when faced with a choice of two ways to update the screen, can choose based on cost.

Parameters

Some capabilities require parameters. For example, the `cup` capability, which describes how to position the cursor, needs the row and column to which the cursor should be positioned. Parameters are easy to support in a driver approach, since arbitrary code can be written to specify the string. In a capability database, handling the wide variety of real terminals is difficult, but with a sufficiently powerful parameter method, it is possible. Terminfo uses a stack and % codes similar to those in `printf` with extensions to support computation. A simple terminal using the ASCII character whose value is the row or column number might use `%c`, for example, the ACT 4 `cup=^T%p1%c%p2%c`. The `%p1` code says to use (push) parameter number 1, and `%p2` uses the second parameter. The `%c` pops a value off the stack and prints it as a character. A terminal using a decimal string of ASCII values might use `cup=\E[%p1%d;%p2%dH`. When a computation is needed, a postfix notation is used.

If a terminal requires numbers starting at 1, and the package numbers rows and columns starting at 0, it is necessary to add one to the number being sent. (This applies to terminfo and ANSI X3.64.) Thus, the substring `%p1%{1}%+%d` means to push the first parameter onto a stack, then to push the integer one, then add the top two elements on the stack (popping the two values and pushing the result), and to print that out in decimal. The capability string `cup=\E[%p1%{1}%+%d;%p2%{1}%+%dH` is a typical way to address the cursor on an ANSI terminal.

This allows fairly complex computations. One older terminal requires cursor addressing to use a BCD notation; this is described with the following capability, split into two lines here for typographical reasons:

```
cup=^O%p2%{10}%/%{16}%*%p2%{10}%m%+%c
    %p1%?%p1%{19}%>%t%{12}%+%;%'@'%+%c
```

Here the column (`%p2`) is encoded in BCD (`%m` is the mod operator), and the second parameter is compared to 19; if greater, an extra offset of 12 is added to force the higher values to begin with 32. The `%? %t %e %;` operation represents if/then/else/endif.

This example displays a message centered both horizontally and vertically on the screen. As before, the message is typed, in quotes, on the command line.

```
#include <term.h>

main(argc, argv)
int argc;
char **argv;
{
        int startcol, startrow;
        char *message;
```

```
      if (argc != 2) {
            printf("Usage: %s 'message'\n", argv[0]);
            exit(1);
      }

      /* required terminfo initialization */
      setupterm(0, 1, 0);

      startcol = (columns - strlen(message)) / 2;
      startrow = lines / 2;

      putp(clear_screen);
      putp(tparm(cursor_address, startrow, startcol));
      printf("%s", message);
      putchar('\n');
      exit(0);
}
```

5.1.5 Curses

The capability database model has built into it the assumption that the screen is manipulated by sending strings of characters to it. The driver approach uses subroutines rather than character strings, but the nature of the calls is very similar. For example, both have primitive operations to address the physical cursor to a particular position.

A higher-level approach is used by the *curses* library. This interface allows the programmer to specify how the screen should look, and lets the library determine the operations necessary to make it look like that.

The user is provided with a WINDOW data-type that represents a software representation of a CRT screen. In effect, it is a two-dimensional array of character values, and additional information such as the cursor position and the current graphic rendition (highlighting mode.) Each character position is a combination of the graphic character and its graphic rendition, for example, an unhighlighted blank in one position, and an inverse video A in another.

Operations on the WINDOW data structure are subroutines whose semantics are similar to typical terminal operations, such as writing characters, positioning the cursor, inserting a line, or setting the current highlighting mode. The important difference is that no output is sent to the screen until a window is flushed using wrefresh. This allows the programmer to make a series of updates to the screen all at once, and moves the job of deciding how to efficiently update the screen from the application programmer to the programmer who implements curses.

Curses Implementation Issues

When a lower-level update is needed, the curses package must be concerned with what is already on the screen, and must send characters intended to change what is currently there with the intended new text.

Making a screen update all at once is an important change. There are many possible ways to actually update a screen. The screen might be physically cleared and redrawn if there are major changes. If only a few changes are made, the cursor can be positioned to the locations to be changed and new text sent. In some cases, many lines of text can be saved from the old screen, but moved to a new position. In this case, operations such as full-screen scrolling, partial-screen scrolling, insert or delete line, and insert or delete character, can reduce the update time to a minimum.

The number of characters sent to update the screen may or may not make much difference. Over a dialup line with a 300 BPS (30 characters per second) modem, cutting a 1000 character screen update from 33 seconds to a 60 character single-line update taking 2 seconds is a critical difference. The same optimization at 9600 BPS reduces the update from 1 to 0.06 second, a far less important savings. On a workstation or personal computer, the line speed may appear to be immediate, but the CPU time spent to update the screen can still be significant.

Nonetheless, it is worthwhile to look at the amount of CPU time spent to reduce the number of characters transmitted. Using a linear full-screen comparison algorithm, it is possible to spend under 0.1 second of processor time on a 1 MIPS machine to save a second of screen updating. On a timesharing machine with many users, or a very slow processor, the tradeoff may be different.

Since the package is free to update the screen any way that makes sense locally, if sending an entire screen is very cheap, it may be faster to redraw the entire screen than to make comparisons to determine what to change. One example of this is when the program is running on a PC, with the screen directly mapped into memory. In this case, an entire screen update can be made by copying from one area in memory to another, taking a very small fraction of a second. (On a bitmapped screen, or a PC where screen memory can only be accessed during a vertical or horizontal retrace period, the update may be slower, but might still be very fast.)

Curses Properties

The curses package is high level in other ways. Rather than being concerned with the type of terminal the user has, the user calls `initscr()`, which handles all terminal-dependent initialization. Rather than worrying about the terminal driver conventions needed to get a single character from the keyboard without line buffering or echoing, high-level functions such as `cbreak()` and `noecho()` are called to portably set the modes. Rather than assuming that the user edits using the ASCII backspace character, the `erasechar()` function can be called to determine local conventions. The details of such system queries, which vary among operating systems, are handled by the curses package itself.

The curses package is not suited for every application. Being high level, it uses a certain model of the screen. It is appropriate for character text-oriented applications, and does not handle graphics. The screen is assumed to be made up of a two-dimensional array of character positions; this is not appropriate for certain bitmapped environments where the characters are not all the same width. (Variable-width fonts are sometimes handled by treating the width of the terminal as a very large number, and discarding text that does not fit on a single line. This approach may be satisfactory for some applications, but will not be transparent to the user.)

This example uses curses to center the message, as before.

```
#include <curses.h>

main(argc, argv)
int argc;
char **argv;
{
        int startcol, startline;

        initscr();  /* required curses initialization */

        startcol = (COLS - strlen(argv[1])) / 2;
        startline = LINES / 2;

        /* We always start with a clear screen */
        move(startline, startcol);      /* move cursor */
        printw("%s", argv[1]);    /* similar to printf */
        addch('\n');              /* similar to putchar */
        refresh();                /* similar to fflush */
        endwin();                 /* required cleanup */
        exit(0);
}
```

5.1.6 Form/Menu Packages

Many applications, designed for ease of use, are built around the concept of *filling out a form*. This approach allows users to be quickly trained to fill out a general form, and then the system can be made self-documenting. There are packages that manage forms, allowing the application programmer to concentrate on the content of the screen. Without such a package, it is possible to write something from scratch, or to build a simple package for the specific application.

A similar approach is built around the concept of a *menu*. Here the user is presented with a menu, which is a fixed list of choices, and allowed to choose any one choice. The computer performs the action associated with the choice, which may be to open up a submenu, to run some program, or to perform some special-purpose action such as exiting to a higher level.

The form and menu concept is often combined into a single package. The user is presented a menu at the top level, and after going through one or two submenus, is given a form to be filled out. Sometimes the form is at the top level, and a menu can be brought up by pressing a button.

Forms

Forms packages allow the programmer to specify, at a very high level, what the fields of the form will be, where they will appear on the screen, what type of data will be typed into each field, and what action to take once the form is filled out and the user presses some key (to request an action). Similarly, menu packages allow the programmer to set up the choices of the menu, specifying an action for each menu choice.

These packages are higher level than C. Often, they are totally driven by a table resident in an external file. This allows the system to be configured by adding a line to a file without changing any C code. (This can be important when a production system is distributed in binary-only form, since there is no easy way to alter the program source.)

For example, each form might be controlled by a file. Here is a typical form configuration file:

```
 5    2    7  LIT Action:
 5   10   10  ACT /usr/lib/form/valid/demo.action
 7    4    5  LIT Name:
 7   10   60  REQ d_name X(20)
 9    1    8  LIT Address:
 9   10   60  REQ d_address X(60)
11    4    5  LIT City:
11   10   20  REQ d_city X(20)
11   46    6  LIT State:
11   53    2  REQ d_state XX
11   61    4  LIT Zip:
11   66    5  REQ d_zip 99999
13    3    6  LIT Phone:
13   10   20  OPT d_phone 999-999-9999
F1 "<Menu" GOTO /usr/lib/form/toplevel
F3 "Bill to" GOTO /usr/lib/form/billto
F6 "Help" GOTO /usr/lib/help/demo
F8 "Action" ACTION
```

This describes a form that appears on the screen like this:

```
 Action: **********

   Name:  _____

Address:  _____

   City:  _____        State: __     Zip: ____

  Phone:  _____


____  ____  ____  ____  ____  ____  ____  ____  ____
 <Menu        Bill to              Help        Action
```

In this form configuration file, each line represents one field in the form (except the last four lines, which represent function keys, discussed below). For each field, the first two columns are the row and column on the screen of the beginning of the field; the third is the width of the field, the fourth is a field type that specifies the type of the field; and any additional fields are parameters specific to the field type. Lines beginning with F indicate a special function key, a label to be displayed on the screen for it, and an action to be taken when the user presses that key.

The LIT (literal) field type indicates that the value is to be displayed literally on the screen, and that no user input is allowed in this field. The parameter is the label to display. The REQ (required) field type indicates a required input field, which the user must fill out for the form to be accepted. The first parameter is a data field name into which the value will be stored, so it can be referenced by other software. The second parameter is a COBOL-style picture, describing the format of the field. It specifies which positions may be any character (X); which must be digits (9); and other special-purpose characters, such as the hyphen, indicating that a literal hyphen will appear at that point. The OPT (optional) field type is similar to REQ, except that the user is not required to fill out the field.

The ACT (action) field type indicates that the field is used for an action. The valid choices for the action are contained in an operations file. Such actions are initiated by entering the appropriate action (e.g., ''update'') into the form field, completing the fields that are required for that action, and then by pressing a special key such as the F8 Action key. For example, the operations file demo.action in the directory /usr/lib/form/valid might look like this:

```
add       NEW $curid
delete    DELETE $curid
update    UPDATE $curid
```

In this example, if the user types add in the action field, a built-in operation called NEW is invoked to add a record to the database, using a built-in macro called $curid. Similar delete and update commands are provided. If the user presses the F3 Bill to key, the package calls another form, /usr/lib/form/billto, so that the user will fill out the ''bill-to'' form and then return to the ''demographics'' form.

Soft labeled function keys (or SLKs) are often associated with forms. If the terminal permits, soft labels can be put up on the screen to show the meanings of the function keys. Special meanings such as `Save`, `Action`, `<Menu`, `Cancel`, `Help` and the like can show the user the current set of choices. These labels can be displayed on the bottom line of the screen if the terminal has no support for SLKs.

Forms like these can be very tedious to create by editing descriptions such as those given. Forms packages usually support a forms editor, allowing a forms developer to create a form by seeing the form displayed directly on the screen.

There are many possible approaches to designing forms[3] and implementing the actions the user may need to take. One alternative is for a special function key, which caused the program to put up the form initially, to indicate the desired action. For example, an `update` function key (or menu choice) might enter a form that is specifically for updates, making the action field unnecessary.

Menus

A menu allows the programmer to present the user with a set of choices. Instead of the user typing the text of the choice as a command, the choice can be selected by some kind of pointing mechanism. Menus are often combined with forms packages, perhaps as the result of a particular action or pressing a `Help` key. Menus are also an important concept on their own.

Many menu packages work with special hardware, such as a bitmapped workstation and a mouse. A nice graphics picture is drawn on the screen, and the mouse can be used to point to a selected choice.

Menus do not require special-purpose hardware, however. With a simple alphanumeric CRT screen, an easily understood menu can be displayed. Thus, a menu such as the following might appear:

```
 --------------
| 1. add       |
| 2. delete    |
| 3. update    |
 --------------
```

From this sort of menu, it is possible to set up the software so that the user has a choice of moving a mouse, using up/down arrow keys, typing the number corresponding to the choice (and pressing return), or typing one of the letters a, d, or u. If a mouse is not available, or if the terminal has no arrow keys, the other input methods are still possible.

---

[3] For more information about good design principles for forms, see Wilbert O. Galitz, *Handbook for Screen Design Format*, QED Information Systems, Wellesley, MA.

Even with a hard-copy terminal, or with a terminal of unknown type, a menu is possible in scroll mode:

```
Operations:
1. add
2. delete
3. update
Choice (1-3, q to quit, ? for help):
```

By writing your application at a high level, calling an operation called menu, driven by a configuration file, you can choose bitmapped menus with mouse-driven selection if the hardware support is available, or alphanumeric menus with arrow keys on a CRT, or scrolling menus as a last resort. The rest of the application need not be rewritten.

5.1.7 Veneering

The technique of *veneering* is very useful. Define the interface you want (in this case, the *curses* interface) and then build that interface in terms of what the system actually provides. For example, here are some possible implementations of the curses erase function for the MS DOS system using Microsoft C. These implementations use unportable code, but the key is that the *interface* (the call to erase, in this case) is portable and high level.

The first version assumes ANSI.SYS is installed.

```
erase()
{
        printf("\033[H\033[J");
        fflush(stdout);
}
```

The second version calls a subroutine screenline, which copies an 80 byte buffer onto a particular line on the screen. This routine can be written using assembly language or Microsoft *far* pointers, but it won't be portable.

```
erase()
{
        register int i;
        char buf[80];

        for (i=0; i<sizeof buf; i++)
            buf[i] = " ";

        for (i=0; i<LINES; i++)
            screenline(i, buf);
}
```

Since typical PC hardware actually uses two consecutive bytes, one for attributes and one for characters, a version of the above routine that passed a 160 byte buffer, with even bytes set to zero, or the appropriate attribute combination, and odd bytes set to blank, might actually be more useful. Of course, the numbers 80 and 160 should actually be tunable macros, it is unwise to hard code these numbers into low-level routines like this.

The next version calls BIOS routine INT 10H through the DOS int86 interface, setting the graphics mode to text, and clearing the screen as a side effect.

```
#include <stdio.h>
#include <dos.h>

union REGS inr;

erase()
{
        inr.h.ah = 0;
        inr.h.al = 2;
        int86(0x10, &inr, &outr);
}
```

The final version makes no assumptions about hardware or software, but sacrifices some functionality. For some applications, this sort of implementation can be extremely portable. This method will work even when the command interpreter has been redirected to a serial port. The disadvantage is that it leaves the cursor at the bottom of the screen instead of at the top. A different programming model, one that does not depend on escape sequences or partial-screen updates, is necessary to generalize this to any additional functions.

```
erase()
{
        register int i;

        for (i=0; i<LINES; i++)
                printf("\n");
        fflush(stdout);
}
```

5.1.8 Terminal Recommendations

When you are faced with the decision of writing a screen-oriented program that you hope to port to many different architectures someday, it is very important to adopt an initial model that will allow you a great deal of flexibility. Understanding the different environments you may be using is a big step toward that flexibility.

In general, you should adopt the highest-level model you can. Write the bulk of your code to use the interface you really want. If that interface isn't already available for the systems you need to support, you should implement it using the facilities that are actually provided.

If your package uses a forms-oriented user interface, you should adopt a forms-oriented interface. You may find a forms package that does what you need available off the shelf. However, since forms packages are not widely standardized, you may be better off to define your own interface and to implement that on each system using whatever forms package is available for it. (There are some public domain packages available from users groups.) On some systems, you may be unable to find a forms package, so it will be necessary to either port an existing package or to write your own. Substitution of another forms package should be transparent to most of your code, which is written for a single interface.

If you want to manipulate the screen with alphanumerics, curses may be right for you. Curses provides a character-oriented interface to a CRT screen or window with fixed-width characters, and to the keyboard. Implementations of curses are available on UNIX systems. In addition, compatible curses packages are commercially available for MS DOS systems.

For personal computers, it is not difficult to write a curses package, supporting only as much of curses as you need for your application, which writes directly to display memory. Most of the work in implementing curses goes into optimization algorithms for low-speed connections and into handling of different terminals that don't all behave exactly the same. On a PC, you don't need to be so concerned with terminal types and bandwidth issues, so a much simpler veneered implementation is possible. The user interface can be kept compatible, even with a different implementation.

If you want a window-oriented interface using menus on a character screen, you might choose curses, or you might choose an interface more oriented to bitmapped windows. The X Windows system has become widely available for bitmapped workstations. AT&T offers a forms package called FMLI.

If you have a low-level, special-purpose application, such as setting tabs on the terminal or writing information to a status line, you should consider a lower-level package, such as terminfo or termcap. If the program is small, it is probably specific to the particular system and can easily be rewritten for each system. If it is large, the parts that use terminfo can be separated into a few higher-level routines, such as `set_tab(column)`.

If you want to be oriented toward byte streams, you might choose a virtual device driver: an interface similar to the virtual terminal driver. You can also consider curses, which can be implemented to generate byte streams.

The virtual device driver approach is also very useful for some applications that are not screen-oriented. For example, desktop publishing software often separates the text processing function from device control. A standard format can be defined, allowing different device drivers to be written to convert the standard format to device specific commands.

5.2 Telephone Calls

Modems, and the mechanisms they use to dial, are not well standardized. In addition to the many command sets and options used by modems, other networks (X.25, TCP/IP, ISDN, OSI) provide similar functionality to the dialup telephone network, using incompatible interfaces. AT&T's Transport Layer Interface (TLI) takes a step toward solving this problem.

The original asynchronous modems were acoustic couplers, designed to contain a telephone handset, with a speaker to activate the handset microphone, and a microphone to listen to the earpiece. No electrical connection was needed or allowed, and all calls were placed by hand. The computer that received the calls had banks of answer-only 103 or 212 modems, directly connected to the telephone line by the telephone company. Eventually, direct-connect modems were sold for call origination, but the call was still placed by hand.

To have one computer dial another, under program control, a special hardware device, called an *automatic calling unit* (ACU), was needed. The ACU would interface to the telephone line and the originating modem, place the call, and then hand the call off to the modem. The UNIX system came with software that supported one such ACU, the DN-11. The UUCP network began in this environment.

As hardware became less expensive and more sophisticated, modems began to appear that were capable of interacting with the user on a terminal. The modem would prompt for a telephone number, the user would type it on the keyboard, and the modem would place the call. Some modems would support additional capabilities, such as a directory of stored telephone numbers, waiting for a second dial tone, and detection of a busy signal.

These intelligent modems supported two types of commands. Some modems were interactive, intended to be user-friendly. They would announce their brand name and version, prompt the user and offer help if the user asked for it. Others were intended to interface to computer programs, and had very brief command sets and responses, designed to be easy for a program to recognize. In practice, the interactive interfaces tended to be as easy to program for as the terse interfaces.

Since each modem was designed either to interface with a human user or to talk to a program that was supplied with the modem, there was no standardization of the command sets. Each command set contained similar capabilities, but a program designed for one modem would not work with another. As a result, the UUCP system, which came configured for only the DN-11, had to be customized for any available modems at each end-user installation. It was necessary to write a dialing subroutine in C for each modem, and often #ifdef was used to select the dialer available on the local system. This especially presented a problem on binary-only systems, which could not be easily customized and often did not have a trained programmer available.

Many solutions to the modem command-set problem have been used. Some of them have been inspired by termcap or terminfo, and others have been inspired by UUCP itself.

Capabilities

A typical terminfo-based solution describes a set of modem capabilities. Sample capabilities include a string to wake up the modem, a prefix to tell it to begin accepting a telephone number to dial, and a suffix to complete the number and tell it to place the call. Capabilities such as waiting for a dial tone in the middle of the number or a blind pause for a few seconds can be indicated with optional capabilities.

For example, the following description might be used:

```
4024|att4024|AT&T 4024 modem,
        speed=2400, init=\r,
        prompt=:, bdial=, edial=\r,
        pause=\054, wsd=;,
        conn=ANSWER,
```

This would indicate that the name of the modem is 4024 with nickname att4024, that it runs at 2400 BPS, it is initialized by sending it CR, and it prompts with a colon. To dial a telephone number, send it the bdial string (null in this case), the telephone number, and edial (CR), and wait for ANSWER. The characters within the telephone numbers that generate a 2-second pause and wait for a secondary dial tone are comma (the pause capability) and semicolon (the wsd capability), respectively.

Chat Scripts

Another method is to use the UUCP *chat script*. UUCP uses an *expect, send, expect, send* sequence to specify a dialog between the program and whatever is on the other end of the connection. For example, the chat script

```
login: nuucp Password: letmein
```

indicates that the program should expect (wait until it sees) login, then send uucp followed by a newline, then expect Password, and then send letmein and a newline.

Extensions to this basic method allow some variations. For example, special codes can be embedded in the *send* string. The sequence \r means to send an ASCII CR (carriage return) character; BREAK means to send a break signal (\b or \B could be used, but BREAK is used for upward compatibility with older UUCP implementations). Finally, \c is used at the end of a string to suppress the newline. (Another design might require \n to explicitly send a newline only when requested. UUCP sends one by default, because it is usually needed when logging into a remote computer.)

Sometimes the expected sequence is never received. A chat script will time out after some reasonable period of time (often 30 seconds) and return a failure indication, unless an alternative is shown in the chat script. These alternatives are embedded in the *expect* string, separated by hyphens. Thus:

```
login-BREAK-login-BREAK-login uucp Password letmein
```

indicates that the program should wait for login, and if it doesn't get it, send a break and again wait for login again. If that fails, it sends a second break and expects another `login`. If that fails, the entire script fails. When any of the expected `login` strings is received, it goes on to send `uucp`. This is useful when the remote computer system uses the BREAK signal to switch between different line speeds, as is common on UNIX systems.

Another variation is to allow a quoted string as part of a chat script. This allows blanks or hyphens to be part of a string to be expected or sent. It also allows the null string to be specified. This script expects the null string (which is always received immediately), sends two CR characters after a delay, expects `Request`, and sends `osgd`. This is useful when a system sends nothing, or answers at the wrong speed, and the caller must send something first.

```
""  \d\r\r\c Request: osgd
```

This technique can be extended to allow different modems to be handled. For example, an interactive modem that prompts with a colon might be specified as follows:

```
""  \r\c : \T ANSWER
```

This indicates that the dialing program should expect nothing, send an isolated CR, wait for a prompt, send the telephone number to be dialed (expanded from `\T`), and wait for the modem to say `ANSWER`.

A program-oriented command set can be handled as follows:

```
""  ATDT\T CONNECT
```

This means that the program should send `ATDT` and the telephone number, and then wait for `CONNECT`.

One necessary extension is to handle different notations for commands during the insertion of the telephone number. Most modems support a command to "wait for another dial tone" or to "pause for about 2-seconds." These are normally indicated with a special character in the telephone number, such as a hyphen, comma, or the letter w for "wait." These two functions are the major functions needed, and the description of the modem should indicate which two characters are used. UUCP uses an extra field, separate from the chat script, made up of pairs of characters:

```
-,=;
```

This indicates that any hyphen in the telephone number should be replaced by a comma, and any equal sign should be replaced by a semicolon. Thus, if the telephone number database uses a dash for a 2 second pause and an equal sign to wait for a secondary dial tone, and the modem uses comma and semicolon for the same purposes, this serves as a translation table. Note that there is no reason to limit the translation to two characters; other functions, such as switching between tone and pulse dialing, may also be needed.

There is currently no international or national standard for the command set used by an intelligent modem. Many manufacturers have products on the market that use their own command sets. However, by 1986, a de facto standard emerged, usually called the Hayes command set, or sometimes the AT command set. The previous example using

`ATDT` is a simple chat script for this command set. Some day it may be safe to assume this command set will be used universally. At the current time, this assumption is unwise because of the installed base of incompatible modems.

In general, dialing a modem is the sort of function that should be hidden in a subroutine. There is no universally supported subroutine for this purpose, although the System V `dial` function provides one possible programmer interface. Unfortunately, `dial` is specific to System V, and is not in the SVID. Some systems were distributed with a `dial` function that did not support the dialing hardware on the system. If you expect to support many modems, you will probably have to write your own subroutine.

5.3 Printers

Printers are similar to terminals in many ways. There are many brands with many different capabilities, and there is no prevailing standard for use of these capabilities. So programs that use a printer must take the marketplace into account.

There are many different kinds of printers. The original mainframes had line printers capable of printing text at very high speeds. They usually had a special-purpose interface designed for the particular computer. These printers were often four or five feet high and stood alone on the floor.

Some of these line printers supported lower-case, but since they were primarily designed for data processing applications, such as billing, high quality print was not as important as speed, and medium-quality upper-case output was commonplace. (This is still true in many mainframe data processing shops.) Only text could be printed, and special instructions such as page eject could be specified using *carriage control,* such as the FORTRAN notion of a 1 in the first column.

Minicomputers were built around special-purpose printers and mass produced third-party printers. These printers were nearly as large as those used on mainframes, although to cut costs, it was common to omit features such as soundproofing and output paper stacking. Two de facto standard interfaces for the third-party printers became established: the Centronics parallel port and the Printronix interface. These interfaces specified the plug, the assignment of pins, provisions for flow control and data rate (eliminating the need for line speed and character size configuration) and that the ASCII character set was to be used. They did not support graphics or special control sequences.

In the late 1970s, inexpensive desktop printers with RS232 serial ports became popular. These were used both as local printers attached to terminals and as printers on microcomputers. Shortly thereafter, desktop printers supporting the Centronics parallel interface appeared on the market, and a de facto standard for the microcomputer ''parallel port'' was established. This standard still does not go beyond the ASCII character set, and while it can be generally assumed that CR, LF, and FF are supported by all printers, no other control sequences are universally supported. (Many widely used printers do not support backspace, and there is no universal interpretation of tabs. Many printers power up with no tab stops set.)

Inexpensive desktop printers can be divided into several classes. Those currently available include *daisy wheel* printers, which use an interchangeable wheel to print high-quality characters from a fixed set; *dot matrix* printers, which construct low- or medium-quality characters from several dots on the print head; and *laser printers,* which use a photocopier mechanism to print very high-quality characters on sheet paper. There are many varieties in each class; for example, dot matrix printers can be found using impact/ribbon technology, ink jets, or thermal paper.

Daisy wheel printers are unable to print graphics, except by using fully formed characters such as periods, hyphens, and vertical lines to draw graphs. In the 1970s, such programs were commonplace. However, since dot matrix and laser printers can now produce similar or better results at faster speeds, the daisy wheel technology is no longer heavily used.

Dot matrix printers can draw graphs by varying the dot patterns used as the print head crosses the paper. This allows graphics to be easily sent. However, there are many different control sequences used to get the same effect. The different printers also support different resolutions, varying from about 70 dots per inch to about 300 or more. Since these dots are large enough to form readable printing characters with as few as eight rows, and the dots are designed to run together, the true resolution is often only 30 to 50 dots per inch.

Laser printers are available with several different resolutions, with the most widely used being 300 dots-per-inch. These dots are quite small, generally supporting a true 300 dot per inch resolution. There are several incompatible methods of printing graphics on laser printers, and no defined international or national standards. In addition, laser printers are typically used for desktop publishing applications, so they usually contain a microprocessor and a great deal of RAM. They also usually support the concept of *downloading fonts* from the host. This allows the host to program a font into the printer once, and then send characters to the printer and let the printer set up the bits of each character from the current font. This is usually much faster than the host sending all the bits in the representation of each character in the document.

While there are no international or national standards covering printers other than ASCII, there is some help from related standards and de facto standards. The X3.64 standard is intended for both CRT terminals and printers, but it is not well suited to such concepts as variable-width fonts and pixel-resolution cursor positioning, so few printers support it. In the desktop dot matrix class, the current de facto standard is often called *EPSON compatibility*. This includes the ASCII character set and escape sequences to print dot-oriented graphics.

The laser printer market has largely gone in a different direction. Several proposed standards have been used, as well as many command sets that are specific to the product. Not all of them use escape sequences. A recently offered interface is called PostScript, and appears to be popular for laser printers. PostScript supports not only the traditional one-directional command sequence, but also has provisions for interaction between the printer and the host.

When writing a program that allows for hard-copy printout, it is first necessary to consider the application and the target class of printers. If all you need is to print text on a printer, and you aren't concerned with typefaces or graphics or color, you can assume the least common denominator: a printer that can print 80 columns of ordinary text. While some printers only support upper-case, the programmer needn't be concerned with this, since these printers or printer drivers will normally automatically map lower-case to upper-case. Most desktop printers support lower-case, but upper-case is still very widely used in data processing environments on mainframes.

If your application requires text with a few extensions, such as positioning the print head for superscripts or overstriking, a capability approach, like terminfo, is very useful. The terminfo database describes printers as well as CRT terminals. Capabilities such as cub1 for backspace and cr to return the cursor to the left margin describe the extent of conformance to basic ASCII, and other capabilities like hu to move half a line up and hts to set a horizontal tab are useful for better control. Additional capabilities involving pixel-level cursor positioning and the ability to enter a 7- or 8-bit graphics mode can be used if needed for the application.

More sophisticated applications often use the driver approach. A setup file or a menu is used to select the printer type from a list of supported printers, and the application calls a standard set of subroutines for the necessary operations.

Desktop publishing applications often use virtual device drivers. The program writes an output stream in a standard format into a file and then calls a filter that translates from this format into the particular commands needed by a particular printer. Then, to support a new printer, it is only necessary to write a new filter. Some vendors provide the source code to a few filters with their package, allowing sophisticated users to write filters for their own printers.

Most desktop publishing applications require some information about the output device in the main program. They must know which fonts are available, and for each font, the width of each character in the font. This allows the application to properly position the characters in each typeface. Additional information is sometimes provided, to account for a different page size or to allow the application to kern appropriate pairs of characters.[4]

For other applications, write the routines modularly, using the highest-level interface possible. If your objective is to print out an exact copy of the screen, call a routine that does just that; many PC operating systems provide a system call to print the screen, even in graphics mode. If your high-level objective is to send a stream of characters to the printer, varying the font and cursor position, use subroutine calls oriented to those operations.

---

[4] Kerning involves positioning two characters closer together than normal, to avoid a big space between the letters. For example, the sequence "oy" can often be kerned because the tail on the "y" extends to the left below the "o."

5.4 Graphics

So far we have dealt only with text-oriented applications. Many applications display pictures graphically, or use bitmapped hardware to achieve a windowing effect. How possible is it to write portable graphics software?

The answer is that any program that uses graphics cannot be very portable. Graphics is a very hardware-specific subject, and there is little consistency among implementations. There are several competing standards for graphics interfaces, and many systems don't support any of these standards.

Two well established standards for programmer interfaces to graphics are CORE[5] and GKS[6] (Graphical Kernel Subsystem). They describe a set of function calls that an implementation makes available from any programming language. There is no clear standard binding of either standard into the C language. These standards each have their own advantages and disadvantages, and no clear winner has emerged.

Other standards are emerging for windows interfaces. Each interface is usually specific to a particular operating system. Some operating systems have one windowing system, and some have more than one. The MS DOS system has, for example, Microsoft Windows, TOPVIEW, and GEM. The UNIX system has `layers` from AT&T, X Windows from MIT, and NeWS from Sun. Some windowing systems will emulate other windowing systems, allowing applications for one to run on another, but such emulations are often incomplete and may be missing some key feature that your implementation may require.

Windowing standards affect three independent parts of the system. Some standards determine the programmer interface to the window system, such as `Xt` from MIT and NPE (NeWS Programming Environment) from Sun Microsystems. Other standards control the network interface between client (application) and server (screen) processes, such as the X11 and NeWS protocols. Other standards determine how the screen appears to users, such as Open Look from UNIX International and Motif from the Open Software Foundation. (Open Look and Motif both exist for X Windows.) The primary standard affecting the portability of the application is the programmer interface, although the user interface will also be visible to the programmer.

The USA National Institute of Standards and Technology issued a proposed Federal Information Processing Standard in 1989 adopting the X11 standards for the X Protocol, Xlib Interface, Xt Intrinsics and Bitmap Distribution Format. Thus, software written to use the Xt library will be more portable than software written for another interface. Unfortunately, the set of *widgets* (menus, scrollbars, buttons, and other decorations on a window) was not standardized, and so there was no portable way to write applications with widgets. As usual, a veneered approach is best for new applications.

---

[5] CORE, *Computer Graphics*, Quarterly Report of SIGGRAPH-ACM, Vol. 11, No. 3, Fall 1977.

[6] GKS, Draft International Standard ISO/DIS 7942, Information Processing, Graphical Kernel System (GKS), Functional Description, ISO TC 97/SC5/WG2 N 163, November 14, 1982.

Another class of de facto graphics standards revolves around specific hardware. The PC class of machines has several kinds of display adapters, including the monochrome display adapter, a 25 × 80 screen with no color or graphics capabilities; the CGA (color graphics adapter) with 320 × 200 4-color and 640 × 200 2-color graphics modes as well as a 25x80 text mode; the EGA (enhanced graphics adapter) with 640 × 350 16-color graphics; the Hercules enhanced version of the monochrome adapter (HGA) (allowing 720 × 348 2-color graphics on monochrome hardware); the VGA (video graphics adapter), new with the IBM PS/2, supporting 640 × 480 15-color graphics; the AT&T enhancements to the CGA allowing a 400 × 640 2-color graphics mode; and the AT&T DEB (display enhancement board) enhancements to their CGA board, allowing 400 × 640 16-color graphics. Most of these support CGA 200 × 320 and 200 × 640 graphics as one of their modes, creating CGA as a de facto standard for PCs.

Operating systems provide some support for text-oriented operations, such as displaying characters and scrolling the screen. In the typical MS DOS machine, there are also calls to display a single pixel and to put the screen into a graphics or text mode. These routines are, in general, a small subset of what is actually needed by a typical application, and most implementations are extremely slow. As a result, many important screen-oriented PC applications do not go through the standard calls, but access the hardware directly.

Direct access to the hardware is not normally a recommended way to write a program, but lack of an alternative has caused a large number of programs to be written this way. As a result, new hardware systems were forced by market pressures to be upward compatible with the original hardware, and a de facto standard for PC display hardware has evolved.

This unfortunate turn of events has made migration to improved products difficult, since the de facto standard interface involves accessing memory in 64K locations beginning with address 0xB8000. New features, such as more than 640K of RAM and multitasking with each process protected from other processes, have been stifled by the need to run the vast array of programs that access the hardware directly.

Graphics Recommendations

How do you write graphics software given the lack of a standard graphics interface? The first step is to decide just what you really need. Do you need color or will monochrome using different patterns or brightnesses do? How much resolution do you require? Do you need hardware or a graphics library that can clip, pan, and zoom? Do you need three dimensions? Is your application based on rasters or shapes, and if on rasters, what will happen if the images are to be displayed on a device with a different resolution? Make your assumptions explicit and decide how much these assumptions limit you. You may only be concerned about one device today, but someday, there will probably be a need to port your program to a different environment.

Once you start to code, it is important to modularize. Write the bulk of your application to use an ideal graphics library, one that provides exactly the functions you need.

Then write the graphics library yourself, using whatever real library or hardware is available on the target machine.

When the time comes to port the program, you can just rewrite the graphics library instead of the entire program. Ideally, your graphics library is a ''veneer'' that is so short it is simple to rewrite it. Chances are good you can start by copying your first library and just change code as needed.

Once you begin to port to additional devices, you will have a collection of *graphics drivers* similar to the terminal drivers described earlier. You can compile in whichever library you need for the particular executable you are generating. Since the set of graphics features tends to vary among personal computers and workstations, it is likely you'll have to recompile for each of them anyway.

Eventually, you may find you run into two problems. One is that you need a single executable program to run on several different kinds of graphics hardware. For example, you may need to deal with graphics terminals, or to handle one of several display boards that might be on a PC.

The other problem is that, as you copy your graphics library to create a new version for new hardware, you duplicate code. As you enhance and maintain this code, you either must update each copy separately or ignore additional copies and only enhance the one of interest.

Both problems are solved by the same mechanism: linking in all drivers and making a run time decision. You can combine similar drivers into one, testing explicit parameters like the screen resolution in the few places where they are needed. (This is similar to the terminfo approach in Section 5.1.4.) Combining also facilitates the inclusion of similar code into common subroutines, cutting down on the size of the program and eliminating duplicate maintenance.

It has been suggested that an approach like curses or terminfo may be appropriate for graphics as well as text. This approach has been tried, but so far it hasn't worked out well. One problem is that the set of graphics capabilities is huge, and the database grows to an excessive size.

Another problem is that many systems use a subroutine call interface rather than escape sequences. Even if it is possible to link in the appropriate libraries, different subroutines must be linked into the program on different systems. These subroutines are not universally available. If you include them all in a distributed application, the resulting program may be excessively large, and there may be licensing problems with distributing the libraries to unlicensed customers.

5.5 Pointing Devices

There are many kinds of pointing devices used to point at a particular location on the screen. The *mouse* has become the most popular and comes in varieties with one, two, three, or rarely more, buttons. A *tablet* with a *puck* is similar, but uses fixed locations instead of relative motion, and has from zero to four buttons. A *trackball* uses relative motion like a mouse, but takes up less desk space, and usually doesn't have any buttons. A *joystick* is hand-held and may be either relative or absolute; it often has a single button. A *light pen* allows the user to ''draw'' on the screen, as well as point, and has no buttons, but may have a switch in the tip to detect being pressed on the screen. A *touch screen* allows the user to touch the screen with a finger or other object, with the processor detecting the location. A *touch pad* is similar, but is placed on the desktop or keyboard instead of overlaying the screen. The *arrow keys* on a keyboard are often used as a poor man's pointing device.

More sophisticated pointing devices have been developed in the lab, such as helmets that allow handicapped individuals to point by moving their head, and even head-mounted devices that determine where your *eyes* are looking. Foot mice (sometimes called ''moles'') and knee bars have been built.

These devices all share the ability to point to a particular location on the screen, and portable software can be written to work with any of them. (Unfortunately, there are few standards for hardware or software interfaces to pointing devices, so the details of the software interface should be hidden behind a veneer.) Additional functions, such as buttons and how they work, vary from one device to another. Some devices can detect separately when a button is pressed or released. Others can only tell that a button has been *clicked* (pressed and released). Some systems are sensitive to the time interval between clicks. One-button mice often use a *double click* (two rapid clicks) to indicate an alternate meaning, something that can be done with another button if present.

While all these devices can point to the screen, the light pen has an important limitation. It can only point at bright areas of the screen. As a result, light-pen-oriented software is usually structured differently: a user points to an object on a menu and drags it to the desired location, or points to a *tracking cross* (a bright object whose purpose is to give the pen something bright to point at) and drags it to new locations. This limitation means that for software to be useful with a light pen, it must be written differently than it would for other pointing devices. Because of the limitations, and the strong popularity of the mouse, most implementors do not bother with the light pen.

Interfaces between pointing devices and computers are far from standard. Some devices are part of the keyboard or plug into it. Some plug into special sockets on the computer or terminal. Some come with a controller that takes up a bus slot. Some plug into an unused RS232 serial port. There are no standard plugs or standard conventions for the signals on the pins. As a result, pointing devices are far from interchangeable; they are made for a specific type of computer or game system.

Programming with Pointing Devices

There is no standard way for a program to access a pointing device either. There are several general methods, each quite different. Some systems mirror (or access directly) the hardware and provide an interrupt whenever the device moves or a button is pressed or released. An interrupt routine can check the new location and button status. Another approach is to access the hardware but not interrupt, requiring that the software poll the hardware periodically. A variation is to consider a move or click an *event* and to pass the details to an event handler called by a routine waiting for an event to occur.

In windowing systems, several applications share the screen and pointing device. The systems will tell each application when the device enters, leaves, or moves within its window.

Another approach is to treat the pointing device as part of the keyboard by encoding moves and presses as keystrokes. (This is especially common if a serial port is used or for a mouse attached to a terminal.) A motion can be encoded as an escape sequence, with parameters giving the new position; a click can be treated just like a function key.

For compatibility with arrow keys, some pointing devices generate the same escape sequences sent by the keyboard's arrow keys, and the buttons emulate existing function keys. (For example, if you plug an AT&T MTG 630 mouse into the keyboard on an AT&T PC 6300, the mouse will send arrow keys when moved, and will send F8, F9, and F10 when the buttons are clicked.) The advantage to this approach is that any character-oriented program that understands arrow keys (including nearly any text editor) will work with the mouse with no software modification. The disadvantage is that resolution is reduced to a box the size of a character, which is not suitable for many graphics applications.

Windowing systems usually require a mouse and encourage applications to run in a window. This usually requires that the windowing system provide an interface to the mouse that gives each window the illusion that the mouse belongs to it alone, while in reality sharing the mouse among windows. Each program only sees mouse motions and button presses inside its own window, and the windowing system handles the mouse on the window borders and on the background. This often involves subroutine calls and interrupt structures specific to the windowing system.

How to deal with this variety? The usual steps apply. First, decide on the degree of portability you want. Do you need to run specifically on one computer, under one windowing system, or do you want to port among several? Are you interested in terminals or only in personal computers? Will you assume a mouse or a generic pointing device? How many buttons do you require? What will your program's fallback strategy be if the expected device, or the required number of buttons, is not present? (Many programs can use arrow keys or function keys when there is no mouse.)

Second, adopt a paradigm. Will you assume interrupts? Keystrokes? Events? Do you use clicks or separate down/up presses? Are menus involved? If so, are you providing your own menu routines or using a menu library built into the system? Since events are very general, and easily emulated with other facilities, they are well suited to new code. Old code based on keystrokes can be converted to use a pointing device by encoding the motions as keystrokes at a low level.

Third, design and code your application modularly. At the high-levels, use high level primitives that make sense to your application.

At lower levels, use generic routines like ''select from a menu'' and ''determine the position of the pointing device''. Avoid making assumptions about the resolution of the device or the size of the window; using a scaled coordinate system may allow your application to run in any sized window. (If you do scale your application, watch out for text, since it often doesn't scale easily.)

At the lowest level, write a veneer library that interfaces to the window system you have. This veneer can be replaced with another driver, and if your design is sufficiently general, the bulk of your program will require little or no modification.

5.6 Operating System Interfaces

The first interface between the user and the operating system was the panel of lights and switches on the computer console. Gradually, card readers, paper tape, and printers made it possible for users without much special training to use computers. As timesharing became popular, half-duplex hard-copy terminals allowed interactive use of the machine, a line at a time. CRT terminals and high-speed interfaces allowed screen-oriented programs and special handling of typed line-oriented input, such as erasing a character when backspace is pressed or not echoing passwords. Bitmapped terminals with mice made windowing interfaces possible. Personal computers changed the nature of the interaction in many ways.

All this evolution in the user interface has taken place over the relatively short lifespan of the computing field, starting in the late 1940s. Each step toward better user interfaces was not instant and universal, however. Panels with binary lights and switches were standard parts of most computer systems until the late 1970s. Card readers and printers are still the paradigm used by the batch job processing facilities that mainframes are built around. But the most ingrained user interface is the line-oriented command system. With few exceptions, operating systems of personal computers and workstations are built around the notion of typing a command name on a command line, adding options and arguments on the end of the command line, and pressing **enter** or **return**. In the interactive computing world, the command-line interface is the least common denominator, a facility that can be assumed to work everywhere. Networks and modems designed to be accessed by anyone with a terminal often assume the user has a *glass tty* interface, essentially a dumb terminal that displays text on the bottom line and scrolls previous lines up to the top. Only the barest minimum assumptions are made: ASCII character set, asynchronous RS232 interface, and a set of known line speeds.

Many older systems use only upper-case, because until the late 1970's, lower-case was considered a rare luxury. (Since many users still work with CAPS LOCK on, or the equivalent, much software is designed to ignore case in user commands. Only in the UNIX system has tradition suggested that an upper-case A command would mean something different from a lower-case a command.) UNIX system applications can be more powerful by using both cases, at the expense of simplicity.

Some newer operating systems, such as the Macintosh operating system, are built around windows and mice. These operating systems do not have a command-line interface. Programs are selected for execution from a menu. Only when calling another system is a terminal emulator called, allowing the remote system to be used with commands.

Command Line Arguments

C programs are passed a list of arguments in the parameter `argv` to the `main` function. This list normally comes from the command line. K&R requires that these arguments be available from the command line. ANSI C has refined the language somewhat, requiring only that the arguments passed be character strings from the host environment. (ANSI C also requires that the arguments be mapped into lower-case if the environment is unable to support both cases, so that programmers don't have to check argument flags for both cases.) There may be no way to generate arguments from an environment that does not have a command-line interpreter.

This issue stems from a philosophical difference among user interfaces. Those who most strongly advocate mice believe that the user always should have mouse-oriented tools available, and that one hand usually should be on the mouse. The keyboard is reserved for typing in text, typically in a document or message, that cannot be selected from a menu. They feel that the mouse, combined with good menus and tools, is far more productive than using a keyboard. Keyboards on systems built with this philosophy tend to have as few keys as possible.

Those who use operating systems built around a command-line environment, such as the UNIX and MS DOS systems, like mice and menus, too, but also have a large collection of existing tools built for the command-line environment. These tools are assumed to be available as the basic system, with the windowing package considered an option. The base of users are already trained to use these tools. Upward compatibility is an absolute requirement.

Designers of such systems tend to make heavy use of *shell windows,* which allow a command-line interface (shell) to be run from inside a window. Programs run by this application, if portably written, will not care whether they are being run from a window. (There is an assumption that the window will be big enough. Since small windows are possible, applications should check that their window is big enough, and resize it or refuse to run, if necessary.)

This conflict leads to two different ways to write programs. One method is to write the program so that it works in the base environment, without use of windows or a pointing device, and take advantage of the upward compatibility feature to run it inside a window. This approach passes arguments from the command line via `argv`. The other approach is to call the program from a menu, using submenus to convey options or file names. This approach generally does not use `argv`.

The issue of argument passing is not well settled yet. The C standards expect a command line, or equivalent, to be available. Not all systems provide this option. A program portable to both environments must detect that it has been called from a menu (possibly because `argc == 1`) and use menus to fill in any required parameters.

Unfortunately, it is not possible for a program to detect portably the difference between being called from a menu and being called from a command line with no arguments. Some programs do something useful when passed no arguments. For example, they may filter standard input to standard output. They might print a usage message. There is no clear cut solution here, so caution and flexibility are advised.

Exercises

Exercise 5-1. The `poscursor` routine from Section 5.1.1 assumes that the terminal supports return and backspace. Modify it to require only return.

Exercise 5-2. Modify `poscursor` to require only backspace.

Exercise 5-3. Modify `poscursor` to assume an ANSI X3.64 conforming implementation, but not to assume that it knows the current row number on the screen. The ANSI "horizontal position" sequence is `\E[%dG`. (Paging programs, such as the UNIX commands `pg` and `more`, and other filters, can make use of column local cursor positioning.)

Exercise 5-4. Modify `poscursor` as in Exercise 5-3, but this time do cursor optimization, so that it sends the smallest possible number of characters to the terminal. How many characters can you save in the best and worst cases? Is it worth the complexity? Consider speeds of 300, 1200, and 9600 BPS. Does it matter if both the row and column must be transmitted to the terminal using the sequence `\E[%d,%dH`.

Exercise 5-5. What are the advantages and disadvantages of placing the terminal type in the environment variable `TERM`?

Exercise 5-6. Compare the driver method with the terminfo method. Discuss the advantages of each. Which is more powerful? Which is more portable? Which will be faster? Which considerations matter more than others?

Exercise 5-7. Many modems return messages other than `CONNECT` when something goes wrong; for example, `BUSY`, `NO ANSWER` and `NO DIAL TONE` are common messages. The method described in this chapter times out waiting for `CONNECT` before it can go on to try something else. A human would recognize the error message and give up at once. Design an alternate specification language that will allow another path to be taken at once when a recognized failure string comes in. Hint: use a finite-state machine.

CHAPTER 6: **NETWORK PROTOCOL DESIGN**

6.1 Protocols

Whenever two processes communicate with each other, the messages they send back and forth form a protocol. Protocols occur in a surprising number of situations. If the processes are on different machines, communicating over a network, it's fairly clear that the data sent over the wire represent a protocol; if one machine changes the form or sequence of the data, the other machine won't understand the transmissions anymore.

The same reasoning applies when the two processes are on the same machine. There is no wire separating the processes, but the communication between the processes is really no different, and still forms a protocol.

Another less obvious application of protocols involves using a disk file to communicate data between two processes. Any program that writes data to a disk or tape, with the intention that the data will be read back by another program (or even the same program) at a later time, in effect forms a protocol. The format of the file must be agreed upon by the portions that write the file and that read the file. Disk files are not generally considered ''protocols'' by the computing community, but the same issues apply to them as to networking and interprocess communication (IPC), and they will be treated the same here.

A related question involves the operating system primitives used for IPC. Older UNIX systems did not provide any general purpose IPC mechanism. Pipes and, to a lesser extent, signals are quite portable, but their functionality is limited. Often it is necessary to communicate through disk files. Networking solutions such as Berkeley sockets and System V's TLI are less portable. In general, if your IPC needs can be satisfied using a pipe, you'll have more portable code.

Whenever a protocol is involved, several issues should be addressed. These issues include (1) hardware dependence, (2) upward compatibility, (3) documentation, and (4) performance. Such issues are generally felt to be part of the International Standards Organization (ISO) presentation layer, but they really apply to all layers and interfaces between processes.

Hardware Dependence

Many protocols contain binary quantities, such as integers and floating point numbers. These protocols are usually not portable, because different machines use different bit orders and byte orders to represent such quantities. Similarly, not all machines use the same number of bits for their representations. For example, some machines have 16-bit integers and others have 32-bit integers. Such hardware dependencies in protocols almost always cause serious problems, because they make it impossible for heterogeneous machines to communicate using the protocol. If machine A sends an integer down the wire in A's native format, and it is received by machine B, which has a different byte order, machine B will receive the wrong value unless special provisions are made.

Upward Compatibility

Programs are always being modified. Bugs are fixed, features are added, and pieces of code are rewritten. When the code is changed, often the protocol is changed as well. If the protocol contains structures, new fields are sometimes added to the structures. If new commands or options are added to the protocol, the program that understands the protocol must be updated to understand the new features. Once the program is released to a few users and has any significant amount of use, you have to worry about old versions of the program on the other side of the connection, and about old files created using the old version of the program.

Documentation

Whenever a protocol has been created, there are two ways the protocol can be defined. One way is "by the code," that is, whatever the program does defines the protocol. (By definition, such programs have no bugs!) The other way is to write a document that defines exactly what the protocol consists of.

Serious problems arise if the code is allowed to define the protocol. These problems appear when the protocol is ported to a new machine, or extensions or changes are made to one copy of the implementation, or features are taken away. A document not only helps provide an open architecture, by defining what another implementation must do to conform to the protocol, but also helps the author find dependencies and inconsistencies in the protocol itself. One disadvantage to a document is that the document can be vague, making it possible for another implementation to conform to the document, but be unable to communicate with the first implementation. Sometimes only the protocol is documented, and the language bindings are not specified, causing divergence among applications. Another problem is that two separate implementations, even when based on the same original source code, may tend to diverge.

Performance

When addressing the above issues, the solutions can sometimes force conversion of the data into a portable or extensible format. With some applications, this can result in excessive CPU overhead or in an overly verbose protocol. A trade-off must be made between performance and portability.

6.2 Protocol Design

When designing a protocol or file format, consideration should be given to all these issues. For some applications, performance is so critical that using a portable or extensible format would produce an unacceptable load on the machine. However, when a network protocol is not portable, two conforming machines may simply not be able to talk to each other. Normally, the portability concerns are the most important.

Text Protocols

One easy way to make a protocol portable is to use straight ASCII text. Since all machines support character strings, and even operating systems that do not use ASCII (such as IBM 370 operating systems that use EBCDIC) support conversion to and from ASCII, it is almost always safe to use text. Numbers are easily encoded as text using existing library routines (possibly with some loss of precision for floating-point numbers). The one thing to watch out for is ASCII characters that may not have a representation in other character sets, such as ˜ and \. A few very old machines have 6-bit character sets that are missing lower-case and many of the punctuation characters. It's usually safe to assume 7-bit ASCII is present, since the 6-bit character sets are all but extinct, and nearly every vendor using a proprietary character set supports conversion to and from ASCII. EBCDIC does not have \ or ˜, but since it is an 8-bit character set, there are unused values that represent these characters. (Unfortunately, there are several standards for how to map between ASCII and EBCDIC. If you can ensure that your environment will always use just one of these standards, you will usually be OK, but watch out for tabs and trailing blanks.)

When using straight text, be sure to watch out for international issues. A protocol that depends on English keywords, or U.S. specific characters like {, |, and }, or on using the eighth bit for additional data, may cause problems in other countries. The only truly safe characters are those allowed in the X.409 Printable String data type. These characters are

Name	Graphic	Name	Graphic	Name	Graphic
Capital letters	A, B, ..., Z	Left parenthesis	(	Full stop (period)	.
Small letters	a, b, ..., z	Right parenthesis	)	Solidus (slash)	/
Digits	0, 1, ..., 9	Plus sign	+	Colon	:
Space	(blank)	Comma	,	Equal sign	=
Apostrophe		Hyphen	–	Question mark	?

Another advantage of text protocols is that they are more easily debugged. With many protocols (including TCP/IP) it is possible to open a terminal connection to any TCP socket and type commands at it. There is no need to write debugging routines that print binary flags and complex data structures, since the printed text of the protocol is often enough to tell what is going on.

Binary Protocols

Where performance considerations prevent the use of a text protocol, another possibility is a well-defined binary protocol. By choosing very ordinary data types (such as 32-bit unsigned integers) and carefully documenting the byte order, and by explicitly converting from the local format to the network format and back, a reasonably portable protocol can be created. One must still watch out for implementations that make invalid assumptions involving word size, negative numbers, and floating point. Since it is quite rare to use negative numbers and floating point in protocols, an implementation allowing them may appear to work for years before a large integer or an erroneous negative number causes a problem.

Using a portable format also turns out to be important for file formats and single-machine protocols. Several UNIX file formats were originally not portable (for example, ar and cpio) since it was assumed they would be read back on the same machine they were created. This assumption turned out to be false. cpio tapes are often used to transfer data between different machines, as are cpio images and ar images over network links. tar format has always been portable, because it is based on ASCII characters. IEEE P1003 is building on the tar and cpio formats for magnetic-tape distributions. Recent versions of ar use a portable ASCII format, and most versions of cpio have a −c option to use a portable format, but the portable format is not the default.

6.3 Compatibility

Single-machine protocols (where both processes are on the same machine) are subject to the same concerns as file formats. It may appear that the protocol will only be used within one machine, but often years later, in a more distributed environment, that protocol or the code that implements it is expected to work over a network connection. Any code that passes an arbitrary block of data can be used to send information that is not portably formatted. It is quite easy for unportable assumptions to pervade a large programming system and make it nearly impossible to upgrade it to work in a network. A distributed environment with processes on different machines communicating is very similar to a single-machine environment with processes on the same machine communicating.

Upward compatibility is another important issue. During initial development, it is quite common to change the protocol often, as the need suits. Many developers regard it as merely an annoying inconvenience to have to recompile the new version on all testing machines or to recreate all the files that were stored in the old format. Once a version of the program is released, the situation changes dramatically. It is not possible for the programmer to create a new version and install it all at once on every machine running the old version. Instead, a phased upgrade process occurs, where each site upgrades first one machine, then the remaining machines one at a time. Some adventurous sites upgrade at once; others that are more conservative or unwilling to pay an upgrade fee wait until they have heard favorable reports from adventurous sites, or sometimes never upgrade at all. Some sites have made local changes to the code supporting the old protocol, and would lose those changes if they upgraded to the new version.

If the protocol changes from one version to the next, there may be problems with new versions talking to old versions. When initially defining a protocol, it is best to assume that there will be future versions, and to design it so that future implementations can talk to older implementations. There are two popular ways to allow different versions of protocols to communicate: version detection and extensible protocols.

Version Detection

Version detection means that the new implementation detects that the other process (or the program that created the disk file) is an old implementation, and treats it differently because it uses the old protocol. One way to do this is to include a version number in the protocol at the beginning of the conversation or of the file. Another way is to detect that an older protocol is being used from the first few characters of the message. Since it is usually hard to predict how the protocol will be enhanced when it is first released, it is unwise to depend on being able to detect the version of the other party without using an explicit version number. Another problem that arises when version detection is being used is that there are usually several releases of the implementation in use at once, and trying to keep each version upward compatible with all previous versions can result in a lot of extra effort and unmaintainable code. Version detection is similar to `#ifdef`, except that the decisions are made at run time instead of compile time, and you can't throw away the old code on any machine as long as there is still one machine on the network that only understands the old code.

For example, the original Netnews article format, known as ``A News,'' had headers such as

```
Aucbvax.123
net.general
decvax!ucbvax!mark
Aug 27 23:01:18 EDT 1981
Important Message
```

The version, ``A,'' was marked with the first character. However, the ``B News'' version changed the format to use a header similar to the Mail Headers described later in this chapter.

```
Path: decvax!ucbvax!mark
Newsgroups: net.general
Date: Aug 27 23:01:18 EDT 1981
Subject: Important Message
Article-ID: ucbvax.123
```

It is fairly easy to tell these two formats apart since A format will begin with an A, and B format will contain a colon in each header line. Note that since the order of the lines in B format does not matter, it would be possible for the `Article-ID` line to come first, making a simple check for A insufficient. (The original B format always began with a `Relay-Version` header, ensuring that the A check would always work, but the `Relay-Version` line was deleted later, after support for A format became unnecessary.) A program can check for both versions like this:

```
read_header(fd)
FILE *fd;
{
        char buf[BUFSIZ];

        fgets(buf, sizeof buf, fd);
        rewind(fd); /* fails if stdin is a pipe */
        if (buf[0] == 'A' && strchr(buf, ':') == NULL)
                read_a_fmt(fd);
        else
                read_b_fmt(fd);
}
```

Extensible Protocols

Some simple protocols are never revised. More complex protocols, however, are often enhanced. If the protocol can be designed initially to be extensible, the code can be kept simple and old versions do not cause a problem. A typical extensible protocol uses text commands with text arguments and a regular syntax. A single routine can be written to decode any command or argument without knowing what the command does.

Many presentation layer protocols are designed to be general purpose and extensible. Two examples of such protocols are the international standard ASN.1 (Abstract Syntax Notation, also known as X.409) and the Sun Microsystems XDR (external data representation) protocols. Both define a syntax for arbitrary combinations of data types. A major difference is that ASN.1 contains two pieces of identification with every data element: a type description and the length. This makes it easy to recognize and ignore new unexpected data elements. Both protocols can represent variable length arrays, from which it is possible to create an extensible protocol.

File Transfer Protocol

One example of an extensible protocol is the TCP/IP FTP (file transfer protocol), using commands such as

    USER SMITH(CRLF)

as part of the user/password validation process ((CRLF) represents the CR and LF characters, which are normally used to terminate lines of text in a networked ASCII environment) with replies such as

    252 Username accepted, send password(CRLF)

Each digit of the numeric code has a meaning defined by the protocol, so that a program can interpret the response without having a list of all possible responses; the English text of the response is intended for humans to read, if necessary.

Protocols such as this can be extended easily by just adding more commands. Note that an implementation must be prepared for commands it does not understand, and new

implementations must be ready to do something reasonable when talking to an old implementation that refuses to accept a command.

Mail Headers

As another example, consider ARPA-style electronic mail headers. These headers are
highly portable and can be easily and transparently extended.

An electronic mail message contains one or more header lines, followed by a blank
line, followed by arbitrary text making up the body of the message. Header lines are a
word, a colon, a blank, text, and a newline. The format is similar to a typical interoffice
memo:

```
Date: 10 Aug 1989 14:22:17 EDT
From: JSmith@ABU.EDU
To: JDoe@ABU.EDU
Subject: Meeting tomorrow
Return-Path: @ABU.EDU:JSmith@ABU.EDU

What time is the meeting tomorrow?

    John
```

The header lines may be in any order. Only the `Date:` and `From:` lines are
required; the rest are optional.

An important property of this format is that new header lines can be easily added
without breaking existing implementations. A typical implementation will search the
message header for any lines it needs. For example, a `reply` command will search for a
`From:` line and generate a response message to the address shown. Any unrecognized
header lines will be ignored.

There are two natural implementations of mail headers. One is to store the entire
message as text and to search for header lines by textual comparison when needed. This
can be slow because of the search time. An improvement is to represent the header and
body as linked lists of text lines.

Another is to read the entire header into a C structure containing a field for each
expected field. The second method may be faster, but if the message is written back into
the text format for storage or transmission to another system, only the recognized header
lines are written out.

Both problems have solutions. The pure text method can keep pointers into the message for commonly used fields or keep memory copies if the fields are not to be changed.
The structure can add an array of character strings to store unrecognized header lines.

Binary Name/Value Pairs

The previous examples all use text formats. Text is a very portable format because all systems can store and transfer text files with few portability problems.

Text formats do have disadvantages. Fixed-width headers with binary contents often generate better performance. Text files containing words are written in a particular natural language, such as English, and may be unportable to countries where other languages are used. After all, the average French office worker may be unwilling to use an electronic mail package where all the header titles, commands, and error messages are in English.

It is possible to design a binary format that is portable, but it requires a bit more care. Special care must be taken to avoid byte-order problems, and to ensure that all header fields are the same size on all systems. Special care is needed to keep such protocols extensible.

One technique for an extensible binary protocol is the use of *name/value pairs*. This is extensible in the same sense as mail headers; the name corresponds to the type of header field, such as From, and the value corresponds to the rest of the line. Names might be character strings, such as From, or integers, such as 7, which might mean ''From''.

One possible design of a *name/value pair list* might consist of an integer representing the number of pairs, followed by an integer name and a character string for each pair. A mail body can be represented similarly, although names are not needed. For example, the previous mail header might be represented as follows:

```
5
3
"10 Aug 1989 14:22:17 EDT"
1
"JSmith@ABU.EDU"
11
"JDoe@ABU.EDU"
7
"Meeting tomorrow"
17
"@ABU.EDU:JSmith@ABU.EDU"
3
"What time is the meeting tomorrow?"
""
"       John"
```

Exercises

Exercise 6-1. Design an implementation of mail headers using the pure text method. The program must read a message from standard input, append the `Date:`, `From:`, and `To:` fields to a log file, and prepend the local host name to the `Return-Path:` header line in the message itself. Thus, if `hostname` returns `xyz.com`,

> `Return-Path: @prev.org:abc@def.edu`

becomes

> `Return-Path: @xyz.com:@prev.org:abc@def.edu`

It must then write out the entire message (with the modified header) for transmission to another system. Use `hostname` to get the current host name, and `popen("/bin/mail%s");` to transmit the message, where the argument is the contents of the `To:` header line.

Exercise 6-2. Design an implementation of mail headers using the structure method. The same operations apply as in Exercise 6-1.

Exercise 6-3. What does the structure method implementation do when it encounters two or more copies of a header line it does not recognize, such as multiple carbon copy fields? What if a recognized field, such as `Subject:`, occurs more than once? How can this be corrected?

Exercise 6-4. Which of the two implementations might alter the order of header lines in messages that pass through it?

Exercise 6-5. Write a Baccus Normal Format (BNF) grammar to describe the binary name/value pair representation of an electronic mail message.

Exercise 6-6. Design the detailed binary representation for mail messages. Use of the ASN.1 notation is recommended.

Exercise 6-7. Suppose the body of the message were also represented as a name/value pair list instead of a value list. What are some advantages and disadvantages of this change?

PART III
COMMON PORTABILITY PROBLEMS

## CHAPTER 7

CONSIDERATIONS IN A PORTABLE PROGRAM

There are many things a programmer can do that may not be portable. In general, they can be divided into two categories: use of documented extensions not generally present in other systems, and use of undocumented properties.[1]

The most obvious problem is making use of a language extension present only on the local implementation. Fortunately, few pre-ANSI C implementations support any language extensions beyond the language supported by System V release 2. (Three extensions that are not portable are AT&T's #ident lines, Microsoft's far and near pointers, and Quantum's @ and -} pointers.) Recent additions to the language have included enumerated types and flexnames (that is, allowing all characters of long names to be significant, rather than the traditional first seven or eight characters). There have been three major definitions of the C language in use recently: the first edition of Kernighan and Ritchie's *The C Programming Language* (K&R); the C compilers on major implementations of the UNIX system available in the mid-1980s, such as V7 and System V release 2; and the ANSI C standard.

Fortunately, the intersection of these definitions is still a very rich language. This intersection turns out to be the same as K&R. The de facto subset supported by most existing compilers, which is the practical limit faced by programmers, is even richer, allowing essentially the full language available on UNIX systems. (Many implementations on other systems support only K&R.) It is fortunate that the most definitive UNIX system dialects of C (System V release 2, 4.2BSD, and V8) agree on the C language.

There is more to portable programming than just language features. A program written with the assumption that it is running on a 32-bit machine (and, hence, that an int can hold numbers ranging into the millions) may do unexpected things when run on a 16-bit machine. There are many other hardware dependencies that can creep into programs if you aren't careful.

The C language itself is very Spartan. It has no provisions for input or output, for example. Instead, these features are provided by a *standard C library*. Lack of I/O has kept some other languages from catching on, but it hasn't been a problem in C. All releases of the UNIX system since 1977 have included a package called "Standard I/O" (stdio), which is supported by nearly all C implementations. In addition, many of the UNIX system calls, such as read, write, open, and close, are usually provided as

---

[1] For additional information about problems to avoid, see Andrew Koenig, *C Traps and Pitfalls*, Addison-Wesley, Reading, MA, 1989.

well. The UNIX system notion of command line arguments being passed in the `argc` and `argv` parameters to the `main` procedure has also become a de facto standard. (Non-UNIX operating systems, which usually just pass a single-string command line to the program, break this string up into individual arguments. Some even interpret the shell redirections <, >, and |, allowing the user to "pipe" one program to another.)

Many standard C functions, such as `getchar` and `strcat`, are provided in nearly every implementation. Others, such as `chown`, are specific to the UNIX system. Some, such as `mount`, are intended for use by the system itself and not by applications, so they may not be portable even among implementations of the same version of the UNIX system. Most implementations will add a few extensions to their C library in order to provide access to some local feature. Use of such extensions will lead to unportable programs.

A program may depend on a compile time feature of the implementation. For example, include files such as <stdio.h> are present in nearly all C implementations, but others, such as <sgtty.h>, may not be safe. Unfortunately, there is no way to check for the existence of an include file in the preprocessor, making it hard to portably use a feature only if it's present. (It is possible to use makefiles and shell scripts to get this effect in the UNIX system. The technique is to write a `Configure` shell script that searches for appropriate include files, shell commands, and functions in the C libraries, and build the appropriate makefiles and header files. Unfortunately, this technique is not portable to other systems.)

The C preprocessor is a powerful tool for increasing the portability of programs. Sometimes a program needs a feature that is present only on a few implementations, or may not have the same interface on all implementations. (For example, the same function is called `strchr` on some systems and `index` on others.) The C preprocessor (`cpp`) can be used to make a program work on many different systems by conditionally compiling different source code. `cpp` must be carefully used, since it is possible to get into trouble by using preprocessor variables that may not extend to future releases.

Finally, a program may depend on features of the run time environment. Certain files or databases may be assumed to exist, to be readable and/or writable, and to be in a certain format. A programmer assuming that an on-line dictionary can be found in the file `/usr/dict/words` will be in for a surprise when the program is moved to a machine where this file is in `/usr/lib/spell/hlista`, in a different format, or to a machine where no on-line dictionary exists. Help files, databases, and the like are often essential, but their use must be properly checked, so that when the program is run and the files aren't there, the application recovers or terminates gracefully.

Part III describes common problems that are often found in unportable programs. By being aware of the issues, it becomes possible to avoid the problems and to write more portable code. After a while, writing portable code becomes second nature. Chapter 8 discusses dependencies on the processor hardware. Chapter 9 covers problems that arise from assumptions about the C language. Chapter 10 deals with unportable dependencies on the operating system.

CHAPTER 8: **HARDWARE DEPENDENCIES**

A totally portable program uses only documented features of the language. It is consistent with the spirit of the language. Observed behavior of a particular implementation should not be taken as a definition of the language.

Keep your program modular and high level. Don't try to figure out what's going on underneath, except when tuning for performance. Assumptions about the underlying implementation may not be true of another implementation. It is best to test a program on several kinds of hardware to ensure that no unintentional assumptions have crept in.

When porting a program to new hardware, most problems encountered tend to be the result of coding errors not caught in the debugging process. One example is uninitialized stack variables, whose initial value happens to be zero in one implementation. Another problem is a program that dereferences a NULL pointer when memory location zero happens to be accessible and contains a zero.

Hardware dependencies account for a sizable portion of porting problems. Different processors have different properties that appear to the programmer. There are a few differences in the hardware that often show up when trying to port software written in C.

8.1 Byte Ordering

Not all processors order bytes within a word in the same way. Some processors place the most significant byte at the lowest address (this order is sometimes called "big endian"),[1] and others place the least significant byte first ('little endian"). There are even hybrids—the PDP-11 uses a mixed order for long words. For the most part, recent DEC products and Intel products use the little endian byte order, and others use the big endian order. A portable program should run correctly on machines with any byte ordering.

Well written programs seldom run into byte order problems unless they attempt to exchange binary data (i.e., not text) among two different processors. For example, since the UNIX filesystem contains long integers in the directory information for each file, it is not possible to directly share filesystem media between a little endian Intel 386 and a big endian AT&T 3B. It would have been possible to make filesystems portable by

---

[1] See *Gulliver's Travels*, by Jonathan Swift, first published in 1726, Part 1, Chapter 4. The term was applied to computer byte order by Danny Cohen, "On Holy Wars and a Plea for Peace," *IEEE Computer*, Vol. 14, October 1981, pp 48-54.

designing a filesystem format that is portable. While this would have enabled different processors to share filesystems across networks, dual-ported disks, and removable disk media, the cost to convert between the portable format and the internal numbers needed would probably have been much more than the benefit of having portable filesystems. (In practice, sharing filesystems is now generally done using network remote filesystem protocols. Floppy disks in UNIX filesystem format are not easily shared among different processors, however, because of byte order and floppy-disk format incompatibilities.)

This problem also shows up when exchanging magnetic tapes or floppy disks encoded with binary numbers. For example, the UNIX system `cpio` program will produce different archives depending on the byte order of the machine on which it is run. Other more severe media change problems exist as well, such as the density of recording, number of sides, number of tracks, and the like.[2]

Any time files are exchanged between processors, the byte order problem can occur. Computer networks make byte ordering considerations very important. Protocols are usually defined to use pure text, or else are defined right down to the byte level. The protocol shouldn't say "the next 32 bits are a long integer"; it should specify the format of the 32 bits, which bits come first, whether there are any sign bits involved, and so on. It is even possible to get into debates about the bit order within a byte, but, fortunately, from a software design point of view, it is fairly safe to assume that an 8-bit byte will arrive in the same bit order it was sent.

A few programs contain assumptions that cause the program to fail when it is moved to a processor with a different byte order. For example, the C code

```
/* This is unportable */
int c, r;
r = read(0, &c, 1);
if (c == '\n')
```

is in error because the second parameter to read is supposed to be a pointer to an array of characters. (Note that reading into the casted lvalue (`char *`)`&c` won't help, since the object being read into is still an integer.) It turns out this will work on a little endian machine because the first byte of c happens to be the least significant byte. It will fail on a big endian machine, setting c to 2^{24} times the desired value. Since `read` will only set the first byte of c, if c contained a value other than zero before the `read`, the results are unpredictable. The proper way to handle this is to declare c as a `char` rather than an `int`. Attempts to get at the "high byte" or "low byte" of an integer are unlikely to be portable, but such practices are rare nowadays, except in code originally written for very old versions of the UNIX system (such as V6, where such practices were commonplace,) and MS DOS system calls. Since the MS DOS system only runs on little endian machines, byte ordering is not usually a concern at this low level.

_____

[2] The `-c` option was added to `cpio` to create a portable format, but, unfortunately, the default remained the unportable format.

8.2 Sign Extension

Some processors have signed characters, capable of holding signed numbers, usually ranging from −128 to +127. Other processors have unsigned characters, which hold values ranging from 0 to +255. ANSI C also allows the explicit types unsigned char and signed char. The type char can be either and usually matches what the hardware provides. The type signed char was new with ANSI C. Many, but not all, older implementations supported unsigned char.

Care should be taken to store only actual nonnegative character text data in char variables. Since EOF is −1, it should never be stored in a char variable. While this may work on a machine with signed characters, it will be stored as some large positive value if characters are unsigned.

There are some older compilers that will not allow the declaration of an "unsigned char" variable. The ANSI signed keyword is new, and was not supported by many compilers released before 1989. Sign extension is important for integers as well as characters, but since most of the problems encountered in practice deal with characters being widened to integers, this section will use characters as examples.

This problem does not affect programs that only manipulate ASCII text in character variables and strings, since the ASCII values range from 0 to 127. (Don't assume the 0-127 property, however; see the section on international considerations.) Problems arise when a programmer needs a "byte" type in which to store other values.

Some programs place the value EOF (which is −1) in a character, and expect it to come out as EOF. This works on a VAX processor, but on a 3B processor, the value retrieved will be 255. Conversely, if 128 is stored in a character, it will come out as 128 on a 3B, but as −128 on a VAX.

There are two solutions to this dilemma. The first is to store such data in short, int, or long variables instead of char variables. This can cause problems with library routines that expect character strings and buffers to be arrays of characters, and can increase space requirements. But for local variables, it's often the easiest solution. (The traditional character variable c used to hold the current character being looked at is usually an int for this reason.)

The second solution is to treat all characters as unsigned, that is, assume only values from 0 to 255 can be stored in a char. When retrieving a value from a char variable, always "and" the result with 0377 (an 8-bit mask of 1's, assuming an 8-bit byte) to force it into this range. Thus:

```
char buf[MAXBUF];
...
if (buf[i] == 145)
```

is not portable—it will never be true on a signed computer such as a VAX processor. However,

```
if ((buf[i] & 0377) == 145)
```

is portable, and will work on nearly all implementations of C. An even better solution is to define a macro to do the same job. Then, porting to a machine with 7- or 9-bit bytes is as easy as changing the value of MASK.

```
#define MASK 0377
#define TRIM(c) ((c) & MASK)

    . . .
    if (TRIM(buf[i]) == 145)
```

Note: another solution may be to just declare the variable unsigned char rather than char. An alternative implementation of TRIM is

```
#define TRIM(c) ((unsigned char)(c))
```

which may run faster and not depend on byte order, but does depend on the presence of the unsigned char type. This will work, in fact, on many C compilers. However, there are many compilers in use today that do not support unsigned characters.

With UNIX System V, developed on the 3B, which has hardware unsigned characters, programmers are now urged not to assume signed characters. The ANSI C standard specifies that both signed and unsigned characters must be supported. Some day, it will be reasonable to just declare characters unsigned. In the meantime, a highly portable program must depend on the C '&' operator, if there is any chance that the value being compared is outside the 0-to-127 range. Ordinary ASCII characters are in this range, but extra care is needed when checking for special flags or international characters.

The simplest rule is *don't use character variables for anything other than characters.* Some programs used the high bit for something else. Such programs later had to be rewritten when 8- or 16-bit character sets were used. It is unnecessary to do any masking when comparing ordinary 7-bit characters. Here are portable methods to compare characters:

```
char a[5], c;
int i;
    . . .
    if (c == '/')
        . . .
    for (i=0; i<5; i++) {
        if (c == a[i])
            . . .
    }
```

It remains to be seen if problems with 8-bit characters will develop, as such characters are not heavily used today. The following method, where Ω is an international character whose value is above 0200, may not be totally portable on machines with signed characters.

```
    if (c == 'Ω')
        . . .
```

As a rule, if the character variable is declared to be `unsigned char` rather than `char`, such comparisons work properly.

Another common portability problem is `getchar`. In the above example, suppose `c` were initialized with

```
c = getchar();
```

`c` is declared `char`. What happens when `getchar` returns EOF?

8.3 Word Size

Programs should be written so that they work even on a machine with an unexpected word size. It is easy to make the assumption that a program will only run on a 32-bit computer. Many once-popular 16-bit machines are obsolete, and many of the more popular processors in use today for the UNIX system are 32-bit machines. However, it is important to realize that there are 8- and 16-bit processors in widespread use today. Some very large computers use larger words, such as 64 bits. MS DOS machines are often 16 bits wide. It is not difficult to write software so that it will run on processors with 16-bit, 32-bit or larger words.

8 Bits

In rare instances, it may be appropriate to consider 8-bit machines. 8-bit processors are primarily used in inexpensive home computers, special-purpose hardware, educational computers, and game machines. Most 8-bit processors deal with 8-bit data and 16-bit addresses. Pointers are usually 16 bits, but since 8 bits is so small, it's likely that a language provides a 16-bit integer type (or even a 48-bit floating point type in BASIC) as an easily used data type.

Memory on an 8 bit computer is often very limited. The chips can architecturally address only 64K, and I/O locations and the operating system often eat up much of that. Some machines have bank switching hardware to allow a bit more memory, often 128K, on the system, but this hardware must be explicitly switched, so memory allocation must be done very carefully. Even the most sophisticated compilers for 8-bit machines usually limit segments (and, hence, arrays) to 64K bytes.

Most 8-bit processors are programmed in either assembly language or BASIC. There are few C compilers available for them, and those that are available are usually limited, supporting only a subset of the language. The operating systems for such computers usually don't even assume a floppy disk drive. It may be unlikely that a program developed in C will be ported to an 8-bit processor.

On the other hand, there have been more 8-bit computers sold than all the 16- and 32-bit computers combined. (This may change as IBM-compatible PCs become more popular in the home and schools.) Some machines are widely used in schools and homes. Depending on the nature of the market, and on memory needs, it may be worthwhile to consider this market.

16 Bits

16-bit processors are also very common. The original IBM PC used the Intel 8088, which looked like a 16-bit machine to software. The AT&T PC 6300 used an 8086, which can be thought of as a faster 8088. (The difference is that the external bus of the 8086 is 16 bits wide, and the 8088 is 8 bits. 8088-based systems tend to be inexpensive, but since two bus cycles are needed for every 16-bit data transfer, they are usually slower.) There are compilers for the 8086 family that use the "small model" (function pointers, data pointers, and integers are 16 bits), the "medium model" (function pointers are 32 bits, and data pointers and integers are 16 bits), the "large model" (function pointers and pointers are 32 bits, but integers are still 16 bits), and the "huge model" (everything is 32 bits.) The medium and large models manipulate the segmentation registers to get the effect of a large addressing space on a small machine. Of course, the price for this is larger, slower code, but it is fairly transparent to the programmer, except for variable size.

Although the 8086 family has taken the world by storm (largely due to its use in the IBM PC), there are some other popular 16-bit processors. The Zilog Z8000 was the host for one of the first ports of the UNIX system, and comes in a strict 16-bit version (Z8002) and a version with segmentation hardware (Z8001).

The DEC PDP-11, a 16-bit processor, is the original processor used for C. It didn't have provisions for anything except the small model. It did allow more than 64K of memory on a physical system, so the operating system (running in a privileged mode) could change segmentation registers.

A feature called "split instructions and data" on the larger PDP-11 models allowed a program to have 64K of program and another 64K of data, for a total of 128K. Larger programs had to be pared down to a version that fit in 64K of instructions and the same amount of data.

Some versions of the UNIX system for the PDP-11 offered a feature that allowed the equivalent of the 8086 medium model. This required help from the operating system to change the segmentation registers, which are not accessible to an ordinary program.

The 8086 has no notion of privileged mode, since it was not intended for a multi user operating system. This means that all programs can change their own segmentation registers. This makes it faster to switch registers on an 8086, but an errant or malicious program has the ability to clobber anything in RAM. Successor processors, such as the 80286, have the necessary modes and memory management hardware to fully support multi-user operating systems.

32 Bits

Currently, 32-bit processors are the most popular machines for more expensive "supermicro" systems. The VAX and 3B processors are 32 bits wide, as are some chips like the AT&T 32200, the National Semiconductor 32032, and the Intel 80386. Many mainframes are based on 32-bit words.

The Motorola 68000 is mixed, with 32-bit pointers and 16-bit data; many C compilers treat it as a full 32-bit machine by providing 32-bit integers. The 68020 is a full 32 bits inside and out.

From a software point of view, the 80386, and it's cheaper cousin the 80386SX, are full 32-bit processors. The 80286 is really a 16-bit processor, although it has some provisions for running programs of various sizes using various memory models and degrees of transparency.

Assumptions about the content of structures can cause problems. It is best to treat a structure as an opaque bundling mechanism. Word sizes matter if you make assumptions about how much fits in an integer, or about what overlays what else in memory. (Overlaying in memory is rarely a good programming practice, but sometimes files or arrays must be carefully layed out.)

For example, given structure declarations

```
struct foo {
        short a;
        char *b;
        int c;
        short d;
} x;
struct bar {
        short a;
        char *b;
        char c1;
        char c2;
        short d;
} y;
```

and the assumption that the d fields are supposed to represent the same memory, we have a nonportable construct. On a 16-bit machine, c will take 2 bytes, the same size as c1 and c2. On a 32-bit machine, c will take 4 bytes and the d's don't match.

Had c been declared short instead of int, the program would be more portable. The declaration short usually produces a 16-bit integer, and long usually 32 bits. You can't be assured of this, however. On an 8- or 64-bit processor, it is likely it will be different. A processor is perfectly justified in providing a 64-bit long, for example. Since the alignment can depend on the particular compiler, in general, the above technique of parallel structures is not portable.

When an overlay or variant record is needed, the fixed part should precede the variant part. Each declaration of d above should be moved after the corresponding b. This is not enough, however, due to uncertainties of alignment and structure size.

The most portable way to handle overlays like this is to use a union.

```
struct twochars {
      char c1, c2;
};
union byteword {
      short word;
      struct twochars byte;
};
struct foo {
      short a;
      char *b;
      char *d;
      union byteword c;
} x;
```

Unfortunately, unions are not very easy to use in C. There are a lot of restrictions on their use (they couldn't be initialized at load time before ANSI C, there are no constants of union type, and values of nonunion types can't be assigned to union variables, even using casts.) The syntax is cumbersome; for example, in the first example, you might refer to x.c1, which in the union version becomes x.c.byte.c1. Some relief is possible by using macros:

```
#define    cw     c.word
#define    cb1    c.byte.c1
#define    cb2    c.byte.c2
```

In practice, most C programmers are willing to assume that a short will get them a 2-byte integer, a char a 1-byte integer, and a long a 4-byte integer. Although this may not work on some supercomputers today, it is more likely to be a long-term problem if the world outgrows 32 bits.

If typedefs are used to give symbolic names to the types used, such programs are usually not hard to port. For example, if you need a pointer to the smallest element of memory available, you might use this.

```
typedef char *memptr;
```

Beware of declaring variables int. Such a declaration means to use whatever size is most efficient on the computer, and the implementation is free to use any size. An int should be used for variables where size doesn't matter, such as flag variables and short counters under 32K in programs. It is a bad idea to include an int in a structure declaration, or in a file format, since the size can vary considerably. (Situations where the size doesn't matter are, however, quite common. Since many compilers optimize int variables, there is no reason to avoid their use in local or global scalar variables.) As K&R says, about all you should count on is that short is no longer than long.

The new ANSI header file <limits.h> is useful if you absolutely must be concerned about the size of basic types. Implementations conforming to ANSI C must support signed and unsigned characters (at least 8 bits), short integers (at least 16 bits), integers (at least 16 bits), and long integers (at least 32 bits).

8.4 Word Alignment

Some processors require that certain kinds of data be aligned on 2-, 4-, 8- or even 16-byte boundaries. Such requirements simplify the hardware logic of the processor, which can retrieve bytes in parallel by varying only a few low bits in an address. Other processors allow data to be aligned any way desired, but are faster if the data are properly aligned. Floating point is often more restrictive about alignment than fixed point, requiring, for example, 4-byte alignment.

For this reason, the C compiler is free to leave gaps in memory to force correct alignment. The first structure declaration above, for example, might have a 2-byte gap if the hardware requires pointers to be on 4-byte boundaries. If you are trying to lay out a structure to match some externally imposed data format, beware of alignment restrictions. Even within one processor type, different compilers may not use the same alignment rules.

The usual bug encountered here is when a pointer has an odd value, and an integer is referenced through the pointer. This often results in the error message "Bus error—core dumped". Such bugs are not always the result of unportable code, however, since the alignment is generally hidden by the C compiler. It's quite possible that the pointer just got a garbage value.

Some processors that run the UNIX system require all multibyte data to be aligned on a 2- or 4-byte boundary. The main potential trouble spot, the memory allocator `malloc`, is conservative on the subject: it always returns an area in memory that is properly aligned for anything you might want to put there.

8.5 Byte Addressing

Not all pointers are the same size. Character pointers on word-oriented machines may need extra bits. Similarly, not all machines have pointers that are the same size as integers.

It is not even safe to assume that characters are all the same size. A simple application running on a Japanese text file may find `getc` returning a mixture of 8- and 16-bit characters. (See the new ANSI multibyte character functions, such as `mbtowc`, for a new, if unportable, way of dealing with large characters.)

The C language is most comfortable on machines with 8-bit bytes, where each byte is addressable with a consecutive address. With the exception of the IBM 360, such machines are relatively new. Most older machines were built around words, with word sizes such as 12, 18, 32, 36, and 60 bits quite common. Each word had a separate address, and you usually couldn't take the address of a specific byte. Many popular mainframes have special word sizes; for instance the Sperry Univac (now Unisys) 1100 series uses a 36-bit word, as does the DEC PDP-10. Many older supercomputers use a 60-bit word, and store 10 characters of 6 bits in each word. The 36-bit machines have various character packings. The Univac started with 6 characters of 6 bits per word, in the days of punched cards when a character set of 64 characters was sufficient, and has moved to 4 characters of 9 bits. The Honeywell 6000 has a 36-bit word with 4 characters of 9 bits, too. The PDP-10 has an architecture capable of using any size characters, but its operating system packs 5 characters of 7 bits each into a 36-bit word, wasting one bit.

Unlike most other programming languages, C measures the size of objects. The unit of measurement is *bytes,* normally the size of a single character. This is consistent with existing implementations on byte-oriented machines, but is not clarified for the case of word-oriented machines. All the I/O and string routines, such as `read`, `write`, and `strncpy`, assume that sizes are measured in bytes. They also assume that if you copy all the characters from one place to another, you have copied all the data. This assumption is true on a machine with 8-bit bytes, but is not true on the PDP-10.

It's quite rare to find the UNIX system ported to a machine that isn't byte-oriented. However, there is a C compiler for the Honeywell 6000 running GCOS. The 9-bit characters often turn up portability bugs in programs. For example, the trick above using the & operation with 0377 does not work on GCOS, where you must & with 0777. Character pointers on the 6000 are longer than integer pointers, too, causing some programs that assume that they are the same size to be nonportable. In practice, this problem is more likely to occur on the 68000, which often has 16-bit integers and 32-bit pointers.

Lately, there has been a strong trend toward byte-oriented machines. The C language has soared in popularity with this trend. The C language is an excellent language for byte-oriented machines, although it is weaker on some word-oriented machines. The word-based machines matter less and less as byte-oriented machines become a de facto standard.

8.6 Shifts

A portable program should avoid the >> and << shift operations, except when doing bit manipulation. If the objective is to multiply or divide by a small power of 2, let the C optimizer determine if implementation with a hardware shift instruction is appropriate.

Shifts are well defined, but are intended to be efficiently implemented on existing hardware. Because of this, sign extension can be a portability problem.

When shifting right, the bits shifted in from the left depend on the implementation and the data type. If a quantity is unsigned, the implementation must shift in zeros. (Not all implementations properly support unsigned characters, shorts, or longs.) For signed quantities, implementations are allowed to shift in either zeros or copies of the sign bit, and portable programs should not assume either implementation.

The shift count for an n-bit word may range from zero up to (but not including) n. Thus, for a 32-bit word, shifting by 32 or by -1 are not allowed.

8.7 Floating Point Hardware

The C language was designed for systems programming, which seldom uses floating point. So floating point support in C often has not received as much attention as some of the other language features.

The K&R C language treats floating point as double precision. Arithmetic operations are carried out in double precision, and floating point parameters to procedures are passed as `doubles`. The `float` type was used primarily to save storage space, not to speed up the program or to guarantee a particular precision in the result. The ANSI C `float` type does not do this automatic expansion.

Many C compilers perform peephole optimizations on the generated code. They form expression trees, reorder expressions, and eliminate common subexpressions to avoid repeated work at run time. Reordering of expressions can be done using mathematical identities, such as the commutative and associative laws of addition and multiplication. As long as overflow does not occur, these laws apply to integers. Unfortunately, they do not always apply to digital floating point numbers because of rounding.

An early draft of the ANSI C standard provided the unary + operator to force grouping of subexpressions, but it was later taken out. The same effect can be had with real compilers by using a temporary variable.

While ANSI C is much more specific about floating point, it is important for programmers who use floating arithmetic and the math libraries to realize that many C implementors take considerably less care with their floating point implementations than their fixed point, and considerable variation of results occurs.

Floating point code should be very defensive. There is a wide variety of hardware, data formats, exception conditions, and default handling of these error conditions. Overflows and underflows, for example, sometimes cause a program to abort.

There are many trouble spots among older floating point implementations. The data format varies widely. The base, word size, exponent bias, and range of numbers supported can all vary. Rounding is not always what you might expect. Some hardware has real bugs; for example, multiplication may not be commutative.

Error handing of floating point operations might cause an abort, a traceback, be ignored, or generate a signal that can be caught by the application. There is no standard way to turn off such exceptions. There may be reserved or special values, such as infinity, NaN (not a number), and unnormalized numbers.

Some implementations might have both +0 and −0. Support for single precision may vary from system to system. Many of the math libraries produce results with which some programmers are unhappy.

The IEEE 754 standard defines floating point data formats and provides detailed definitions of the operations. This standard has become widely implemented in new hardware. It offers hope for truly portable floating point applications.

8.8 Disk Space

Some programs require large amounts of disk space for their code, library files, or data. Others require only a little disk space. Still others will work with data of any size. Many systems have only floppy disks, which might hold only 360K each. Your program will be more widely useful if it can be used on small systems as well as large systems.

Floppy-disk based systems have special considerations. It is common for a floppy-based system to have two disk drives. The boot disk is kept in the first drive, and the user data is kept in the second drive. Sometimes the user prefers to keep the application program on the boot drive, and sometimes on the second drive. For example, a file transfer program might be used to copy data onto an unrelated disk, so it is likely it will reside on the boot disk.

Unfortunately, there is no portable way to determine whether there is enough disk space. The best you can do is write the data and check to see if it succeeded. Even the UNIX system df command is not portable, since the formats vary, the units are not consistent from system to system, and the command is not required by POSIX.

8.9 Assembly Language

A computer's instruction set is rarely a portability problem, since it is hidden by the C language. Of course, if you use any assembly language, this automatically restricts your program to the particular processor whose assembly language you're using.

This section discusses some techniques for using the asm directive while salvaging *some* portability. However, it is important to realize that *using assembly language is highly unportable, and should normally be avoided.* This section is intended for the programmer who has already decided that a particular section of code must be rewritten in assembly language, and is looking for a way to do so with minimal damage to the program's portability.

Many compilers support an extension to the C language to allow assembly language to be called from C. The format is often asm ("*instructions*"), although there are others. Use of this directive is the same as using assembly language, so it reduces portability as well.

For most sections of most programs, the performance to be gained by using assembly language is relatively minor, and is quickly offset by the added cost of maintaining assembly language code for several processors. In some cases, however, a performance analysis will determine that one or two small parts of the program, somewhere inside an inner loop, or a heavily used subroutine, account for a large fraction of the running time of the program. In these cases, optimization of the particular part of the program can make a big difference.

Recoding in assembly language is rarely a useful approach to such optimization, but in a few cases it can make a difference. Be sure to consider other ways to speed up your program, such as not using the critical section of code so much, and using register variables. Examination of the generated assembly language can sometimes help to reveal a way to recode more efficiently in C, although such insight may not apply to other hardware. This section is intended to be helpful for those rare circumstances. In general, it is strongly recommended that portable C programs be coded entirely in the C language.

If you have determined that you absolutely must use assembly language for a critical section, you may be able to use #ifdef and asm to do it without losing too much portability. The use of #ifdef is often preferable to having separate source files that are only used on certain machines, because it results in only one copy of common code, making maintenance easier.

Most C compilers provide a predefined preprocessor variable for the processor you're on, for example, u3b2, pdp11, vax, or mc68000. *Use of processor names is strongly discouraged.* Any time a particular processor seems to require some change, try to find out why. Often you'll find a more general reason for the difference, such as a different release of the operating system. If you must code processor names into your program, find out the name for your processor from your C compiler manual, or from the vendor. This feature permits code such as that which follows. Note that this example is very fragile and makes assumptions about register assignments. These assumptions can turn out to be wrong if a new compiler is installed or if an optimizer is used. Assembly language is not even totally consistent among different operating systems on the same processor.

```
                     cnt = bp->b_nleft;
                     bp->b_nleft -= cnt;
                     to = bp->b_ptr;
        #ifdef vax
                     asm("movc3 r8,(r11),(r7)");
        #else
                     memcpy(to, src, cnt);
        #endif
                     bp->b_ptr += cnt;
```

Use of asm is somewhat tricky. In C, values are in variables with names. In assembly language, some values are in memory locations with names, some are in registers with register numbers, and some are on the stack at a known offset from the stack pointer. It's up to you to know your machine and compiler well enough to know which variables go where. (You can look at the assembly code your compiler generates to find out what it puts where.) Be careful about assuming register numbers, stack offsets, and the like— some day you may need to use a different compiler, with different allocation conventions, on the same processor.

Another trick is to create a subroutine call that does the same as a hardware instruction, such as memcpy in the previous example. If there is no hardware instruction, the subroutine, written in C, can be called. If there is hardware support, you can have the C compiler treat it normally (e.g., generate the subroutine call) and then postprocess the assembly language output of the compiler. The 4.2BSD VAX UNIX system kernel has rules like this in the Makefile:

```
af.o: ../net/af.c
        $(CC) -I. -c -S $(COPTS) ../net/af.c
        $(C2) af.s | sed -f asm.sed | $(AS) -o af.o
        rm -f af.s
```

These rules insert an extra step in the compilation process, passing the assembly language generated by the compiler through a `sed` script called `asm.sed`, before passing the results to the assembler. The file asm.sed has lines in it to change assembly language C calls into direct machine instructions.

```
s/calls $3,_memcpy/movc3 8(sp),*(sp),*4(sp)\
        addl2 $12,sp/
```

This technique, while useful on many systems, only works on one given machine, but since the details are usually hidden in the Makefile and don't appear in the C source, the same C source can be compiled with a different Makefile on another system and still work. The dependency on the specific machine has been isolated in one place, in this case, the makefile, where it can be easily changed for other machines.

Beware of the C preprocessor names for different processors. There is no documented standard for any particular convention, only word-of-mouth conventions, and a few documented names such as u3b2. Some day you may be using the same processor or a compatible one that has a different preprocessor variable name. If you know the set of widely used names for your processor or processor group, you can factor the ifdefs:

```
#if u3b2 || u3b5 || u3b
...
#endif
...
#if m68 || mc68000 || m68000 || m68k
...
#endif
```

In general, portability is completely sacrificed if you want to make any processor specific assumptions, such as use of assembly language. Don't use it unless you have a *lot* to gain. Generally, assembly language is only justified for access to special hardware instructions that can't be accessed from C, or for critical inner loops that can drastically improve the overall performance of the program by recoding in assembly language. If you must use it, try to use one of the methods described here, so you don't sacrifice so much portability.

CHAPTER 9: **C LANGUAGE DEPENDENCIES**

Until the ANSI C standard was written, there was no single official definition of the C language. For years, the language was defined by Ritchie's C compiler. In 1978, Kernighan and Ritchie wrote the K&R ''C book,'' which has served as the major public domain definition of the language. (The K&R book was updated in 1988.) Many non-AT&T written C compilers (those not derived from the Ritchie compiler or Johnson's portable compiler) used K&R as the definition of the language, and supported only the 1977 version of the C language.

In 1986, the definition of C was generally taken to be ''what the System V release 2, 4.2BSD, and V8 C compilers do.'' Fortunately, these major compilers in use on UNIX systems and UNIX-derived systems all pretty much agreed on the C language, so there were few conflicts.

The ANSI X3J11 committee proposed a C language standard in the mid-1980s. The ANSI C language is generally a superset of the C language supported by System V release 2. There are also several areas where the language specification has been clarified, making some existing programs invalid. The enhancements include `const`, `volatile`, and `signed` attributes, and a way for C to check the types of parameters to functions. Several new functions and include files are also defined.

If you target an application for UNIX System V release 2, or a more recent release, you should assume they all understand the same dialect of C, including flexnames.

New applications should be written to conform to ANSI C, as well as K&R, since ANSI C compilers are expected to become popular over the next several years. If you assume the presence of new ANSI C features, you will restrict the application roughly to System V release 4 or later, and to other operating systems for which ANSI C compilers are available, such as the MS DOS system. When porting old code to ANSI compilers, the biggest areas to watch for are liberties taken with the preprocessor, such as comments after preprocessor statements, and programs that contain assumptions about the order of evaluation of the code generated by a particular compiler. For the C library, see the tables in Appendix G.

The ANSI C language supports a new feature called *function prototypes*. This allows the programmer to state the number and type of function parameters in a header file, so that the compiler can check for correct usage.

Older versions of the language only allowed function parameters to be declared with the function definition. When the function is called, the compiler usually does not know the types of the parameters. To work with both kinds of compiler, function prototypes must be omitted or conditionally compiled.

The following example shows conditional compilation of function declarations to take advantage of ANSI C prototypes while still working on older implementations. A separate #ifdef has been used for each declaration to make software maintenance of each pair more reliable. Grouping all the ANSI prototypes together would result in a shorter header file, but makes it more likely that an update to a function would be made to only one of the declarations.

```
#ifdef __STDC__
char *f(int, char *str);
#else
char *f();
#endif

#ifdef __STDC__
int g(void);
#else
int g();
#endif
```

A traditional programming style has been to mark #else and #endif lines with the name of the condition being checked to aid the matching of nested conditional compilation.

```
#ifdef BIT32
# ifdef REVERSED_BYTE_ORDER
# else REVERSED_BYTE_ORDER
# endif REVERSED_BYTE_ORDER
#endif BIT32
```

This practice was forbidden in ANSI C, and newer compilers will consider this an error. A portable version of the same practice is to use comments.

```
#ifdef BIT32
# ifdef REVERSED_BYTE_ORDER
# else /* REVERSED_BYTE_ORDER */
# endif /* REVERSED_BYTE_ORDER */
#endif /* BIT32 */
```

Not all compilers evaluate function parameters in the same order. When a function such as f(a, b, c) is called, and the parameters are expressions, some compilers will evaluate a first, then b, and then c. Others will evaluate c, b, and then a. This matters if the parameters contain side effects, such as autoincremented variables or calls to input/output functions such as getc. Portable programs will not depend on the order of evaluation.

If you aim at "most of the UNIX systems in the marketplace," you can assume the language accepted by the System V release 2 C compiler as the lowest common denominator. This means names need not be unique in the first eight characters. Systems based on 4.2BSD support essentially the same language. For the C library, see the tables in Appendix G. Again, don't do anything forbidden by ANSI C.

If you are aiming at targets including implementations of C that are not based on an AT&T compiler, you will find that many of them use the ''K&R C book'' as the definition of the language. K&R was written in 1977, shortly before V7 came out, and omitted the features just described. Since none of these features are present in the C book, many vendors do not include them. Enumerated types are less useful in C, as their implementation is often very restrictive. Structure operations are quite useful, but can easily be avoided by passing pointers to the structures instead of the whole structures, and avoiding making local changes to the structure, since the structure is now being passed by reference instead of by value. Passing a pointer is also often more efficient than forcing an entire structure to be copied, but beware of structuring problems, since pointers are to data as goto's are to programs.

There are a few very old C compilers still in use, based on the V6 compiler. Since this compiler was missing a large number of features that are commonly used today, such as #include with <> brackets, the *op=* form of assignment statement, the = to initialize values, and unions, the cost to avoid these features is usually too high to consider. Such compilers can be considered obsolete, and it is usually reasonable to disregard them.

Many compilers in use today have warnings built into them to discourage the V6 constructs. In some cases, these warnings will mistake a legal program for a V6-style program, generating incorrect code. For example,

```
i=-1;
```

is a legal C assignment, assigning the value −1 to the variable i. Many older compilers will instead treat it as

```
i =- 1;
```

which was the V6 way of writing

```
i -= 1;
```

Such compilers print a warning and generate code to subtract one from i instead of assigning −1 to it. Be sure to separate any operator that might be mistaken for a V6-style operator (an = followed by a binary operator, especially − and *) with a space to avoid any such problems.

```
i = -1;
```

This problem arises often in for loops.

```
for (i=-1; i < n; i++)
```

should be written

```
for (i = -1; i < n; i++)
```

9.1 Stack Growth

Some machines have stacks that grow up (toward larger addresses). Others have stacks that grow down (toward smaller addresses). Some align parameters on 2-byte boundaries, others on 4-byte boundaries. In general, assumptions about the layout of parameters passed to functions are unsafe, as the compiler is free to organize these any way it wishes. If you find yourself thinking about how items are organized on the stack, you are probably thinking of writing unportable code.

One reason for wanting to access parameters on the stack is to use your own interface to `printf`, taking a variable number of arguments. For example, it's handy to have a debugging routine that only does a `printf` if a debug flag is set.

Taking the address of a parameter and following it up the stack is very unportable. You can't depend on whether the stack grows up or down. Some machines pass the first several parameters in registers instead of the stack.

The recommended portable way to write a function with variable parameters, such as `printf`, is to use `#include <varargs.h>` (see `varargs(5)`). This only works, however, if you reinvent your own `printf`. (Note that ANSI C supports a new `stdarg` mechanism that is similar. If you are willing to assume ANSI C, the `stdarg` mechanism is preferable.)

ANSI C and System V release 2 provide a handy routine called `vprintf`, which can be called by your printf-like routine. There are variants `vsprintf` and `vfprintf` to print to strings and files, as well.

`vprintf` is useful for libraries such as curses. This library needs a facility like this to implement the `printw` and `wprintw` functions. Before `vprintf`, curses used unportable code to make low-level changes to standard I/O bits and fields to get the same effect. In System V release 2, the higher-level interface was moved into standard I/O and documented as a standard feature.

Unfortunately, there is no equivalent feature for `scanf`. In practice, most programs only need the `printf` capability, so this doesn't matter very often. If you must build your own `scanf`-like function, the implementation will probably have to use one of the unportable techniques that follow.

On systems without `vprintf`, it is necessary to use unportable techniques. These methods include using a direct interface to an internal part of `printf`, often called `_doprnt`, declaring several sample `int` parameters, and writing your own `printf`.

It is possible to write `printf` entirely in C. The UNIX System III implementation of `printf` was written entirely in C, using `varargs`. Eventually, it was decided that since `printf` was such a heavily used function, it should be written in assembly language to get better performance.

System V generally uses a `printf` written in assembly language, gaining speed at significant portability expense. This requires `printf` to be rewritten for each UNIX system port. Users of UNIX System III or System V systems with source code can usually find a `printf` written entirely in C by looking in the directory

`/usr/src/lib/libc/port/print`, although this may vary with different UNIX system releases.

One trick used when you need a quick-and-dirty `printf` is to pass several integer variables, and to pass them along to `printf`. Typical code looks like this:

```
dprintf("x is %d\n", x);
...
dprintf(fmt, p1, p2, p3, p4)
char *fmt;
int p1, p2, p3, p4;
{
        if (!debugging)
                return;
        fprintf(trace, fmt, p1, p2, p3, p4);
}
```

This approach is inherently dangerous, but in practice seems to work quite well on most C implementations. The major pitfall is that the caller might need more parameters than the routine provides (e.g., five or more with the above example). Note also that floating point variables will usually take up two of the parameters, as will long integers on a 16-bit machine. It's fine for debugging, but not a good idea for a documented interface in a product.

9.2 Uninitialized Variables

The C language specifies that all global variables are initialized to zero, unless otherwise initialized. Some programmers think this means that all variables start at zero. What it really means it that all static memory is set to zero when the program starts up. Local variables (on the stack) and register variables are not initialized; they retain whatever garbage was previously there. The first time a routine is called, it may be zero, or it may be whatever value the most recent function call left on the stack. Programs that assume a local or register variable is initially zero will eventually fail. You should explicitly initialize such variables to zero if needed. It's not a bad idea to explicitly initialize a global or static variable to zero, just to emphasize that you really expect it to be initially zero, and to form the habit so you won't forget when you need to initialize a local variable. Explicit initialization to zero is also a documentation aid for others who may later read your program. (Beware, however, that explicitly initializing large arrays to zero may move the array from the BSS to the DATA region, resulting in a larger executable file.)

In the following example, it is safe to assume that a, b, and d are initialized (once, when the program starts) to zero. The variables c and e will be left with garbage in them, and f will be initialized (once) to either zero or some other known value, as specified in its defining declaration elsewhere.

```
int a;
static int b;
funct()
{
      int c;
      static int d;
      register int e;
      extern int f;
}
```

9.3 Multiple Definitions

One common portability problem involves the way global variables are declared. A popular way to declare a global variable is to put a group of related declarations, such as

```
#define NAMELEN 64
int gflag;
char curdir[NAMELEN];
```

in a header file, and #include the header file in each source file that uses any variable in the file. (An even simpler method is to put all globals in a single header file, and #include that file in *all* of the source modules.) This works fine in most versions of the UNIX system, but in general won't work on other operating systems.

The problem is that each source file that includes the declaration behaves as if the declaration were directly in the source file, and generates a loader directive that allocates space for the variable. If there is more than one source file, the loader complains that the variable is multiply defined, and refuses to create an executable file. The loader can't tell that all these storage allocations are really supposed to be for the same variable; it thinks that several separate variables all have the same name. It works on the UNIX system only because a special class of storage allocation in the UNIX system loader is used, allowing multiple instances to be treated as the same.

Before we look at methods to portably declare global variables, let's step back a minute and ask a more fundamental question. *Why are we using global variables?* Global variables are usually used to communicate between two or more parts of the program. Another method of communication is to use explicit parameters. Many experienced C programmers feel that parameters are a better mechanism because they make the lines of communication more visible when reading the program and this forces the programmer to think about these lines of communication when designing and coding the application. Many well-written programs use global variables sparingly and instead use subroutines with parameters for almost all communication.

Another technique is to use local variables in the section of the program that logically "owns" the variable. Declare the variable outside functions, like a global, but only declare it in the one source file that "owns" it. For the rare circumstances when another part of the program must access the variable, use an explicit extern declaration. It may be a bit extreme to competely avoid global variables, just as it is a bit extreme to completely avoid the `goto` construct, but it is worthwhile to treat each new global declaration suspiciously, and to use an alternative unless you are convinced it is really necessary.

The portable way to declare a global variable is to allocate space for it in exactly one place, using

```
int gflag;
```

Other source files that reference it should declare

```
extern int gflag;
```

If your programming style is to avoid declaring variables in header files, but instead to declare the variable near the "owning" function, and use `extern` for all other references, you won't run into this problem. You will, however, run into the maintenance problem described below.

It is hard to get exactly one ordinary declaration if the variable is declared in a header file. One method is to put the `extern` declaration in the header file, and put the regular declaration in just one module, or in a separate file used only for such declarations.

The disadvantage to this is that you now have at least two copies of the variable declaration, causing some maintenance problems. If you change the type or size of the variable, you must update all the declarations. If there is only one declaration, this is automatic. If there is more than one, you may miss one, resulting in inconsistent declarations. The compiler and linker may not catch this error, unless the `extern` declaration is in a header file visible to the local declaration. and you'll have a strange run time error. (This problem also applies to separate explicit `extern` declarations, used as needed.)

One way to work around this is to play a game with the preprocessor. Declare the variable using another keyword in place of `extern`, such as

```
#ifndef global
# define global extern
#endif
...
#define NAMELEN 64
global int gflag;
global char curdir[NAMELEN];
```

Then include the file normally in all but one source file. In one file, define `global` before the `#include`:

```
#define global /* empty */
#include "globals.h"
```

This will ensure that the variables are allocated exactly once. (This method may only be worthwhile for a large program.)

Another method is to put all globals into a single structure. The header file contains the structure definition, and hence the only copy of the members.

```
#define NAMELEN 64
struct global {
      int gflag;
      char curdir[NAMELEN];
};
extern struct global g;
```

One C source file must declare

```
struct global g;
```

Now the source files can reference `g.gflag` without extra declarations. The major difficulty here is that all references must have the `g.` prefix to mark them as a structure member. One way to look at this is that the extra prefix serves the purpose of clearly marking global variables to enhance the clarity of the program.

All of these methods are cumbersome and unappealing. The only reasonable method, a single declaration in a header file, isn't portable. The recommended way to deal with this problem for new code is to write two duplicate external declarations (an `extern` in a header file, and a regular declaration in one defining module) for new code.

```
/* globals.h */
extern int gflag;
#define NAMELEN 64
extern char curdir[NAMELEN];

/* main.c */
int gflag;
char curdir[NAMELEN];
```

If the defining module includes the header file, the compiler should detect the inconsistency if only one is changed.

Recommendation: for new code, use two declarations, as in the last example. For porting existing code containing many unportable single declarations in a header file, the program can be ported using the `global` macro method, if necessary.

9.4 Name Length

Many older compilers truncate the names of identifiers to a certain length, often eight characters, to make them fit in their symbol table. This means that all names that have the same first eight characters are treated as the same by the compiler. The UNIX system loader once truncated at eight, too, but since external names (function names and global variables) had an underscore prepended to them by some C compilers, truncation sometimes occurred after seven characters. Local variables, macros, and structure names had the full eight characters.

Recent versions of the UNIX system (4.0BSD, V8, and System V release 2, and their successors) have a feature called "flexnames." This means that all characters of all names are significant. (In practice, they may be truncated at 256 characters, but people seldom use names longer than 16 characters, making 256 effectively infinite. Unfortunately, some programs, such as C++ compilers, may generate longer names.) Both the compiler and loader support flexnames.

Other operating systems use their own loader, which has more restrictive conventions. It's quite common for a loader on an older operating system to consider upper- and lower-case letters the same. Length restrictions as short as six characters also exist on a few operating systems.

ANSI C requires 31 significant characters for internal names, and 6 for external names. Although it is generally safe to assume 31 characters on UNIX and MS DOS systems, there are some older implementations still in use that truncate at 7 or 8.

For example, this program fragment fails in an environment without flexnames, because of the two names that are not unique in their first eight characters.

```
if ((pp = getprotobyname("telnet")) == NULL)
        pp = getprotobynumber(23);
```

The following fragment fails only in an environment with flexnames, because of a misspelling beyond the eighth character that is not detected by a traditional compiler:

```
for (i=0; references[i]>0; i++)
      if (reference[i] == j)
          . . .
```

If older environments are a concern, it is recommended that programmers take an application back and forth between a flexnames environment and an eight character environment periodically to check for names that conflict in the first eight characters. If you develop in an eight character environment, it's still a good idea to test your application with flexnames, as it often catches typing mistakes past the eighth character.

If you must support an environment without flexnames, and find the short names to be a serious problem, you may be able to deal with the problem by using a modified C preprocessor. Preprocessors have been written that turn long names, or names that are not unique in the first seven characters, into unique names. It's harder to use debuggers on such programs, since the names have been changed, and such a tool is a fair amount of work to write, but it may allow you to use the longer names you prefer.

Do not use the same name for variables, functions, and other symbols that may be visible to the compiler or linker. For example, having a variable called `read` in addition to the built-in function called `read` will work on some systems, but fail on others.

It is a bad idea to choose names that are the same except for different cases; for example, if you have one function called `putchar` and another called `Putchar`, you may run into trouble eventually. IBM MVS, Honeywell GCOS, and DEC VMS, for example, only support one case in the linker, and would treat `putchar` and `Putchar` as the same name.

In addition to variable names, programs can be unportable if they assume long file names. Many UNIX systems permit file name components only up to 14 characters each.

Others permit virtually unlimited file names. Some other operating systems restrict names even further; for example, MS DOS allows eight characters for the file name, followed by an optional period and three character extension. Many older systems allowed only six character file names. In general, it is best to let the user choose file names. When the application must choose a name, have it choose a short one.

9.5 Order of Evaluation

Some operations in C have a well-defined order of evaluation, and others are left up to the compiler to determine the most efficient way to evaluate an expression. Some trouble spots in other languages, such as "Boolean expression" evaluation of the "and" and "or" operations, are not a problem in C, which provides the explicit "short-circuit" operators && and ||.

Other operations with side effects can be a problem if you code carelessly. When an index is autoincremented or autodecremented using ++ or −−, the change in value might happen before or after the rest of the expression is evaluated. If the rest of the expression references the variable, it might use the old or the new value. For example, the statements

```
i = i++;
j = i + a[i++];
++i++;
*p++ = f(p);
```

are not portable.

Lists of values passed to functions may also be evaluated in any order. Some compilers evaluate left to right, and some right to left. Code such as this, which depends on the order of evaluation, is unportable.

```
i = 1;
printf("%d, %d\n", i, ++i);
```

It is possible to have functions with side effects, resulting in problems that are even harder to track down. Depending on the compiler, this prints 1 4 or 5 4.

```
int i, j;

main()
{
        i = 1;
        j = 2;
        printf("%d, %d\n", i, seti(j));
        ...
}
```

```
seti(x)
{
        i = 5;
        return x+2;
}
```

This problem occurs in most languages, but it's more severe in C, because of the ++ and −− operators, and because the preprocessor makes it so easy to hide in-line code. Some standard functions, such as `toupper` and `putc`, may be implemented as macros that reference their argument more than once. If the argument has a side effect, such as an autoincrement, the side effect may occur twice. Since you are seldom sure whether a function is implemented as a macro, or how many times it might reference its arguments, it's a good idea to assign any complex expression, especially one with side effects, to a temporary variable before passing it to a function.

```
printf("%c\n", toupper(*p++));
```

is unportable, but this is portable.

```
char ch;
...
ch = *p++;
printf("%c\n", toupper(ch));
```

9.6 Macro Arguments

If you're writing a macro, be sure to put all the arguments in parentheses in the definition body, since you never know what sort of expression might be passed. While the macro writer can't do anything about side effects, it's important to be concerned about priorities. It is also important to carefully document any side effects caused by the macro, or constructions where arguments with side effects cause a problem, both in the source code and the documentation of the macro.

Consider this fragment:

```
#define twice(x)    2*x
        ...
        i = twice(a+5) * 3;
```

i will be assigned the value `2*a + 5*3` when the value intended was most likely `(2 * (a+5)) * 3`. Use of parentheses around the argument and around the entire macro body will solve this problem.

```
#define twice(x)    (2*(x))
```

9.7 New ANSI C Features

The new X3J11 ANSI C standard goes further than merely formalizing the de facto standard dialect of C that the various UNIX system compilers have supported for several years. It adds several new features to the language that had not been implemented in any major compiler. As a result, even though these features are required by the definition of the language, it will be a while before they can be assumed to be present in typical systems. Many operating systems have new releases every two or three years. The old compilers are used until the new release comes out. Some compilers are released more often than the operating systems on which they run, but some features may be associated with the C library (which may come with the operating system or the compiler) or with the operating system itself. Unless you are very sure of the set of compilers you will be using, it is wise to stay away from the new features until you are satisfied they are widely implemented. It seems reasonable to expect that ANSI C will be widely supported by 1991, although many older systems will continue to be in use for years.

In some cases, it is possible to emulate the feature on an old compiler well enough to get the program compiled. For example, the new `const` attribute can be freely used because a program using it can add the line

```
#define const /* nothing, emulate ANSI C "const" keyword */
```

to get rid of all uses of `const` if the compiler doesn't know about it.

Similarly, the `(void)` cast, which was added after V7, can be emulated on older compilers by using

```
#define void int
```

The command line `-Dvoid=int` will have the same effect, on the UNIX system, allowing the dependency to be hidden away in a makefile. Other features, such as `volatile` and `signed`, cannot be emulated, but by defining them as macros that expand to nothing, an acceptable approximation may sometimes be formed.

The remainder of this section is a list of the major new features defined by ANSI C that were not previously considered standard parts of the language.

Trigraphs allow the entry of special characters on systems that do not have these characters. For example, to get the [character on a keyboard without a [, type ?? (. This is useful on some EBCDIC systems, and on overseas systems where the native character set has assigned local characters, such as ü in German, to locations used in ASCII for the C characters. This feature is controversial and should be avoided if possible.

The \a sequence generates an audible alarm, generally, the control-G bell character.

K&R requires that eight characters be unique for internal names, such as macros and structure fields. It concedes that existing linkers for other operating systems sometimes allow only six characters, and often consider upper- and lower-case to be the same. The ideal system of K&R was considered to be the UNIX system, which considered eight characters significant in external names, but prepended an underscore, resulting in seven significant characters.

ANSI C requires that internal names be significant to at least 31 characters. External names are still allowed to be cut off at six characters, with upper- and lower-case ignored, but this is considered a concession to existing implementations. As a rule, portable UNIX system code can assume flexnames if it is to run on System V release 2 or later, or 4.0BSD or later. Flexnames are also portable to most newer operating systems, such as MS DOS. Portable code can use names a long as you like, but they should be unique in the first seven (external) or eight (internal) characters, and consistently spelled even past the eighth character. Older systems with fixed-symbol table loaders are the cause of the restriction in the standard.

The new header files `<limits.h>`, `<float.h>`, `<locale.h>`, `<stdarg.h>`, `<stddef.h>`, and `<stdlib.h>` were defined by ANSI C.

Three new reserved words were created: `const`, `signed`, and `volatile`.

The new data type `long double` has been added. Previously, the only floating point types were `double` and the second class citizen `float`.

A new data type constructor `enum` was added. (This change first appeared in V7, so it is already present in most modern implementations, but enumerated types were not part of K&R.)

A new casting type `void` was added to explicitly ignore status values returned from functions such as `sprintf`, whose primary purpose is something other than returning a value. Generic pointer variables can also be declared `void *`, which is large enough to hold any pointer. (This change first appeared in System III, so it is already present in most modern implementations, but it is not part of K&R.)

The floating point suffixes `f` and `l`, and the unsigned suffix `u`, were added. Previously, all floating point constants had type `double`.

Hexadecimal character constants and string elements using the `\xnnn` notation were added. Previously, characters could only be explicitly encoded in octal.

Structure fields need no longer be unique, except within a structure. This in turn requires that all structure references must be fully qualified. Previously, structure names were in a single symbol table, and their offset could be applied to nearly anything. This feature was added shortly after V7.

The new type specifiers `const` and `volatile` have been added to the language. `const` indicates that any attempts to modify the value are illegal and unintended, so the compiler can place the data in a read-only area of storage. (Read-only areas can be easily shared among several running copies of the program.) `volatile` is used to describe special hardware registers that might change without any explicit action on the part of the program, such as an I/O register. A more common use would be a variable that could be changed at any time by a signal handler. This is used to defeat optimization efforts to improve code by reusing the value already loaded from that variable. It is possible to have both type specifiers on the same variable, as in `extern volatile const int real_time_clock;`.

In one of the most significant changes, functions are allowed to declare the types of their arguments in a function prototype. Previously, the compiler did not keep track of the arguments expected by a function. This meant that it couldn't check for parameter errors at compile time, and it couldn't do any type casting that might be needed, such as from an `int` to a `long`. The old syntax has been retained for upward compatibility, and a function that takes no parameters can be declared using `void`.

Character string constants are now considered read-only. Most programs treat them as read-only anyway, and some programs are compiled using special-purpose tools that move all the strings to a read-only area. The language did not, however, prevent a program from modifying a string, and some programs do modify string constants. The UNIX system function `mktemp`, for example, does this.

A parameter is considered to be declared among the local variables at the front of the function definition. Previously, the parameters were a separate scope, and the local variables were another block within the function. This allowed a function parameter to be redeclared inside the function, creating two variables with the same name and making it impossible to use the parameter. This type of error was not detected by the compiler and was difficult to find.

The new preprocessor directive `#elif` has been added to mean ''else if.''

Text after such preprocessor syntax as `#else` and `#endif` is no longer ignored, unless it is placed inside `/* ... */` delimiters. This means that many existing programs using the programming style

```
#ifdef FOO
...
#else FOO
...
#endif FOO
```

must be changed to read

```
#ifdef FOO
...
#else /* FOO */
...
#endif /* FOO */
```

String literals adjacent in the source program are concatenated at compile time. For example, a file name may be built from a parameterized directory name and a constant like this:

```
#define DIRNAME "/usr/lib"
    ...
    fd = fopen(DIRNAME "/defaults", "r");
```

The concatenation function was previously accomplished on most UNIX systems using an undocumented coding trick: placing a macro argument inside a character string. For example, the previous example was previously coded as

```
#define DIRNAME(file) "/usr/lib/file"
   ...
fd = fopen(DIRNAME(defaults), "r");
```

This undocumented trick is no longer allowed by ANSI C, and programs using this method must be changed.

The new preprocessor structure # *arg* is used to generate double quotes around a macro argument, since the previous coding trick is no longer allowed. For example, the DIRNAME macro above could be implemented as follows:

```
#define DIRNAME(file) "/usr/lib/" # file
```

This achieves the same result using string constant concatenation.

New tokens can be built using ## to attach separate preprocessor items together. FOO ## BAR will become the single token FOOBAR, even if FOO or BAR is the result of a macro expansion. This was previously done with another coding trick: an empty comment: FOO/**/BAR, which worked with some compilers because comments were stripped off by the preprocessor, while the tokens were still considered separate. A new-line, quoted with a backslash, served the same purpose.

The construction

```
#line 123 "main.c"
```

to identify the true line number and file name from which the code in question originates has been documented. This worked with many recent compilers, but was unofficial. It is useful so that better error messages can be generated.

A new preprocessor line

```
#error any sequence of tokens
```

can be used to generate an error message and terminate compilation.

A new implementation defined facility called #pragma has been added, so that programs can give special instructions to their local compilers without undue concern about its portability to other implementations. Pragmas that are not supported by a particular compiler will be ignored. Use of pragmas cannot be considered portable because there is no standard set of arguments. Nonetheless, they may provide a useful way to give unportable directions to one compiler without interfering with the operation of others.

A number of predefined macros are specified, including __LINE__, __FILE__, __DATE__, __TIME__, and __STDC__.

New definitions for size_t, ptrdiff_t, and offsetof have been added in <stddef.h>.

The concept of *locales* has been added to the library, so that a program can arrange to use local conventions for items that vary from country to country, such as the character used for a decimal point, or the format of a date or time, or which characters are considered letters.

The new signal definition SIGABRT has been defined. This is not a new signal, but just a portable name for the particular signal to be generated by the abort function.

The raise function has been added as a new way for a process to send itself a signal without using UNIX system dependent functions such as kill and getpid.

The old varargs mechanism has been replaced with the stdarg mechanism. The two are similar, but stdarg fits in with function prototypes.

The ellipsis token , ... has been added as part of the stdarg mechanism.

Several new macros have been added to <stdio.h>, including fpos_t, _IOFBF, _IOLBF, _IONBF, OPEN_MAX, SEEK_CUR, SEEK_END, SEEK_SET, and TMP_MAX.

Standard I/O now distinguishes between text and binary files. Files are assumed to be text files by default, but a file can be opened in binary mode by passing the b flag to fopen. This doesn't matter on the UNIX system, but on other operating systems, text files often end in CRLF rather than \n, and standard I/O must remove the CR characters on input and generate them on output.

A new function, remove, has been added as a portable way to delete a file. This is similar to the unlink function in the UNIX system, but the semantics of remove are more portable.

A new function, rename, has been added as a portable way to rename a file.

A new printf format conversion specifier %p has been added to print a pointer.

A new printf format conversion specifier %n has been added, allowing the program to determine the number of characters generated at this point.

Two new functions fgetpos and fsetpos are similar to ftell and fseek, but use the type fpos_t rather than long. This is necessary for files larger than 4 gigabytes and for operating systems where an integer does not adequately describe a file position.

The new include file <stdlib.h> is provided, with many new types and macros, including div_t, ldiv_t, RAND_MAX, and the functions atof, atoi, atol, strtod, strtol, and strtoul.

A new function atexit has been added to arrange for one or more user functions to be called when the program exits.

A new function strcoll has been added to convert character strings into a canonical representation that will sort according to locale-specific rules using strcmp or memcmp.

Two new functions difftime and mktime are provided to compare values of type time_t and to convert a struct tm into a time_t.

A new function strftime provides a printf-like capability to format times in a locale-specific way.

CHAPTER 10: **OPERATING SYSTEM DEPENDENCIES**

A truly portable program will read from standard input, write to standard output, and do little else. It will run on the UNIX system, as a filter, or interactively. It will also run from a card deck on a batch machine such as IBM's OS/MVS. There are a few applications that can really run like this; for instance, statistics packages like SPSS and MINITAB are written in FORTRAN and work in this kind of environment.

Unfortunately, for an application to be truly successful today, it frequently has to do something more. Often it is screen-oriented. Some programs use graphics, or color. Perhaps it accepts characters as they are typed by the user, rather than buffering a line, with erase/kill processing, and returns the line to the program all at once. It may need to communicate with other processes or other computers. It may need some kind of real time behavior.

The early UNIX systems didn't have all these features. Different groups have needed this kind of functionality, so they have added them. However, there are many ways to do these sorts of things, and many arbitrary decisions must be made. Each implementation group invented its own way of doing the job. The result is that there are several different UNIX system versions, each of which has a different way of doing the same thing.

If it's just a case of a handy subroutine, such as `getopt` or `index`, you can easily get around the problem by writing the function yourself. Many of the functions in the C Library chapter fit into this category. Some operations, such as `alarm`, can't be emulated with a subroutine. If the operating system doesn't already support it, it is necessary to either enhance the operating system or live without the feature.

In many cases where such true additional functionality was required, the system developers added a feature to the operating system. When such enhancements were made, any application that used them became unportable. Some applications, such as `vi`, need to do something (for example, put the terminal into the character-at-a-time mode), but this is done differently on different systems. These programs contain #ifdefs in order to do it differently. Sometimes, an application can run in degraded mode without a feature. If this is the case, an #ifdef can be used to use the feature, if present, and avoid it otherwise.

When programming in C, the #ifdef is the traditional way to handle such a decision. For example, suppose you need to turn on "cbreak" mode (where input from the keyboard is passed to the application one character at a time, rather than a line at a time) in the terminal driver. Typical code might read:

```
#ifdef SYSV
# include <termio.h>
struct termio nbuf, obuf;
#else
# include <sgtty.h>
struct sgtty nbuf, obuf;
#endif

...
/*
 * Save current terminal driver state in obuf, change
 * to cbreak mode, put new state in nbuf.
 */
cbreak()
{
      int r;
#ifdef SYSV
      /* System V method. */
      r = ioctl(0, TCGETA, &obuf);
      if (r < 0) error("cbreak: ioctl TCGETA failed");
      nbuf = obuf;
      nbuf.c_lflag &= ~ICANON;
      /* Must fix VMIN, VTIME since they overlay VEOF, VEOL */
      nbuf.c_cc[VMIN] = 1;
      nbuf.c_cc[VTIME] = 0;
      r = ioctl(0, TCSETAW, &nbuf);
      if (r < 0) error("cbreak: ioctl TCSETAW failed");
#else
      /* V7, 4.2BSD method */
      r = ioctl(0, TIOCGETP, &obuf);
      if (r < 0) error("cbreak: ioctl TIOCGETP failed");
      nbuf = obuf;
      nbuf.sg_flags |= CBREAK;
      r = ioctl(0, TIOCSETN, &nbuf);
      if (r < 0) error("cbreak: ioctl TIOCSETN failed");
#endif
}

      ...
```

```
/* Go back by restoring state from obuf. */
nocbreak()
{
      int r;
#ifdef SYSV
      r = ioctl(0, TCSETAW, &obuf);
      if (r < 0) error("nocbreak: ioctl TCSETAW failed");
#else
      r = ioctl(0, TIOCSETN, &obuf);
      if (r < 0) error("nocbreak: ioctl TIOCSETN failed");
#endif
}
```

Here, we assume that SYSV has been defined, perhaps in a header file, or perhaps by an option in the makefile, if the computer runs UNIX System V (or System III, which is very similar). As a standard coding convention, we recommend the use of the preprocessor names SYSV for UNIX System V and UNIX System III, BSD for 4.nBSD, V7 for systems similar to the Seventh Edition, and MSDOS for the MS DOS and PC DOS operating systems. When specific versions matter, it is possible to use numerical suffixes, such as BSD42 or SYSV31 for 4.2BSD and System V release 3.1, respectively, or to use integer numerical values such as #define BSD 42, which allows #if to be used with the preprocessor > operator:

```
#if BSD >= 43
        /* Use a feature new to 4.3BSD */
#else
        /* workaround */
#endif
```

Sometimes you want to use a feature, if it's present, but run in a degraded mode otherwise. If the feature has a corresponding #define (such as an ioctl name), the ifdef can key on the name itself:

```
        int n, r;
        ...

#ifdef FIONREAD
        r = ioctl(1, FIONREAD, &n);
        if (r >= 0 && n > 0)
                return;
#endif
```

In this case, FIONREAD would have been defined by a header file. FIONREAD is a feature of V7 that checks for waiting input on a file descriptor, returning the number of characters waiting to be read without actually having to read them. It is useful to check for type ahead on the keyboard in a highly interactive program.

If FIONREAD is available, a positive result will cause this function to return immediately (possibly avoiding some unnecessary work), and a negative or zero result would cause it to continue. If FIONREAD is not available, the program will just continue on, making a conservative guess that FIONREAD would have indicated that the work must be done.

A popular coding custom in C programs is to #ifdef out unused code, rather than to comment it out. Commenting out code does not work if the code itself contains comments. For example, this doesn't work, because the first */ will terminate the comment:

```
/*
for (i=0; i<n; i++)       /* for each subject */
        examine(a[i]);
*/
```

The internal comment will confuse the compiler. This problem does not occur with #ifdefs, since ifdefs can nest:

```
#ifdef notdef
        for (i=0; i<n; i++)       /* for each subject */
# ifdef EXAM_A
                exam_a(a[i]);
# else
                exam_b(a[i]);
# endif
#endif
```

The name notdef is not special to the compiler; it's simply a word that is unlikely to ever be defined. (Some programmers also use a long block comment bracketed with #ifdef comment, #endif.)

10.1 Terminal Driver

One major source of differences is the terminal driver. The UNIX 3.0 (and hence System III) terminal driver was a major change, with a completely different interface. This driver is very clean, packing all the related information in a large structure, allowing the state to be gotten and set with a single pair of ioctls (input/output controls).

The 4BSD terminal driver has several structures, each manipulated separately with a different pair of ioctls. The advantage to this structure is upward compatibility as far back as the V6 terminal driver. The disadvantage is in needing to do several ioctls to get at everything, and incompatibility with the UNIX 3.0 descended terminal drivers.

From a functionality point of view, the 4BSD terminal driver appears better to the user, since it has nice features like word erase, correct echoing and erasing of control characters and tabs, and line retype. The System III/V terminal driver appears better to the sophisticated programmer because it provides access to many options in the hardware and software separately, rather than bundling several features into one bit as in V7. (Some simple applications, such as turning on cbreak mode, may be easier to do in the V7/4BSD terminal driver, since only a single bit need be changed.)

It is best to avoid use of the terminal driver interface at all, if possible. Most modern applications can use the curses package to hide these differences. By using curses, unless you need an unusual bit setting, you can usually get the effect you want without writing unportable code. Curses itself is highly portable, and has been tested on a number of hardware/software combinations. This portability is attained by the extensive use of ifdefs in the implementation of curses. It does the dirty work so you don't have to.

If you must access the terminal driver directly, the example in the previous section of this chapter shows how for System V and V7/4BSD systems.

10.2 Interprocess Communication

Until 1983, there was no Interprocess Communication (IPC) mechanism in any UNIX system, except for signals (which carry little information), disk files, and pipes. System V included an IPC, called `msgop`, based on one done in the CB-UNIX system. The System V `msgop` provides reliable, unacknowledged messages, and works only within a single UNIX machine. System V also supports a semaphore-based IPC mechanism and a shared memory mechanism. 4.2BSD has an IPC built for the networking implementation, commonly referred to as "sockets." The 4.2BSD IPC is based on datagrams or connections at the option of the application. System V release 3 defines an interface to its new "streams" mechanism, called the Transport Layer Interface (TLI). The AT&T TCP/IP package also emulates sockets using TLI. None of these interfaces is part of ANSI C or IEEE P.1003 yet.

Programmers needing IPC must look into their crystal ball to guess what will become the industry-standard IPC in the future. The System V `msgop` was intended for a single machine and will not extend to a distributed environment, nor to a virtual circuit environment. The Berkeley socket mechanism is very powerful and has become very popular, but it is complex and the internal implementation is felt by some not to be as clean as streams. AT&T is promoting TLI as a new standard.

Until a clear winner emerges, it is best to isolate IPC under a layer of software and make as few assumptions about the nature of the provided IPC as possible. Call the subroutines your application really wants, and implement those subroutines using whichever IPC is available on the system in question.

The semantics of the socket and TLI interfaces are actually very similar. Their main difference is the syntax. Sockets have a separate system call (or subroutine call) for each operation. Some of these subroutines have names that are not unique in the first seven characters, making flexnames essential. TLI uses an operation similar to `ioctl`, with a separate control for each operation. The set of operations (bind, accept, connect, and so on) for the basic primitives is essentially the same. This means it should not be difficult to emulate either one in terms of the other.

Since both 4.2BSD and System V release 3 support the socket interface for TCP/IP (either directly or by an emulation library), a program written to use sockets with TCP/IP will run on either system, assuming the TCP/IP module is installed. It is not clear, however, that this situation will continue forever.

10.3 Networking

Networking and interprocess communication are closely related, since most sophisticated networking is a method for two processes on (possibly) different computers to exchange data. The advice in the IPC section above is of interest, in addition to the protocol-related advice here.

High-speed networking is an area that did not become widely used in UNIX systems until 4.2BSD was released in 1983. Until then, inexpensive local area network (LAN) hardware was unavailable, and each vendor used a proprietary protocol, unable to talk to anyone else. By 1986, Ethernet hardware was quite common and other LAN technologies were becoming standardized. The TCP/IP protocol family is widely used; the ISO/CCITT OSI (Open Systems Interconnection) protocol family is expected to become even more widely used over the next several years.

Other than UUCP (Unix to Unix CoPy, a low-cost file transfer mechanism used primarily over dialup telephone lines), the early UNIX systems did not have networking. 4.2BSD was the first to support TCP/IP over popular media such as Ethernet, and now its use is commonplace.

Deciding which protocols to support can be an art. By 1987, most proprietary protocols had faded from the scene. (Some proprietary protocols, such as IBM's SNA and DEC's DECNET have a large enough user base to withstand this trend for the time being.) The de facto standard has become TCP/IP, which is widely supported for the UNIX, MS DOS, and other operating systems.

OSI is gaining considerable popularity in Europe, where CCITT has considerable influence, but by 1989 OSI has still not caught on in the United States. Nonetheless, most major computer vendors have announced their intention to support OSI or some part of it, such as General Motors' MAP (Manufacturing Automation Protocol), and the feeling is that someday OSI will become dominant in the United States.

There is disagreement as to when OSI will prevail, however. Some said it would happen by 1987, although it didn't. Some predict that it may be as late as 2000 before TCP/IP is completely gone. The later OSI catches on, the more time TCP/IP has to gather a support base, and the harder it will be to eliminate. It is possible that OSI will go the way of the CCITT V.22 1200 BPS modem standard: it was mandated by law in Europe, but ignored in the United States, where the 212 modem represents a de facto standard with a huge installed user base. Only time will tell.

If you are designing software to use a network, you should try to design it in a way that doesn't depend very much on a specific protocol family. If you can use a connection-oriented transport service, such as TCP/IP's TCP or OSI's TP4, you'll find that your application makes sense almost everywhere. If you need unreliable low-cost datagrams, you may have to assume a LAN, but the application should still work with either family. (Datagrams implemented over an X.25 long-haul network may not be very efficient, but they will work.)

If you need reliable messages, or a transaction facility, you may find that the network services offered are not exactly what you need, and you may have to build your own protocol. In this case, you should watch the OSI standardization effort closely, and track their proposals. X.410 and its successor X.ROS are transaction protocols, and the advantages of standardization may be worth something later. (Beware, however, of performance issues. The early implementations of ASN.1, upon which X.ROS is based, had severe performance problems.)

If you can hook into an existing network that a customer may have, you'll be more likely to sell your product than if the customer has to throw away all its equipment and replace it with yours. Proprietary protocols are unpopular, especially when there is a standard protocol to do the same thing. If your protocol is something new that no standard covers, it is often worthwhile to promote it as a new standard, and try to get it adopted by standards organizations such as CCITT, ISO, IEEE, ANSI, NBS, ECMA, and DARPA.

One area to watch out for is if specific properties of a particular protocol family creep into your code. For example, TCP/IP uses a 32-bit host address and a 16-bit port number. If you assume that the host address and port will fit into a pair of integers, you may be in for a surprise when you try to port your application to OSI's 20-byte host addresses. An assumption that an electronic mailing address is a pair of 8-byte character strings (host and user) will get you into trouble when you try to use ARPA domains, which use a single, arbitrarily long, character string. The character-string model will also cause problems when you try to convert to X.400, which uses a sequence of name/value pairs of attributes to describe the destination of electronic mail.

The Berkeley socket mechanism was developed for TCP/IP, and while it was intended to be used for other protocol families, it's easy to have port numbers and the like creep into your code. It's best to just pass around pointers to structures of protocol dependent information, and let lower-level routines handle the contents of the structures.

You must provide some sort of user interface, however. Try to avoid having anything protocol-specific in the interface. Use of names like "telnet" (the name of the TCP/IP protocol to log in to another machine) or dotted host numbers (the TCP/IP syntax for network-level host addresses) should be avoided. Electronic mail syntax is something that's hard to hide, but you can provide a good reply command, and an easy way to alias a simple name into an address stored earlier (from user information or from the address field of an old piece of mail) to minimize the dependence on it.

Even host names can often be hidden from the user. They may not really care what host is involved, but might instead want access to a resource. The resource may be implicit in the operation or dependent on some information that can be found in an on-line database. The user may never be aware that a network is being used.

Sometimes, the user does want to access a specific machine, for example, to log in to it. In this case, the user will have to either select the machine from a menu or type in the name. You will probably have given each machine a character-string name, which can be selected or typed as text. Assuming that a machine name is a character string is a lot safer than building in information about 32-bit addresses. Assuming there is a generic "remote login" service is safer than knowing about "telnet" or "port 23." Try to hide specific details of the protocol in a subroutine or in a server process, so that your program will not care whether it's in a TCP/IP or OSI environment.

Exercises

Exercise 10-1. Modify the `ioctl` code at the beginning of the chapter to turn off echoing. Package the result into a pair of subroutines called `noecho` and `echo`.

Exercise 10-2. Modify the `ioctl` code at the beginning of the chapter to turn off any mappings between newline and return or return linefeed. Package the result into a pair of subroutines called `nonl` and `nl`.

PART IV
REFERENCE

CHAPTER 11: **C LIBRARY SUBROUTINES**

This chapter deals with functions that are present in the C library, generally thought of as "subroutines" in the UNIX environment. Functions that are considered "system calls" are covered in Chapter 12. The distinction is that system calls are primitive operations provided by the UNIX operating system, but subroutines are written in terms of system calls and other subroutines.

The subroutine/system-call distinction is not an absolute one, since different operating systems will have different sets of system calls. The functions considered system calls here, in fact may be subroutines, implemented in terms of the different system calls of another operating system.

Nonetheless, since C is so historically derived from the UNIX system, this organization is traditional. It also helps separate some of the more UNIX specific functions, since the system calls were intended to be UNIX specific. Although many C libraries include emulations of many of the UNIX system calls, they should still be considered less portable than standard subroutines.

The C language itself, like ALGOL 60, has no provisions for input and output. (These, and all other built-in functions, are provided separately by the C library.) However, unlike ALGOL, C was first implemented and then publicized. For C to be useful, a complete library was needed from the beginning. This library might as well be a part of the language, and most implementations tend to copy the UNIX C library. ANSI C was the first standard to require a complete library for functions such as I/O. The exact content of this library varies quite a bit from implementation to implementation, even among UNIX variations.

This chapter is organized alphabetically by function or group of functions. Only functions available in at least two separate implementations, or in one of the standards documents, are listed. (See Appendix G for the list of implementations and documents used.) Any function present in your manual but not described here should be considered unportable, unless it has appeared in a standards document and has become widely implemented after this book was written.

The portability of each function is rated, using an adjective and one to five stars and an optional mark. The more stars, the more portable the function at the time this book was written.

Functions that are new but are part of one of these standards have been given, in addition to their one to three stars, a bullet mark •. This mark indicates that as the appropriate standard becomes more widespread, the portability of the function will also increase. At the time of this writing, • can be estimated to be worth one additional star in 1991 and possibly two additional stars a few years beyond that.

One star, *, means a function is *unportable,* meaning that it is specific to one system, such as System V, 4BSD or a particular MS DOS C compiler.

Two stars, **, means a function is *portable among UNIX systems,* meaning that it can be expected to work on any UNIX system since V7.

Three stars, ***, means a function is *fairly portable,* meaning that it is present on a significant fraction of C implementations, but there are many implementations that do not support it.

Four stars, ****, means a function is *very portable,* meaning that it is present in nearly all implementations of C.

Five stars, *****, means a function is *extremely portable,* meaning that it is supported essentially everywhere.

By 1989, three major C-related standards had emerged: ANSI C (X3J11), POSIX (IEEE 1003.1), and AT&T SVID. It is intended that a function required by one of these standards will be widely available. In practice, it will take a few years before it it safe to assume widespread support of these standards. The star ratings given here are appropriate for 1989, and give any function required by ANSI C at least three stars, by POSIX at least two stars.

Over time, it is expected that many implementations will announce that they conform to one or more of these standards. The standards will be like the layers of an onion skin: an implementation conforming to SVID should also conform to POSIX, and a C implementation conforming to POSIX will likely conform to ANSI C.

As this is written, it is not clear how fast systems will move toward conformance with the standards. The most recent major releases of System V (releases 2, 3, and 4) occurred in 1983, 1986, and 1989. The 4.2BSD and 4.3BSD Berkeley releases were in 1983 and 1986. Thus it is possible that it will be an additional one to three years until a completely conforming system will be released to vendors, incorporated into most existing products, and released to the public.

Beware of claims alleging conformance to a standard. Many standards have several versions. By 1988, AT&T had released two issues of the SVID corresponding to System V releases 1 and 3. The first SVID specified only the C library, and the latter issues also included shell commands. Although the second issue of the SVID has been available for some time, there are many claims alleging SVID conformance that really comply with only the first SVID issue. In 1987, at least one product was on the market claiming that it conformed to ANSI C (which had not been approved yet). This product did not support locales or trigraphs.

POSIX has several sections: 1003.1 covers the operating system interface, and 1003.2 covers user commands. Several other sections are working on issues such as validation and bindings for languages such as Ada and FORTRAN. Future versions of POSIX may go into more detail on issues currently unresolved, such as handling of graphics and time zones. ANSI C is likely to release only infrequent revisions, so version confusion is less likely to be a problem with this standard.

In the discussion that follows, the strengths and weaknesses of each function are described from a portability viewpoint. Systems that support the function, and other special considerations are discussed.

Finally, for the programmer who really needs the functionality of the routine in question, but finds it isn't portable enough to meet the requirements, guidelines are suggested to get the same functionality without losing too much portability.

abort   terminate program abnormally   ****

This routine is part of a typical C library, so it is very portable. Beware, however, of trappings that surround the call. On the UNIX system, it is traditionally necessary to first restore the abort signal to a default status, and this abort signal varies from SIGIOT on the PDP-11, to SIGILL on the VAX, to not being present on an MS DOS PC. If you haven't caught the signal in the first place, you generally don't have to worry about restoring it.

One way to portably abort is to conditionally compile the signal-catching code, like this.

```
#include <signal.h>
...
#ifdef SIGABRT
        signal(SIGABRT, SIG_DFL);
#endif
#ifdef SIGILL
        signal(SIGILL, SIG_DFL);
#endif
#ifdef SIGIOT
        signal(SIGIOT, SIG_DFL);
#endif
        abort();
```

On many operating systems, there is no way to dump core. On such systems, calling abort is not very different from calling exit, except that an error-exit status is returned. In general, abort should be considered a debugging tool, not a part of a production program.

The signal SIGABRT is a new addition to various C standards, including ANSI C and P1003, and is not present in many current implementations. A typical implementation will probably treat it as a duplicate of an existing signal number, not as a new signal. Since you don't know which name to use, all three cases above are necessary for truly portable code.

abs   integer absolute value   ****

This routine is part of most C libraries, so it is very portable.

assert   verify program assertion   ***

This routine is part of many C libraries, so it is fairly portable. Be sure to include
<assert.h> since this is generally implemented as a macro.

Since the implementation of assert is fairly simple, if you want very high portability, you may prefer to write your own custom version. Then you can modify it as needed
for new environments. Here is one implementation:

```
#ifndef NDEBUG
# define assert(ex) \
        {if (!(ex)){ \
                fprintf(stderr, \
                "Assertion failed: file %s, line %d\n", \
                __FILE__, __LINE__); \
                abort();}}
#else
# define assert(ex) ;
#endif
```

The #define assert macro has been expanded above into six lines for typographic
reasons. In your program you should join it into one long line, without the terminating
\'s.

The use of __FILE__ and __LINE__ are only fairly portable, because prior to ANSI
C, they were generally not documented. If you port your program to a new environment
that doesn't support them, you can always substitute a simpler call that doesn't identify
the file and/or line, such as this:

```
#ifndef NDEBUG
# define assert(ex) \
        {if (!(ex)){ \
                fprintf(stderr,"Assertion ex failed\n"); \
                abort();}}
#else
# define assert(ex) ;
#endif
```

The trick of expanding the argument ex inside quotes isn't strictly portable, since it's
also generally not documented, but it does tend to work with most older UNIX system C
implementations. This trick is *forbidden* by ANSI C, however, so it should be considered very unportable. ANSI C provides a different way to accomplish the same thing.
The __FILE__ and __LINE__ variables are part of ANSI C.

You can include this as your own assert.h and use it only if there is no system file
by that name, if you prefer.

atof   ascii to floating   ***

This routine is part of most C libraries, so it is fairly portable. On many systems, however, `atof` is not very accurate. An even more portable alternative to `atoi`, `atol`, and `atof` is to use `sscanf`.

Note: the use of `<math.h>` to declare `atof` is not portable, as it is a recent addition to the language. ANSI C uses the new include file `<stdlib.h>` for the declarations. *If you use this function, make sure it is declared!*

```
double atof();     /* portable, nonprototype declaration */
```

atoi   ascii to integer   ****

This routine is part of most C libraries, so it is very portable.

atol   ascii to long   ****

This routine is part of most C libraries, so it is very portable.

Note: the use of `<math.h>` to declare `atol` is not portable, as it is a recent addition to the language. It is better to declare it in your own header file. *If you use this function, make sure it is declared!*

```
long atol();       /* portable, nonprototype declaration */
```

bsearch   binary search   *

This routine is part of most System V derived C libraries, but it is not very portable. It is required by the SVID, POSIX, and ANSI C standards, so it is likely that it will eventually become very widely used. However, until it is safe to depend on ANSI C, this function should be considered specific to System V.

If you need a binary search routine and your program must be portable to environments that do not support ANSI C, you can write your own binary search function, resulting in completely portable code.

calloc   allocate zeroed memory   *****

This routine is part of most C libraries, so it is extremely portable. Strictly speaking, you don't need `calloc`, since you can get the same effect using `malloc` and then zeroing out the memory. However, every implementation known to the author includes all the basic memory-allocation routines: `calloc`, `free`, `malloc`, and `realloc`.

`calloc` is part of the original standard I/O, and is documented in K&R, but `malloc` is considered a low-level UNIX function. This makes `calloc` slightly more portable than `malloc`, although in practice nearly every implementation supports it.

ceil, fabs, floor   float to integer   ****

These routines are part of most C libraries, so they are very portable. They are missing only from a few libraries that do not support full floating-point libraries, and from the standard I/O and K&R documents.

It is fairly safe to depend on the include file <math.h> to declare these functions or to declare that they return a double.

cfree   free memory   *

The cfree subroutine was originally intended as a portable version of free, much like calloc is a portable malloc, or fopen is a portable open. In practice, implementations have treated the two as identical, and cfree normally just calls free with its first argument, ignoring any additional arguments. cfree is usually not documented in UNIX manuals, or in UNIX or C standards, but it has historically always been present (without documentation) in the UNIX systems.

Since it is not widely used, and not documented, it is recommended that cfree not be used, but rather that memory allocated with calloc be freed using free.

clearerr   clear stdio error   ****

This routine is part of standard I/O, so it is very portable. It is missing from only a few systems, because it was not in the original standard I/O document. Since it is often implemented as a macro, the file <stdio.h> must be included to use clearerr.

crypt, setkey, encrypt   encrypt password   **

These routines are present on most UNIX systems, so they are fairly portable within UNIX systems. They may not be in versions available outside the United States.

Many current UNIX systems use the same encoding algorithm. This allows encrypted passwords from /etc/passwd to be copied from one system to a different implementation and still work. The standards do not, however, require this algorithm, and it is possible for the encrypted passwords to be incompatible.

It is important to note that these routines are intended *only* for the encryption of UNIX system passwords. They are not general-purpose encryption functions, and support one-way encryption; no decryption is possible or needed for password checking.

More recent releases of the UNIX system hide the encrypted password from most programs. For this reason, portable programs should not make use of encrypted passwords.

clock   get CPU time   ***

This routine is part of ANSI C, but is not yet widely implemented. It is currently supported by TSO, GCOS, and System V, and can be expected to become more widely implemented as ANSI C is more widely supported.

ANSI C provides a type `clock_t` and a value `CLK_TCK` to indicate the number of ticks per second; and an include file `<time.h>` in which these are defined. Existing implementations return a `long` integer representing the number of microseconds since the first call to `clock`. While it is unwise to assume microseconds, or to assume that the first call will return zero, it is important to realize that the typical implementation will overflow after about 36 minutes of CPU time. If the programmer anticipates the possibility of 36 minutes or more CPU time being used in a calculation, extra care should be taken.

For example, the `time` function can be used to watch elapsed real time, making a sanity check to ensure that the real time is at least as great as the CPU time. If intermediate checkpoints can be made with `clock`, wraparound can be checked for. Use of the `alarm` call, on UNIX and POSIX systems, can be used to ensure reasonable checkpoints.

ctermid   generate terminal name   *

This routine is part of System III derived C libraries, so it is not very portable.

The `ctermid` function is present only in System III, System V, and the related standards, including SVID and POSIX. It is not part of ANSI C.

This function normally returns the string `/dev/tty`, which is assumed to refer to the proper terminal when opened. It is almost equivalent, and certainly more portable, to refer to `/dev/tty` explicitly in your program.

If you want the true name of the terminal, the most useful function is `ttyname`. This does not work if you don't have a file descriptor, but most programs can use `fileno(stdin)` or `fileno(stderr)` to get this information, first checking that it is indeed a terminal with `isatty(fileno(stdin))`. Programs with `stderr` redirected are likely to be invoked in the background, with no controlling terminal.

The only reason you would need the controlling terminal (as opposed to the terminal that the standard error file is connected to) is if you are concerned about signals generated by the interrupt or quit characters on the keyboard. In practice, it's rare for a programmer to be concerned about this.

ctime, asctime   date/time to string   ***
gmtime, localtime

These routines are part of the UNIX C library, so they are fairly portable. They are present in all UNIX libraries, and a few non-UNIX libraries. They are also part of ANSI C.

Beware, however, that `ctime` does not produce any time-zone information in the output. It also produces a string in a format that, while widely used, is different from the ISO standards. Future standards work may create some minor incompatibilities in the future.

Conventions involving input to `ctime` for information such as the time-zone conventions are not portable. Some systems convey the time zone using the `ftime` call. Others use an environment variable called `TZ`. Many other systems do not support the concept of a time zone and just run in local time.

The variable passed to `ctime` can safely be assumed to be a `long`. Some implementations have a built-in type `time_t` for this, defined in `<sys/types.h>`, but the effort needed to include this (the definition may be in `<time.h>` or `<sys/time.h>` or `<stdlib.h>`, for example) outweighs any portability advantage at this time.

The underlying routines `localtime`, `gmtime`, and `asctime` are typically present if `ctime` is, but there is seldom a reason to use them.

`curses`   character screen library   **

Implementations of this library are part of 4.2BSD and System V, so programs using only the common subset are portable to most UNIX versions. Although curses was designed for portability, it is not included in any C language standard. Nevertheless, because the alternatives aren't very portable either, curses is a useful tool for portable screen-oriented software. See Chapter 5 for a more detailed discussion.

There are several implementations of curses. Two of the major ones are the Berkeley curses, present in 4BSD, and the AT&T curses, present in System V. For the most part, the Berkeley curses is a subset of the AT&T version.

The AT&T System V curses uses the terminfo database, and the 4.2BSD curses uses termcap. A portable program using curses should be tested on both terminfo and termcap versions of curses.

There are a few termcap specific features present only in the Berkeley curses, notably certain global variables. Use of these variables is not portable:

```
AM, BS, CA, DA, DB, EO, GT, HZ, IN, MI, MS, NC, OS, UL, XN,

AL, BC, BT, CD, CE, CL, CM, CR, DC, DL, DM,
DO, ED, EI, HO, IC, IM, IP, LL, MA, ND, NL,
SE, SF, SO, SR, TA, TE, TI, UC, UE, UP, US,
VB, VE, VS, PC,

NONL, UPPERCASE, normtty, _pfast, _tty
```

The routines present in all major versions of curses are `addch`, `addstr`, `box`, `crmode`, `clear`, `clearok`, `clrtobot`, `clrtoeol`, `delch`, `deleteln`, `delwin`, `echo`, `endwin`, `erase`, `getch`, `getstr`, `getyx`, `inch`, `initscr`, `insch`, `insertln`, `leaveok`, `longname`, `move`, `mvcur`, `newwin`, `nl`, `nocrmode`, noecho, nonl, noraw, overlay, overwrite, printw, raw, refresh, scanw, scroll, scrollok, standend, standout, subwin, touchwin, unctrl, waddch, waddstr, wclear, wclrtobot, wclrtoeol, wdelch, wdeleteln, werase, wgetch, wgetstr, winch, winsch, winsertln, wmove, wprintw, wrefresh, wscanw, wstandend, and wstandout. It is also safe to assume that LINES and COLS are defined by <curses.h>

There are some differences, however, in a few of the functions. The box function must be passed a pair of printing characters in the Berkeley version, but either character may be passed as 0 in the AT&T version to indicate a default. mvcur is a low-level routine, and should be avoided by a typical high-level curses application. getstr is merely a loop, calling getch in the Berkeley version, but handles echoing and backspacing in the AT&T version. Different bugs may be present in different versions, especially in the less used functions.

In general, if your application is simple, and if you can restrict yourself to initscr, endwin, crmode, noecho, nonl, addch, addstr, printw, move, clear, erase, clrtoeol, refresh, and getch, you'll have a more portable program. Most curses programs run in the combination of crmode (cbreak), noecho, and nonl modes. Programs that want the system to do echoing or line buffering are more likely to run into unexpected results.

If you need the lower-level terminfo and termcap functions, see the entries for termcap and terminfo in this chapter.

cuserid   get user login name   *

This routine is part of System III derived C libraries, so it is somewhat portable within System III and System V. It is not required by the SVID.

This routine is basically a front-end routine that first calls getlogin, and if that fails, calls getpwnam(getuid()). If what you really want is the getlogin value, then cuserid is an appropriate interface to use. On systems that don't have cuserid, it's easy to write it yourself. *The security problems associated with* getlogin also apply to cuserid. Do not trust the name returned for authentication purposes!

dbminit, fetch, store   database library   *
delete, firstkey, nextkey

The Data Base Management (DBM) library is present only in V7 derived systems, such as 4.2BSD. It is not present in System V, nor in non-UNIX C libraries. Other systems often do not provide similar functionality, presenting developers with a serious portability problem.

The source code to DBM is fairly short, self-contained, and portably written. However, since the code is part of UNIX V7, it is proprietary to AT&T, and is covered by the UNIX source license.

One way of dealing with this is to put #ifdefs in your code for DBM. If the #ifdefs are present, the hashed database is used. If not, a text file is sequentially read. Many large production programs, such as Berkeley's sendmail and the Usenet B news software, do this. It can sometimes mean that programs running without DBM are terribly slow, suitable only for environments where the program isn't run very often or small databases.

Another possibility is to store the database as a sorted text file, one line per entry. A binary search routine can be written to quickly find elements in the database. This isn't as fast as a hashed database, but is much faster than a sequential search, and in practice is usually ''fast enough.'' Here is a sample binary search routine, to be used with sort -f.

```
/*
 * filebinsearch(): look up key in ascii sorted database.
 * Binary searches a la the V7/4BSD look command.  Sort -f to
 * fold cases.  File format for each line: key \t value
 * Returns 0 for OK, -1 key for not found, -2 for no database.
 * Based on "smail" routine written by Christopher Seiwald.
 * This does not work properly for very small databases;
 * it should use sequential search in those cases.
 */
#define DATABASEFILE "/your/name/goes/here"
#include <stdio.h>
#include <ctype.h>

int
filebinsearch( key, result )
char *key;          /* what we are looking for */
char *result;               /* where the result value goes */
{
    long pos, middle, hi, lo;
    static long pathlength = 0;
    register char *s;
    int c;
    static FILE *file;
    int flag;

    if( !pathlength ) {     /* open file on first use */
        if( ( file=fopen( DATABASEFILE, "r" ) ) == NULL ) {
            (void) fprintf(stderr,
                "can't access %s.\n", DATABASEFILE );
            pathlength = -1;
        } else {
            /* find length */
            (void) fseek( file, 0L, 2 );
            pathlength = ftell( file );
        }
    }
```

```
        if( pathlength == -1 )
                return -2;            /* No database file. */

        lo = 0;
        hi = pathlength;
        (void) strcpy( result, key );
        (void) strcat( result, "\t" );
        /*
         * "Binary search routines are never written right the
         *  first time around." - Robert G. Sheldon.
         */
        for( ;; ) {
                pos = middle = ( hi+lo+1 )/2;
                (void) fseek( file, pos, 0 ); /* find midpoint */
                if ( pos )  /* to beginning of next line */
                        while((c=getc(file)) != EOF && c != '\n');
                for( flag = 0, s = result; !flag; s++ ) { /* match? */
                        if ( *s == '\0' )
                                goto solved;
                        c = getc( file );
                        flag = tolower( c ) - tolower( *s );
                }
                if ( lo>=middle ) /* failure? */
                        return -1;  /* not found in database */
                if ( c != EOF && flag < 0 ) /* close window */
                        lo = middle;
                else
                        hi = middle - 1;
        }

        /* Now just copy the result. */
solved:
        while( ( c=getc( file ) ) != EOF && c != '\n' )
                *result++ = c;
        *result = '\0';
        return 0;   /* success */
}
```

difftime   compare times   ***●

This routine is part of ANSI C, but is new with that standard. No existing implementations supported it before ANSI C. It should be considered unportable unless you either assume ANSI C, or use #ifdef __STDC__.

opendir, readdir, rewinddir   directory library   *●
closedir, seekdir, telldir

These routines are fairly new, and although they are designed to be portable, they are not yet widely implemented. The four routines `opendir`, `readdir`, `closedir`, and `rewinddir` are required by POSIX and the SVID.

The original method of reading a directory on UNIX systems was to open the directory using `open` or `fopen` and then read in 16-byte structures, as defined by `struct direct` in `<sys/dir.h>`. This method made low-level assumptions about the implementation of the file system, and was not especially portable, but it did work on traditional UNIX systems.

In 4.2BSD, Berkeley reimplemented the filesystem, and one change allowed arbitrary length file names. The structure of a directory file changed, and the fixed-structure method no longer worked. Berkeley defined these six routines as a more portable interface, and made available a public domain implementation of the routines for the traditional file system.

In 1985, /usr/group and IEEE added four of these routines to the POSIX standard, and AT&T included them as standard parts of System V release 3. All six functions are currently available in 4.2BSD and 4.3BSD, and in System V release 3, and other systems conforming to the SVID or POSIX will be offering four or more of them in time. The `telldir` and `seekdir` functions are present in the 4BSD and System V implementations, but not required by the SVID or POSIX, because their implementation may not be possible on some filesystems.

Beware of the include file name. 4.2BSD uses the file `<sys/dir.h>` and POSIX and System V use the file `<dirent.h>` The Berkeley public domain implementation uses `<ndir.h>`. None of the systems supports alternate file names. All systems require that `<sys/types.h>` be included first.

The structure name is also different: Berkeley uses `struct direct` and POSIX and the SVID use `struct dirent`. One way to deal with this is to use the preprocessor:

```
#ifdef IEEE1003
# include <dirent.h>
#else
# include <sys/dir.h>
# define dirent direct
#endif
```

The typical application program needs only `opendir`, `readdir`, and `closedir`. POSIX requires these three and `rewinddir`, but not `telldir` or `seekdir`. Programs using `telldir` or `seekdir` are not quite as portable as those that don't.

Even though these routines are not yet universally implemented, they still define a fairly portable interface. If you need to examine all files in a directory, use of `opendir`, `readdir`, and `closedir` is recommended. If you must port your program to an environment without the directory routines, it is not difficult to write your own version or to find a copy of Berkeley's public domain version. (Their implementation is about 200 lines of C.) For operating systems other than the UNIX system, it is often possible to implement the same interface using appropriate primitives.

Some operating systems have case-insensitive file systems, where the names `myfile`, `MYFILE`, and `MyFile` are considered equivalent. This is usually transparent to an application, but if a user program is searching a directory for files whose names match a particular pattern, it may be necessary to do a case-insensitive comparison. Although there is no portable function to do the locally appropriate comparison, it would be prudent to isolate the comparison so that a function other than `strcmp` can be easily substituted.

`div, ldiv`   integer division   ***

These routines are part of ANSI C, but are new with that standard. No existing implementations supported them before ANSI C. They should be considered unportable unless you either assume ANSI C, or use `#ifdef  __STDC__`.

`drand48, erand48, jrand48`   48-bit random numbers   *
`lcong48, lrand48, mrand48`
`nrand48, seed48, srand48`

These routines are specific to System V. They are part of all releases of System V. The SVID requires them. They are also present in Lattice C. However, in general, they are not portable beyond System V.

`ecvt, fcvt, gcvt`   float to ascii   **

These routines are part of many UNIX C libraries, so they are fairly portable. They are sometimes viewed as an ''undocumented internal function'' used by `printf`. In general, you should use `sprintf` if you want to portably format a number.

`erf, erfc`   error functions   *

These routines are part of System V, but are not supported by many other implementations. They should be considered unportable outside System V.

`exit`   terminate program   *****

This routine is part of all C libraries, so it is extremely portable. Some very old libraries (before standard I/O) may not automatically flush all buffers before they exit.

exp   exponential   ****

This routine is part of most C libraries, so it is very portable. It may not be present in machines that do not support math routines.

fclose   close stdio file   *****

This routine is part of the core standard I/O, so it is extremely portable. Be sure, however, that the argument passed to `fclose` is a value returned by `fopen`, and that the file has not already been closed. The results of passing garbage to `fclose` are unpredictable and will usually result in a program abort.

fdopen   UNIX fd to stdio fp   **

This routine is part of all UNIX C libraries, so it is portable within the UNIX system. It is defined in terms of the UNIX file descriptor, which is not a portable concept. For this reason, `fdopen` is not very portable outside the UNIX system.

The UNIX `fdopen` function is considered part of standard I/O. It is present in all UNIX versions since V7.

Some implementations of C have a notion similar to the UNIX file descriptor, and may support `fdopen`. This just means that the implementation has a more complete emulation of the UNIX system than usual.

feof   test end of stdio file   *****

This routine is part of standard I/O, so it is extremely portable.

Note that `feof` is often implemented as a macro, so it is unwise to pass it an expression with side effects or to redefine your own version.

ferror   test stdio file error   *****

This routine is part of standard I/O, so it is extremely portable.

Note that `ferror` is often implemented as a macro, so it is unwise to pass it an expression with side effects or to redefine your own version.

fflush   flush stdio file   *****

This routine is part of standard I/O, so it is extremely portable.

By custom, when a program exits, all buffered output is flushed. While this property tends to be true of most implementations, it is still wise to explicitly close all files before exiting. It is safe to assume that closing a file will call `fflush` or the equivalent.

Under some operating systems, such as MS DOS 2.11, flushing a file does not necessarily force an immediate write to disk. If the program later aborts, the data may not appear in the file. This can be frustrating during debugging, but otherwise should not affect the behavior of a correct program.

On the UNIX system, flushing the file to disk does not force an immediate write, due to buffering in the operating system. The sync system call can be used to force scheduling of the actual write, but this call can return before the actual write occurs. Since the sync call will force *all* disk buffers to be written out to disk, a sync on a large system can impact system performance. The 4.2BSD fsync call forces a write for the particular file, but this call is not portable. Similar functionality can be found on System V release 3 with the O_SYNC option to open and fcntl.

fgetc   get stdio character   ***

This routine is part of standard I/O, but it is redundant with getc, so it is little used. Not all implementations support it. If you need a nonmacro version of getc, you can easily and portably write your own.

fgets   get stdio line   *****

This routine is part of standard I/O, so it is extremely portable. In general, this routine may be portably used to read a line from a text file, or a line typed at the keyboard. If the purpose is to copy an arbitrary input file to an arbitrary output file, then fread is recommended. One reason for this is that arbitrary files sometimes contain binary data, and it is possible that fgets will transform binary data in an attempt at text compatibility. Another is that sometimes very long lines occur in files, which fgets may separate into two lines if the buffer isn't large enough.

fileno   stdio fp to UNIX fd   **

This routine is part of all UNIX C libraries, so it is very portable within the UNIX system. It is defined in terms of the UNIX file descriptor, which is not a portable concept. For this reason, fileno is not very portable outside the UNIX system. (In practice, most C implementations do support it.)

The UNIX fileno function is considered part of standard I/O. It is present in all UNIX versions since V7.

Some implementations of C have a notion similar to the UNIX file descriptor, and may support fileno. This just means that the implementation has a more complete emulation of the UNIX system than usual.

fmod   floating modulus   ****

This routine is part of most C libraries. They are missing only from a few libraries that do not support full floating-point libraries, and from the standard I/O and K&R documents.

Many implementations do not correctly implement the floating-point modulus. Beware of incorrect values returned by this function.

fopen   open stdio file   *****

This routine is part of the core standard I/O, so it is extremely portable. It is safe to assume it will be present in nearly any implementation of C. Be careful, however: the interpretation of the arguments may be subject to local operating system interpretation.

The first argument is a file name. The syntax for file names is different on different systems. If the file name has any operating system syntax in it, such as the UNIX system ''/'', or the MS DOS '':'' or ''\'', the call isn't portable.

Possible ways to portably use this call include having the user type the file name from the keyboard, using short simple file names containing only letters and digits, or using a configuration file to tailor the file names for each system. The use of `#ifdef` is also a possibility, using a different name for each system as part of the configuration procedure.

The second argument can portably be either `"r"`, `"w"`, or `"a"` if the file is a text file. Input and output will use local text conventions. For the UNIX system, this generally means the bytes written and read will be exactly what is in the file. For other operating systems, it's common for lines in text files to terminate with the two characters CR and LF. For text files, the C library will automatically translate newlines into native representations such as CR/LF, and vice versa.

If you need to do both input and output on the same file descriptor, you can add a + after the r, w, or a. This isn't quite as portable as a single-letter argument, since some older UNIX versions did not support it; in particular, PWB, 32V, and 3BSD did not have this feature. The + feature was not in the original standard I/O, but was added in about 1978.

If you have to do both input and output, you must make a choice between using two file descriptors for the same file or using the + feature. The awkwardness of using two file descriptors (and the potential for clobbering your file if the two buffers get in each others way) probably outweighs any portability problems.

If you intend the file to be a binary file, the call won't be as portable. On the UNIX system, there is no concept of text or binary modes, so the same usage is needed. For other operating systems, it's common to add another character to the second argument, such as b, to indicate a binary file. For binary files, no translation is done on input and output.

Unfortunately, the second argument for binary files is not very portable yet. It is part of ANSI C, but wasn't previously implemented widely. For one or two calls within a

program, this isn't a major problem to fix, but it can be hard to find the problem when
porting. One recommended way to open a binary file is to include a define in a header
file:

```
#ifdef unix
# define WRITEBIN "w"
#endif
#ifdef msdos
# define WRITEBIN "wb"
#endif
```

and then opening the file like this:

```
fd = fopen(filename, WRITEBIN);
```

This way, if you port the program to a new operating system, you'll get a diagnostic that
WRITEBIN is undefined, which should be easy to find. The fix is to add another operating system condition to the header file.

Another approach is to always include the trailing b anyway. Most implementations
that don't look for it will ignore it. While this isn't guaranteed to work all the time, in
practice, it may be a pragmatic and relatively elegant solution.

The owner of a newly created file will be the same as the uid of the process, but the
group might be either the gid of the process (the V7 and System V behavior) or the group
of the parent directory (the 4.2BSD behavior). Some systems allow either source of
group. For example, the merged System V release 4 uses the parent directory's group if
the SGID bit is set on the directory, otherwise, the gid of the process. POSIX allows
either interpretation and provides the new feature _POSIX_GROUP_PARENT to allow a
C application to determine what the current implementation will do. The FIPS standard
requires the Berkeley behavior, so future implementations may migrate toward using the
parent's group. In general, in the rare case where the group of a new file is important, an
application should use chown to ensure that the file has the correct owner and group.

fprintf   formatted stdio print to file   *****

This routine is part of standard I/O, so it is extremely portable. See printf for comments about specific formatting options.

It is not portable to make use of the value returned by fprintf, since many documents do not state what this value is. While ANSI C and the SVID state that the value is
the number of bytes printed, this was not true of 4.2BSD and many of its descendents.

fread   read stdio file   *****

This routine is part of the core standard I/O, so it is extremely portable. Be sure, however, that the arguments passed to fread are proper values, and that the file has not
already been closed.

The size argument should be carefully constructed. The best way to construct the argument is to use the `sizeof` operator on the object being written.

This call is best suited for binary files. It can also be used for straight copies of arbitrary files (in binary mode.) For text handling, routines such as `scanf` and `fgets` are probably better.

Most implementations merely treat `fread` as a series of calls to `getc`. Although this makes the call quite portable, it also makes it somewhat inefficient. `getc` is usually a macro that checks for an empty buffer and does a read if necessary. Calling `getc` in a loop, as `fread` does, causes a check to be made at every character. Some implementations (notably UNIX System V) contain special-purpose code to avoid these repeated, unnecessary checks, but many just loop on `getc`.

Usually calls to `fread` are incidental to program execution, and portability outweighs efficiency. If you are doing a straight memory dump with a large file and you find that performance is too slow using `fread`, try using `read` directly. This may gain speed at a minor decrease in portability.

freopen   redirect stdio file   ****

This routine is part of all C libraries, so it is extremely portable. It was not present in the original K&R book, but it is part of standard I/O.

In practice, `freopen` is not heavily used, except when converting a large program that reads from `stdin` to be able to process a named file instead. When writing a new program, it is usually better to explicitly open and read or write the files named.

frexp, ldexp, modf   manipulate floating-point numbers   ****

These routines are part of most C libraries, so they are very portable. They are missing only from certain libraries that do not fully support floating point, and from the standard I/O and K&R documents.

These routines may cause undesired rounding on some machines, such as the IBM s/370. The 4.3BSD routines `scalb` and `logb` may work better in some cases, but are unportable.

fseek, ftell, rewind   stdio file positioning   ****

These routines are part of the core standard I/O, so they are very portable. In order to have a truly portable program, however, the only offset value ever passed to `fseek` should be a value returned by `ftell`. It is also generally safe to use the value `0L` to seek to the beginning or end of a file. Although most implementations do use byte offsets as seek tokens, the byte offset for a text file may not be what you expect, due to the use of the ASCII CR (return) and LF (linefeed/newline) characters instead of newlines. Other possible implementations encode block, record, and byte values. ANSI C requires that the offset be a byte offset, and the CR-LF / newline problem is the only one you're likely to run into in practice.

Seeking is not meaningful on all devices. Seeking on standard input or output, in particular, is not recommended. If these files are attached to a pipe, or a terminal, the seek is likely to fail. Seeks on tapes, or raw disk devices, may not work either. Seeking should be reserved for ordinary disk files.

On the other hand, if you open a standard I/O file for both input and output, you must do a seek on it in between reads and writes. This is necessary to switch the standard I/O buffering between reading and writing. In this case, a seek is not only permissible, but required. Since you can't expect the seek to work properly, a seek that doesn't do anything should be used:

```
fseek(fd, OL, 1);
```

This is important in some situations where you wouldn't expect it, for example, if you have a network connection open with a read/write file descriptor.

Some care should be taken with the type returned by `ftell`. Most implementations use a `long`, although some mask this as an `offset_t`, which is normally a `long`. ANSI C has defined a pair of functions, `fsetpos` and `fgetpos`, that serve the same purpose, but use the type `fpos_t` passed as an argument. These are intended for situations when the file position cannot be represented as an integer, such as a file over 2 billion bytes in size, or a need for information such as extent, record, and offset.

Historically, another function called `tell` has been provided as a non-standard I/O version of `ftell`. The `tell` routine was documented in V7 (in `lseek(2)`) and described as obsolete. The function is still present, but undocumented, in AT&T System V release 2, and in 4.2BSD. Since the same effect can be gained with `lseek`(*fd*, `OL`, `2`), there is no reason to use it. The `tell` function was a mainstream function for a short period between V6 and V7, since it required `long` integers, which V6 did not support, and was obsoleted by standard I/O.

fwrite   write stdio file   *****

This routine is part of the core standard I/O, so it is extremely portable. Be sure, however, that the arguments passed to `fwrite` are proper values, and that the file has not already been closed. The results of passing garbage to `fwrite` are unpredictable and will usually result in a program abort.

The size argument should be carefully constructed. The best way to construct the argument is to use the `sizeof` operator on the object being written. Sometimes this isn't possible, however. For buffers that might be incomplete, you'll have to calculate the size, ideally by using the value returned by a call to `fread`.

This call is best suited for binary files. It can also be used for straight copies of arbitrary files (in binary mode.) For text handling, routines such as `printf` and `fputs` are probably better.

Most implementations merely treat `fwrite` as a series of calls to `putc`. While this makes the call quite portable, it also makes it somewhat inefficient. `putc` is usually a macro that checks for buffer overflow. Calling `putc` in a loop, as `fwrite` does, causes a check to be made at every character. Some implementations (notably UNIX System V) contain special-purpose code to avoid these repeated, unnecessary checks, but many just loop on `putc`.

Usually, calls to `fwrite` are incidental to program execution, and portability outweighs efficiency. If you are doing a straight memory dump with a large file, and you find that performance is too slow using `fwrite`, try using `write` directly. This may gain speed at a minor decrease in portability.

gamma   log of abs of math gamma   **

This routine is part of many UNIX implementations, but is not supported by any other systems. It should be considered unportable outside the UNIX system. Since it is required by the SVID, but not by POSIX, it is not completely portable within the UNIX system, but it is present in both 4.2BSD and System V.

NOTE: in 4.3BSD, this function has been renamed `lgamma` in order to be consistent with conventional notation and the FORTRAN library. This function returns the log of gamma, not gamma itself. While the SVID requires `gamma` to return the log of gamma, the 4.3BSD manual indicates that "programmers should not assume that lgamma has settled down."

If you use this function in many places in your program, one useful defensive programming technique is to always call a routine `lgamma`. On systems other than 4.3BSD, you can add `-Dlgamma=gamma` to the compiler command line or

```
#define lgamma gamma
```

to a header file. Standardizing on the name `lgamma` allows you to write a different routine called `gamma`, or to use such a routine provided by the C library, to get the gamma value itself. If both names are to be used, it is easier to detect which is which by using conventional mathematical names. Also, this method will produce a quick error message if you mistakenly get the wrong version of `gamma`.

getc   get stdio char   *****

This routine is part of all C libraries, so it is extremely portable.

Be sure to treat the value returned from `getc` as an `int`, not as a `char`, until you have checked it for end of file. On machines with signed characters, the EOF value (-1) may store properly in a `char` variable, but on unsigned machines, it may come back out as 255.

Because it may be implemented as a macro, `getc` may incorrectly handle an argument with side effects. It is likely that the argument will be evaluated more than once.

getchar   get stdio char from stdin   *****

This routine is part of all C libraries, so it is extremely portable. The getchar function is probably *the* most portable input function in the C environment.

Be sure to treat the value returned from getchar as an int, not as a char, until you have checked it for end of file. On signed machines, the EOF value (−1) may store properly in a char variable, but on unsigned machines, it may come back out as 255.

getcwd   get current directory   *

This routine is part of System V, but is not supported by many other implementations. It is also present in Microsoft C for the MS DOS system. It should be considered unportable outside System V.

4.2BSD has a similar function called getwd. The 4.2BSD function takes only one argument, a pointer to the result buffer, whereas the System V version takes two arguments, a pointer to the result buffer and the size of the buffer.

getenv   get environment variable   ***

This routine is part of many C libraries, so it is fairly portable. Environments first appeared in V7 and UNIX/TS 2.0. (It is possible to emulate them, using disk files, for simple uses like the terminal type or home directory.) Environments may not exist on other operating systems, although they do exist in MS DOS systems in essentially the same form.

Attempts to change the environment by altering the value returned by getenv, or assumptions that the value can be altered without changing the environment, are not portable.

The particular set of values that can be expected in the environment varies greatly from system to system. It is widely agreed that TERM refers to a terminfo or termcap name for the controlling terminal type. Most UNIX systems also provide HOME as a name for the home directory, and PATH as the Bourne-shell format search path. The variables TZ and LOGNAME are present on System III derived systems and the POSIX standard, but the user can change them to any value. The variables SHELL and MAIL are present on both systems, by convention, but are not always present. The Berkeley equivalent of LOGNAME is USER. The early PWB systems used LOGDIR instead of, or in addition to, HOME.

In general, the users can set the environment to whatever they like, so it is unwise for a program concerned about security to trust anything it gets from the environment.

`getgrent`, `getgrgid`, `getgrnam`   read group file   **
`setgrent`, `endgrent`

These routines are part of most UNIX libraries, so they are portable among UNIX systems. They were not present in V6 or PWB, but are essentially identical in later systems. They are generally not available outside UNIX systems.

Some systems use hashed password and group files, or provide similar functionality with nameservers over a network. These systems generally provide a different implementation of the `getgrent` routines, with a compatible user interface. Programs that use these routines will require only recompilation when ported to such new systems; often only relinking is needed.

The recommended routines for most applications would be `getgrgid` and `getgrnam`.

`getlogin`   get login name   **

This routine is part of most UNIX C libraries, so it is portable among UNIX systems.

This routine typically looks for the current terminal in the `/etc/utmp` file, and returns the character string stored there. Normally, this is the same login ID that was typed when the user logged in, and is the value printed by the `who` command. It is possible that, due to suid (the file-mode bit) or the `setuid` function, the value returned by `getlogin` will be different from the result of looking up `getuid` in `/etc/passwd`. It is also possible to get a different result because of multiple entries in the password file with the same uid.

Since this subroutine uses the owner of the terminal attached to standard input or standard output, it is possible for an intruder to redirect these files at another terminal, and deceive an authentication mechanism. Do not use this function for authentication. Use `getuid` *or* `geteuid` *instead.*

The application programmer should give some thought to which value is really wanted: the logged-in string, the current effective or real uid, or the value of `LOGNAME` or `USER` in the environment. `getlogin` will fail if called from a background server, or from `cron` or `at`. `getuid` may tend to return a name such as `root` if the user has run `su`. Environment variables can be set by the user, which allow the user more freedom to specify what he or she wants, but which may also pose a security problem.

Often an appropriate scheme is to try one, and if that fails, to try something else. For example, when an electronic mail application determines the return address for a piece of outgoing mail, a programmer not worried about security might write code to check the environment first, then `getlogin`, and finally `getuid`. Some programs also use the convention that a file in `$HOME` whose name begins with a dot, such as `$HOME/.exrc` for the `vi` program, is checked.

getopt   get command-line options   *●

This routine is part of System III and System V, but it is only moderately portable to other systems.

The getopt routine is a mainstream routine used in System V, and AT&T is firmly behind it. It has been well received in the UNIX community, and 4.3BSD includes a version. However, it is not present in POSIX or ANSI C, and is not present in most non-UNIX C implementations.

Beware that other operating systems may not use the UNIX option conventions involving the hyphen. It may be necessary to rewrite getopt to use options beginning with another character, such as a slash, or to get options from a menu or using a mouse. On some operating systems, it may not be possible to use getopt at all.

The opterr variable was undocumented in early versions of getopt, and some implementations did not support it. Another variable, optopt, is present but undocumented in some implementations. Use of optopt is unportable.

Two implementations of getopt have been placed into the public domain: one by Henry Spencer at the University of Toronto, and one by AT&T. You should only use getopt if you have access to one of these implementations or if you are willing to assume System V or 4.3BSD. The Toronto version is about 60 lines long. The AT&T version is about 250 lines, and supports additional functionality. The AT&T version source code is shown in Appendix F.

getpass   get password   **

This routine is part of most UNIX C libraries, but it is not generally available outside the UNIX system.

getpw   get password line   **

This routine is part of most UNIX C libraries, but its use is not recommended. It is provided primarily for upward compatibility with previous UNIX versions. In V6 and PWB, getpw was the only routine available for reading the password file. When getpwuid became available in V7 and UNIX/TS 2.0, there was no longer any need for getpw.

While getpw is more widely available than getpwuid, it is not as portable. The calling function must interpret the fields of the password file, and there are slight variations in the format.

The PWB system did not include the concept of a group, so the group field was missing from the password file. Some systems do not implement the password file as a text file, but rather use a hashed binary file, or an alternate file without the encrypted passwords, or a network client that queries a server on another machine. The UNIX standards (SVID, /usr/group, and POSIX) do not include getpw.

getpwent, getpwuid, getpwnam   read password file   **
setpwent, endpwent

These routines are part of most UNIX libraries, so they are very portable. They were not present in V6, but are essentially identical in later systems. They are generally not available outside UNIX systems.

While in practice all UNIX systems have these routines, and they are considered to be the preferred way to access information in the password file, they are not required by the base-level SVID. (They are required by POSIX.)

Note that, for security reasons, the encrypted password may be stored in a protected auxiliary file, such as /etc/shadow in System V release 3.2. There is no portable way to verify passwords.

Some systems use hashed password and group files or provide similar functionality with nameservers over a network. These systems generally provide a different implementation of the getpwent routines, with a compatible user interface. Programs that use these routines will require only recompilation when ported to such new systems; often only relinking is needed.

The recommended routines for most applications would be getpwuid and getpwnam.

Many systems use the pw_gecos field to store extra information about the user, such as the full name, office, phone extension, or home phone number. Other systems use it to store accounting information used for submitting RJE jobs to mainframes. The field was originally intended for RJE to GCOS systems, but few systems have GCOS connections.

Some software uses the pw_gecos field to extract information such as the full name. Unfortunately, there is no completely portable way to do this. On a traditional Berkeley system, the full name is the first part of this field, terminated by a comma; an & should be replaced by the login name. On a traditional System V system, the field consists of an RJE number, a hyphen, the full name, a left parenthesis, an RJE number, a right parenthesis, and the number of a bin in which to place printed output. An obvious algorithm is to use the information up to a comma or left parenthesis, and to start over if you find a hyphen. The problem here is that some people have hyphens in their names. Here is a routine that depends on a #define for RJE if the RJE convention is locally in effect.

```
/*
 *  BUILDFNAME -- build full name from gecos style entry.
 *      This routine is taken from B news.
 *
 *      Parameters:
 *              p -- name to build.
 *              login -- the login name of this user (for &).
 *              buf -- place to put the result.
 */
```

```
buildfname(p, login, buf)
register char *p;
char *login;
char *buf;
{
      register char *bp = buf;

      if (*p == '*')      /* ignore leading star */
            p++;
      while (*p != '\0' && *p != ',' && *p != ';' &&
            *p != ':' && *p != '(') {
#ifdef RJE
            if (*p == '-') {
                  bp = buf;     /* start over */
                  p++;
            }
#endif
            else if (*p == '&') {    /* full name */
                  strcpy(bp, login);
                  /* Capitalize first letter of word */
                  if ((bp == buf || !isalpha(bp[-1]))
                              && islower(*bp))
                        *bp = toupper(*bp);
                  while (*bp != '\0')
                        bp++;
                  p++;
            }
            else
                  *bp++ = *p++;
      }
      *bp = '\0';
}
```

gets   get string from stdin   *****

   This routine is part of standard I/O, so it is extremely portable. In general, this routine
may be portably used to read a line of text typed at the keyboard (or on standard input.)
Nonetheless, use of gets is strongly discouraged. If the purpose is to copy an arbitrary
input file to an arbitrary output file, then fread is recommended. One reason for this is
that arbitrary files sometimes contain binary data, and it is possible that gets will
transform binary data in an attempt at text compatibility. Another is that sometimes very
long lines occur in files, which may gets to overflow the buffer if it isn't large enough.
For security reasons, the use of gets is strongly discouraged. It is sometimes possible
to break into a computer system by intentionally overflowing the gets buffer and
overwriting the return address on the stack. This was one of the methods used by the
ARPANET worm in 1988.

gets is not quite as portable as fgets. In the original standard I/O, it was intended as an upward compatibility routine. In practice, it has become a popular part of C. Most C implementations do support gets, but not MVS.

Another advantage of fgets over gets is that fgets is more robust in the case of long lines. The fgets function is passed the length of the buffer, so it won't overflow the buffer you provide, no matter how long the line of input. Beware, however, that gets strips the trailing newline, but fgets leaves it there.

getw, putw   stdio get/put word   *

These routines are part of standard I/O, but they are not very portable, and they are seldom used. One problem is that the size of a ''word'' is not well defined. (It is generally taken to be the same as sizeof int.)

The second problem is that the order of bytes within a word is not universal. This suggests that getw be used primarily for fast copying of quantities a word at a time. In practice, however, getw usually merely calls getc two or four times, so there is actually an efficiency *loss*. Since you must also deal with odd numbers of bytes to be copied, it is generally better to use byte- or block-oriented routines such as getc or fread.

The putw function suffers the same problems. It is generally better to use putc or fwrite.

hypot   Euclidean distance   **

This routine is part of most UNIX implementations, so it is very portable within the UNIX system. It is not required by ANSI C or POSIX, but is required by the SVID. It should be considered unportable outside the UNIX system.

A limited number of non-UNIX C libraries support hypot. These include GCOS, Microsoft C, and Mark Williams C. The typical implementation of hypot is probably more accurate than an implementation likely to be written by a casual programmer.

index, rindex   search string   *

These routines are part of V7 derived systems, such as 4.2BSD. Functions called strchr and strrchr, which have the same arguments and same semantics, are required by all the standards. See the entry for strchr in this chapter for more details.

isalpha, isupper,   classify characters   ****
islower, isdigit, isalnum, isspace,
ispunct, isprint, iscntrl, isascii

The ctype routines are isalpha, isupper, islower, isdigit, isalnum, isspace, ispunct, isprint, iscntrl, and isascii. These routines are part of most C libraries, so they are very portable. They are usually implemented as macros, so you must include <ctype.h>.

Many implementations of C augment this set with additional routines. In particular, System V supplies isxdigit and isgraph.

K&R documents only isalpha, isupper, islower, isdigit, and isspace, so an implementation claiming only K&R support may be missing the others. Beware that the space character is considered a printing character by isprint, although not by isgraph.

Beware that these functions were originally well defined only if their values range from 0 to 127. ANSI C requires that they work for arguments in the range of unsigned char (often 0 to 255) or EOF (often −1.) On an EBCDIC system, values can range as high as 255. Passing garbage to a ctype function can result in a garbage result, except for isascii. Unfortunately, isascii was left out of ANSI C, due to the name and the difficulty in generalizing it to other character sets. If there is any doubt about the validity of a character, check it with isascii first:

```
if (isascii(c) && isdigit(c))
```

isascii is not defined on MVS, and may be missing on other systems conforming to ANSI C. If you do wind up porting your code to such systems, you can define your own version that always returns true or checks that the argument is between −1 and 255, as appropriate.

Some implementations of ctype look up the value in a table. Others do one or more comparisons. If the argument has any side effects, you may run into a problem with the side effects being run more than once. Thus, calls such as isdigit(*p++) are not portable.

Beware that these routines are often defined under the assumption that a 7-bit environment is being used. Efforts were made in the mid 1980s so that software would work in an 8-bit environment (to handle European extended character sets) or 16- or 32-bit environments (for Japanese and other Asian languages.) Assumptions involving the number 0177 or being able to store an extra bit of information in the high bit of a character will get you into trouble when someone tries to port your program to an international environment, so it's best to avoid them early. (The 16- and 32-bit character sets do not require you to use more than 8-bit characters. Just pass 8-bit characters normally and terminal-handling software will find groups of characters and join them appropriately. See also the new ANSI C multibyte character functions such as mbtowc for a potential long-term solution.)

isatty   is a terminal   **

This routine is part of all UNIX C libraries, so it is extremely portable within the UNIX system. Some non-UNIX implementations also support it, although some are not fully standard. One MS DOS implementation, for example, returns true only if the file descriptor refers to the console. Another returns true for the console, a terminal port, or a parallel or serial printer port.

The SVID and POSIX standards require isatty, but ANSI C does not.

j0, j1, jn, y0, y1, yn   Bessel functions   **

These routines (the "Bessel functions") are part of most UNIX implementations, so they are very portable within UNIX systems. They are not required by ANSI C or POSIX, but are required by the SVID. They are also supported by Microsoft C. They should be considered generally unportable outside the UNIX system.

log, log10   math logarithm   ****

These routines are part of most C libraries, so they are very portable. They may not be present in machines that do not support math routines.

log10 is a fairly new addition to the math library. It was not present in V6, V7, or System III, but was present in 3BSD and System V and their descendents.

logname   get login name   *

This routine is part of the PWB library, and it is not portable. Although it is present in System V, it is not required by the SVID or other standards. The use of cuserid is more portable, although still not very portable.

Some early implementations of this function called getenv("LOGNAME"). Current versions call cuserid.

On System V, it is necessary to include -lPW on the linker command line to get this function. This library will not be present in future System V releases.

malloc, free, realloc   memory allocation   *****

These routines are part of all C libraries, so they are extremely portable.

The malloc and free routines are considered the primary memory-allocation and deallocation routines for C. realloc is nearly as portable. calloc has a slightly different interface, which should be viewed as multiplying the two parameters to yield the desired number of bytes. In practice, calloc is most convenient when the area to be allocated must be initialized to all zeros, and malloc is more appropriate when the initial value does not matter.

Part of the V7 folklore allows free to be called on a buffer before calling realloc on it, to exploit the allocation strategy. Although many systems allow this for upward compatibility, the practice is not portable and is not recommended. Once a section of memory has been freed, all pointers to it should be considered invalid and no longer used.

Although `malloc` is quite portable, on many systems it is not fast enough for some applications. In the traditional implementation, each call to `malloc` would search the arena of available memory, one buffer at a time, looking for free space to satisfy the request. For an application that calls `malloc` many times before ever calling `free`, it would search the entire arena without finding any free space, and wind up lengthening the arena with a lower level routine such as `sbrk`. This has led to many improved versions of `malloc`, each of which tends to do better for some applications. System V has an alternate version, with tunable parameters, available by indicating `-lmalloc`. Berkeley has a version designed for large virtual-memory applications.

For the most part, these alternate versions of `malloc` all are implemented using `sbrk`. Since all UNIX systems provide `sbrk`, these memory allocators tend to work unmodified on other UNIX versions, assuming source is available and can be legally copied to the other system and recompiled.

It is also possible to write your own memory allocator. One approach is to merely buffer calls to `sbrk` when `malloc` is called, and for `free` to do nothing. This is very fast, but freed memory is never given back, so it is only appropriate for a few applications.

Another approach is to call `malloc` only a few times, getting a large chunk of memory each time, and to subdivide this yourself. This is especially useful if you have many standard-sized structures, so you can keep a free list for each size.

`mallinfo, mallopt`   malloc options   *

These routines are part of System V, but are not supported by many other implementations. They should be considered portable only within System V.

In System V, these routines are only available as part of the *malloc* library. You must add the option `-lmalloc` when linking the program. This causes the use of an alternate implementation of `malloc`.

`matherr`   math error function   *

This routine is part of System V, but is not supported by many other implementations. It should be considered unportable outside System V. It is present in Microsoft C and Lattice C.

`memchr, memcmp`   memory functions   ***
`memcpy, memset`

These routines are part of most System V derived C libraries, so they are somewhat portable. The related routines `memccpy` and `memmove` are less portable.

The four main routines `memchr`, `memcmp`, `memcpy`, and `memset` are present in System V, ANSI C, GCOS, and Microsoft C. The `memcmp`, `memcpy`, and `memset` routines are also present in MVS.

System V and Microsoft C, but not ANSI C, have memccpy. ANSI C has memmove, so even though all implementations will eventually support memmove, it won't be widely available for some time. A good approach would be to go ahead and use memmove, and include in a header:

```
#ifndef __STDC__
# define memmove memcpy
#endif
```

Beware of the include file used to declare these functions. System V uses either <memory.h> or <string.h>. ANSI C uses <string.h>. The long-term direction is to use <string.h>. It is safest just to use <string.h> and to not use any return values.

The similar Berkeley functions are bcopy(src, dest, count) (same as memcpy(dest, src, count)); bcmp(s1, s2, count), (same as memcmp(s1, s2, count)); and bzero(s, length) (same as memset(s, 0, count)); all of these are documented in bstring(3). Note that Berkeley uses a different argument order for bcopy.

The memcpy and memmove routines are similar, except that memcpy is optimized for speed, but memmove guarantees that the right thing happens, even if the source and destination areas overlap. It is unwise to assume that memcpy will handle overlapping areas properly, even if it does handle them in one implementation.

mktemp   make temporary file name   **

This routine is part of most UNIX C libraries, so it is very portable within the UNIX system. Some MS DOS implementations also support it, or a similar routine, but, in general, this function should be considered UNIX specific, because of the UNIX pathname that must be passed to it.

The mktemp function may modify its argument. Some programs use the following technique:

```
/* Unportable! */
char *tfn, *mktemp();
int fd;

tfn = mktemp("/tmp/abcXXXXXX");
fd = open(tfn, 2);
```

This is not portable because a constant string is modified.

A slightly better, but still unrecommended, technique is this:

```
char *tfn, *mktemp();
int fd;
static char tfnbuf[15] = "/tmp/abcXXXXXX";

tfn = mktemp(tfnbuf);
fd = open(tfn, 2);
```

This works properly as long as the above code is called only once during the lifetime of the program. If it is called a second time, the value actually passed to mktemp is the first file name, such as /tmp/abca12345. Since this does not end in the required six X's, it is incorrect. Nonetheless, many implementations of mktemp work properly given such input.

A truly portable method looks like this:

```
char *tfn, *mktemp();
int fd;
char tfnbuf[15];

strcpy(tfnbuf, "/tmp/abcXXXXXX");
tfn = mktemp(tfnbuf);
if (tfn == NULL)
        perror("mktemp");
fd = open(tfn, 2);
if (fd < 0)
        perror(tfn);
```

Of course, be sure to check that mktemp did not return NULL, and that open returns a legal file descriptor.

Also beware that /tmp may not have much free space on some systems. Many UNIX systems are distributed with small root filesystems, and /tmp is often part of the root filesystem. By convention, /usr/tmp is on the /usr filesystem, which traditionally has more free space. If your temporary file is likely to be large, you should consider placing it in /usr/tmp. The trade-off is that some systems have /tmp optimized to be faster than other filesystems. The related functions tempnam and tmpfile have their own portability and functionality trade-offs. The programmer should carefully choose between them.

nargs   number of arguments   *

This routine is obsolete, and cannot be reliably implemented on many machines, so it is very unportable. It attempted to return the number of arguments passed to the current function.

The nargs function was popular up to V6, so that a function that used a variable-argument list, such as printf or execl, could tell how many arguments it had been passed. Since different arguments can take up different amounts of space on the stack, and since parameter-passing conventions may include the use of registers or the stack, and since there is no requirement that the stack be marked to show the beginning and end of the arguments, it is usually not possible to implement this.

A programmer needing to implement a function supporting variable arguments should use the `varargs` facility.

`nlist`	search symbol table	**

This routine is part of most UNIX C libraries, but it is not portable. This routine is not required by the SVID, POSIX, or ANSI C.

The `nlist` function has been present in every UNIX version since V6. The interface has changed somewhat over time, from a manually declared structure in V6; to including `<a.out.h>` in V7, 3BSD, System III, and System V release 1; and to including `<nlist.h>` in 4BSD and System V release 2.

The reason `nlist` is not portable is that it is normally used to extract symbol-table addresses from a file such as `/unix`, `/vmunix`, or `/xenix`. The application then reads the special file `/dev/kmem` to get the value of a variable from the running copy of the operating system. This involves making assumptions about the implementation of the kernel, as well as the name of the system executable file. (The file containing the kernel tends to have a different name on each system, so as to respect trademarks such as **UNIX**.)

If you must poke around in `/dev/kmem`, you will probably be writing code specific to one system. There may be some elements of the kernel that are fairly consistent from one UNIX version to another, but such elements are not required in order to conform to any of the UNIX or C standards. In general, programs that look inside the operating system are not portable.

`perror`	print error message	***

This routine is part of many C libraries, so it is very portable within the UNIX system, and somewhat portable to other systems.

The underlying variables `errno`, `sys_nerr`, and `sys_errlist` are equally portable within UNIX systems.

One problem area occurs when add-on applications have their own error numbers. For example, core UNIX System V has a certain set of error numbers available to `perror` and in `<errno.h>`. One networking add-on package may define additional error numbers and provide its own version of `perror` and `<errno.h>`. Another package may also add error numbers, providing *its* own version of `perror` and `<errno.h>`. An application calling `perror` cannot possibly satisfy both sets of error numbers without some merging occurring. This problem has not yet occurred in source-based UNIX distributions, such as 4.2BSD, since new error numbers are defined by adding them to the base system. There is little the application can do about this, except to be sure to check `errno` against `sys_nerr` before accessing `sys_errlist`.

While the `perror` call may be portable, the specific set of available errors is not. Use of some of the E variables from `<errno.h>` is likely to be less portable.

popen, pclose   stdio pipe creation   **

These routines are part of most UNIX libraries, so they are very portable among UNIX systems. They are required by the SVID. They are not required by POSIX or ANSI C, and are not part of any non-UNIX libraries.

The `popen` and `pclose` functions are inherently specific to the UNIX system, because they imply a multitasking operating system, and more importantly, because the command itself is something understood by the command interpreter. Since different operating systems have different command interpreters, commands passed to `popen` are rarely portable beyond the local operating system.

For security reasons, the use of `execlp`, `execvp`, `popen`, `pclose`, *and* `system` *is strongly discouraged. Since these operations go through the shell, programs using them have been exploited by intruders to break into computing systems. It is better to use* `fork` *and* `execl` *directly, without going through the shell or path mechanism.*

In general, the only portable uses of `popen` involve either using a well-known UNIX command with well-known options, such as `who`, or else have the user type the command at the keyboard, as in an editor like `vi` accepting a command such as `:r !tail myfile`, which might read in the output of the command.

Although `system` is much more portable than `popen`, it is difficult to take advantage of this. It is possible to call `system` and then use `fopen` to read in a file, or use `fopen` to write out a file, and then call system. The problem is that using system with input or output connected to a file requires use of the shell < or > syntax, which is also specific to the UNIX system. Many other operating systems do support the < / > syntax, either in their native command interpreter or in their C startup library. Use of `system` and < / > restricts you to systems supporting < / >. and you must also limit your commands to those typed by the user. Few UNIX commands can be assumed to be present on other systems.

pow   math power function   ****

This routine is part of most C libraries, so it is very portable. Many implementations of pow are not very accurate. It may not be present in machines that do not support math routines. Do not forget to declare that `pow` returns a `double`, and that the arguments should have type `double`.

printf   formatted print to stdout   *****

This routine is part of all C libraries, and is probably the most portable routine in C. `printf` and `putchar` are even available to device drivers inside the UNIX operating system kernel, which does not have access to the C I/O library. `printf` dates back to before standard I/O, so a few implementations may be derived from the V6 or earlier rules. Some care must be taken, however, that only widely implemented formatting options are used. The function value returned by `printf` is not portable.

The `%c`, `%d`, `%o`, `%s`, `%u`, and `%x` options are portable, and work essentially everywhere. (Terminfo does not support `%u`.) If your system supports floating point, then it is also safe to assume that `%f`, `%e`, and `%g` work.

It is also nearly universally safe to assume that `%%` will print a single `%` sign, that the `%` may be followed by a `−`, that *width* and *precision* may be specified as decimal integers, and that an `l` may be included to indicate that the argument is a `long`. Most implementations also support `*` to indicate that the widths are read from the argument stream.

Certain other features are less portable. Recent additions include the `+`, blank, and `#` characters after the `%`; the use of upper-case `%E` and `%G` as synonyms for the lower-case version but with an upper-case `E` in the output; and the use of upper-case `%X`, which is the same as `%x`, but with an upper-case `X` in the output. All of these were added in UNIX 3.0 and have propagated into System V and ANSI C. Very recent additions that are present in ANSI C, and that should eventually become portable, are the `h` and `L` modifiers for half-word and long double arguments; and the `%i`, `%n`, and `%p` conversions for decimal integer, number of characters output, and pointer, respectively. Obsolete features include the use of upper-case to indicate a `long` argument (replaced with the `l` prefix) and the `%r` conversion to take a format from the argument list (replaced with the `vprintf` series of functions). `%r` was documented in PWB and present in some early V7 descendents.

Features that are specific to one implementation, and hence nonportable, include the 4.2BSD `#` prefix *after* the width and precision (interpreted as a modifier for various formats), the GCOS `%b` for BCD, and the Microsoft `F` and `N` modifiers for far and near pointers, respectively.

putc, fputc   stdio output char   *****

These routines are part of all C libraries, so they are extremely portable.

Because it may be implemented as a macro, `putc` may incorrectly handle an argument with side effects. It is likely that the argument will be evaluated twice. `fputc` is normally implemented as a function.

putchar   output char to stdout   *****

This routine is part of all C libraries, so it is extremely portable. It can even be called from inside the UNIX operating system.

putenv   change environment   *

This routine is part of System V, but is not supported by many other implementations. It is present in Microsoft C. It should be considered unportable outside System V.

It is possible to write your own version of putenv, by using environ and manipulating the list directly. Beware of overflowing the list of pointers or a particular environment variable. It is in general necessary to use malloc when enlargement is needed.

The environ external variable, and indeed the entire concept of environments, is not portable outside the UNIX system or to UNIX versions that predate V7.

puts, fputs   stdio write string   *****

These routines are part of nearly all C libraries, so they are extremely portable. Note that puts will add a trailing newline, but fputs will not.

qsort   quicksort   ****

This routine is part of most C libraries, so it is very portable.

raise   generate signal   **●

This routine is part of ANSI C, but is new with that standard. No existing implementations supported it before ANSI C. It should be considered unportable unless you either assume ANSI C or use #ifdef __STDC__.

With a typical UNIX implementation, this function can be emulated, if not present, as follows:

```
#ifndef __STDC__
raise(sig)
int sig;
{
      kill(getpid(), sig);
}
#endif
```

rand, srand   pseudorandom number generator   ****

These routines are part of most C libraries, so they are very portable, if used with care.

The problem with rand is that the range of values it returns is not consistent across systems. In V7 and UNIX/TS 2.0, running on the 16-bit PDP-11, rand returned a positive int, which was a 16-bit quantity, ranging from 0 to $2^{15}-1$. The VAX version of V7, UNIX/32V, also returned an int, but this time the value contained 32 bits, ranging from 0 to $2^{31}-1$. This created some problems with portable software, which wanted to divide the number by an appropriate integer to use the high order bits. UNIX 3.0, however, was changed to always return a number in the range from 0 to $2^{15}-1$. Subsequent versions of System V also used this range.

Eventually, ANSI C will make it possible to get the range from the RAND_MAX macro defined in <stdlib.h>. In the meantime, it is safe to extract the low-order 15 bits:

```
r = rand() & 077777;
```

Since an ANSI implementation can be detected by the presence of __STDC__, a portable call might look like this.

```
#define RAND_USE 077777
long
randrange(rangewanted)
int rangewanted;  /* want result in range 0 ... rangewanted-1 */
{
      long r, ret;

      r = (rand() & RAND_USE) * rangewanted;
      ret = r / RAND_USE;
      return ret;
}
```

This example uses its own macro called RAND_USE instead of the ANSI built-in macro called RAND_MAX, because not all implementations support ANSI C. Also RAND_MAX can be as large as 31 or 32 bits, causing this example to overflow. The disadvantage is that this example extracts the low-order 15 bits of the random number, and the most random bits are often the most significant bits. A portable application should assume it can only get 15 random bits from rand.

The above example has some limitations. The parameter rangewanted should be at least 2, and no more than 32,767. Since the traditional rand implementation is a linear congruential pseudorandom-number generator, the discussion in Knuth[1] applies.

Existing applications can be slightly more portable by replacing the line that calls rand with this:

---

[1] *The Art of Computer Programming*, Volume 2, *Seminumerical Algorithms*, Addison-Wesley, Reading, MA, 1969, page 9.

```
#ifdef __STDC__
        r = rand();
#else
        r = rand() & 077777;
#endif
```

The randomness properties of the traditional implementation of rand are not really very random, according to some of the manual pages. System V has added a family of random-number generators based on 48-bit arithmetic, grouped under drand48(3C). Berkeley has added a generator, based on a variable-sized state vector, called random(3). Both of these sets of routines are more random, more complex, and portable only within System V and 4.2BSD, respectively.

The value passed to srand can safely be any int or unsigned int, although it should not be a long if you want portability to a 16-bit machine. One way to portably pass a 32-bit value (such as the result of a time call) on a 32-bit machine, is to cast it to an (int), for example,

```
long t;

time(&t);
srand( (int) t);
```

scanf, fscanf, sscanf   formatted input   *****

These routines are part of nearly all C libraries, so they are extremely portable. They are not quite as mainstream as printf, however, and are not so widely used. Like printf, some conversions are more portable than others.

The %c, %d, %o, %s, and %x options are totally portable, and work essentially everywhere. If your system supports floating point, then it's also safe to assume that %f, and %e work. (Many systems do not support %g, which was added much later than the others, much later than %g was added to printf.)

It is also nearly universally safe to assume that %% will match a single % sign, and that %[abc] and %[^abc] will match strings of characters containing and not containing, respectively, abc. It's also fairly safe to assume that the % may be followed by a *, that width may be specified as a decimal integer, and that an h or l may be included to indicate that the argument is a short or long.

Certain other features are less portable. Recent additions include the %g conversion as a synonym for %f; the use of upper-case %E, %G, and %X as synonyms for the lower-case version; %u for unsigned integers, all of which were added in UNIX 3.0, and have propagated into System V and ANSI C. Very recent additions that are present in ANSI C, and that should eventually become portable, are the L modifier for long double arguments; and the %i, %n, and %p conversions, for arbitrary integer, number of characters output, and pointer, respectively.

Obsolete features include the use of upper-case to indicate a `long` argument (replaced with the `l` prefix.)

Features that are specific to one implementation, and hence nonportable, include the the GCOS `%b` for BCD, the Digital Research `%h` for a half-word integer (equivalent to the more portable `%hd`.) and the Microsoft `F` and `N` modifiers for far and near pointers, respectively.

`setbuf, setvbuf`   buffer output   *****

`setbuf` is part of all C libraries, so it is extremely portable. `setvbuf` was new with System V release 2 and ANSI C, and it is portable only within ANSI C or System V release 3 (or later) environments.

Unfortunately, `setbuf` was intended for filters and other noninteractive output, under the assumption that unbuffered output is adequate for interactive terminals. It has since been discovered that enormous performance improvements are possible if the output is line buffered.

Berkeley's original enhancement is called `setlinebuf` and takes only the file-pointer argument, assuming a buffer has already been allocated; another call `setbuffer` is similar to `setbuf`, but allows the user to specify the size of the buffer.

System V (and ANSI C) use a more general `setvbuf` primitive. This allows flags and buffers of any size to be attached with a single call.

Unfortunately, even though the documentation for `setvbuf` has been consistent since System V release 2, the implementation reversed the order of the second and third arguments in System V release 2. The implementation was changed to match the documentation in System V release 3. Because of this, `setvbuf` cannot be used in applications that must work on System V release 2 without using the preprocessor.

Because the `setlinebuf`, `setbuffer`, and `setvbuf` calls are incompatible, it is usually best to depend on the default buffering provided by standard I/O; this is usually appropriate. Use of `setbuf` is portable, but only appropriate if you are printing large amounts of output (screenfulls) on a terminal, and then you should be careful to `fflush` the buffer at appropriate times, such as when expecting input. (The line-buffering mechanisms all automatically flush `stdout` before reading from `stdin`, if you use standard I/O routines.)

`setjmp, longjmp`   nonlocal goto   *****

These routines are part of nearly all C libraries, so they are extremely portable. The routines were first introduced in PWB, using an array of three integers as a buffer. The `#include <setjmp.h>` and `struct  jmp_buf` were added in V7 and have become a part of most implementations.

The routines `sigsetjmp` and `siglongjmp` were added by POSIX, with similar functionality, but also saving and restoring signal masks. These routines should be considered unportable until POSIX catches on.

In V6 and PWB, a similar pair of routines called `setexit` and `reset` were used for this purpose. These two routines took no parameters. In effect, there was a single global `struct jmp_buf` that had to be shared among all applications.

sin, cos, tan   trig   ****
asin, acos, atan, atan2

These routines are part of most C libraries, so they are very portable. They are considered basic to any math library. The `atan2` function is newer than the others, and may not be present in a few systems that support the others.

Several techniques for calculating the trigonometric functions are used by math library implementations. Both floating-point modulus and division have been used to perform trigonometric range reduction (mapping large arguments into smaller ones, for example, mapping into the range $[0,2\pi]$). The accuracy of the value of π used in the range reduction can vary from about 30 to several thousand bits. Using arguments outside the range $[0,2\pi]$ may be unportable. Using arguments that are already in the range $[0,2\pi]$ is more portable.

There is no portable method of dealing with illegal values, such as `asin(10.0)` and `atan2(0.0,0.0)`.

sinh, cosh, tanh   hyperbolic trig   ****

These functions are part of most C math libraries, so they are very portable.

The status value returned by range errors may vary from system to system.

sleep   pause program   ***

This routine is part of all UNIX C libraries, so it is portable within the UNIX system. Although required by ANSI C, `sleep` is generally not present in non-UNIX C libraries.

sprintf   formatted output to string   *****

This routine is part of standard I/O, so it is extremely portable.

See `printf` for comments about specific formatting options. It is not portable to make use of the value returned by `sprintf` since this value is often not documented.

sqrt   square root   ****

This routine is part of most C libraries, so it is very portable. It may not be present in machines that do not support math routines.

The call `sqrt(-1.0)` is undefined and unportable. Unfortunately, so is `sqrt(-1.0E-200)`.

strbrk, strtrm   string search   *

These routines are present in GCOS and MVS, but are not supported by other implementations. They should be considered unportable.

The `strbrk` function is similar to the standard `strpbrk`, except that `strbrk` returns an integer offset instead of a pointer.

strcat, strncat   string concatenate   *****

These routines are part of all C libraries, so they are extremely portable.

These routines were new in V7, but have become de facto standards. Historically, `strncat` was originally named `strcatn`, but the name was changed to keep the names unique in the first six characters for systems, such as GCOS, that truncate external names to six characters. The change was made between the time UNIX/32V branched off from V7 and the time when V7 was released. As a result, UNIX/32V documented `strcatn`, but also provided `strncat` for compatibility. 3BSD used the same documentation, and much user code was written to call `strcatn`. By 4BSD, the Berkeley documentation was updated and the use of `strcatn` was gradually phased out.

strchr, strrchr   string search   ***

These routines are part of many C libraries, but they are only marginally portable. In many C libraries, they are called `index` and `rindex`.

`index` and `rindex` were new in V7, along with the other string routines. V7-derived UNIX systems, including 4.2BSD, use `index` and `rindex`, and do not support `strchr` and `strrchr`. Shortly after V7 was released, AT&T changed the names to `strchr` and `strrchr` for consistency with the other *str* functions, and did not include upward-compatibility code to support `index` and `rindex`. As a result, there is no completely portable way to use the built-in versions of these functions.

The C standards all require `strchr` and `strrchr`. 4.3BSD includes versions of `strchr` and `strrchr` that call `index` and `rindex`.

The only completely portable way to gain this functionality is to provide your own version of `strchr` and `strrchr` in your source code. The disadvantage of this is that if your machine has special instructions to search for characters and the library version uses these instructions, you'll lose speed.

In practice, most programmers decide to stick with one set and use macros to use the other on appropriate systems. For example, in a header file, you might include

```
#ifdef BSD
# define strchr index
# define strrchr rindex
#endif
```

Another option, in a system-specific makefile, is to add the flags -Dstrchr=index -Dstrrchr=rindex to CFLAGS to get the same effect.

strcmp, strncmp   string compare   *****

These routines are part of all C libraries, so they are extremely portable.

These routines were new in V7, but have become de facto standards. The comments about strncat also apply to strncmp, which was once called strcmpn.

strcpy, strncpy   string copy   *****

These routines are part of all C libraries, so they are extremely portable.

These routines were new in V7, but have become de facto standards. The comments about strncat also apply to strncpy, which was once called strcpyn.

strdup   duplicate string   *

This routine is part of System V and is new in System V release 3. It is not part of any standard except for the SVID release 3. It should be considered unportable outside System V. It is easily written from scratch using strlen, malloc, and strcpy.

strerror, strstr, fstrtoul   string functions   ***

These routines are part of ANSI C, but are new with that standard. No existing implementations supported them before ANSI C. They should be considered unportable unless you either assume ANSI C or use #ifdef __STDC__.

strlen   string length   *****

This routine is part of all C libraries, so it is extremely portable.

Beware that the length returned by strlen does not include the trailing null character. If you use this value as an argument to malloc, be sure to add 1 to allocate space for the null.

strlwr, strupr   case translation   *

These routines are present in GCOS and Microsoft C, but are not supported by other implementations. They should be considered unportable.

It is important to note that these routines cannot simply be implemented as follows:

```
/* unportable */
#include <ctype.h>
char *
strlwr(str)
char *str;
{
        register char *p;

        for (p=str; *p; p++)
            if (isupper(*p))
                    *p = tolower(*p);
        return str;
}
```

The above function works properly in the United States, but is inadequate for some countries with different alphabets. For example, in German, the β (ess-tset) lower-case character is equivalent to the two upper-case letter sequence SS. Some languages have no concept of upper- and lower-case, and some Far East languages use 16-bit characters.

If you need translation between upper- and lower-case, one very flexible method is to implement functions similar to strlwr and strupr in your own program, and to allow different implementations of these functions to be configured in for different conventions. A somewhat better interface would pass both a source and destination buffer, or the buffer and buffer size, since the length of the result could be larger than the original string.

strpbrk, strspn, strcspn, strtok   string operations   *

These routines are part of most System III derived C libraries, including System V, and are required by ANSI C, so they are portable within System III and ANSI C derived systems.

No similar functions exist in V7 or 4.2BSD. 4.3BSD supports all four functions for System V compatibility. All the C standards require these functions, but prior to these standards, the only major non-UNIX libraries to support them were Microsoft C and Lattice C. Lattice C did not support strtok, but did have a similar function called stptok with different calling conventions.

strtod, strtol   string to number   ***

These routines are part of System V and ANSI C. Few existing implementations, other than System V, supported them before ANSI C. (MVS and GCOS include them, and Lattice C supports `strtol`.)

`strtol` first appeared in System V release 1, and `strtod` first appeared in System V release 2. They should be considered unportable unless you assume ANSI C or System V.

swab   swap bytes   *

This routine is part of most UNIX C libraries, but its use is not recommended.

The `swab` function dates from V6, which only ran on the 16-bit PDP-11. When the UNIX system was ported to 32-bit machines, byte swapping became an unportable concept: sometimes it was necessary to swap 2 bytes, sometimes 4.

If you need to copy data from one machine to another, see Chapter 6.

system   run shell command   ****

This routine is part of most C libraries, so it is very portable if used carefully. Although originally intended to support UNIX shell commands from inside C, it turned out to be very useful for general "shell escape" commands, such as the ! command found in interactive programs such as `ed` and `write`.

For security reasons, the use of `execlp`, `execvp`, `popen`, `pclose`, *and* `system` *is strongly discouraged. Since these operations go through the shell, programs using them have been exploited by intruders to break into computing systems. It is better to use* `fork` *and* `execl` *directly, without going through the shell or path mechanism.*

The `system` subroutine is present in all UNIX implementations. It is also provided by GCOS, MVS, Microsoft C, Lattice C, and Mark Williams C. (The MVS version takes two extra optional arguments, which can be ignored without sacrificing much portability.)

The SVID requires `system`, as does ANSI C. /usr/group and POSIX have gone back and forth between including `system` and not requiring it.

Even though the function itself is generally present, the meaning of the command can vary widely from system to system. If you restrict your program to run on the UNIX system, you can safely use commands that are universally present, such as `date` or `cat`. If your program is intended to run on other operating systems, you should only use commands typed by the user, who then assumes responsibility for the command working.

The `system` routine is best used to implement ! commands, or as low-level implementations of semiportable functions such as `mkdir`.

tempnam   make temp file name   *

This routine is part of System V, but is not supported by many other implementations. It should be considered unportable outside System V.

termcap   terminal library   ***

This library consists of the functions `tgetent`, `tgetstr`, `tgetnum`, `tgetflag`, `tgoto`, and `tputs`. It is present in all Berkeley releases and can be linked in by including the flag `-ltermcap` or the obsolescent `-ltermlib` on the command line. The same functions are available, with a compatible interface, in the System V curses library, using the flag `-lcurses`. Unless you need the additional functionality of the terminfo library, using the termcap library calls is more portable. Using the higher-level curses library is even more portable.

terminfo   terminal library   **

This library consists of the functions `setupterm`, `tparm`, `tputs`, `putp`, `vidputs`, and `vidattr`. It is present in System V release 2 and later, and is required by the SVID. These functions can be linked in by including the flag `-lcurses` on the command line.

timezone   get time zone   *

This routine is part of V7-derived systems, such as 4.2BSD, but is not supported by many other implementations. It should be considered very unportable outside 4.2BSD.

System V uses an external variable called `timezone` as part of the `ctime` functions. This name conflicts with the V7 `timezone` function. There is no way, without some cleverness, for an implementation to be compatible with both uses. As a result, it is recommended that applications avoid use of *either* of the two meanings of `timezone`. If a meaning must be used, it should be protected by `#ifdef`.

tmpfile   open temp file   ***

This routine is part of many C libraries, so it is somewhat portable. It is not present in many V7-derived systems, including 4.2BSD and 4.3BSD, nor in most current non-UNIX implementations. It is required by all the C standards, including ANSI C.

The `tmpfile` function depends on the ability to create a file that will be automatically removed from disk when the file is closed or the program terminates. Not all operating systems have this ability. On the UNIX system, it is implemented by creating the file and then unlinking it while keeping it open. Since there are no references to it in the file system, once the file descriptor is closed, the last reference will be gone and the file will be deleted.

Other operating systems may be unable to assure that the file will be automatically deleted. Although it is possible to alter the `fclose` and `exit` functions to check for and delete the file, complications such as abnormal program termination and the equivalent of `fork` or `exec` can make this difficult or impossible, depending on the file system. Some UNIX network file systems may have trouble implementing this if the temporary file is on another machine and a remote unlink request deletes the file.

For these reasons, and since only a few current implementations support this function, it is recommended that this function be avoided, unless you are convinced it will be supported on all target systems. If you explicitly delete your file when you are finished with it, you will have fewer portability problems.

tmpnam   make temp file name   *

This routine is part of many C libraries, but it is not very portable.

The function was not part of the original standard I/O, but was added shortly thereafter. The original implementation created a unique file name in the current directory, so it failed if the current directory was unwritable. It also did not check to see if the filename already existed.

This older implementation appears undocumented in V7-derived systems such as 4.2BSD. It was not used very much, in favor of `mktemp`, which generated better names. In System V, the implementation was improved to place the file in `/tmp` and use `mktemp` to create a good name.

`tmpnam` is required by all the C standards, but was not present in many mid-1980s implementations. It was not present in 4.2BSD, but was in 4.3BSD. It is safe to use only in System V or ANSI C conforming implementations. If you are willing to assume one of these environments, the use of `tmpnam` is very portable, since you need not be concerned with system-specific filename syntax as you must with `mktemp`. A good compromise is to use `tmpnam` but to provide your own implementation of `tmpnam` for systems that either do not support it or don't generate good names.

toascii   trim high bit   *

This routine is part of System V and some other C libraries, but is not very portable. Its semantics are unclear on EBCDIC systems and on systems with larger than 7-bit characters. In general, since 8-bit ASCII is becoming more important for international programs, this routine (and any equivalent & 0177 operation) should be avoided. If masking is required, use a symbolic constant that is part of the configuration of the program. 0177 and 0377 are common values, and 0777 and 0177777 are other possibilities.

On MVS, this routine does EBCDIC-to-ASCII translation, which is quite different from the other systems. Although you can view the 7 bit trimming done on ASCII implementations as a translation from the local character set into ASCII, this is not the intent of the function.

`tolower`   upper-case to lower-case   ✱✱✱

This routine is part of many C libraries, but is not very portable. All implementations will change upper-case letters into lower-case letters. If you pass it anything other than an upper-case letter, the behavior is undefined. Some implementations return the unaltered character, and others alter it by the difference between upper- and lower-case (32 in ASCII.) Some implementations have a function `_tolower`, which does the constant shift, and another `tolower`, which checks for an upper-case letter. (The constant shift is used on V7 and 4BSD, and K&R has a constant shift implementation in mind.)

In general, you may be better off to write your own versions of these macros. A simple, portable, implementation would look like this:

```
#define _lower(c) ((c) - 'A' + 'a')
#define lower(c) (isupper(c) ? _lower(c) : (c))
```

If you are willing to assume ANSI C, the standard requires an implementation that checks the argument to ensure it's upper-case.

Beware that in some languages, these functions may not make sense. Some languages do not have the concept of upper- and lower-case. Other languages have letters that do not have single character equivalents in the other case. For example, the German lower-case letter β (ess-tset) is mapped into the two letters SS when converting to upper-case. Translation between cases is best done by copying from one buffer to another buffer of possibly different length, translating while copying. No standard routines are provided for this purpose, and the actions of such routines depend on the locality. It is best to isolate this functionality in one part of the program, so it can be easily changed as needed.

`toupper`   lower-case to upper-case   ✱✱✱

This routine is part of many C libraries, but is not very portable. All implementations will turn lower-case letters into upper-case letters. If you pass it anything other than a lower-case letter, the behavior is undefined. Some implementations return the unaltered character, and others alter it by the difference between upper- and lower-case (32 in ASCII.) Some implementations have a function `_toupper`, which does the constant shift, and another `toupper`, which checks for an upper-case letter. (The constant shift is used on V7 an 4BSD, and K&R has a constant shift implementation in mind.)

In general, you may be better off to write your own versions of these macros. A simple, portable, implementation would look like this:

```
#define _upper(c) ((c) - 'a' + 'A')
#define upper(c) (islower(c) ? _upper(c) : (c))
```

If you are willing to assume ANSI C, the standard requires an implementation that checks the argument to ensure it's lower-case.

See the comments in `tolower` about portability to other languages.

`ttyname`   get name of terminal port   **

This routine is part of all UNIX C libraries, so it is extremely portable within the UNIX system. Some implementations for the MS DOS system support a somewhat non-standard interface that returns the string `CON:`. In general, however, this function is intended for the UNIX system, and doesn't make sense on other systems, because it's often used in an environment with UNIX specific assumptions. For example, the string generally begins `/dev/` and this value is typically stripped off so the result can be used to consult a system-specific table.

Beware that `ttyname(0)` may not always work, because standard input may be redirected. It is best to try 0, 1, and then 2, and take the first one that works. It is less common for 2 to be redirected, but it does happen. If all three descriptors are redirected, you might consider using `/dev/tty`, but this is only useful for `ioctl` calls, not for table indexing.

`tzset`   set time zone   *

This routine is specific to System V, so it is not portable. It is also provided by Microsoft C, which uses the same time-zone conventions as System V.

There is no equivalent function in other systems, but `tzset` is normally called automatically by `asctime`, so there is generally no need to call it explicitly.

`ungetc`   push stdio char back   *****

This routine is part of all C libraries, so it is extremely portable.

There are different implementations, however, so nonstandard use of the function can lead to implementation-defined results. For example, attempting to push back more than one character may not always work, although sometimes it will. Attempting to push back a character before reading anything is not allowed by some older implementations, although it is required by ANSI C. The position returned by `ftell` may or may not be one less after an `ungetc`. Pushing back a character other than the one read is generally safe, and can be depended upon not to affect the external file. Writing into the stream after an `ungetc` may also produce varying results.

Calling `ungetc` is intended for lexical analyzers that want to look ahead in the input stream by one character. It is generally assumed that the stream is read-only and that it will be sequentially read all the way through. Uses considerably different from this may be less portable.

Pushing back `EOF` will sometimes work, and sometimes not. This is a very common problem with routines written in `lex` and `yacc`.

va_start, va_arg, va_end   variable arguments   ***

These routines are part of most UNIX C libraries, and they were once very portable within the UNIX system. The include file <varargs.h> was present (and undocumented) in V7, and was subsequently documented in 4.0BSD and System V release 2. ANSI C is changing all that.

The original varargs feature was implemented entirely in the include file, with knowledge of the stack structure of the machine present in the macros. This can be easily implemented on systems that pass all arguments on the stack, but causes problems if some arguments are passed in registers. It also causes problems for lint, which needs an extra /*VARARGS*/ to turn off a warning about inconsistent argument use.

ANSI C is much better about checking arguments to ensure they match those expected by a function. This extra checking can generate compiler errors, so an extension to the syntax was made: a new token, . . ., was added, to take the place of the dummy "last argument" traditionally passed. This breaks va_start, which needs to be able to reference the va_alist dummy argument. ANSI C changed the calling conventions by adding a second argument to va_start, the argument *before* the . . . in the list.

Here is a reasonably portable programming style, using varargs, allowing for the new and old methods. This example implements the UNIX execl function in terms of execv.

```
#ifdef __STDC__
# include <stdarg.h>
#else
# include <varargs.h>
#endif

#define MAXARGS 100

#ifdef __STDC__
execl(file, ...)
char *file;
#else
execl(va_alist)
va_dcl
#endif
{
    va_list ap;
    char *args[MAXARGS];
    int argno = 0;
#ifndef __STDC__
    char *file;
#endif
```

```
      va_start(ap);
#ifndef __STDC__
      file = va_arg(ap, char *);
#endif
      while (++argno < MAXARGS && args[argno] =
            va_arg(ap, char *))
                  ;
      /* in case of overflow */
      args[MAXARGS-1] = (char *) 0;

      va_end(ap);
      return execv(file, args);
}
```

Another implementation moves all the ifdefs to the front of the file, and might be appropriate if you have several functions that use varargs. An implementation of a C library that is upward-compatible with the older varargs might also be created along these lines.

```
#ifdef __STDC__
# include <stdarg.h>
# define va_dcl /* nothing */
# define va_list ...
#else
# include <varargs.h>
#endif
#define MAXARGS 100

execl(va_alist)
va_dcl
{
      va_list ap;
      char *args[MAXARGS];
      int argno = 0;
      char *file;

      va_start(ap);
      file = va_arg(ap, char *);
      while (++argno < MAXARGS && args[argno] =
            va_arg(ap, char *))
                  ;
      /* in case of overflow */
      args[MAXARGS-1] = (char *) 0;

      va_end(ap);
      return execv(file, args);
}
```

vprintf, vfprintf, vsprintf   varargs printf   ***

These routines are part of System V derived C libraries, so they are somewhat portable.

The vprintf functions were added to the C library in System V release 2. Although they are a mainstream part of System V, being present both in the implementations and in the SVID, other implementations were slow to support them. For many years, Microsoft C for the MS DOS system was the only implementation outside System V with support for vprintf. ANSI C requires these functions.

The primary use for these functions is to be able to write your own printf style function. This can be very useful for debugging, logging, or the implementation of a library with a printf function available to the user. The vprintf functions provide a way to portably write such routines.

Before vprintf, it was necessary for such functions to make assumptions about the implementation of printf in the standard I/O library. A typical function looked like this:

```
/*
 * This is really a modified version of "sprintf".  As such,
 * it assumes that sprintf interfaces with the other printf
 * functions in a certain way.  If this is not how your
 * system works, you will have to modify this routine to use
 * the interface that your "sprintf" uses.
 *
 * This version works only on 4.2BSD on a VAX computer.
 */
logent(fmt, args)
char    *fmt;
int     args;
{
        FILE    junk;
        FILE    *lf;
        char    buf[BUFSIZ];

        /* This is essentially what sprintf does. */
        junk._flag = _IOWRT + _IOSTRG;
        junk._ptr = buf;
        junk._cnt = 32767;
        _doprnt(fmt, &args, &junk);
        putc(' ', &junk);

        /* The result of the printf is now in buf. */
        lf = fopen(LOGFILE, "a");
        fputs(buf, lf);
        fclose(lf);
}
```

Another alternative, even less portable, but very simple to implement, is to declare several dummy arguments, and pass them directly to the `printf` routine. Although this seems very unportable on the surface, in practice, it works quite well on most implementations, and is perfectly adequate for a debugging tool that is not part of a product. The same `logent` function would look like this:

```
logent(fmt, a1, a2, a3, a4, a5, a6, a7, a8)
char   *fmt;
int    a1, a2, a3, a4, a5, a6, a7, a8;
{

    FILE   *lf;

    lf = fopen(LOGFILE, "a");
    fprintf(lf, fmt, a1, a2, a3, a4, a5, a6, a7, a8);
    fclose(lf);
}
```

Exercises

Exercise 11-1. How portable is the `filebinsearch` routine shown in the dbm section? Why? How much does it matter?

Exercise 11-2. Determine exactly how small a database must be for `filebinsearch` to fail to work correctly.

Exercise 11-3. Modify `filebinsearch` to work properly for a database of any size.

Exercise 11-4. The `while` loop in the `buildfname` routine in the `getpwent` section considers the string terminated if it finds one of several terminating characters. Is it possible, using a `string` function, to shorten the condition? How portable would the result be? How efficient would the result be?

Exercise 11-5. Implement `logent` (shown in the `varargs` section) portably. What is the portability trade-off between using `varargs` and `stdarg`?

CHAPTER 12: **OPERATING SYSTEM CALLS**

This chapter discusses each of the widely implemented UNIX and MS DOS system calls. These correspond to Chapter 2 of the *UNIX Programmer's Manual*, which is often distributed in a document called the *UNIX Programmer's Manual, Reference Guide* or the *UNIX System V, Programmer Reference Manual*. The rating system used here is the same as that used in Chapter 11. The difference is that it is the norm for these functions to exist only on UNIX systems. Some of them may be widely available in other C implementations, but this is because they are emulating part of the UNIX system. Use of any function in this chapter is less portable than the standard I/O functions and other extremely portable functions from the C library.

access   check for file access   ✳✳

This routine is part of all UNIX libraries since V7, so it is very portable among UNIX systems. Some other operating systems provide a version of `access` molded to the permissions supported by that operating system. For example, on a single-user system such as MS DOS, some compilers implement `access`, but have only a single set of permission bits to check; these are generally treated as *owner* permissions. Systems that allow users to be in multiple groups at the same time, such as 4BSD, check for access by any of the current groups.

`access` was not present in V6, but it was in PWB, V7, and their descendents.

Use of standard include files, such as POSIX's `<unistd.h>` to define symbolic constants for `access`, is not portable. Most versions of the UNIX system do not provide symbolic constants, but instead use the hard-coded numeric values 0, 1, 2, and 4.

While the presence of the `access` call is quite portable, its semantics are not always what the programmer wants. This call is intended for suid programs that want to determine if the user that called them has permission. It uses the real user id and group, not the effective user id and group. Since the real operating system calls use the effective user id and group, `access` does not always make an accurate prediction of whether an attempt to open or create a file will succeed or fail. A program not intended to be run in this hybrid mode may still be called from a parent running that way. Since in most UNIX implementations, a call to `access` is nearly as expensive as a call to `open`, this call should not be used just to check for permission. It should only be used in a suid program, where there is no other way to determine if the real user id has permission to open or create a file. Another case where `access` can be useful is when you risk running out of file descriptors. The `open` call requires another file descriptor, but `access` does not.

acct   turn accounting on/off   **

This routine is part of most UNIX libraries, but it is not part of any UNIX standard, so it should be viewed as not portable.

There is seldom a reason for a user application to call `acct`. Only the super user is allowed to use this call. This system call is intended for use by system administration software, not applications.

alarm   set alarm clock   **

This routine is part of most UNIX libraries, so it is very portable among UNIX systems.

The `alarm` call was not present in V6, but was in PWB, V7, and their descendents.

The granularity of the `alarm` system call is one second. This is fine for long timeouts, but for applications that need fast response, such as real-time video games, this call is not appropriate. Different systems round to the nearest second differently, causing variations in response.

Since `alarm` is tied to `signal`, and since `signal` is not totally portable, caution is indicated when an alarm goes off. The most portable way to react to the alarm is to use `longjmp` to abort the operation in progress, taking a timeout branch from the `setjmp` call. (Calling `longjmp`, or any other function, in a signal handler is considered undefined by ANSI C. It is generally safe, however, as long as you're sure the function called by the handler cannot be in the process of being called when the signal comes in.)

bdos   DOS BIOS call   *

This routine is part of some MS DOS libraries, but it is not part of any standard, so it should be viewed as not portable, even among MS DOS systems, unless you assume a particular DOS compiler.

The function is provided by Microsoft C, Turbo C, and Lattice C under the MS DOS system, to make a DOS system call. The arguments are essentially compatible. (Lattice treats the registers as signed, Microsoft as unsigned, and Turbo C as a pointer and an unsigned integer, but in each case, they are really a 16-bit value that depends on the particular system call.) The Lattice call `bdosx` is not provided by Microsoft C; if it is needed, see the lower-level call `intdosx`.

brk, sbrk   low-level memory allocation   *

These routines are part of most UNIX libraries, so they are fairly portable among UNIX systems. Use of these routines is not recommended.

The `brk` and `sbrk` system calls are not part of the SVID. Some emulated UNIX systems, built on top of another system, may not be able to implement `brk` and `sbrk`.

Another reason not to use `brk` is that it may interfere with `malloc`. The `malloc` routines use `sbrk` and assume they have exclusive use of the heap. Standard I/O routines call `malloc` for their buffers.

`brk` and `sbrk` should be viewed as low-level routines to be used only in the implementation of `malloc`, and not for use by applications.

This system call was deleted from POSIX in favor of `malloc`.

`chdir`   change directory   ***

This routine is part of all UNIX libraries, so it is very portable among UNIX systems. It is also provided by a few non-UNIX C implementations.

Although `chdir` is present in all versions of the UNIX system, use of `chdir` on single-tasking operating systems, such as MS DOS, should be made with caution. The `chdir` call changes the current directory of the current process, and of all processes that derive from the current process via an `exec` or `fork` call. On single-tasking systems, the parent shell is included among those affected.

Normally, use of `chdir` will restrict a program to the UNIX system. `chdir` implies the presence of a hierarchical file system, and often implies assumptions about the contents of that file system.

`chmod`   change file permissions   **

This routine is part of all UNIX libraries, so it is very portable among UNIX systems.

This routine is virtually unchanged in all versions of the UNIX system. some MS DOS C implementations provide a subset, but only the owner bits are meaningful.

Use of include files such as `<sys/stat.h>` to define the bits is not portable. In the past, most programs hard coded the octal numbers, and this practice won't break with most anticipated new UNIX systems. A more robust approach is to use the POSIX definitions such as S_IRUSR, and to define them if they are missing.

```
#ifndef S_IRUSR
# define S_IRUSR 0400
# define S_IWUSR 0200
# define S_IXUSR 0100
# define S_IRGRP 0040
# define S_IWGRP 0020
# define S_IXGRP 0010
# define S_IROTH 0004
# define S_IWOTH 0002
# define S_IXOTH 0001
#endif
...
    chmod(file, S_IRUSR|S_IWUSR|S_IXUSR);
```

The semantics of the "sticky bit" can vary from system to system. It is unwise to count on this bit in a program – it is generally set by hand.

On some systems, writing a file or changing the owner clears the suid and sgid bits in the interest of improved security. Setting these bits from the chmod system call should be considered unportable except for the super user.

chown   change file owner   **

This routine is part every UNIX version since V7, so it is fairly portable among UNIX systems, for the super user *only*. There is one major incompatibility between the two main UNIX branches. In many V7-derived UNIX systems, chown is restricted to the super user. In PWB-derived UNIX systems, chown may be used by ordinary users as long as the old owner of the file is the same as the effective user id of the calling process. POSIX allows both chown behaviors.

This incompatibility often does not cause a problem, because many programs do not make this call unless being run by the super user. However, in file unpacking programs such as cpio and tar, care should be taken. If the program is written under the assumption that the chown call will fail if the caller isn't the super user, it may behave differently than intended on System V. Once a file or directory is given away, it can't be reclaimed without help from the other user or the super user. When combined with a conservative umask setting, it may not even be possible to read or remove files in directories that have been created and given away.

The pre-V7 versions of the UNIX system, V6 and PWB, had an incompatible chown call, with the *group* parameter missing. PWB did not support groups, and V6 passed both user and group in separate bytes of the second argument.

The chown call is not portable to other systems. The concepts of the integer user id and group are specific to the UNIX system. The DRI MS DOS C library provides the routine, but it's a dummy, since the MS DOS system doesn't have these concepts.

close   close file descriptor   ***

This routine is part of all UNIX libraries, so it is extremely portable among UNIX systems. In addition, many non-UNIX C implementations support close.

creat   create new file   **

This routine is part of all UNIX libraries, so it is very portable among UNIX systems. Popular use is gradually moving away from creat and toward open with a third parameter. However, the three-parameter open is not universally supported yet, so creat is still the portable way to create a file with a given mode. (Note, however, that fopen is even more portable.)

The value of a umask may affect the actual permission bits of the new file. Since system default umasks can vary widely (000, 022, 007, 027, and 077 are common values), the resulting mode can be quite different from the value specified.

Also note that if the file already exists, the resulting mode will be the original mode of the file, not the value specified here.

Traditional values given for the mode are 0666 and 0777; any other value may lead to unexpected results.

The owner of a newly created file will be the same as the uid of the process but the group might be either the gid of the process, (the V7 and System V behavior) or the group of the parent directory (the 4.2BSD behavior). Some systems allow either source of group. For example, the merged System V release 4 uses the parent directory's group if the SGID bit is set on the directory; otherwise, it uses the gid of the process. POSIX allows either interpretation and provides the new feature _POSIX_GROUP_PARENT to allow a C application to determine what the current implementation will do. The FIPS standard requires the the Berkeley behavior, so future implementations may migrate toward using the parent's group. In general, in the rare case where the group of a new file is important, an application should use chown to ensure that the file has the correct owner and group.

dup   duplicate file descriptor   **

This routine is part of all UNIX libraries, so it is very portable among UNIX systems.

dup2   duplicate file descriptor   **

This routine is part of some UNIX libraries, so it is somewhat portable among UNIX systems.

V6 and PWB did not have dup2. Neither do System III, or System V releases 1 or 2. It is present in V7 and V7-derived systems, System V release 3, and the portable operating system standards.

System III and V have similar (but slightly different) functionality in an option to fcntl.

Older UNIX versions achieve the same goal by first closing the desired target file descriptor, then using dup. This does not work in the general case, but the primary use of dup and dup2 is to redirect file descriptors 0, 1, and 2, and the ordinary dup call is sufficient for this:

```
/*
 * The following is equivalent to:
 * dup2(fd, 0);
 * dup2(fd, 1);
 * dup2(fd, 2);
 */

(void) close(0);
(void) close(1);
(void) close(2);

(void) dup(fd);    /* 0 */
(void) dup(fd);    /* 1 */
(void) dup(fd);    /* 2 */
```

For a simple case involving standard in, out, and error, where you are sure that all lower file descriptors are open, it is safest to just use dup. For a more complex case, you can use dup2, and if you port your program to a System III or V implementation without dup2, you can include the following:

```
#ifdef NODUP2
#include <fcntl.h>
int
dup2(fildes, fildes2)
int fildes, fildes2;
{
        (void) close(fildes2);  /* F_DUPFD won't close it */
        return fcntl(fildes, F_DUPFD, fildes2);
}
#endif
```

execl, execv   overlay new program   **

These routines are part of all UNIX libraries, so they are very portable among UNIX systems.

Beware of the last argument; to be truly portable, you must cast it to (char *) 0 to ensure that it is the same size as the character pointers. (Otherwise your program may not run on 68000 or 8086 machines, where pointers can be 32 bits but integers are only 16 bits.)

Although the execl call is available on all UNIX versions, a program using it may be making assumptions that the program being loaded exists and can be found in a particular place on the filesystem. Such assumptions may not be valid. In particular, watch out for programs that live in /bin on some systems and in /usr/bin on others. A program in a local directory has a worse dilemma, since popular local directories include, but are by no means limited to, /usr/lbin, /usr/local, /usr/local/bin, /local/bin, and $HOME/bin.

For security reasons, it is recommended that these problems be solved with `execl` and `execv`, rather than using `system` or `popen`. One possible method is to enumerate some likely alternatives that cannot be altered by changing the environment, trying them in sequence until one succeeds.

```
execl("/bin/mail", "mail", dest, 0);
execl("/usr/bin/mail", "mail", dest, 0);
execl("/usr/lbin/mail", "mail", dest, 0);
execl("/usr/local/bin/mail", "mail", dest, 0);
```

Some systems, such as 4BSD, support shell scripts in the `exec` calls. Other systems, such as System V, support them from the shell. Use of `exec` with a program that might be a shell script is less portable, but usually more efficient, than use of `system`. The notion of a *suid shell script* is easier to support from the operating system than from the shell. There are also security problems associated with suid shell scripts. It is recommended that suid shell scripts be avoided, as they are unportable and present potential security problems.

`execle`, `execve`   overlay new program, new environment   **

These routines are part of most UNIX libraries, so they are very portable among UNIX systems. The concept of an *environment* was first introduced in V7 (and UNIX/TS 2.0), so V6 and PWB did not have these calls. Their purpose is to pass an environment, other than that of the parent, to the child.

Comments about `execl` and `execv` above apply to these routines as well.

An alternative method sometimes used to alter the environment is to write over the string returned by `getenv` or to alter what the external variable `environ` points to. These methods will generally work on UNIX systems, but may not work on other operating systems. If you are deleting a value, writing zeros on top of it is not sufficient; the elements after it in the list should be copied up in the array. If you are adding a new element, or making an existing element longer, you must allocate new space (preferably with `malloc`) and alter an appropriate pointer to reference the new space. Since changing a value has the potential to make the value longer (especially if the user already has a very short value, such as `TERM=s4`) or to make the list longer if the name isn't present, well-written code must generally allow for this case. A general `putenv` routine is non-trivial to write. One is provided in System V, starting with release 2, but few other implementations support it.

`execlp`, `execvp`   overlay new program   **

These routines are part of most UNIX libraries, so they are fairly portable among UNIX systems.

Comments about `execl` and `execv` apply to these routines as well.

For security reasons, the use of execlp, execvp, popen, pclose, *and* system *is strongly discouraged. Since these operations go through the shell, programs using them have been exploited by intruders to break into computing systems. It is better to use* fork *and* execl *directly, without going through the shell or path mechanism.*

When depending entirely on the search path, care is indicated. A program running suid, or as root, should use explicit path names to prevent a user from providing his own version of the program ahead of the standard one in his PATH. It is also possible for a nonstandard PATH to be missing some important directory, causing this call to fail.

If your objective is merely to get the standard version of a program, whether it is in /bin, /usr/bin, or /usr/ucb, it is usually better to explicitly exec each possible location, rather than depend on the path.

```
execl("/usr/ucb/mail", "mail", "root", (char *) 0);
execl("/bin/mail", "mail", "root", (char *) 0);
execl("/usr/bin/mail", "mail", "root", (char *) 0);
```

fcntl   file control   **

This routine is part of System III, 4.2BSD, their descendents, and the POSIX standard, so it is fairly portable among UNIX systems. It is a relatively recent addition, and so older systems such as 4.1BSD do not have it.

The 4.2BSD version of fcntl is slightly different from the System III/POSIX version. The flags passed to F_GETFL and F_SETFL are different sets, and are not spelled the same. 4.2BSD supports FNDELAY, FAPPEND, and FASYNC. System V supports O_RDONLY, O_WRONLY, O_RDWR, O_NDELAY, and O_APPEND. (System V release 3 added O_SYNC.) The semantics of FNDELAY and O_NDELAY are similar, as are FAPPEND and O_APPEND.

Beware of the value returned by read in O_NDELAY mode when no data is waiting. On some systems it is 0, and on others it is −1.

fork   copy process   **

This routine is part of all UNIX libraries, so it is very portable among UNIX systems.

The semantics of fork are all the same on all UNIX versions. (The Berkeley vfork call, however, has different semantics; the two processes share memory, so one process can change a variable and cause the variable to be changed in the other process.)

The efficiency of fork may vary considerably, however. On many versions of the UNIX system, including many swapping systems (V7, System III, and System V releases 1 and 2), a call to fork results in a complete copy of the process being made in memory and on the swapping device. (If the executable program text is shared, that part is usually not copied.) This copy is often immediately thrown away by a subsequent exec.

Some versions may be much faster, implementing a feature known as *copy on write*, which preserves the illusion of two separate address spaces and copies only when absolutely necessary. Other versions achieve similar performance by requiring the programmer to call vfork. If efficiency is a concern, you can use #ifdef to decide which function to use:

```
#ifdef VFORK
        pid = vfork();
#else
        pid = fork();
#endif
        if (pid == 0) {
                ... rearrange file descriptors ...
                ... exec child program ...
        }
```

The define for VFORK becomes one of the configuration parameters of the program. This sort of code is safe only if the child immediately calls exec. If the child process changes any variables or blocks, the parent may be affected.

For many situations involving fork and exec, the same result can be more easily and more portably had by using system. Beware, however, that system causes an extra shell process to be called to interpret the arguments, so there may be some additional run time overhead. Also beware that system in essence uses execvp, so its special considerations apply as well.

fprompt   set keyboard prompt   *

This routine is part of the TSO and GCOS libraries, but is very specific to those two systems. It is used to set an operating system level prompt for all terminal input. This function is unportable.

Since these two systems are half duplex, the operating systems took special measures with prompts to handle the case where the user and the system typed at the same time. There were also significant performance considerations. In both cases, the operating system needs to know the prompt. These routines should be considered generally obsolete, although special-purpose code may be needed for these two systems.

ftime   get time   *

This routine is part of all V7-derived UNIX libraries, but it is not part of any UNIX standard, or of System V, so it should be viewed as not portable outside V7. V7-derived systems supporting ftime include 4.2BSD and Xenix. The ftime call is also supported on MS DOS systems by Microsoft C.

The ftime call is often used to find out the time of day with better than one-second resolution, or to find out the local time zone and daylight conventions. The local time zone can be found in System V by calling tzset or ctime, and then inspecting the external variables timezone and daylight, as documented in ctime(3C).

The local time of day, with better than one-second resolution, cannot be directly obtained with functions available in POSIX or System V release 3. If your objective is to measure elapsed real time with better than one second resolution, the `times(2)` system call return value serves this purpose. Beware, however, of the method used to determine the units returned by `times`. Some implementations return it in `HZ` in `<sys/param.h>` or `<param.h>`; others conform to POSIX, which requires it to be in `CLK_TCK` defined in `<time.h>` or `<limits.h>`; and some do not make the value available. Popular values include 60 or 50 (the line frequency, used in System V on DEC hardware), 100 (used on AT&T 3B hardware), and 18.2 (used on the PC and similar hardware.) See the section on `times` in this chapter for suggested ways to determine this value.

getpgrp   get process group   **

This routine is part of some UNIX libraries, so it is somewhat portable among UNIX systems.

The usage is not always the same. In System V, `getpgrp` takes no arguments, and returns the process group of the current process. In 4BSD, `getpgrp` takes one argument, the process ID for which the process group is desired or 0 for the current process.

Since extra arguments are generally ignored, it is fairly portable to call `getpgrp(0)` to get the process group for the current process. ANSI C compilers, however, will probably complain about extra arguments. It is better to use `#ifdef` if practical.

The interpretation of this value may be nonportable.

getpid   get process id   **

This routine is part of all UNIX libraries, so it is very portable among UNIX systems.

It is often used as part of a temporary file name when a unique file name is desired. Such use only makes sense on the UNIX system. Other operating systems may not have the concept of a process ID, and single-tasking operating systems don't normally need to be concerned about uniqueness of temporary file names, unless a shared file server is involved.

A program using `getpid` to generate a unique file name may be assuming the UNIX filesystem, e.g.,

```
long pid = getpid();
sprintf(tempfile, "/tmp/xyz.%ld", pid);
```

The routines `mktemp`, `tmpnam`, `tempname`, and `tmpfile` are intended to partly or wholly solve this problem. Unfortunately, they are not currently very widely implemented. A good solution is to use `tmpfile`, and if you port your program to a system not supporting `tmpfile`, write your own implementation for the particular system, including it only conditionally:

```
#ifdef BSD
#include <stdio.h>
FILE *
tmpfile()
{
      FILE *r;
      char namebuf[50];

      sprintf(namebuf, "/tmp/xyz.%d", getpid());
      r = fopen(namebuf, "w+");
      if (r != NULL)
            unlink(namebuf);    /* causes delete-on-close */
      return r;
}
#endif
```

getppid   get parent process id   **

This routine is part of many UNIX libraries, so it is fairly portable among UNIX systems. It first appeared in System V release 1 and in 4.2BSD. If you must find out a parent process ID in an older UNIX version that does not support getppid, it may be possible to call getpid before a fork, save the value in a global variable, and use the variable in the child process. (The value can be saved in a file if an exec is involved.)

Some versions of the UNIX system may include getppid in the C library without documenting it.

getuid, geteuid, getgid, getegid get user/group id   **

These routines are part of most UNIX libraries, so are very portable among UNIX systems.

V6 and PWB had a different interface. The getuid and getgid routines returned 16-bit quantities, with the high 8 bits containing the effective ID and the low 8 bits the real ID. When user and group IDs were widened from 8 to 16 bits in V7, the routines were separated. Typical V6 code to use the uid would read:

```
      uid = getuid() & 0377;
```

If your program must work on pre-V7 UNIX systems, it is necessary to use #ifdef. Otherwise you would restrict your users to an 8-bit user and group ID.

Some applications use an array to store a separate value for each user ID on the system. This method was appropriate for V6, which had only 256 possible user IDs. In V7 and later systems, the uid can be any 16-bit value. Some systems use values as high as 65535, for example, a user ID with the high bit on may be a student account with fewer privileges than an ordinary user. (These numbers may be considered negative on some systems.) 32-bit values are possible in future systems. It is unwise to place any interpretation on the value, other than testing for equality with a stored value or with zero.

gtty, stty   get/set terminal modes   **

These routines are part of most UNIX C libraries, so they are fairly portable. They are no longer documented in System V, but are present in many UNIX system releases.

Ironically, because these system calls are based on the V6 and V7 calls, they currently represent one very portable way to do terminal manipulation on UNIX. As long as the programmer avoids the CBREAK and TANDEM bits, these two calls will work compatibly between systems. (System V's stty and gtty system calls emulate UNIX/TS 2.0, which did not have CBREAK or TANDEM.) Nonetheless, use of these functions is not recommended.

In practice, it is better to use #ifdef to handle the systems separately. The stty and gtty calls have been declared obsolete, and are no longer documented, in favor of ioctl. While current systems still support them, they may go away, or change in meaning, at any time.

Another reason to avoid stty is that, on some versions of System V, the emulation turns off the ECHOE bit, no matter how it was originally set. Since setting ECHOE is quite popular, it is unfortunate to have it turned off. Use of the proper ioctl not only allows the programmer direct control over ECHOE, but it also allows access to the equivalent of CBREAK by turning off ICANON and appropriately setting VMIN and VTIME.

int86, int86x   8086 interrupt   *

These routines are part of some MS DOS libraries, but they are not part of any standard, so they should be viewed as not portable, even among MS DOS systems, unless you assume a particular DOS compiler.

These functions are provided by both Microsoft C and Lattice C for the MS DOS system to make a ROM BIOS call. The arguments are compatible. It is possible that these calls will eventually become a de facto standard for MS DOS systems.

intdos, intdosx   MS DOS system call   *

These routines are part of some MS DOS libraries, but they are not part of any standard, so they should be viewed as not portable, even among MS DOS systems, unless you assume a particular DOS compiler.

These functions are provided by both Microsoft C and Lattice C for the MS DOS system to make a DOS call. The arguments are compatible. It is possible that these calls will eventually become a de facto standard for MS DOS systems.

`intss`   test for interactive process   *

This routine is part of the TSO and GCOS libraries, but never caught on in other implementations. It returned zero if the program was running as a batch job and nonzero if running interactively.

The intent was to determine if a user is available to consult in case of trouble. If the program is interactive, it could be assumed that printing on the standard error and then reading from standard input was a reasonable way to get an answer to a policy question. For example, the UNIX `rm` command will ask, if the file being removed is not writable by the user, if it's really OK to remove it. This is the sort of question intended for `intss`.

On the UNIX system, similar functionality can be gained by calling `isatty(fileno(stderr))` and `isatty(fileno(stdin))`. This call may be somewhat portable to a few other systems. If you need to tell if the program is interactive, one good approach is to write your own `intss` function, with an `isatty`-based implementation under the UNIX and MS DOS systems, and using the built-in function under MVS and GCOS. For some operating systems, the function might always just return 1.

Beware that with systems supporting job control (such as 4.2BSD), the standard input may appear to be a terminal, yet attempting to read from it will suspend the program. There is no easy or portable way to detect this or compensate for it, but the consequences are minor, only resulting in a user inconvenience.

`ioctl`   input/output control   *

This routine is part of most UNIX libraries, but it is unportable, even among UNIX systems. There are two distinct branches of `ioctl` functionality: the V7/4BSD branch and the System III/V branch. Each of these has its own core set of `ioctl` calls, and many of them have local additions.

Even within one UNIX version, the values used by `ioctl` are very dependent on the hardware, both in the internal value that the name expands to and the layout of the parameter often depends on the hardware. This makes it unportable to send `ioctl` calls over a network, which in turn makes the implementation of remote filesystems harder than it would otherwise be. POSIX has specified an interface called *termios* that is similar to the System V method, although it uses calls such as `tcgetattr` and `tcsetattr` instead of the traditional `ioctl`.

In general, systems programming often requires the use of `ioctl`, but typical applications need it only for a small set of operations, such as going into cbreak mode in the terminal driver. The best policy is to use a standard library routine where possible, such as `cbreak` or `noecho` in curses, or letting curses set `LINES` and `COLS` to the current screen size. If no standard library is available with the required functionality, write a subroutine that does what you really want, and bury the `ioctl` call in the subroutine. Then you need only rewrite the subroutine as appropriate for other systems. (But be prepared

for the possibility that another system may not support the same functionality, and you'll
have to live without it.)

kill   send signal   **

This routine is part of all UNIX libraries, so it is very portable among UNIX systems.

There are some differences in interpretation among the different UNIX versions. In
all cases, if the given process ID has the same user ID as the current process, or if the
current process is root, and if the signal is an integer in the range from 1 to the highest
defined signal number, the signal is sent, and an accurate error indication is returned to
the caller if the signal could not be sent.

If the process ID is zero, the signal is sent to all processes in the same process group
as the sender. (Processes in the same process group with a different uid may or may not
be sent the signal, depending on the system and whether the signal was generated by
kill or by a key being pressed on the terminal.) If the process ID is negative, the call is
unportable, because different systems give different interpretations.

The method of sending signal number zero to test whether a process ID still exists,
without bothering the process, first appeared in System III and in 4.2BSD. This is useful
to check lock files to see if the process holding the lock has gone away.

Signal values over 15 are not portable. V7 had no such signals, System III defined
one set of additional signals, and 4.2BSD defined a different set. Some widely defined
signals may not be portable either; for example, SIGIOT is specific to processors with
the IOT instruction. See signal for more discussion of the portability of signals.

ANSI C defines a new function raise that can portably send a signal to the current
program.

link   create hard link   **

This routine is part of all UNIX libraries, so it is very portable among UNIX systems.

lockf   file/record locking   *

This routine is part of the POSIX standard, but is not yet widely implemented in earlier systems. In UNIX System V, it first appeared in an intermediate release shortly
before System V release 3, and was fully supported in release 3 as well. 4.2BSD and
4.3BSD do not have this function, but a similar function named flock.

File and record locking has been a controversial issue for years. There are proponents
of advisory locking and of mandatory locking. Some feel that only advisory file locking
is needed. Locking is difficult to implement reliably when the filesystem is mounted over
a network from another computer. Special caution is needed here until the issue becomes
more clearly defined.

lseek   position within file   ***

This routine is part of most UNIX libraries, so it is very portable among UNIX systems.

In V6 and PWB, a similar routine `seek` was provided. Since 32-bit integers were not supported by the V6 C compiler, and file sizes in V6 were 24-bit quantities, `seek` took 16-bit arguments, whose values were internally shifted left by 8 bits by adding 3 to the second argument.

Between V6 and V7, the `long` data type was added to the language, and the cleaner `lseek` routine was added, implemented using the `seek` primitive. By V7, `lseek` had become the standard call and `seek` was no longer supported.

Since the K&R book was written between V6 and V7, there is discussion of `seek` and `lseek` as equals. In practice, `seek` is obsolete, and most programs use either `lseek` or the even more portable `fseek`.

Seeking is appropriate only on disk files. Attempts to seek on a pipe, tty, tape drive, or network connection may or may not work. Seeking on a raw disk or tape device is normally supported, but only to physical sector boundaries. Seeking on a "cooked" tape drive usually works, but the "cooked" tape drive feature has faded into disuse, since the small records wasted most of the tape and large amounts of CPU time, so it is unwise to use this feature. Some tape drives do support more functionality, but use of this functionality is generally not portable.

mkdir, rmdir   make/remove directory   ***

These routines are part of some UNIX libraries, but are required by POSIX and the System V release 3 SVID. They will be portable across UNIX and POSIX systems someday, but currently are available only in 4.2BSD, System V release 3, Microsoft C for the MS DOS system, and their derivations.

In the absence of the `mkdir` and `rmdir` system calls, it is possible to write your own subroutine to have the same effect. This subroutine must call the shell `mkdir` and `rmdir` commands, either by use of `system`, or the less portable, slightly faster, and considerably more secure `fork` and `execlp`. Since it's rare for a call to `mkdir` to be made very often, speed is generally not important, but for security reasons, don't use `system`. For example:

```
int
mkdir(dirname, mode)
char *dirname;
int mode;
{
        int r;

        r = fork();
        if (r < 0) return r;
```

```
        if (r == 0)
                execl("/bin/mkdir", dirname);

        wait(&r);
        chmod(dirname, mode);

        return r;
}
```

Note that /bin/mkdir was spelled out fully. While this might slightly hurt portability to systems where mkdir is in another directory, it defends against Trojan horse
programs called mkdir that might be run from the path-searching versions of exec.

mknod   create filesystem inode   *

This routine is part of most UNIX libraries, but it is very unportable. The mknod system call is used to create special device files, usually in the /dev directory. It is very
unusual for a program to need to call mknod from C. This system call is primarily
present for the mknod shell command, which is used for system administration.

The mknod system call is also used on System III and System V to create FIFOs
(also known as named pipes). This use is somewhat more portable, but is not supported
on V7-derived systems such as 4BSD.

According to the /usr/group 1984 standard, when using mknod to create a FIFO, the
final parameter to mknod must be 0 for the call to be defined.

This system call was deleted from POSIX in favor of the new mkfifo function.

monitor, profil   measure process execution   *

These routines are part of most UNIX libraries, but they are not part of any UNIX
standard, so they should be viewed as not portable.

These functions are special-purpose low-level functions used by the profiling option
of the C compiler. They should not be called by users. Although they are present in most
UNIX systems, they may change, or be totally omitted, in future systems. They are not
likely to be present in POSIX emulations built on other systems.

mount, umount   mount/umount filesystem   **

These routines are part of most UNIX libraries, but they are not part of POSIX, so
they should be viewed as not portable. The set of arguments varies from system to system.

The mount and umount calls are special-purpose low-level functions used by the
user-level mount and umount commands, to mount filesystems. They should not be

called by users. In general, filesystems are usually mounted from the shell level, and the methods of mounting (possibly remote) filesystems are considered system- and network-specific.

Although they are present in most UNIX systems, they may change, or be totally omitted, in future systems. These functions are required by the SVID (issue 1 only,) but not by POSIX. They are not likely to be present in POSIX emulations built on other systems.

If you must call `mount` or `umount` from your program, consider using `system` to use the `mount` shell command. If the C call must be used, consider using only the first two arguments, since additional arguments are often optional.

nice   change priority   *

This routine is part of most UNIX libraries, but it is not part of any UNIX standard, so it should be viewed as not portable.

This function is a special-purpose advisory function used by programs to declare that they take a low (or sometimes high) priority in operating system scheduling. While it is present in most UNIX systems, it may change, or be totally omitted, in future systems.

The semantics of this system call are not the same on all systems. Current systems add the parameter to the current ''niceness'' (priority) value, within certain limits. (The higher the ''niceness'' value, the lower the priority of the process.) Systems older than V7 (including V6 and PWB) set the current niceness value to the argument, discarding any previous value.

In the event that a program needing `nice` must be ported to a system that neither supports it, nor provides a dummy function, the easiest approach is probably to provide a dummy function or to use a makefile macro to get the same effect:

```
CFLAGS= '-Dnice(prio)='
```

open   open file   ***

This routine is part of all UNIX libraries, so it is very portable among UNIX systems.

The name in the first argument, and values 0 (read only), 1 (write only), and 2 (read/write) are very portable. An alternative method is to use

```
#ifndef O_RDONLY
#define O_RDONLY 0
#define O_WRONLY 1
#define O_RDWR   2
#endif
```

Unfortunately, this method still suffers from the problem of knowing what file to include to get the definitions.

Using the third argument, any value other than 0, 1, or 2 for the second argument, or include files such as <fcntl.h> are not portable. 4.2BSD uses the include file <sys/file.h>, and older systems support only hard-coded integers. The additional values for the second argument first appeared in System III and 4.2BSD, as did the third argument.

To specify a third argument, or the TRUNC or CREAT flags, it is more portable to use the creat system call. The NDELAY, APPEND, EXCL, and O_SYNC features are not supported in older systems.

pause   wait for signal   **

This routine is part of most UNIX libraries, so it is very portable among UNIX systems. The pause function is rarely called from user applications. Its primary purpose, along with alarm, is implementation of the sleep subroutine. It is sometimes used in coordinating multiple processes or waiting for an externally generated signal.

V6 did not have pause or alarm, but instead sleep was a system call. Releases beginning with PWB 1.0 had pause and alarm.

pipe   create pipe   **

This routine is part of all UNIX libraries, so it is very portable among UNIX systems. Pipes traditionally provide one-directional byte-stream communication between pairs of processes.

Although the pipe function is highly portable, it is becoming obsolete. Improved networking functions have better functionality and often better performance. Some new networking facilities, such as System V's TLI and Berkeley's sockets, allow two-directional communication, and do not require that the processes share a common cooperating ancestor or even be on the same computer. At the same time, some systems have enhanced, bidirectional pipes.

Because pipes are becoming viewed as special cases of more powerful constructions, some systems implement pipes using the more powerful, higher-performance primitives. This means that the semantics of pipes may vary from implementation to implementation. Beware of assumptions about the behavior of pipes that are not documented.

For example, the size of the buffer (the amount ahead that the writer can write before the reader reads), traditionally 4096 or 5120 bytes, can vary. Some implementations may not have a fixed size. Some applications will fstat the pipe to see if there is anything to read; this is not portable. Most implementations guarantee that writes are atomic, that if two or more processes write to the same pipe at the same time, the results of each write will be contiguous. It is unwise to depend on this property.

Some implementations support pipes only at the shell level. A command such as

```
tbl file | eqn | nroff -mm
```

may be treated by the shell as if it were

```
tbl file > temp1
eqn < temp1 > temp2
nroff -mm < temp2
rm temp1 temp2
```

ptrace   debug process   *

This routine is part of most UNIX libraries, but it is not part of any UNIX standard, so it should be viewed as not portable.

This function is a special-purpose low-level function used by various debuggers. It should not be called by users. Although it is present in most UNIX systems, it may change, or be totally omitted, in future systems. It is not likely to be present in POSIX emulations built on other systems.

read   read from file   ***

This routine is part of most C libraries, and it is extremely portable among UNIX systems. Although ANSI C does not require read to be present, it is in fact present on most implementations.

Normally, a program will use fread or other standard I/O routines instead of read. The appropriate times to call read are when standard I/O has a serious performance impact or when standard I/O causes some unwanted buffering property.

It is unwise to depend on O_NDELAY, although this is becoming more and more portable. This feature first appeared in System III, and was added to 4.2BSD. A more portable version, O_NONBLOCK, was defined in POSIX, and is probably the best model to use for nonblocking read. On systems with neither O_NONBLOCK nor O_NDELAY, such as V7, 4.2BSD, and their descendents, the FIONREAD ioctl can be used to emulate O_NONBLOCK functionality as follows:

```
nbread(fd, buf, nbytes)
int fd, nbytes;
char *buf;
{
#ifdef O_NONBLOCK
        /* assume fd was put into O_NONBLOCK mode when opened */
        return read(fd, buf, nbytes);
#else
```

```
# ifdef FIONREAD
        n = ioctl(fd, FIONREAD, 0);
        /* n is number of bytes available to read immediately */
        if (n <= 0) {
                /* nothing waiting to be read */
                errno = EAGAIN;
                return -1;
        }
        return read(fd, buf, nbytes);
# else
        /* guess that there's something there, hang if wrong */
        return read(fd, buf, nbytes);
# endif
#endif
}
```

remove   remove file   ***

This routine is part of ANSI C, but is new with that standard. No existing implementations supported it before ANSI C. It should be considered unportable unless you either assume ANSI C, or use `#ifdef __STDC__`.

The `unlink` routine, theoretically less portable and specific to the UNIX system, is in practice quite portable, even outside the UNIX system. Since the two are compatible, on a system that does not support `remove`, you can just add the definition `-Dremove=unlink` and usually get your program to work.

rename   rename file   ***

This routine is part of ANSI C, but it is implemented in only some systems, so it should be viewed as not portable until ANSI C can be assumed.

The `rename` function is implemented on 4.2BSD, Amiga, Microsoft C, Lattice C, and Mark Williams C; and missing in GCOS, MVS, Digital Research C, V7, and System V release 3. As ANSI C is more widely implemented, more systems will support it.

Beware of the order of the arguments to `rename`. Some older implementations have the arguments in the order `rename(new, old)`. ANSI C, and most other implementations, including Microsoft C version 4.0, use the order `rename(old, new)`.

The ANSI C standard requires that `rename` works on files, but does not specify that it work for directories. (Indeed, systems supporting C need not have the concept of a directory.) POSIX requires that the call work on files, or on directories, but the shell-level semantics of naming an existing file and an existing directory, and referring to the old filename being newly created in the directory, are not supported. In addition, POSIX specifies that `rename` on directories may be restricted to the super user. This makes `rename` unportable for programs that do not run as the super user.

If you must rename files on systems that do not have this system call, it will be necessary to use lower-level functions to emulate it. On the UNIX system, the following code is roughly equivalent:

```
char *old, *new;
...
if (link(old, new) == -1)
        return -1;
return unlink(old);
```

If the process is interrupted, or the system crashes, between the two operations, this call may leave both names in place. This method does not work for directories, unless the program is running as the super user. An alternative may be to use `system` to call the user-level `mv` command, although this may not always work. (In System V, the `mv` command will rename directories only if both the old and new names are in the same directory.)

On other operating systems, there may be a system-specific way to do a rename. Another possible method of renaming files is to copy the old file to the new file, and then to delete the old file. This does not preserve properties of the file, such as the creation date and the permissions, but it may be the best you can do.

setgid   set group id   **

This routine is part of most UNIX libraries, so it is very portable among UNIX systems. It can be depended upon to set the real and effective group id's of the process to the value given, if the current effective gid is the value given or if the current effective uid is the super user. It may be implemented in many different ways; in 4.2BSD, for example, it is a subroutine that calls the `setregid` system call.

setpgrp   set process group   *

This routine is part of most UNIX libraries, but the usage is not the same in all versions, so it is only somewhat portable among UNIX systems.

In System III derived systems, `setpgrp` takes no arguments and sets the process group of the current process to the current process id. In addition, POSIX specifies that the association between the current terminal and the process is broken.

In 4.2BSD, `setpgrp` takes two arguments: the process to set and the value to set it to. The process will default to the current process, but not the value.

A truly portable call to `setpgrp` looks like this:

```
setpgrp(getpid(), getpid());
```

The arguments will be ignored on System V, but are harmless. (The `lint` program will complain about the extra arguments, but this may be preferable to the use of `#ifdef`.)

In practice, the usual reason for calling `setpgrp` is either to put a server process into the background, immune from signals, or else to detach a process from a terminal so that the process, or its descendents, can become associated with another terminal.

For example, a window manager or network server may need to spawn a shell on a software pseudoterminal device. The shell must be properly attached to the new terminal. There is no completely portable way to do this. In general, you must set the process group of the current process to a new number, and also clear out the controlling terminal from the current process. Setting the process group can be accomplished as shown above. Clearing out the controlling terminal cannot always be done, and when it can be done, it isn't portable. Sometimes an `ioctl` can be used to clear out the controlling terminal. Sometimes `setpgrp` will automatically do it. You'll need to use `#ifdef` for each system you support.

`setuid`   set user id   **

This routine is part of most UNIX libraries, so it is very portable among UNIX systems. It can be depended upon to set the real and effective user id's of the process to the value given, if the current effective uid is the value given or is the super user. It may be implemented in many different ways; in 4.2BSD, for example, it is a subroutine that calls the `setreuid` system call.

It is not portable to depend on being able to set the user id's *back* to the previous value. System V saves the original user id, so that it is possible for a program without special privileges to switch back and forth between the original real and effective user id. V7-derived systems overwrite all copies of the original user id when `setuid` is called, and cannot change back.

`signal`   catch signal   ***

This routine is part of all UNIX libraries, but the set of signals is different, and the semantics are different in 4.2BSD, so it is only somewhat portable among UNIX systems. Signals were originally designed to deal with unexpected events, but they have been widely used as a primitive interprocess communication mechanism.

The original signal mechanism can be convenient for programming, but for some applications, it isn't completely reliable. The problem is that signals are reset when caught, and the first thing the signal routine is supposed to do is to catch the signal again. If the signal is raised a second time before the routine can catch it, the default behavior for the signal occurs, resulting in either a lost signal or a terminated program.

In 4.2BSD, Berkeley changed the semantics of signals. The new mechanism, which they called *reliable signals*, causes all incoming signals to be queued until the first signal-handler function exits. There is a change to the method for returning to the interrupted code. In other UNIX versions, if a slow I/O was interrupted (such as a `read` waiting for keystrokes to be pressed on a terminal) and the signal handler returns, the system call fails with error number EINTR. In 4.2BSD, the I/O call is resumed as if nothing had happened. This is an improvement, but it isn't compatible with previous versions of 4BSD or with System V.

The relevant standards, including ANSI C and POSIX, allow either behavior. System V release 3 provides an implementation of signal with the old behavior, but also provides a new system call sigsys with the reliable behavior. POSIX specifies a set of routines such as sigaction to provide reliable signals and an optional set of facilities to support Berkeley-style job control.

It used to be that the only truly portable way to use signal was to never return from the signal handler. Instead, the handler would terminate with exit, exec, or more commonly longjmp. Unfortunately, ANSI C has made this behavior undefined, out of concern that a signal handler might call a function that is already being called when a signal comes in.

Today there is no truly portable way to use signals. Calls to longjmp from the signal handler are undefined. ANSI C specifies that signals generated with means other than abort, raise, or hardware traps causing SIGFPE must terminate by returning from the handler. On some systems, this will terminate the call; on others, execution will resume where it left off. It is necessary to have all read calls on slow devices (such as the terminal) check for error returns:

```
if (read(0, &buf, sizeof buf) < 0 && errno == EINTR)
        longjmp(jmpbuf, 1);
```

Unfortunately, this will not work on 4.2BSD, because the read call will resume without any error indication.

You should also be careful which signals you catch. SIGINT is supported not only on the UNIX system, but by the Microsoft C compiler for the MS DOS system, and ANSI C. ANSI C requires SIGINT, SIGABRT, SIGFPE, SIGILL, SIGSEGV, and SIGTERM, but indicates that these signals may only be portably raised with raise.

Signals available in every UNIX version include SIGINT, SIGHUP, SIGQUIT, SIGKILL, SIGFPE, SIGPIPE, SIGALRM, and SIGTERM. (Of course, some signals, such as SIGKILL, cannot be caught by signal.) Signals that appear in every UNIX version, but that depend somewhat on the underlying hardware, include SIGTRAP, SIGIOT, and SIGEMT. In addition, although SIGILL, SIGSEGV, and SIGBUS are hardware dependent, they tend to have the same meaning on all UNIX systems. Portable among System III, System V, and POSIX, but not V7-derived systems, are SIGUSR1 and SIGUSR2.

In the calling routine, it is best not to rely on any parameters being passed. If you must use the arguments, it is fairly safe to depend on the signal number being passed as the first argument. Any additional arguments are unportable.

It is common for an application to be bulletproof and to catch or ignore all signals. Unfortunately, there is no completely portable way to catch all signals, because there is no way to know how many signals are defined, or even to know whether the signal numbers are sequential. Because of the structure of the `wait` system call, it is unlikely that there will be signal numbers higher than 127.

Some systems define `NSIG` as the upper bound, but some do not. POSIX applications can call `sigfillset` and `sigismember` to determine which signals are defined. The functions `sigemptyset`, `sigfillset`, `sigaddset`, `sigdelset`, `sigismember`, `sigaction`, `sigprocmask`, `sigpending`, and `sigsuspend` are inventions of the POSIX committee, and will not be portable until POSIX conformance becomes widespread. In general, the only portable signal functions are `signal`, `alarm`, and `sleep`.

It is also possible that a signal may represent a real problem, such as a segmentation violation indicating a bug in the program. Since the number of signals can't always be predicted, and since there are signals in the middle that cannot or should not be ignored, this method is not recommended.

Instead, a truly bulletproof program (such as a background network server) should run as two processes. The parent forks and waits for the child to exit. The child is the real server. When the parent detects, with `wait`, that the child has exited, it records this fact to a log file, pauses for 30 seconds or so to avoid thrashing in the event of a loop, and forks off another child. The parent should also detect looping conditions (where the child exits more often than reasonable) and take some appropriate action. Looping can cause log files to fill up the disk and is a symptom of some serious problem requiring human intervention.

Some systems make use of the signal mechanism to implement job control. It is possible for an application to ignore job control or to catch signals such as `SIGCONT` when job control actions take place. Since many systems do not offer job control, portable applications should not depend on it.

The most portable method of dealing with job control is to ignore it. A line-oriented application, or a filter, can ignore job control and allow the shell to handle it. Screen-oriented applications, or applications that change the terminal mode settings, probably need to fix things when exiting to the shell and when resuming the application. Code that catches such signals should be conditionally compiled:

```
#ifdef SIGCONT
        signal(SIGCONT, redisplay_screen);
#endif
```

sigpause   reliable signals   *

This routine is part of newer UNIX libraries, but it is not part of any UNIX standard, so it should be viewed as not portable.

The `sigvec` facilities of System V release 3 are similar to the `jobs` library of 4.1BSD. The `sigpause` function is also present in the default C library in 4.2BSD. All these versions are compatible.

The function is not present in earlier systems, and there is no reliable way to get the same effect. Unreliable means, such as `signal`, are needed to get a similar effect.

In general, given a choice between portability and reliability, there are no pretty solutions. On older systems, there is way to reliably catch signals. If they come in too fast, the application will abort. Many applications expect only an occasional signal, so this may not matter. Conditional compilation can be employed to use reliable signals when the system supports them, and unreliable signals otherwise. There is no portable built-in macro to key on, so it will be necessary to define one as a configuration parameter.

stat, fstat   get file status   **

These routines are part of most UNIX libraries, so they are very portable among UNIX systems.

The fields that can reasonably be depended on are `st_mode`, `st_ino`, `st_dev`, `st_uid`, `st_gid`, `st_size`, and `st_mtime`. The sizes of the data items in the `stat` structure may vary.

The inode number `st_ino` and the device number `st_dev` may have different interpretations on different systems. It is best to restrict use of these two fields to determining if two names refer to the same file. If the inode and device numbers from two calls to `stat` or `fstat` both match, the two names can usually be assumed to reference the same file. (Even this assumption may not be true over a network, because there is no global management of inodes and device numbers. There is no easy way around this problem.)

The `st_ctime` field has had different interpretations over the years and different implementations. Sometimes it's been the time the file was created, sometimes the time the inode was last changed, and sometimes the same as `st_mtime`. It is best to use `st_mtime` and, with less portability, `st_utime` to determine the status of the file.

The `st_nlink` and `st_atime` fields are currently present and portable across all UNIX and POSIX implementations.

stime   set time of day   *

This routine is part of many UNIX libraries, but it is not part of any UNIX standard, and it should be viewed as not portable.

The `stime` call has historically been present in all UNIX versions since V6. User applications, however, rarely need to call `stime`. Only the UNIX `date` command makes this call, and resetting the clock is done with `date`. In essence, `stime` is a low-level system call, not to be called by applications.

In recent history, some events have made `stime` less portable, if more important, for applications. 4.2BSD replaced `stime` with the new function `settimeofday`, which allows the time to be set to microsecond precision, as well as setting the systemwide time zone. Although it would be easy to write an `stime` routine in terms of `settimeofday`, no such routine was provided.

Another event is that network time daemons have become popular with the advent of networks. Such daemons must set the local time of day. A daemon cannot be completely portable without using `#ifdef`, but this is a minor problem.

In general, it is rare that an application will need to set the clock. The method for setting the clock is not portable. The `stime` function is only present in older UNIX systems and in System V, and is not required by any of the standards. Any application that sets the time will not be completely portable.

`sync`   force write to disk   **

This routine is part of most UNIX libraries, but it is not part of POSIX, so it should be viewed as somewhat portable within UNIX systems.

Historically, this call has been present in all UNIX systems since V6. It is still present in all current implementations, and is required by the SVID, but not by POSIX. Since the function is really advisory to the system, if it is not present on some other system, you can write a function called `sync` which has a similar effect (if possible) or does nothing.

An implementation of `sync` that does nothing may have the intended effect on filesystems that are fully synchronous, such as MS DOS. (A synchronous filesystem always completes a write to disk before the `write` call returns. This is more robust, but usually implies slower performance.) Otherwise, an empty function will allow the program to link and run adequately, although the risk of a system crash losing some recent data may still exist. Since the UNIX system does not guarantee that data has been written out when `sync` returns, there is only a small loss in reliability.

System V release 3 supports a file mode O_SYNC, which can be specified on `open` or with `fcntl`. It causes *all* writes to the affected file or device to be synchronous. The `write` system call will not return until the data is safely written to the physical media. The caveat on the `fsync` system call also applies to O_SYNC.

The Berkeley systems, and System V release 4, support a related `fsync` call. This call also affects only one file. It guarantees that when the call returns, all outstanding disk blocks have been written out, at least as far as the operating system can control. (It may, in fact, have only made it out to a disk controller or to a hosted operating system.) The `fsync` call is not portable.

`time`   get time of day   ***

This routine is part of all UNIX libraries, so it is extremely portable among UNIX systems.

In V6, the usage of `time` was slightly different. There was no support for the `long` data type, so the parameter passed was an array of two short integers. The time value had to be returned in the array, since functions could not return a long. For this reason, it is slightly more portable to pass a pointer to a long rather than depending on the value returned by `time((long *)0)`. On modern systems, it really only matters for 16-bit machines, and then only because you have to be sure to declare that `time` returns a long, and worry about bugs developing from passing longs. It's also likely that better code will be generated.

Some implementations recommend that the type `time_t` be used instead of `long`. If `time_t` is ever expanded to more than 32 bits, this could become an issue. (There has been some interest in being able to represent times before 1970 or after 2106.) In practice, enough standards document the data type as a `long` rather than a `time_t`, and the location of the files to include that define `time_t` vary enough among the standards that it's probably better to just use `long`. Better yet, define your own `time_t` type as a `long`.

`times`   get CPU times   **

This routine is part of most UNIX libraries, so it is very portable among UNIX systems.

The values returned in the structure are quite portable, although you should take care to get the units right. (Some systems use 60th's of a second, some 50th's, some 100th's, and some other values. There is no portable way to get this value, other than a loop calling `times` and `time` to see how many *ticks* of wall-clock time a program can use in several *seconds* of wall-clock time, and taking the ratio.)

It is unwise to depend on the wall-clock value returned as the function value. This feature exists in System III and V, and in POSIX, but not 4BSD.

If you are using this for a benchmark, which will often be carried around from system to system, it's worthwhile to include the check on the units. For other applications, it's often worthwhile to configure in the frequency per second as an `#define` in a header file.

Here is sample code to determine the clock frequency. It should be run on an otherwise idle machine.

```
int
findtps()
{
        int TPS;    /* number of clock ticks per second is placed here */

#ifdef SYSV
        long t1, t2, ct1, ct2;
#else /* V7/4BSD */
# include <sys/timeb.h>
        struct timeb tb1,tb2;
#endif
```

```
#ifdef SYSV
      time(&t2);
      for (;;) {
            time(&t1);
            if (t1 > t2)
                  break;
      }
      /* start off at an even second boundary */
      ct1 = times(&tbuf1);

      /* burn exactly one second of real time (idle system) */
      for (;;) {
            time(&t2);
            if (t2 > t1)
                  break;
      }
      ct2 = times(&tbuf2);
      TPS = ct2 - ct1;
#else /* V7/4BSD */
      ftime( &tb1 );
      /* wait for clock to tick once */
      do {
            ftime( &tb2 );
      } while( tb1.millitm == tb2.millitm );
      /* check how many ms it ticked. */
      TPS = 1000/(tb2.millitm-tb1.millitm);
#endif
      return TPS;
}
```

ulimit   set maximum file size   *

This routine is specific to System V. It is part of System V and the SVID, but missing from most other UNIX versions.

4.2BSD has a similar system call `setrlimit`, and 4.1BSD has a similar call `vlimit`. Either of these Berkeley calls, which are specific to Berkeley's system, can be used to emulate `ulimit`. Berkeley also has a disk quota mechanism that limits the total disk space a user can occupy. This can result in a failed `write` call, much like `ulimit` can.

It is rare that a program will call `ulimit` directly; this function is normally called by a shell to affect all programs called from the shell.

One common problem is that, on System V, the default value of `ulimit` is typically 1, 2, or 4 megabytes, but the default on V7 and Berkeley systems is unlimited. This sometimes causes programs, or users who are used to the unlimited behavior, to create files of the maximum size, and then fail. Network servers are especially vulnerable if they are to create files, since they run with a default `ulimit` value.

It is recommended that server programs running under System V increase their `ulimit` value or provide a way for the client to request a larger limit. Another technique is to break up large files into smaller pieces.

umask   set default file permissions   **

This routine is part of most UNIX libraries, so it is very portable among UNIX systems.

The `umask` system call first appeared in V7 and UNIX/TS 2.0. Earlier systems, such as V6 and PWB, did not have this feature. In the earlier systems, the umask value was effectively 777.

Only a few umask values are commonly used. These include 000 (no protection), 077 (high secrecy), and 022 (read only). The values 027 and 002 also make sense. Other values are unusual, and may cause unexpected results. The default umask value varies from system to system.

It is common to see the umask value set to 000 on development machines where the users are not concerned with security. Software developed in such an environment may not work well when run in in a more protected environment, especially multiuser software such as a mail, bulletin board, or shared database application. A developer would be well advised to test the application on systems with 077, and possibly 022, umask values in place.

It is rare for a program to change the umask value, since this is normally handled by the shell `umask` command from `/etc/profile` or `.profile` or `.login`. Usually, the only reason for a program to change the value is to work around the effect of an existing mask setting or to force a particular file mode when a file is created. (Use of `chmod` after the `creat` will behave differently if the file already exists.) This may apply, for example, when creating a new general-purpose file or directory for a shared application.

uname   get system name   *

This routine is part of System III derived UNIX libraries, so it is somewhat portable among UNIX systems. Nonetheless, it is recommended that `uname` be treated as an unportable routine, and isolated in a separate subroutine.

Most applications use `uname` to find out the name of the local computer system, that is, the `nodename` field. The other fields are rarely useful to a program, and their interpretation and format are not necessarily consistent from one system to another.

System V through release 3 allowed only 8 characters in the host name. 4.2BSD and System V release 4 allow up to 256 characters.

System V release 4 has the `domainname` shell command, which can be concatenated onto the `nodename` to get the fully qualified host name. From C, use the `INFO_SRPC_DOMAIN` option to the new `sysinfo` system call. See also the new System V release 4 library `-lmail`, which contains a function `maildomain` that gets the domain but can be overridden by the mail configuration file.

4.2BSD-derived systems have the `gethostname` system call to get the same result. V6 and V7 had no similar facility, and by convention the name was found in the include file `<whoami.h>` in V7. PWB 1.0 had a `uname` call, but it returned a single character string with a recommended 8-byte format.

The Xenix system uses a text file to contain the host name. Releases before 1987 supplied the `uname` system call, but this call did not return any useful information.

Host names are evolving, and, as this is written, it is unclear what sort of structure will be needed in the long term to represent a host name. The result might be a character string or it might be some more complex structure. While the standardization efforts have so far endorsed `uname`, it does seem clear that 8 bytes is too short for a general host name. This makes it likely that some other system call will eventually become a de facto standard.

The best way to find out the current host name is to use a subroutine that returns the local host name, and length, in a buffer. (If you're willing to assume the name will be a character string, or can be encoded as one, you can get by without the length, although it's still a good idea to pass the length of the buffer you provide to the routine. This assumption is probably a fairly safe one.) You can then provide several different implementations of the subroutine, either calling `uname`, `gethostname`, or reading a file. (Some implementations open `/usr/include/whoami.h` and look for an appropriate `#define`; others open a file such as `/etc/ident` or `/usr/include/whoami` and treat the entire contents of the file as a newline terminated name.)

If you assume the name is a character string, the `gethostname` interface is well suited to such a subroutine. By adopting the `gethostname` interface, you can emulate `gethostname` by using `uname` or by reading a file.

Here is one possible subroutine. It is controlled by configuration parameters: UNAME to use the `uname` system call, GHNAME to use `gethostname`, UUNAME to use a file whose name is defined as UUNAME, and HDRFILE to use a file such as `<whoami.h>` to read a line of the form `#define sysname "myname"`.

```
/*
 * Configurable function to get local host name.
 * Does not make use of System V release 4 INFO_SRPC_DOMAIN option.
 */
#define MAXHOSTNAME 64
```

```
char *
myname()
{
        static char retbuf[MAXHOSTNAME];

#ifdef UNAME
        struct utsname ubuf;

        uname(&ubuf);
        strcpy(retbuf, ubuf.nodename);
        return retbuf;
#endif

#ifdef GHNAME
        gethostname(retbuf, sizeof (retbuf));
        return retbuf;
#endif

#ifdef        UUNAME
        FILE *uucpf;
        register char *p;
        /* uucp name is stored UUNAME */

        if (((uucpf = fopen(UUNAME, "r")) == NULL) ||
                fgets(retbuf, sizeof (retbuf), uucpf) == NULL) {
                        fprintf(stderr, "no sysname in %s\n", UUNAME);
                        return NULL;
        }
        p = index(retbuf, '\n');
        if (p)
                *p = '\0';
        if (uucpf != NULL)
                fclose(uucpf);
        return retbuf;
#endif /* UUNAME */
```

```
#ifdef HDRFILE
        FILE *fd;

        fd = fopen(HDRFILE, "r");
        if (fd == NULL) {
                fprintf(stderr, "Cannot open %s\n", HDRFILE);
                exit(1);
        }

        for (;;) {   /* each line in the file */
                if (fgets(buf, sizeof buf, fd) == NULL) {
                        fprintf(stderr, "no sysname in %s\n", HDRFILE);
                        fclose(fd);
                        exit(2);
                }
                if (sscanf(buf, "#define sysname \"%[^\"]\"", retbuf) ==
                        fclose(fd);
                        return;
                }
        }
#endif
}
```

unlink   remove file   ***

This routine is part of most UNIX libraries, so it is very portable among UNIX systems. In fact, most non-UNIX implementations also supply unlink.

ANSI C supplies a new function called remove, which takes the same argument and does approximately the same thing as unlink. Although in theory remove should be more portable, in practice it first appeared in X3J11 in 1986, and few implementations currently have it.

There are some slight variations in semantics between unlink and remove. The unlink call is specific to the UNIX system, and certain properties of the traditional UNIX implementation are considered defined properties of unlink. These properties include the notion of multiple links to the same file, so that removing one of several links does not cause the file to go away. Also, if the file is open at the time it is unlinked, the program or programs with the open file can continue to use it until the file is closed. This turns out to be useful for creating temporary files without having to remember to remove them later; the tmpfile routine depends on this property.

The remove routine is less UNIX-specific; it merely requires that the file be deleted from the filesystem, and the exact properties of how this is done may vary among implementations. Many implementations of unlink actually are more like remove. Even on the UNIX system, it is possible for the file to be immediately deleted on some remote filesystem implementations, such as Sun's Network File System (NFS).

A good programming practice would be to use whichever routine best does what you want, and use the preprocessor to emulate the other call where needed. For example, if you want to just remove an ordinary file, write your code using `remove`:

```
remove(file);
```

and on systems that don't support `remove`, add the command-line flag `-Dremove=unlink` or the line

```
#define remove unlink
```

in some header file.

ustat   get free space on disk   *

This routine is part of PWB-derived UNIX libraries, so it is somewhat portable among UNIX systems. It is not present on V7 or 4.2BSD. It is present on Xenix.

According to the /usr/group standard, only the `f_tfree` and `f_tinode` fields are required; use of `f_fname` or `f_fpack` are unportable.

The size of the blocks referred to in `f_tfree` are not documented, so there is some possibility of variation among implementations, but generally 512-byte blocks are implemented.

This call was deleted from POSIX, because the device passed as the first parameter is system-specific and that this call might compromise system security.

utime   set file access/modify times   **

This routine is part of most UNIX libraries, so it is very portable among UNIX systems. The `utime` call was not present in V6, but it appeared in PWB and V7, and their descendents.

The use of include files and the `struct utimbuf` parameter are, unfortunately, not portable. The structure first appeared in System III, and although it is present in System III derived UNIX systems, it is not in V7 or 4BSD. In addition, the particular include file that defines the `struct utimbuf` varies from system to system.

In System III and System V, the structure is declared in `<sys/types.h>`. The /usr/group standard declares it in `<unistd.h>` and requires that `<sys/types.h>` be included before including `<unistd.h>` to get the definition for `time_t`. It also specifies that only the `modtime` field is required, and that the `actime` field is optional. POSIX moves the /usr/group convention from `<unistd.h>` to `<utime.h>` and puts back the requirement that the `actime` field be available.

Microsoft C implements `utime` on the MS DOS system, but supports only the `modtime` field, because MS DOS systems do not keep track of the access time. The MS DOS emulation does provide the `actime` field in the structure, but the value is ignored by the call.

4.2BSD has replaced the call with a similar call `utimes`, which provides resolution down to the microsecond, and declared the `utime` call to be obsolete. Fortunately, it provides a `utime` subroutine in section 3C, implemented using `utimes`, which supports the old interface.

Because of the variation among the various systems and standards, the most portable way to use `utime` is the original convention. Create an array of two `time_t` (or `long`) values and pass a pointer to the array. Times are of type `time_t`.

```
#include <sys/types.h>

time_t utbuf[2];


    . . .
    utbuf[0] = access time;
    utbuf[1] = modification time;
    (void) utime(path, utbuf);
```

wait   wait for child to finish   **

This routine is part of all UNIX libraries, so it is very portable among UNIX systems.

The `wait` system call is one of the few system calls returning a structured value whose interface is still defined in terms of bits and masks by the SVID and POSIX standards.

4.2BSD has created a `union wait` structure, defined in `<sys/wait.h>`, and an enhanced version of the call called `wait3`, but these are specific to Berkeley. POSIX created a call `waitpid`, which is similar to `wait3`.

Portable code should call `wait` and pass an `int *` parameter.

write   write to file   ***

This routine is part of most C libraries, and it is extremely portable among UNIX systems. Although ANSI C does not require `write` to be present, it is in fact present on most implementations.

Normally, a program will use `fwrite` or other standard I/O routines instead of `write`. The appropriate times to call `write` are when standard I/O has a serious performance impact or when standard I/O causes some unwanted buffering property.

In addition to the C language and the C library, an important part of any working C program is the set of system header files, such as <stdio.h>. These files are needed to access even the most basic library functions and facilities, such as input and output.

Unfortunately, the names and contents of header files vary as widely as any other feature of the language. Extensions are often implemented trivially by adding a macro to an include file.

Only a small group of header files can be expected to be present in most C implementations. This chapter describes the core set of include files, and what can be portably expected of each file.

The new ANSI C standard created several new header files. Until ANSI C becomes widespread, these new header files must be considered unportable. The new files defined by ANSI C are <float.h>, <limits.h>, <locale.h>, <stdarg.h>, <stddef.h>, and <stdlib.h>. In addition, POSIX has defined <unistd.h>, which should be given the same treatment.

A missing include file is difficult to deal with portably. If the program tries to #include a header file that is not present, a fatal compilation error usually results. There is no way to check, using a #if line or similar feature, to determine whether a particular include file exists.

If you need a feature that is present in a header file, but the header file is not widely available, it will be necessary to use #ifdef to include it only when it is available. The choice of method to key on the #ifdef can be tricky.

Sometimes it will be possible to use a definition from a portable header file to make the decision. For example, to determine whether to #include <sgtty.h> with 4.2BSD or <termio.h> on System V, a portable header file such as <stdio.h> can be included, and the contents can be inspected. System V defines the variable L_ctermid, but 4.2BSD does not. This makes the following code fragment possible:

```
/* This often works, but is dangerous */
#include <stdio.h>

#ifdef L_ctermid
# define SYSV
#endif

#ifdef SYSV
# include <termio.h>
#else
# include <sgtty.h>
#endif
```

The method above can be made to work, but it is inherently dangerous. The problem is that, sooner or later, some system will create a hybrid of the two systems, and the test will fail. (In fact, this problem arose on Sun workstations as early as the mid-1980s.) Whether L_ctermid is defined or not has nothing to do with the choice between <termio.h> and <sgtty.h> it just happens to work on the two systems tried. Some systems based on 4.2BSD contain some System V features to ease compatibility. If such a system defines L_ctermid in <stdio.h>, the test will fail.

A safer method, if less automatic, is to set up a configuration section to be handled manually. The flag SYSV may be defined from an external source, allowing the person installing the software to personally decide which compile time options to enable.

There are several methods to configure such flags. For short programs, a section near the front of the program can contain declarations like this:

```
#define SYSV          /* System V */
/* #define BSD           4.2 BSD */
```

The /* comment marker can be moved around to enable or disable a particular option.

Unfortunately, the construct

```
/* #define BSD          /* 4.2 BSD */
```

is not portable because some compilers see the extra /* inside a comment, and, thinking a programmer may have omitted a trailing */ somewhere, will issue a warning.

Another method is to create a private header file with a name like config.h with all local configuration options present. This directs the installer's attention to one place, especially if the installation instructions point out the configuration step and file.

Another method is to define the flags in the makefile. It is common to see a list of options, each prefixed by −D or −U, at the front of the makefile.

```
OPTIONS=    -DSYSV -UBSD
CFLAGS=     -c -O $(OPTIONS)
```

Since the −U option will be ignored for flags not already defined, the effect is to have commented out the BSD option, preserving it for subsequent editing. True comments can also be used if you prefer:

```
OPTIONS=      -DSYSV
# OPTIONS=    -DBSD
CFLAGS=       -c -O $(OPTIONS)
```

Of course, in either case, you should provide documentation explaining what the various options are for and when each should be enabled. The best place for this is in the makefile or header file, and a copy in the written documentation is not a bad idea either.

```
# Compile time options:
#           SYSV  Defined for System V systems.
#           BSD   Defined for 4.2BSD systems.
#
OPTIONS=      -DSYSV
# OPTIONS=    -DBSD
CFLAGS=       -c -O $(OPTIONS)
```

Similar methods can be used for features that are sometimes present in a header file that you are sure is there. (Perhaps you are sure the header file is there because it is described as portable in this chapter, or perhaps because the code in question is already inside an #ifdef that only applies if the file is present.)

You can key on the feature itself, if it is in the form of a macro, or on some related macro from the file.

For example, suppose you want to use the FIONREAD ioctl command, but your program must also run on systems that don't support it. Fortunately, FIONREAD is a macro, and you can key as follows:

```
/* This assumes <sys/ioctl.h> has already been #included. */
#ifdef FIONREAD
      ... code to use FIONREAD ...
#else
      ... code to avoid FIONREAD ...
#endif
```

Some features of header files do not use macros and cannot be detected by the preprocessor. For example, the same built-in type is called ushort on System V and u_short on 4.2BSD. There is no way the preprocessor can tell which one you have; any such uses must be based on a configured symbol such as SYSV. (Don't use a complex solution when a simple one will do: in this example, it's easier and far more portable to just declare your variables as unsigned short.)

If your application will be cross-compiled, beware that the translation environment may be different from the execution environment. Since the preprocessor is in effect executing in the translation environment, any computations done may not be the same as in the run time system. For example, tests such as the following test the translation hardware, not the execution hardware.

```
#if 32767 + 1 < 0
```

The remainder of this chapter discusses the most widely available system header files and their contents. Any header file not described here should be considered unportable, as it is present on only one of the systems surveyed or is present but still considered unportable.

For example, most of the `<sys/*.h>` header files on the UNIX system are intended to be specific not only to the UNIX system, but to the implementation of the operating system kernel itself. In practice, a few of these files have become a standard part of the UNIX system environment and are even present in some other operating systems. Most of the `<sys/*.h>` files, and other header files whose names contain a slash, are not portable.

A feature is described here only if it is in either a standards document, such as ANSI C or POSIX, or if it is present in more than one system. Features specific to one system are omitted to save space.

These tables *should not* be taken as a rating of specific products or releases of products. It is recognized that newer releases will often support more features. The purpose of these tables is to rate the *portability of the feature*. Older releases have been deliberately used to better show the degree to which any given feature has historically been in the mainstream.

The tables for each header file show the name of the feature and for each feature, the status of that feature in each system supporting the header file. Systems not listed do not include the header file.

E   indicates that the feature is supported and is an `enum`.

F   indicates that the feature is supported and is a function. (Functions whose declarations are present in header files are not listed here, unless they are conventionally implemented as macros.)

J   indicates a macro that is only present on systems supporting job control.

M   indicates that the feature is supported and is a macro.

O   indicates that the feature is optional and may or may not be present in any given system conforming to this standard.

S   indicates that the feature is supported and is a `struct`.

T   indicates that the feature is supported and is a `typedef`.

-   indicates that the feature is not supported.

The following abbreviations are used for the columns:

4.2   Present in the header file in 4.2BSD.

ANSI   Required in header files of systems conforming to ANSI X3J11 C.

DOS-MS   Present in the header file of the Microsoft C compiler, version 4.0, for the MS DOS system.

DOS-TC   Present in the header file of the Borland Turbo C compiler, version 1.0, for the MS DOS system.

POSIX   Required in header files of systems conforming to IEEE P1003.2.

SVID   Required in header files of systems conforming to the System V Interface
               Definition, Issue 2, in the basic subset (e.g., BA_OS) or terminfo extension
               (e.g., TI_LIB).

SVR2   Present in the header file in System V release 2.

SVR3   Present in the header file in System V release 3. (Used when the header is
               new in SVR3.)

n   The feature is present in *n* of the systems listed.

<a.out.h>

This header file is specific to the UNIX system. It has historically described the format of an executable file, often called an *a.out* file. Usually, a program needing this information is part of the standard software that comes with the computer system or as a language-processing add-on specifically intended for that particular system. These programs include compilers, assemblers, loaders, debuggers, and programs that manipulate the symbol table, such as nm and ar.

When a user program includes this file, it is usually because it uses the nlist function. Some systems have documented the nlist interface in a more portable way, using the file <nlist.h>. Even these programs tend to look into the UNIX kernel, which is not a very portable thing to do.

In general, use of <a.out.h> should be considered highly system-specific and unportable. For some applications, it may be possible to attain an acceptable level of portability among UNIX systems, but this usage will not generally port to other systems.

a.out.h			
MACRO	V7	4.2	SVR2	n
exec	S	S	S	3
N_ABS	–	M	M	2
N_BSS	–	M	M	2
N_DATA	–	M	M	2
N_EXT	–	M	M	2
N_FN	–	M	M	2
N_TEXT	–	M	M	2
N_TYPE	–	M	M	2
N_UNDF	–	M	M	2

`<ar.h>`

This file defines the contents of system archives, normally used as binary object libraries, but sometimes used as a convenient grouping tool. Unfortunately, the archive format and usage varys considerably from system to system, and among these variations, there is no portable way to manipulate archives using this header file.

Fortunately, all the major variants of the UNIX system have standardized on the same archive format, sometimes called the *portable archive format*, developed by Dennis Ritchie. Rather than using a binary header, portable archive headers are a single line of ASCII text. This ensures that archives can be copied to other computer systems and still be read. It is even possible to mail archives electronically and easily extract the individual files on another system. The portable archive format first appeared in V8, 4.0BSD, and System V release 2. UNIX systems based on older releases may use other, less portable formats.

ar.h			
MACRO	4.2	SVR2	n
ARFMAG	M	M	2
ARMAG	M	M	2
ar_hdr	S	S	2

`<assert.h>`

This header file is quite portable in practice, along with the `assert` function. It is present in nearly the same form on nearly all systems. The use of the compilation flag `NDEBUG` to disable assertions is also widely supported.

assert.h					
MACRO	DOS-MS	DOS-TC	4.2	SVR2	ANSI	n
assert	M	M	M	M	M	5

`<ctype.h>`

This header file is universally available, since it is part of the standard I/O package. Not all macros are present everywhere, however. The macros `isalnum`, `isalpha`, `iscntrl`, `isdigit`, `islower`, `isprint`, `ispunct`, `isspace`, `isupper`, and `isxdigit` are present in modern systems.

The `isascii` and `toascii` macros are generally implemented, but not required by POSIX or ANSI C, since their utility is questionable in an international environment.

The `tolower` and `toupper` macros are implemented as functions in System V, so their use is quite portable, as long as the arguments do not have side effects. (Constructions such as `tolower(*p++)` are not portable, because some systems implement these as macros.)

The less well-known `_tolower` and `_toupper` macros are present in many, but not all, systems, and are not required by the standards. Since their only use is a more efficient version of `tolower` and `toupper`, there is seldom a good reason to use them.

In the following table, macros marked with an `F` are present, but implemented as a function rather than a macro.

ctype.h							
MACRO	DOS-MS	DOS-TC	4.2	SVR2	SVID	ANSI	n
isalnum	M	M	M	M	M	M	6
isalpha	M	M	M	M	M	M	6
isascii	M	M	M	M	M	–	5
iscntrl	M	M	M	M	M	M	6
isdigit	M	M	M	M	M	M	6
isgraph	M	M	–	M	M	M	5
islower	M	M	M	M	M	M	6
isprint	M	M	M	M	M	M	6
ispunct	M	M	M	M	M	M	6
isspace	M	M	M	M	M	M	6
isupper	M	M	M	M	M	M	6
isxdigit	M	M	M	M	M	M	6
toascii	M	M	M	M	M	–	5
tolower	M	F	M	F	F	M	3
toupper	M	F	M	F	F	M	3
_tolower	M	M	–	M	M	–	4
_toupper	M	M	–	M	M	–	4

`<curses.h>`

The curses package is present only on UNIX Systems, although it is available for some other systems, such as MS DOS, as a third party add-on. The System V and Berkeley versions of curses are quite different, however. In general, the System V curses includes most of the features of the Berkeley version, and a large number of extensions.

Symbolic constants and variables present in both versions are COLS, ERR, FALSE, LINES, OK, and TRUE.

The type WINDOW is defined and portable among the two systems. The type SGTTY is defined on both systems, but since it is a `struct sgtty` on one system and a `struct termio` on the other, any use of the fields of this type is unportable. The type `bool` is present on both systems, although since its use has little to do with screen management, it is not recommended. Use of the `reg` macro in Berkeley's `<curses.h>` file is strongly discouraged.

The built-in window pointers `stdscr`, and `curscr` are defined in both versions. Use of `stdscr` is quite portable. Use of `curscr` should be restricted to the `clearok` function, since the two implementations are quite different.

curses.h									
MACRO	4.2	SVR2	SVID	n	MACRO	4.2	SVR2	SVID	n
addch	M	M	M	3	mvaddstr	M	M	M	3
addstr	M	M	M	3	mvdelch	M	M	M	3
bool	T	T	T	3	mvgetch	M	M	M	3
chtype	–	T	T	2	mvgetstr	M	M	M	3
clear	M	M	M	3	mvinch	M	M	M	3
clrtobot	M	M	M	3	mvinsch	M	M	M	3
clrtoeol	M	M	M	3	mvwaddch	M	M	M	3
COLS	M	M	M	3	mvwaddstr	M	M	M	3
curscr	M	M	M	3	mvwdelch	M	M	M	3
Def_term	M	M	–	2	mvwgetch	M	M	M	3
delch	M	M	M	3	mvwgetstr	M	M	M	3
deleteln	M	M	M	3	mvwinch	M	M	M	3
erase	M	M	M	3	mvwinsch	M	M	M	3
ERR	M	M	M	3	OK	M	M	M	3
FALSE	M	M	M	3	refresh	M	M	M	3
getch	M	M	M	3	SCREEN	–	T	T	2
getstr	M	M	M	3	SGTTY	T	T	–	2
getyx	M	M	M	3	standend	M	M	M	3
inch	M	M	M	3	standout	M	M	M	3
insch	M	M	M	3	stdscr	M	M	M	3
insertln	M	M	M	3	TRUE	M	M	M	3
LINES	M	M	M	3	ttytype	M	M	–	2
move	M	M	M	3	winch	M	M	M	3
mvaddch	M	M	M	3	WINDOW	T	T	T	3

`<dirent.h>`

This header file is new in POSIX, and should be considered somewhat unportable until POSIX becomes widespread. AT&T System V release 3 was the first release of System V to support this file. Its purpose is, however, similar to header files present in older Berkeley systems as `<sys/dir.h>` or `<ndir.h>`. There are minor differences between the header files that may affect portability, such as the use of `struct direct` in Berkeley systems and `struct dirent` in POSIX. Only the d_name field should be considered truly portable, although the d_ino field will also be generally present.

The directory routines described in Chapter 11 can be ported to any UNIX system, if it doesn't already come with the system. It is not a major undertaking to port programs that use these routines.

If you are faced with a task that requires a sequential scan through a directory, these routines are probably the most portable method to use. Use of `read` into 16-byte structures is very unportable, as it assumes the presence of the original UNIX filesystem. Since 4.2BSD uses a different filesystem format, as do MS DOS and distributed systems such as RFS and NFS, this assumption is quickly becoming invalid.

dirent.h		
MACRO	POSIX	n
dirent	S	1

`<errno.h>`

This header file is specific to the UNIX system. It is required by POSIX and SVID, but not by ANSI C. Some non-UNIX implementations do support <errno.h>, but many do not. The `errno` notion should be considered portable only among UNIX systems.

Within UNIX systems, the set of possible error numbers includes a standard core, and many system-specific extensions. Errors such as EACCES and EEXIST are supported everywhere. Others, such as Berkeley's ECONNREFUSED, only make sense under some circumstances. Still others, such as ENAMETOOLONG, are new and not universally available.

If you really need to use an `errno` value, and it is not universally supported, you can check for it using `#ifdef` and conditionally compile your test accordingly. Be sure to check for an unexpected `errno` value and take appropriate action.

Most <errno.h> header files declare the `errno` variable, but some do not. It is most portable to declare it yourself.

Note that EDOM and ERANGE may be defined in <errno.h> or <math.h> or both.

errno.h						
FUNCT	DOS-MS	DOS-TC	4.2	SVR2	SVID	POSIX	n
E2BIG	M	M	M	M	M	M	6
EACCES	M	M	M	M	M	M	6
EAGAIN	M	M	M	M	M	M	6
EBADF	M	M	M	M	M	M	6
EBUSY	M	M	M	M	M	M	6
ECHILD	M	M	M	M	M	M	6
EDEADLK	–	–	–	M	M	M	3
EDOM	M	M	M	M	M	–	5
EEXIST	M	M	M	M	M	M	6
EFAULT	M	M	M	M	M	M	6
EFBIG	M	M	M	M	M	M	6
EINTR	M	M	M	M	M	M	6
EINVAL	M	M	M	M	M	M	6
EIO	M	M	M	M	M	M	6
EISDIR	M	M	M	M	M	M	6
EMFILE	M	M	M	M	M	M	6
EMLINK	M	M	M	M	M	M	6
ENAMETOOLONG	–	–	M	–	-	M	2
ENFILE	M	M	M	M	M	M	6
ENODEV	M	M	M	M	M	M	6
ENOENT	M	M	M	M	M	M	6
ENOEXEC	M	M	M	M	M	M	6
ENOMEM	M	M	M	M	M	M	6
ENOSPC	M	M	M	M	M	M	6
ENOTBLK	M	M	M	M	M	–	5
ENOTDIR	M	M	M	M	M	M	6
ENOTTY	M	M	M	M	M	M	6
ENXIO	M	M	M	M	M	M	6
EPERM	M	M	M	M	M	M	6
EPIPE	M	M	M	M	M	M	6
ERANGE	M	M	M	M	M	M	6
EROFS	M	M	M	M	M	M	6
errno	–	M	–	–	M	–	2
ESPIPE	M	M	M	M	M	M	6
ESRCH	M	M	M	M	M	M	6
ETXTBSY	M	M	M	M	M	–	5
EUCLEAN	M	M	–	–	–	-	2
EXDEV	M	M	M	M	M	M	6
EZERO	M	M	–	–	–	-	2

<fcntl.h>

This header file and the associated `fcntl` system call were new additions to UNIX System III. They are not present in older systems, nor in non-UNIX systems. The SVID and POSIX require `fcntl`. 4.2BSD has a nearly compatible `fcntl` call.

In general, it is more portable to use the options to the `open` call than the `fcntl` call, but there can be portability problems here, too. The use of `#include` to get symbolic constants such as `O_RDONLY` is not portable to older systems. Not all options are supported on all systems. In general, it is better to use the `fopen` standard I/O call.

Another complication is that the System V `O_NDELAY` option has been replaced in POSIX by the similar `O_NONBLOCK` option. Some careful use of the preprocessor can avoid a problem here.

```
#include <fcntl.h>

#ifndef O_NONBLOCK
# define O_NONBLOCK O_NDELAY
#endif
```

The difference between `O_NDELAY` and `O_NONBLOCK` is in the value returned by `read` when the call would have otherwise blocked. System V's `O_NDELAY` returns 0, which cannot be distinguished from a real read of no data. 4BSD's `O_NDELAY` returns an error, EWOULDBLOCK, and applies the behavior to all file descriptors with the same file open. `O_NONBLOCK` returns an error EAGAIN in this case. Although the calls are not interchangable, they are similar enough that some applications may be able to use either flag.

fcntl.h							
MACRO	DOS-MS	DOS-TC	4.2	SVR2	SVID	POSIX	n
FD_CLOEXEC	–	–	–	·	–	M	1
F_DUPFD	–	–	M	M	M	M	4
F_GETFD	–	–	M	M	M	M	4
F_GETFL	–	–	M	M	M	M	4
F_SETFD	–	–	M	M	M	M	4
F_SETFL	–	–	M	M	M	M	4
O_APPEND	M	M	M	M	–	M	5
O_BINARY	M	M	–	–	–	·	2
O_CREAT	M	M	–	M	M	M	5
O_EXCL	M	M	–	M	M	M	5
O_NDELAY	–	–	M	M	M	–	3
O_NONBLOCK	–	–	–	·	–	M	1
O_RDONLY	M	M	M	M	M	M	6
O_RDWR	M	M	M	M	M	M	6
O_TEXT	M	M	–	–	–	·	2
O_TRUNC	M	M	–	M	M	M	5
O_WRONLY	M	M	M	M	M	M	6

`<float.h>`

This file is a new creation of ANSI C and should not be considered portable until ANSI C is available on all systems in which you are interested.

Since it is possible to create an appropriate `<float.h>` file by hand, an acceptable compromise is to use the quote syntax:

```
#include "float.h"
```

and to supply an appropriate file when porting to an implementation not supporting this file.

float.h			
MACRO	DOS-TC	ANSI	n
DBL_DIG	M	M	2
DBL_MAX_EXP	M	M	2
DBL_MIN_EXP	M	M	2
FLT_DIG	M	M	2
FLT_MAX_EXP	M	M	2
FLT_MIN_EXP	M	M	2
FLT_RADIX	M	M	2
FLT_ROUNDS	M	M	2
LDBL_DIG	M	M	2
LDBL_MAX_EXP	M	M	2
LDBL_MIN_EXP	M	M	2

`<grp.h>`

This file is available on all UNIX systems since V7 in essentially the same format. Although it is rare to need this file, it is portable among UNIX systems. The file and the group concept it represents are specific to the UNIX system and should be considered unportable to other environments.

grp.h			
MACRO	4.2	SVR2	POSIX	n
group	S	S	S	3

<limits.h>

This file is new with ANSI C and POSIX, and should be considered unportable until these standards become widespread. For example, it was first supported by System V in release 3. Since it defines local information, an acceptable compromise can be built, as described under <float.h> above. It is possible to write a small program to automatically generate much of this file; use it as part of your configuration procedure.

One complication is that although ANSI C requires a list of 15 standard values in this header file, POSIX goes further, requiring an additional 22 values. If you need a value on the POSIX list, such as OPEN_MAX, your program may not port to other environments. Some POSIX environments not supporting ANSI C may not provide the ANSI limits.

limits.h					
MACRO	DOS-MS	DOS-TC	POSIX	ANSI	n
ARG_MAX	–	–	M	–	1
CHAR_BIT	M	M	–	M	3
CHAR_MAX	M	M	–	M	3
CHAR_MIN	–	M	–	M	2
CHILD_MAX	–	–	M	–	1
CLK_TCK	–	–	M	M	2
INT_MAX	M	M	–	M	3
INT_MIN	M	M	–	M	3
LINK_MAX	–	–	M	–	1
LONG_MAX	M	M	–	M	3
LONG_MIN	M	M	–	M	3
MAX_CANON	–	–	M	–	1
MAX_INPUT	–	–	M	–	1
NAME_MAX	–	–	M	–	1
NGROUPS_MAX	–	–	M	–	1
OPEN_MAX	–	–	M	–	1
PATH_MAX	–	–	M	–	1
PID_MAX	–	–	M	–	1
PIPE_BUF	–	–	M	–	1
SCHAR_MAX	M	M	–	M	3
SCHAR_MIN	M	M	–	M	3
SHRT_MAX	M	M	–	M	3
SHRT_MIN	M	M	–	M	3
UCHAR_MAX	M	M	–	M	3
UINT_MAX	M	M	–	M	3
ULONG_MAX	M	M	–	M	3
USHRT_MAX	M	M	–	M	3

`<locale.h>`

This file is new with ANSI C and should be considered unportable until ANSI C becomes widespread. Since it was a relatively recent addition to ANSI C, the concept of a locale is not supported in some C implementations that claim conformance to ANSI C. Locales will eventually become a valuable tool for creating highly portable programs for the international community. Until that time, you may wish to make use of them, and provide a simple emulation library that supports only the local locale for systems that do not support them.

locale.h		
MACRO	POSIX	n
LC_ALL	M	1
LC_COLLATE	M	1
LC_CTYPE	M	1
LC_NUMERIC	M	1
LC_TIME	M	1

`<malloc.h>`

This file should be considered unportable. Although it is present in System V, it is only used by the optional `-lmalloc` library, which is not usually used.

Note that although DOS-MS (Microsoft C) supports the `<malloc.h>` header file, the file does not define any macros.

malloc.h				
MACRO	DOS-MS	SVR2	SVID	n
M_GRAIN	–	M	M	2
M_KEEP	–	M	M	2
M_MXFAST	–	M	M	2
M_NLBLKS	–	M	M	2
mallinfo	–	–	S	1

<math.h>

Although this file is almost always present, the contents vary widely. ANSI C requires only that EDOM, ERANGE, and HUGE_VAL be defined. (The first two are values also found in <errno.h>.) Since existing implementations generally do not define these values, it is not safe to assume they are present.

Existing header files based on System V include DOMAIN, HUGE, OVERFLOW, PLOSS, SING, TLOSS, and UNDERFLOW. These are sometimes supported on other systems, too.

The value HUGE is traditionally present, although the standards are migrating this into HUGE_VAL instead. HUGE often was just MAXFLOAT, a possible legal floating-point value. On IEEE 754 compliant machines, HUGE_VAL may be ∞.

The exception structure found in System V and the MS DOS system should be considered unportable, as it is not widely implemented, and not required by any standard.

math.h							
MACRO	DOS-MS	DOS-TC	4.2	SVR2	SVID	ANSI	n
complex	T	T	–	–	–	-	2
DOMAIN	M	–	–	M	M	–	3
EDOM	–	M	–	–	–	M	2
ERANGE	–	M	–	–	–	M	2
exception	S	S	–	S	–	–	3
HUGE	–	–	M	M	M	–	3
HUGE_VAL	M	M	–	–	–	M	3
M_1_PI	–	M	–	M	–	–	2
M_2_PI	–	M	–	M	–	–	2
M_2_SQRTPI	–	M	–	M	–	–	2
M_E	–	M	–	M	–	–	2
M_LN10	–	M	–	M	–	–	2
M_LN2	–	M	–	M	–	–	2
M_LOG10E	–	M	–	M	–	–	2
M_LOG2E	–	M	–	M	–	–	2
M_PI	–	M	–	M	–	–	2
M_PI_2	–	M	–	M	–	–	2
M_PI_4	–	M	–	M	–	–	2
M_SQRT2	–	M	–	M	–	–	2
OVERFLOW	M	–	–	M	M	–	3
PLOSS	M	–	–	M	M	–	3
SING	M	–	–	M	M	–	3
TLOSS	M	–	–	M	M	–	3
UNDERFLOW	M	–	–	M	M	–	3

`<memory.h>`

This file is present in a few systems based on System V, but is not part of POSIX or ANSI C. Systems supporting this header file include SVR2, the SVID, and MS DOS. The file consists of declarations of memory functions.

`<nlist.h>`

This file is present in recent UNIX versions, including 4.2BSD and System V release 2. It is useful for some applications to use calling `nlist`, but, in general, should not be considered portable.

The only fields in the `nlist` structure that are at all portable between Berkeley and System V are n_name, n_value, and n_type, and there are minor differences between the types the two systems use for n_value (Berkeley uses `long`, System V uses `unsigned long`) and n_type (Berkeley uses `unsigned char`, System V uses `unsigned short`). Any program using `nlist` is likely to contain assumptions about the internal representation of another program.

nlist.h			
MACRO	4.2	SVR2	n
nlist	S	S	2

`<pwd.h>`

This file is present in all UNIX systems, and is required by POSIX but not by the SVID. In general, it should be considered unportable outside the UNIX system, and its portability within UNIX systems, while high, may become questionable in the future.

pwd.h				
MACRO	4.2	SVR2	POSIX	n
passwd	S	S	S	3

`<search.h>`

This file should be considered specific to System V. Although required by the SVID, it is not present in other standards or implementations. It contains declarations of constant macros used by `hsearch` and `tsearch`. The Microsoft MS DOS `<search.h>` is an unrelated file, containing function declarations used for `bsearch`, `lsearch`, `lfind`, and `qsort`.

search.h				
MACRO	DOS-MS	SVR2	SVID	n
ACTION	–	T	T	2
ENTRY	–	T	T	2
VISIT	–	T	T	2

`<setjmp.h>`

This file is extremely portable, present in all C implementations since V7. As long as the programmer assumes only the declaration of the `jmp_buf` type, the only portability concerns should be those associated with the `longjmp` call itself. See Appendix A for a description of these concerns, as described by ANSI C.

The POSIX standard requires the presence of this file, but defines only the type `sigjmp_buf` and the functions `sigsetjmp` and `siglongjmp`. Since it defines these functions in terms of the ANSI `setjmp` and `longjmp` it seems virtually certain that a POSIX implementation will also support these.

setjmp.h								
MACRO	DOS-MS	DOS-TC	4.2	SVR2	SVID	ANSI	POSIX	n
jmp_buf	T	T	T	T	T	T	T	6
sigjmp_buf	–	–	–	-	–	-	T	1

`<sgtty.h>`

This file is generally considered unportable, but under some circumstances, it can be the most portable choice. The file and the associated `stty` and `gtty` calls are highly specific to the UNIX system and do not make sense elsewhere.

System III contains a rewritten terminal driver and replaces `<sgtty.h>` with `<termio.h>` using a very different interface. Although no standards document requires `<sgtty.h>`, in practice it is usually provided as an upward-compatibility aid. Thus, for programs with simple needs, this service may be more portable than a conditionally compiled mass of `TIOCSETP` and `TCSETA` `ioctl` calls.

The programmer should probably avoid this call on an interactive user's terminal. Many System III and System V implementations of stty and TIOCSETP clear the popular ECHOE bit in the enhanced termio driver, which may make users unhappy. Also beware that the CBREAK and TANDEM modes are not supported by the System III derived emulation. TANDEM mode should be avoided at all costs.

sgtty.h							
MACRO	4.2	SVR2	n	MACRO	4.2	SVR2	n
ALLDELAY	M	M	2	EXTA	M	M	2
ANYP	M	M	2	EXTB	M	M	2
B0	M	M	2	FF0	M	M	2
B110	M	M	2	FF1	M	M	2
B1200	M	M	2	FIOCLEX	M	M	2
B134	M	M	2	FIONCLEX	M	M	2
B150	M	M	2	HUPCL	–	M	1
B1800	M	M	2	LCASE	M	M	2
B200	M	M	2	NL0	M	M	2
B2400	M	M	2	NL1	M	M	2
B300	M	M	2	NL2	M	M	2
B4800	M	M	2	NL3	M	M	2
B50	M	M	2	NLDELAY	M	M	2
B600	M	M	2	NOAL	–	M	1
B75	M	M	2	ODDP	M	M	2
B9600	M	M	2	RAW	M	M	2
BS0	M	M	2	sgttyb	S	S	2
BS1	M	M	2	TAB0	M	M	2
BSDELAY	M	M	2	TAB1	M	M	2
CBREAK	M	–	1	TANDEM	M	–	1
CR0	M	M	2	TBDELAY	M	M	2
CR1	M	M	2	TIOCEXCL	M	M	2
CR2	M	M	2	TIOCGETP	M	M	2
CR3	M	M	2	TIOCHPCL	M	M	2
CRDELAY	M	M	2	TIOCNXCL	M	M	2
CRMOD	M	M	2	TIOCSETP	M	M	2
ECHO	M	M	2	VTDELAY	M	M	2
EVENP	M	M	2	XTABS	M	M	2

`<signal.h>`

The `signal` function and header file are widely available, but the set of required signals varies from system to system. Only a few signals, such as `SIGINT`, make sense on operating systems other than the UNIX system. ANSI C requires `SIGFPE`, `SIGILL`, `SIGINT`, `SIGSEGV`, and `SIGTERM`.

Unportable signals include `SIGEMT`, `SIGIOT`, `SIGSYS`, `SIGUSR1`, and `SIGUSR2`. `SIGABRT` is new with ANSI C and is not portable until it catches on. `SIG_DFL` and `SIG_IGN` are universally available.

In this table, `J` indicates that the function is present only on systems with job control.

signal.h								
MACRO	DOS-MS	DOS-TC	4.2	SVR2	SVID	POSIX	ANSI	n
NSIG	M	–	M	M	–	–	–	3
SA_CLDSTOP	–	–	–	-	–	J	–	1
SIGABRT	–	–	–	-	–	M	M	2
sigaction	–	–	–	-	–	M	–	1
SIGALRM	–	–	–	M	M	M	–	3
SIGBUS	–	–	M	M	–	M	–	3
SIGCLD	–	–	–	M	–	J	–	2
SIGCONT	–	–	M	–	-	J	–	1
SIGEMT	–	–	M	M	–	M	–	3
SIGFPE	M	M	M	M	M	M	M	7
SIGHUP	–	–	M	M	M	M	–	4
SIGILL	–	M	M	M	M	M	M	6
SIGINT	M	M	M	M	M	M	M	7
SIGIOT	–	–	M	M	–	M	–	3
SIGKILL	–	–	M	M	M	M	–	4
SIGPIPE	–	–	M	M	M	M	–	4
SIGQUIT	–	–	M	M	M	M	–	4
SIGSEGV	–	M	M	M	–	M	M	5
SIGSTOP	–	–	M	–	-	J	–	1
SIGSYS	–	–	M	M	M	–	-	3
SIGTERM	–	M	M	M	M	M	M	6
SIGTRAP	–	-	M	M	M	M	-	4
SIGTSTP	–	–	M	–	-	J	–	1
SIGTTIN	–	–	M	–	-	J	–	1
SIGTTOU	–	–	M	–	-	J	–	1
SIGUSR1	–	–	–	M	M	M	–	3
SIGUSR2	–	–	–	M	M	M	–	3
SIG_DFL	M	M	M	M	M	M	M	7
SIG_ERR	–	M	–	–	–	M	M	3
SIG_IGN	M	M	M	M	M	M	M	7

`<stat.h>`

This file is not generally available. UNIX systems always have the file `<sys/stat.h>` available for the UNIX-specific `stat` system call. Only System V provides `<stat.h>`. Most applications should use `<sys/stat.h>` if `stat` must be called.

stat.h			
MACRO	SVR2	SVID	n
stat	M	M	3

`<stdarg.h>`

This file is new with ANSI C and replaces the similar `<varargs.h>` present in older systems. The files are not entirely compatible, since ANSI C uses the ellipsis for variable argument lists, but it is not difficult to port a program from one environment to the other.

stdarg.h			
MACRO	DOS-MS	DOS-TC	ANSI	n
va_arg	M	M	M	3
va_end	M	M	M	3
va_list	M	M	M	3
va_start	M	M	M	3

`<stddef.h>`

This file is new with ANSI C and should be considered unportable until it catches on. The `offsetof` macro was added to ANSI C late in the standardization process, and some implementations claiming ANSI compatibility may be missing this macro.

stddef.h			
MACRO	DOS-MS	DOS-TC	ANSI	n
errno	M	M	M	3
NULL	M	M	M	3

`<stdio.h>`

This file is present in all C implementations since PWB, since it is the core file of the standard I/O package. Not all macros are supported in all systems, however, so care should be taken to consult the table. Some macros, such as `P_tmpdir`, are specific to one system. Others, such as `OPEN_MAX`, are new with ANSI C, and may duplicate values that POSIX places in `<limits.h>`.

stdio.h								
MACRO	DOS-MS	DOS-TC	4.2	SVR2	SVID	POSIX	ANSI	n
BUFSIZ	M	M	M	M	–	–	M	5
EOF	M	M	M	M	M	–	M	6
feof	M	M	M	M	–	–	–	4
ferror	M	–	M	M	–	–	–	3
FILE	T	T	T	T	T	T	T	7
fileno	M	M	M	M	–	–	–	4
getc	M	M	M	M	–	–	–	4
getchar	M	M	M	M	–	–	–	4
L_ctermid	–	M	–	M	–	–	–	2
L_tmpnam	M	M	–	M	M	–	M	5
NULL	M	–	M	M	M	–	–	4
OPEN_MAX	–	M	–	–	–	-	M	2
putc	M	M	M	M	–	–	–	4
putchar	M	M	M	M	–	–	–	4
P_tmpdir	M	–	–	M	M	–	-	3
SEEK_CUR	M	M	–	–	–	-	M	3
SEEK_END	M	M	–	–	–	-	M	3
SEEK_SET	M	M	–	–	–	-	M	3
stderr	M	M	M	M	M	–	M	6
stdin	M	M	M	M	M	–	M	6
stdout	M	M	M	M	M	–	M	6
SYS_OPEN	M	M	–	–	–	-	–	2
TMP_MAX	M	M	–	–	–	-	M	3
_iob	M	–	M	M	–	–	–	3
_IOFBF	–	M	–	–	M	–	M	3
_IOLBF	–	M	–	–	M	–	M	3
_IONBF	–	M	–	–	M	–	M	3
_NFILE	M	–	M	M	–	–	–	3

`<stdlib.h>`

This file is new with ANSI C and should be considered unportable until it catches on. Some of the types and values it declares, such as `div_t`, `ldiv_t`, and `RAND_MAX`, are not present in some early ANSI C implementations.

stdlib.h				
FUNCT	DOS-MS	DOS-TC	ANSI	n
sys_errlist	M	M	–	2
sys_nerr	M	M	–	2

`<string.h>`

This file is present in many C implementations, and consists entirely of function declarations. Berkeley uses a similar file called `<strings.h>`. The include file should be considered portable only within System V until ANSI C catches on.

`<sys/stat.h>`

This file, like all `<sys/*.h>` include files, is intended to be specific to the UNIX system. In practice, it is also supported by some MS DOS implementations, with not all fields being present. Many of the mode functions and symbolic bit names are new with POSIX.

Some file types are specific to their respective systems. These include Berkeley's `S_IFLNK` for symbolic links and `S_IFSOCK` for sockets, and System V's `S_IFIFO` for named pipes.

sys/stat.h						
FUNCT	DOS-MS	DOS-TC	4.2	SVR2	POSIX	n
stat	M	M	M	M	–	4
S_IEXEC	M	M	M	M	–	4
S_IFBLK	–	–	M	M	–	2
S_IFCHR	M	M	M	M	–	4
S_IFDIR	M	M	M	M	–	4
S_IFMT	M	M	M	M	–	4
S_IFREG	M	M	M	M	–	4
S_IREAD	M	M	M	M	–	4
S_IRGRP	–	–	–	.	M	1
S_IROTH	–	–	–	.	M	1
S_IRUSR	–	–	–	.	M	1
S_IRWXG	–	–	–	.	M	1

sys/stat.h						
FUNCT	DOS-MS	DOS-TC	4.2	SVR2	POSIX	n
S_IRWXO	–	–	–	-	M	1
S_IRWXU	–	–	–	-	M	1
S_ISBLK	–	–	–	-	M	1
S_ISCHR	–	–	–	-	M	1
S_ISDIR	–	–	–	-	M	1
S_ISFIFO	–	–	–	-	M	1
S_ISGID	–	–	M	M	M	3
S_ISREG	–	–	–	-	M	1
S_ISUID	–	–	M	M	M	3
S_ISVTX	–	–	M	M	–	2
S_IWGRP	–	–	–	-	M	1
S_IWOTH	–	–	–	-	M	1
S_IWRITE	M	M	M	M	–	4
S_IWUSR	–	-	-	-	M	1
S_IXGRP	–	-	-	-	M	1
S_IXOTH	–	-	-	-	M	1
S_IXUSR	–	-	-	-	M	1

<sys/timeb.h>

This file, like all <sys/*.h> include files, is intended to be specific to the UNIX system. In practice, it is not even portable within UNIX systems. The related ftime function is supported on V7, 4.2BSD and a few MS DOS implementations only.

sys/timeb.h			
MACRO	DOS-MS	4.2	n
timeb	M	M	2

<sys/times.h>

This file, like all <sys/*.h> include files, is intended to be specific to the UNIX system. The header file and the related times system call are present in all UNIX and POSIX systems.

sys/times.h					
MACRO	4.2	SVR2	SVID	POSIX	n
tms	S	S	S	S	4

<sys/types.h>

This file, like all <sys/*.h> include files, is intended to be specific to the UNIX system. In practice, this file is heavily used to define standard types. Unfortunately, the names for these types are not consistent across different UNIX systems.

For example, an unsigned integer is uint in System V and u_int in 4.2BSD. An unsigned long integer is u_long in 4.2BSD and an unsigned character is u_char, but neither of these types is defined by System V. ino_t is short in System V but u_long in 4.2BSD. The types daddr_t, caddr_t, time_t, dev_t, and off_t are compatibly defined in both systems.

sys/types.h						
MACRO	DOS-MS	4.2	SVR2	SVID	POSIX	n
caddr_t	–	T	T	–	–	2
clock_t	–	–	–	·	T	1
daddr_t	–	T	T	–	–	2
dev_t	T	T	T	T	T	5
ino_t	T	T	T	T	T	5
label_t	–	T	T	–	–	2
mode_t	–	–	–	·	T	1
nlink_t	–	–	–	·	T	1
off_t	T	T	T	T	T	5
physadr	–	T	T	–	–	2
size_t	T	–	T	T		
time_t	T	T	T	T	T	5
uid_t	–	–	–	·	T	1
ushort	–	T	T	T	–	3

`<sys/utsname.h>`

This file, like all `<sys/*.h>` include files, is intended to be specific to the UNIX system. It is not present in V7- and 4.2BSD-derived systems, but rather is a part of System III and System V. It is required by POSIX. See the `uname` discussion in the previous chapter for a more portable method of determining the host name.

sys/utsname.h				
MACRO	SVR2	SVID	POSIX	n
utsname	S	S	S	3

`<time.h>`

This header file is nearly universally available, but the contents vary considerably from system to system. A portable program can only assume that `struct tm` is declared. 4.2BSD distributed this file as `<sys/time.h>`, requiring a special `#ifdef` around the `#include` lines:

```
#ifdef BSD42
# include <sys/time.h>
#else
# include <time.h>
#endif
```

time.h							
MACRO	DOS-MS	DOS-TC	4.2	SVR2	SVID	ANSI	n
CLK_TCK	–	–	–	·	–	M	1
clock_t	–	–	–	·	–	T	1
daylight	M	M	–	M	–	–	3
timezone	M	M	M	M	–	–	4
time_t	T	T	–	–	–	T	3
tm	S	S	S	S	S	S	6
tzname	M	–	–	M	–	·	2

`<unistd.h>`

This file is new with POSIX and should be considered unportable until it catches on. For example, it first appears (with only a few of the options defined) in System V release 3, which was released when POSIX was still in draft form. (For this reason, the table for this section uses SVR3 instead of SVR2.) The SEEK defines are also required by ANSI C in `<stdio.h>`.

Some of these macros are defined only if an implementation supports the corresponding option. These macros are shown with an O rather than an M to indicate that they are optional.

unistd.h			
MACRO	POSIX	SVR3	n
F_LOCK	M	M	2
F_OK	M	M	2
F_TEST	M	M	2
F_TLOCK	M	M	2
F_ULOCK	M	M	2
GF_PATH	–	M	1
PF_PATH	–	M	1
R_OK	M	M	2
SEEK_CUR	M	M	2
SEEK_END	M	M	2
SEEK_SET	M	M	2
STDERR_FILENO	M	–	1
STDIN_FILENO	M	–	1
STDOUT_FILENO	M	–	1
W_OK	M	M	2
X_OK	M	M	2
_PC_CHOWN_RESTRICTED	M	–	1
_PC_CHOWN_SUP_GRP	M	–	1
_PC_DIR_DOTS	M	–	1
_PC_FCHR_MAX	M	–	1
_PC_GROUP_PARENT	M	–	1
_PC_LINK_DIR	M	–	1
_PC_LINK_MAX	M	–	1
_PC_MAX_CANON	M	–	1
_PC_MAX_INUT	M	–	1
_PC_NAME_MAX	M	–	1
_PC_NO_TRUNC	M	–	1
_PC_PATH_MAX	M	–	1
_PC_PIPE_BUF	M	–	1
_PC_UTIME_OWNER	M	–	1

unistd.h			
MACRO	POSIX	SVR3	n
_PC_V_DISABLE	M	–	1
_POSIX_CHOWN_RESTRICTED	M	–	1
_POSIX_JOB_CONTROL	O	–	1
_POSIX_NO_TRUNC	M	–	1
_POSIX_SAVED_IDS	O	–	1
_POSIX_VERSION	M	–	1
_SC_ARG_MAX	M	–	1
_SC_CHILD_MAX	M	–	1
_SC_CLK_TCK	M	–	1
_SC_EXIT_SIGHUP	M	–	1
_SC_JOB_CONTROL	M	–	1
_SC_KILL_PID_NEG1	M	–	1
_SC_KILL_SAVED	M	–	1
_SC_NGROUPS_MAX	M	–	1
_SC_OPEN_MAX	M	–	1
_SC_PASS_MAX	M	–	1
_SC_PGID_CLEAR	M	–	1
_SC_PID_MAX	M	–	1
_SC_SAVED_IDS	M	–	1
_SC_UID_MAX	M	–	1
_SC_VERSION	M	–	1

\<utmp.h\>

This file is specific to the UNIX system, but can be found in essentially identical form on all UNIX systems. It is not required by any standard. Use of this header file, and the /etc/utmp file, should be avoided if at all possible. The file format is not portable, and, in particular, the order of the entries in the file is not portable.

utmp.h			
FUNCT	4.2	SVR2	n
utmp	S	S	2

`<varargs.h>`

This file is available on all UNIX systems since V7 and on many non-UNIX C implementations. A few implementations pass the first few arguments as register variables and may not implement varargs.

ANSI C has defined a feature called stdargs, a new syntax involving the ellipsis, and a new header file `<stdarg.h>` to define the macros. Although most ANSI C implementations can be expected to continue to support varargs for upward compatibility, the stdarg mechanism can be considered the future direction of this feature.

Most implementations implement `va_end` as a no-op. A truly portable program will use `va_end` as documented, just in case some implementation requires it.

varargs.h					
MACRO	DOS-MS	4.2	SVR2	SVID	n
va_arg	M	M	M	M	4
va_dcl	M	M	M	M	4
va_end	M	M	M	M	4
va_list	T	T	T	T	4
va_start	M	M	M	M	4

CHAPTER 14: **PREDEFINED VARIABLES**

The C library normally discourages the use of global variables to communicate among differing subprograms. There are, however, a few global variables whose use can be considered portable. This chapter discusses global variables provided by the C library. Standard macros, such as NULL, are discussed in Chapter 13 with their respective include files.

There are actually many global variables in the C library. Most of them are undocumented and are considered to be for the internal use of the library. Although most such variables are declared static and are invisible to application programs, some variables are in the extern storage class.

It is possible for an application to access and make use of these undocumented variables. Such use is highly unportable, and strongly discouraged. They are discussed here only to make programmers aware that these names are used in some C libraries, so a collision could occur if the application programmer uses the same name. For this reason, these names should be treated as reserved words, and avoided by programmers, much the same as names of library functions should be avoided.

The trend among standards bodies is to discourage the use of these global variables. Even those that have historically always been present are often not documented in the standards in order to allow alternative implementations on other systems. As a rule, if you have a choice between a function interface and a variable interface, the function interface is more portable. For example, the perror function is more portable than the sys_errlist array.

As a rule, implementations that must add variables to the library should choose names that are unlikely to conflict with names chosen by the programmer. According to ANSI C, the way to do this is to begin external names with an underscore, and to begin other names with an underscore followed by another underscore or an upper-case letter. Applications needing hidden internal names should begin them with an underscore followed by a lower-case letter or digit. See Section 4.1.2.1 of the ANSI C standard, and, in particular Section 4.1.2.1 of the ANSI C Rationale.

___Argv   argument vector   *

This variable is used in UNIX System V by the monitor function. It is not documented, and should not be used by an applications programmer.

251

_bigpow   float conversion   *

This variable is used in UNIX System V by the `ecvt` and `atof` functions. It is not documented, and should not be used by an applications programmer.

_bufendtab   stdio   *

This variable is used in UNIX System V by the `stdio` package. It is not documented, and should not be used by an applications programmer.

_ctype, _ctype_   ctype table   *

These variables are used in UNIX System V and 4BSD by the `ctype` functions. They are not documented, and should not be used by an applications programmer.

_debug   dialing debug output   *

This variable is used in UNIX System V by the `dial` function. It is not documented, and should not be used by an applications programmer.

Note: because of the name of this variable, it is important that programmers take care to avoid this variable name.

_doserrno   DOS error number   *

This variable is used in the MS DOS system by the `perror` function. It is documented, but its use is highly MS DOS specific.

_fmode   text/binary file mode   *

This variable is used in the MS DOS system by the `fopen` function to control the default mode (CRLF vs. newline) of files opened. It is documented, but MS DOS specific.

_iob   stdio buffers   *

This variable is used in UNIX System V and 4BSD by the `stdio` package. It is not documented, and should not be used by an applications programmer.

_lastbuf   stdio buffers   *

This variable is used in UNIX System V and 4BSD by the `stdio` package. It is not documented, and should not be used by an applications programmer.

_litpow   floating conversions   *

This variable is used in UNIX System V by the `ecvt` and `atof` functions. It is not documented, and should not be used by an applications programmer.

_osmajor, _osminor   DOS version   *

These variables are used in the MS DOS system as part of the C library. They are documented, but are highly MS DOS specific.

_psp   program segment prefix   *

This variable is used in the MS DOS system as part of the C library. It is documented, but is highly MS DOS specific.

_sctab   scanf table   *

This variable is used in 4BSD by the scanf function. It is not documented, and should not be used by an applications programmer.

_sibuf, _sobuf   standard input buffers   *

These buffers are used in UNIX System V and 4BSD by the stdio package. They are not documented, and should not be used by an applications programmer.

Note: the _sibuf and _sobuf buffers have served as traditional buffers to use when calling setbuf on the stdin and stdout file pointers. Although this can serve as an effective way to save space, the total savings of 2*BUFSIZ are generally not worth the lack of portability caused. Unless extreme space problems can be solved by reusing these buffers, it is better to allocate your own buffers.

_stdbuf   standard I/O buffer   *

This buffer is used in UNIX System V by the stdio package. It is not documented, and should not be used by an applications programmer.

LogFile, LogMask   system log   *
LogStat, LogTag, SyslogAddr

These variables are used in 4BSD by its syslog function. They are not documented, and should not be used by an applications programmer.

countbase   profiler counter   *

This variable is used in UNIX System V by the monitor function. It is not documented, and should not be used by an applications programmer.

daylight   daylight time flag   **

This variable is used in UNIX System V by the ctime function. It is documented, and is part of the SVID and present in the MS DOS system. It is not present in 4BSD, and is not required by POSIX or ANSI C. If you require access to time zone information, you should isolate this in one part of your program. The time zone conventions are different on V7-derived systems such as 4BSD.

end, edata, etext   end of segment   **

These symbols are used in UNIX System V, 4BSD, and most other UNIX system implementations to mark the end of the text, data, and bss segments. Although they are compatible across these implementations, they are not present in other operating systems, and are not part of ANSI C, POSIX, or the SVID. Since they are very low-level symbols, used primarily by sbrk and by subroutines that save and restore memory to a file, they should be considered unportable.

errno   error number   ***

This variable is used in the perror function of most C implementations. It is documented, and is probably the most portable global variable. The meanings of the particular error values are not standardized, however, so care is indicated.

The value of errno is set when an error occurs. If no error occurs, errno may have a value remaining from the most recent error (possibly generated internally by a successful subroutine). It is only appropriate to check the value of errno after an unsuccessful operation that is known to set errno on failure.

Note: ANSI C defines errno as a macro to be defined in <stddef.h>. This include file is new with ANSI C. Users of the errno variable should take care to conditionally include the file:

```
#ifdef __STDC__
#include <stddef.h>
#endif
```

Users of errno should be careful. If your intention is to check for certain well-known errors, you can portably use symbolic names:

```
#ifdef EAGAIN
        if (errno == EAGAIN)
                /* error action */
#endif
```

It is also possible to portably call the perror function, although in some systems, this function may not know about added error numbers, such as networking errors, not present in the base system. (In this case, perror will print the integer number.)

If you intend to use the value yourself, as an index into sys_errlist or into your own table, be careful. The set of error numbers used by another system may not be the same as your system. While it is common to use the same integers, even this isn't assured. Some systems define error names with out-of-range numbers if the error can't possibly be returned on that system, as in the following from an MS DOS implementation.

```
#define EAGAIN -1
```

environ   environment   ***

This variable is used in many C implementations by the `getenv` and `putenv` functions. It is documented, and is safe only among systems that have the concept of an environment. It is required by the SVID and POSIX, but not by ANSI C. It is present on UNIX System V, 4BSD, and MS DOS systems.

numctrs   monitor   *

This variable is used in UNIX System V by the `monitor` function. It is not documented, and should not be used by an applications programmer.

optarg   getopt argument   **

This variable is used in UNIX System V and 4.3BSD by the `getopt` function. It is documented, and is as portable as `getopt`.

opterr   getopt error   *

This variable is used in UNIX System V and 4.3BSD by the `getopt` function. It is documented in UNIX System V, but is not quite as portable as `getopt`.

The `opterr` variable is documented, but was a recent addition to the UNIX System V C library, first appearing in System V release 2. As a result, the first public domain implementation of `getopt` from the University of Toronto did not support it. The 4.3BSD implementation supports, but does not document, `opterr`.

The recommended programming practice is to go ahead and use `opterr` if you need it. If, when porting your application to another system, you receive a diagnostic that `opterr` is undefined, remove the keyword `extern` in the declaration. This will allow the program to compile, but not suppress, the diagnostic.

Another alternative is to use the AT&T public domain `getopt` function provided in this book. This restricts `getopt` to the UNIX system conventions, but ensures that `opterr` will be supported.

optind   getopt index   *

This variable is used in UNIX System V by the `getopt` function. It is documented, and is as portable as `getopt`.

realloc_srchlen   realloc search length   *

This variable is used in 4BSD by the `realloc` function. It is not documented, and should not be used by an applications programmer.

`rexecoptions`   remote execution options   *

This variable is used in UNIX System V by the `rexec` function. It is not documented, and should not be used by an applications programmer.

`sys_errlist`   list of system errors   ***

This array is used in UNIX System V and 4BSD by the `perror` function. It is documented, but its use restricts the application to some C libraries. This array is supported by System V, the SVID, 4BSD, and MS DOS systems. It is not required by POSIX or ANSI C.

`sys_nerr`   number of system errors   *

This variable is used in UNIX System V and 4BSD by the `perror` function. It is documented, but its use restricts the application to some C libraries. This array is supported by System V, the SVID, 4BSD, and MS DOS systems. It is not required by POSIX or ANSI C.

`sys_siglist`   list of system signals   *

This variable is used in 4BSD by the `psignal` function. It is documented, but is specific to the 4BSD system.

`timezone`   local offset from UTC   **

This variable is used in UNIX System V by the `ctime` function. It is documented, and is part of the SVID and present in the MS DOS system. It is not present in 4BSD, and is not required by POSIX or ANSI C. If you require access to time zone information, you should isolate this in one part of your program. The time zone conventions are different on V7-derived systems such as 4BSD.

`tzname`   time zone name   **

This array is used in UNIX System V by the `ctime` function. It is documented, and is part of the SVID and present in the MS DOS system. It is not present in 4BSD, and is not required by POSIX or ANSI C. If you require access to time zone information, you should isolate this in one part of your program. The time zone conventions are different on V7-derived systems such as 4BSD.

CHAPTER 15: **USER COMMANDS**

The UNIX system consists not only of an operating system, C compiler, and library, but also a set of tools. These tools are *user commands*, sometimes called *shell commands*, often typed by the user at the keyboard. Other operating systems usually provide a set of tools, sometimes typed on a command line, sometimes called from a menu-oriented user interface.

As a rule, the set of available commands is not important to the portability of a C program. There are, however, some situations when the set of user commands can be important. The `system` and `exec` functions depend on the presence of the command they call. The program source code may include tools to help compile it, such as a *makefile* or a *shell script*, either of which may invoke user commands.

The set of available commands will be limited by the particular operating system. In this category, if you assume that user commands such as these are available, you are generally limiting yourself to UNIX systems, POSIX systems, and systems that are very similar and very compatible. This chapter applies only to such systems. Use of features described in this chapter is not generally portable beyond UNIX systems.[1]

The shell itself can be a source of unportability. The UNIX system allows each user to specify any program as the command interpreter. In practice, this program is usually one of a small set of shells: the *V6 shell* on V6 systems; the *Mashey shell* on PWB 1.0; the *Bourne shell* on V7, System III, System V, and 4BSD; the *C shell* on 4BSD and System V release 4; or the *Korn shell* on System V release 4 and other systems. All systems since V7 have supported the Bourne shell `/bin/sh`, and some additionally include the C shell `/bin/csh` and the Korn shell `/bin/ksh`.

The Mashey shell was an enhanced V6 shell. The Bourne shell descended from the V6 shell, with major changes and enhancements. The C shell is descended from the V6 shell, with many Bourne and Mashey shell features included. The Korn shell is more recent, descending from the Bourne shell, with many C shell features included.

The V6 and Mashey shells are not present in current systems. All UNIX systems will support the Bourne shell, and some may also support the C shell and/or the Korn shell.

The shells all have common elements, but use of extensions specific to one shell can cause problems when a user with a different shell compiles or uses your program. While

---

[1] Toolkits such as the Mortice Kern (MKS) Toolkit for the MS DOS system make many of these commands available in other environments.

the Korn shell is mostly a superset of the Bourne shell, the C shell is derived from the V6 shell, and is not compatible with the Bourne and Korn shells in some ways. More detailed information can be found in the sh section.

Shell scripts should always be written in Bourne shell. C shell scripts are not portable, since many systems do not offer csh. The C shell and Korn shell enhancements mainly benefit interactive users, so they are not usually important for shell scripts. (There are some useful programming features only in the Korn shell, but it is usually worthwhile to avoid them in the interest of portability.)

There have been some features added to the Bourne shell since V7 that are not portable. These include the : operator used with parameter expansion: ${x:-y} and the use of # for comments. Systems derived from V7, such as 4BSD, do not support these features. The test or [commands also vary from system to system.

The remainder of this chapter consists of discussion of specific user commands. This chapter also contains advice about specific commands present in System V and 4.2BSD. The syntax shown for each command is a portable subset. For commands defined in P1003.2, the options required by that standard are shown. For other commands, the options and arguments shown are those present in all major systems containing the command.

This chapter is guided by the IEEE POSIX 1003.2 standard, draft 9. P1003.2 was in draft form as this was written in 1989. Since the standard was incomplete at that time, some changes may occur between the publication of this book and the final 1003.2 standard.

The portability of each command is rated using 1 to 5 stars and an optional mark. The more stars, the more portable the command at the time this book is written. A mark means that since the command is required by a standards document, as that standard becomes widely implemented in the future, an additional star should be added. Ratings apply *only* to the portability of the command itself among systems released by 1988. Star ratings do not imply that all options to the command are portable, nor do they reflect whether the command is required by a standard. Some commands have been downrated, because, while the command itself may be widely available, the command cannot be used as portably by a typical application.

One star, *, means a command is *unportable,* meaning that it is specific to one system, such as System V or 4.2BSD.

Two stars, **, means a command is *portable within a family,* meaning that it was present in either V7 or System V release 1, and the descendents of that system (its family).

Three stars, ***, means a command is *fairly portable,* meaning that it is present in both System V and 4.2BSD, but was added to both systems at a later date.

Four stars, ****, means a command is *very portable,* meaning that it was present in V7 and System III, and all their descendents.

Five stars, *****, means a command is *extremely portable,* meaning that it was present in some form in V6 and all its descendents.

Some commands are inventions of the POSIX P1003.2 committee and were not present in earlier systems. In other cases, P1003.2 took an unportable command (often one specific to System V) and incorporated it into the standard. In practice, it will take a few years before it it safe to assume widespread support of these standards.

Over time, it is expected that many implementations will announce that they conform to the POSIX P1003.2 standard. As this is written, it is not clear how fast systems will move toward conformance with the standards. The most recent two major releases of System V (releases 2 and 3) occurred in 1983 and 1986. System V release 4 is scheduled for late 1989, before the P1003.2 standard is complete. Thus it is possible that several additional years will elapse until a completely conforming system is released to vendors, incorporated into existing products, and released to the public.

Commands that are new but are part of one of these standards have been given, in addition to their stars, one or two bullet marks •. These marks indicate that as the appropriate standard becomes more widespread, the portability of the command will also increase. In 1989, a bullet mark should be considered worth no stars, but in 1993, it may be worth a full star.

arbitrary_comment   comment   ****

The use of lines beginning with # as comments is supported by the C shell, the Korn shell, and modern Bourne shells. The feature was added to the Bourne shell in System III; the V7 Bourne shell and its descendents do not support it. Indeed, a widespread convention on Berkeley UNIX systems was that if a shell script begins with #, it is assumed to be a C shell script; otherwise it is assumed to be a Bourne shell script. Berkeley obsoleted this convention by adding an *executable-shell-script* feature: if a shell script begins with the two characters # !, the operating system will read the remainder of the first line and will take the name (and arguments, if provided) of the shell interpreter from there. For example, #! /bin/csh −f means that the script is written for the C shell and that the −f option should be passed to the shell.

Even though the technique of detecting C shell scripts by their first character is obsolete, it lives on in many C shell implementations. A one line comment in a Bourne shell script can be more portably (if less readably) created using the : built-in command. For a more extensive shell script requiring serious comments, one approach is to begin the script with a : comment, and then to use # freely in the remainder of the script.

The executable-shell-script feature, although desirable, is not in current releases of System V. Security problems remained to be solved at the time this was written. This will tend to make C shell scripts even more troublesome.

It is not necessary to write portable Bourne shell scripts without comments. The : (colon) command, although less flexible than the # comment, avoids any confusion between different shells. It is easy to delete comments, if necessary, with sed or egrep −v as part of the installation process.

alias [*name*[=*word*]...]   define alias   **

This command is not portable. It is present in System V release 3 and the Korn shell. POSIX supported aliases in an early draft, but removed them in favor of functions. In general, portable shell scripts should not contain aliases.

ar −d[lv] *archive_name file_name* ...   file archiver   ***
ar −p[v] *archive_name* [*file_name*] ...
ar −r[cluv] *archive_name file_name* ...
ar −t[v] *archive_name* [*file_name*] ...
ar −x[v] *archive_name* [*file_name*] ...

This command is part of the POSIX Software Development Environment, and so is portable among POSIX conforming systems as part of a compilation tool, makefile, or shell script. It may not be present on systems with no compiler, so it is not portable from `system`.

Although the POSIX standard does not specify the archive format, the major UNIX system versions (4.2BSD, System V release 2, V8) and their descendents all use the same format.

If `ar` is being used to build a library of object files to be searched by the loader, it is sometimes necessary to take special steps to build a table of contents. This is done with the `ranlib` program on some systems (especially V7-derived systems.) This is not necessary on System V, whose `ar` command automatically builds a table of contents.

as [−o *objfile*]   assembler   **

This command is not part of the POSIX P1003.2 standard, so it should be considered unportable. Some makefiles pass the assembly language generated by the compiler through an editor script to improve the performance of the program. This technique is inherently unportable, since the assembly language varies from system to system.

In addition, it is perfectly permissible for a compiler to generate binary object code directly from C source without going through an assembly language step. Although traditionally many C compilers generate assembly language, compilers for other languages traditionally generate binary object code directly.

The assembly language step slows down the compilation process. The UNIX system favors simplicity over speed, and the adoption of assembly language as an intermediate form passed from the compiler to the optimizer, and from the optimizer to the assembler, simplifies the development and support of the compiler. This design decision is internal to the compiler, however, and other implementations of the UNIX system are free to avoid the assembler step entirely.

For text files in a single directory, an even more portable format is the shell archive, described in Chapter 4. Shell archives can be easily shipped to other systems, even using electronic mail or Netnews.

asa [*file_name* ...]   carriage control   *••

This command is required by the POSIX P1003.2 standard FORTRAN development environment. It is present in System V release 3, but is a fairly new command. Until it is safe to assume P1003.2, asa should be considered unportable.

at *time* [*date*]   queue for later   ***
batch   *

These commands are not part of POSIX, so it should be considered less portable. The at command is present in V7 and its descendents. It was also added to System V release 2.

The batch command is specific to System V. It was new with System V release 2. It should be considered unportable.

These commands may appear in the POSIX 1003.2a user interface standard. In general, the most portable way to set up deferred command execution is to use cron entries that are installed by hand.

awk [-F *ere*] *program file*   awk language   ****
awk [-F *ere*] [-f *progfile*] *file*

This command is part of the POSIX mandatory execution environment, and so it is portable among POSIX P1003.2 conforming systems. Awk scripts are a popular way to combine the power of the shell script calling awk, the power of programming constructs such as arithmetic and printf, and the versatility of an interpretive string-processing language. When execution is less important than development time, awk can be a very useful tool. It was once very portable among UNIX systems based on V7 or later. The 1985 enhancements to awk have introduced the possibility of incompatibilities. System V release 3 provides the 1985 version as nawk, with the intent that System V release 4 would offer this version as the standard awk. The version of awk required by POSIX is the nawk version.

banner *word* ...   print banners   *

This command is not part of the POSIX P1003.2 standard, so it should be considered less portable.

4.2BSD has a /usr/games/banner program that prints sideways block letters up to 132 columns tall with variable width, like this:

$ /usr/games/banner hi

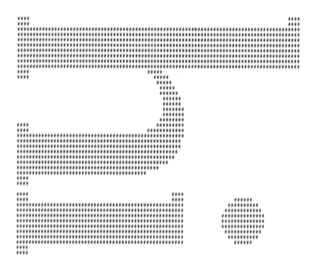

The System V `banner` command prints upright block letters from a fixed-size matrix. This "upright" `banner` command is only present on System V derived systems. Its output looks like this:

```
$ banner hi
```

```
    #      #      #
    #      #      #
    ######        #
    #      #      #
    #      #      #
    #      #      #
```

The two commands are dissimilar enough that they are not both useful for any single task.

basename *string* [*suffix*]   base name of file   ****

This command is part of the POSIX mandatory execution environment, and so it is portable among POSIX P1003.2 conforming systems.

bc [-l] [*file_name* ...]   calculator   ****

This command is present on all major UNIX systems. It is also required by POSIX P1003.2. The command should be considered portable.

bg [*job*]   background job   *

This shell built-in command was part of an early draft of the POSIX P1003.2 standard, but it was removed later. It was required *only* on systems supporting job control. Systems derived from 4.0BSD or System V release 4 support job control. This command is terminal-oriented, and is generally not useful from a shell script.

break [*n*]   break from loop   ****

The break primitive is used in writing shell scripts. It is required by POSIX, and should be considered portable.

cal [*month*] *year*   calendar   ****

This command is not part of the POSIX P1003.2 standard, so it should be considered less portable. The command is present on nearly all UNIX systems, so in practice, it is quite portable.

calendar [-]   calendar   ****

This command is not part of the POSIX P1003.2 standard, so it should be considered less portable. The command is present on nearly all UNIX systems, so in practice, it is quite portable.

cancel [*ids*] [*printers*]   cancel print job   *

This command is not part of POSIX P1003.2.

This command is specific to the System V printer spooler. The equivalent command in 4.2BSD is called lprm.

case *word* in   control structure   ****
    patterns) *list*;; ...
esac

The case shell syntax is present in the Bourne and Korn shells. It is a part of P1003.2. A different syntax is used in the C shell. This structure is portable among Bourne shell scripts.

cat [-u] [-c] [*file_name*]   concatenate files   *****

This command is part of the POSIX mandatory execution environment, and so it is portable among POSIX P1003.2 conforming systems.

Although the cat command is one of the most fundamental UNIX commands, some of the options are not present in every system. In general, only the −u option can be considered universal, and even this option was new with V7. The −v option is present in 4BSD and System V, but was not in earlier systems, and is not in V7, V8, and V9. The −n, and −t options are specific to 4BSD. 4BSD supports a −s option to cause single spacing. System V supports a −s option to cause silence in the presence of errors. This conflict has been resolved in merged systems by causing −s to mean silence, and in POSIX systems, −c causes single spacing.

c89 [−cO] [−D*name*[=*define*]] [−I *dir*]   C compiler   *●●
 [−L *dir*] [−o *outfile*] [−U*name*] *object* [−l*library*]
cc [−cO] [−D*name*[=*define*]] [−I*dir*]   C compiler   ****
 [−o *outfile*] [−U*name*] *object* [−l*library*]

This command is part of the POSIX C Development Environment, and so is portable among POSIX conforming systems as part of a compilation tool, makefile, or shell script. It may not be present on systems with no compiler, so it is not portable from system.

The command is usually called cc on UNIX systems, but was renamed c89 by the POSIX committee to allow a method to force invocation of an ANSI C compiler. The cc command is much more likely to work (****), but may or may not support ANSI C. In general, a makefile should always parameterize the name of the compiler:

```
CC=c89
...
a.out:       $(OBJS)
        $(CC) $(OBJS) $(LIBS)
```

Since the make command supports the CC variable, this also covers implicit references to it. In general, a makefile can be made more portable by replacing all references to cc with $(CC) and including a locally appropriate line such as CC=cc or CC=c89 at the front to be easily overridden or customized for other environments.

The C compiler is the primary command present in C compiler packages, often called *software generation systems* or *development environments*. This book refers to systems with such packages as *systems with a C compiler*.

It is safe to count on the −c, −l, −O, and −o compiler options. The −p, −E, and −S options are fairly portable, but may be missing in a few systems.

The cc command will portably pass some options to the preprocessor. These always include −D −I −U and −C. These options were new with V7, but have become universal.

It is also safe to use cc as either a compiler or a linker. (If the input files are object files ending in .o, and the −c option is not used, the cc command is being used as a linker, not a compiler.) Some options are passed though to ld. These will nearly always include −l, −o, −s, and −u.

Other options, such as −S to generate assembly language and −r to relocate all data to a read-only text region, are less portable. The −S option is present on all implementations supporting an assembler, but generation of assembly language is not required. (In practice, it is generally present on UNIX systems.)

The default executable output file name is usually a.out, but some systems use a different default, such as x.out or the name of the first object file. It is safest to always explicitly use the −o option.

cd [*directory*]   change directory   *****

This shell built-in command is part of the POSIX mandatory execution environment, and so it is portable among POSIX P1003.2 conforming systems.

Because of the multitasking nature of the UNIX system, this command affects only the process invoking it and its descendents. This requires that the shell command be built into the shell. When used from a makefile or from system, it is important to remember that each text line is processed by a separate shell invocation. For the cd command to affect subsequent commands, it must precede the other commands on the same text line. From a C program, it is usually preferable to use the chdir system call.

In early UNIX system releases, the cd shell command was spelled chdir. In V6, the cd spelling was supported, but undocumented. By V7, the Bourne shell and C shell officially spelled the command cd. The older spelling has been kept (also undocumented) for upward compatibility, but since this command is built into the shell, it becomes a reserved word. Recent shell releases, including the Korn shell, and the System V release 3 Bourne shell, support only cd.

chmod [−R] *symbolic_mode file_name* . . . change file mode   *****

This command is part of the POSIX mandatory execution environment, and so it is portable among POSIX P1003.2 conforming systems. Note that only the symbolic modes, such as u+w, are portable, and that the numeric modes, such as 755, have been declared deprecated by the POSIX standard. In practice, both forms are quite portable. New shell scripts should use the symbolic form.

The −R option is a POSIX invention and is not present on older systems.

chown [−R] *who file_name* . . .   change file owner   ****
chgrp [−R] *who file_name* . . .   change file group   ****

These commands are part of the POSIX mandatory execution environment, and so they are portable among POSIX P1003.2 conforming systems. The commands were given only four stars because of their semantic incompatibility. As long as these commands are being run by the super user, they can be considered extremely portable (*****).

The semantics of the underlying system calls are slightly different among UNIX systems. V7-derived systems permit these calls (and hence these commands) only to the super user. System III derived systems permit these calls and commands to either the super user or the owner of the file, and may clear the SUID and SGID permissions bits on the file if they are set.

In 4.2BSD, these commands were moved from /bin to /etc. Since they are normally only run by the super user, who should have /etc in the PATH anyway, this usually doesn't matter on a 4BSD system.

The -R option is a POSIX invention and is not present on older systems.

cksum [*file_name* . . .]   show checksum   *••

This command is part of the POSIX mandatory execution environment, and so it is portable among POSIX P1003.2 conforming systems. The command is an invention of POSIX, and is not present in older systems. Older systems have a less consistent sum command.

cmp [-ls] *file1 file2*   compare files   *****

This command is part of the POSIX mandatory execution environment, and so it is portable among POSIX P1003.2 conforming systems. It is essentially similar on all UNIX systems.

colldef [-e] *file_name*   define collation sequence   *••

This command is part of the POSIX mandatory execution environment, and so it is portable among POSIX P1003.2 conforming systems. This command is an invention of POSIX. It is not present in earlier UNIX systems, and should be considered unportable until it becomes safe to assume POSIX conformance.

: *comment_words*   comment   *****

The colon command is used for comments in shell scripts. It is portable in Bourne and Korn shell scripts, but the comparable C shell feature uses the # character.

Beware that, although the arguments are ignored by the : command, the arguments are evaluated. If the arguments contain any shell syntax, a syntax error may result. An easy workaround is to enclose the entire comment in quotes.

```
: 'Word Processor; version (2.1), 11/*/88'
```

comm [-123] *file1 file2*   find common lines   *****

This command is part of the POSIX mandatory execution environment, and so it is portable among POSIX P1003.2 conforming systems. It is essentially similar on all UNIX systems.

command [*argument...*]   execute simple command   *••

This command is part of the P1003.2 mandatory execution environment. It is an invention of the POSIX committee, and will not be portable until P1003.2 conformance is widespread. Some older systems can achieve the same functionality with shell aliases.

continue [*n*]   control structure   ****

This shell built-in command is part of the POSIX mandatory execution environment, and so it is portable among POSIX P1003.2 conforming systems. It is available in all implementations of the Bourne shell.

cp [-ipfR] *source_file ... target*   copy files   *****

This command is part of the POSIX mandatory execution environment, and so it is portable among POSIX P1003.2 conforming systems. The -R option is an invention of the POSIX committee, and corresponds to the 4.2BSD -r option. The -p option was new with 4.3BSD and P1003.2.

cpio -o[acBv]   copy files in/out   **
cpio -i[Bcdmrtuv6] [*patterns*]
cpio -p[adlmruv] *directory*

This command is not part of the POSIX standard. The POSIX group has settled upon both tar and cpio formats as the standard interchange formats. POSIX has settled on the new pax command to create archives in either format. The cpio format comes from PWB and its descendents, including System III and System V.

The default file format created by the cpio -o command uses a multibyte binary format that depends on word size and byte order. This format is not portable. The -c option causes cpio to create an image in a portable format.

Because of these problems, the use of cpio is not recommended in a portable program, script, or distribution package. Beware especially of using cpio format for a distribution, since some systems will be unable to unpack the distribution.

The cpio command is particularly well suited for two situations. Since images created with cpio are usually smaller than images created with tar, they are useful for situations where the size of the image is important. This is due to the handling of headers and blocks. cpio uses headers of only about 100 bytes,[2] compared to 512 bytes in tar.

---

[2] 77 bytes plus the length of the file name.

Both commands pad the last block with garbage to reach a 512-byte boundary. If the image is to be compressed, however, the size advantage may be lost.

Another advantage to `cpio` is that it uses a list of file names on the standard input. This makes it well suited for incremental backups. Some versions of `cpio` have provisions for pausing after a certain amount of data, allowing large backups to be written to smaller reels of tape, or even to floppy disks.

For text files in a single directory, an even more portable format is the shell archive, described in Chapter 4. Shell archives can be easily shipped to other systems, even using electronic mail or Netnews.

`create [-dfnpqtP]`   create temporary file   *••
  `[-m` *mode*`]  [-x` *prefix*`]` *name...*

This command is an invention of the P1003.2 committee, and should be considered unportable until POSIX conformance becomes widespread. Use of shell names such as `/tmp/mycom$$` is more portable. The name `mycom` represents a name that depends on the name of the shell script, such as `/tmp/sort$$` for a sorting shell script. This command was called `mktemp` in an early draft of P1003.2.

`crontab` [*file*]   schedule command execution   *
`crontab -r`
`crontab -l`

This command is not part of the POSIX standard. It is specific to System V release 2 and later releases. Earlier UNIX versions and their descendents used a single file `/usr/lib/crontab` that could only be updated by having the super user edit it.

The most portable way to get deferred execution is to use `cron`. Write a shell script or command to be invoked from `cron`, and a `crontab` line to invoke it at certain times. Include a procedure in the documentation to manually install this line in the appropriate `crontab`. That may be `/usr/lib/crontab` or it may be in a user-specific file in the `crontab` directory. There is no portable way to control the user id of the resulting process, so if it matters, use the suid bit to force a particular user id.

`csplit  [-sk]  [-f`*prefix*`]` *file arg . . .*   context split   *

This command is not part of the POSIX standard. It is specific to System V. In some cases, it may be possible to use `dd` or `sed` to achieve similar functionality in a more portable way.

cut −c *list* [*file_name* ...]   cut selected columns   **•
cut −f *list* [−d *char*] [−s] [*file_name*]

This command is part of the POSIX mandatory execution environment, but it is specific to System III and System V. Public domain versions of cut and paste exist, but are generally not available on other systems.

cut and paste are quite useful in shell scripts and makefiles, especially for extracting certain fields from the output of commands that were intended to be read by a person. Unfortunately, this has led to many scripts that are not portable. Where possible, it is recommended that sed or awk be used instead. If your application is written specifically for System V, such as a 3B2 software distribution floppy disk, it is safe to assume the presence of these commands.

cxref [−cs] [−w*num*] [−o *file*] *file* ...   cross reference   *

This command is not part of the POSIX standard. It is specific to System V.

date [−u] [+*format*]   print date/time   *****

This command is part of the POSIX mandatory execution environment, and so it is portable among POSIX P1003.2 conforming systems for printing (but not for setting) the system date. The command is present on nearly all UNIX systems, so in practice, it is quite portable, as long as no arguments are given.

There are differences between V7 and System V in the details of the command. The differences fall into two categories: controlling the format of the output, and setting the time.

The V7 and 4BSD date commands print the date and time in the standard format only. The System V date command prints the date in the same format by default, and has options to print all or part of the date in other formats. A portable application cannot use any arguments or options to the date command. Use of a format will restrict the application to System V.

To set the date, all systems accept the format

        date *mmddhhmm*

from the super user. Only V7 and 4BSD allow the *mmdd* to be omitted.

dd [*operand*] ...   copy data   *****

This command is part of the POSIX mandatory execution environment, and so it is portable among POSIX P1003.2 conforming systems. The command is present on nearly all UNIX systems, so in practice it is quite portable.

df [*file_system*] . . .   show free disk space   **

This command is not part of the POSIX standard. It is present on all UNIX systems, but cannot be considered portable.

Shell scripts to install software often use the df command to determine if there is enough free space to install the package. Unfortunately, the output format of this command is intended to be read by people and not programs. The System V df command produces a different format from the V7 command, and 4.2BSD uses a third format.

The units used by this command differ among systems. V7, System III, and many System V implementations use *blocks* of 512 bytes. (Amdahl UTS System V release 2 uses 4096-byte blocks.) 4BSD uses *KB* of 1024 bytes each. When comparing between the two systems, it is necessary to multiply or divide by 2.

For example, suppose you have a distribution image that occupies 5 MB. If the 4BSD df command tells you that a filesystem free count is 7500, it will fit, because 7500 4BSD blocks equal 7.5 MB. If a System V df command tells you that the free count is 7500, it will not fit, because 7500 System V blocks equal 3.75 MB.

diff [-bcer] [-C *n*] *file1 file2*   file differences   *****

This command is part of the POSIX mandatory execution environment, and so it is portable among POSIX P1003.2 conforming systems.

Some options are present only on 4BSD. In particular, the −c context option and the ability to compare all files in a directory are not present in diff commands other than the 4BSD and POSIX versions. The −C option and the explicit use of −r are new with P1003.2. Berkeley systems imply −r if both arguments are directories.

dircmp [-ds] *dir1 dir2*   compare directories   *

This command is not part of the POSIX standard. It is specific to System V, and is similar to the 4BSD diff command when applied to directories.

To portably compare subdirectories, use a shell variable or makefile variable to control the name of the command: DIRCMP="diff-r" and call $(DIRCMP) in the body of the command. This allows easy configuration of the shell script or makefile with the appropriate local command, either diff −r, diff, or dircmp.

dirname *string*   directory part of filename   **•

This command is part of the POSIX mandatory execution environment, and so it is portable among POSIX P1003.2 conforming systems. The command is specific to System III and System V.

`dis [-oVL] [-F` *function*`]`   disassembler   *
    `[-i` *string*`]` *file* `...`

This command is not part of the POSIX P1003.2 standard, so it should be considered less portable. This command is specific to System V release 2 and later releases.

Since the output of the `dis` command contains the specific assembly language of the local system, this output is not portable, even among systems with this command. Different implementations of `dis` may produce output in different formats.

`.` *shell_script*   read commands   ****

The dot command causes the current shell to read commands from the named file. It is portable in Bourne and Korn shell scripts. The comparable C shell feature is the `source` command.

`du [-as]` *name*   disk usage   **

This command is not part of the POSIX standard. It is present in all UNIX versions. The output format is usually the same, even on different systems. Unfortunately, the units are not the same on all systems. 4BSD uses K bytes, but System V uses 512-byte blocks. See the `df` command for a discussion of the differences.

`echo [`*argument*`] ...`   show arguments   ****

This command is part of the POSIX mandatory execution environment, and so it is portable among POSIX P1003.2 conforming systems.

The echo command itself is quite portable, but the special options are a portability problem. Systems descended from V7 use the form

```
    echo -n Enter name:
    read name
```

to suppress the trailing newline in order to prompt the user on the same line. Systems derived from System III use the equivalent syntax

```
    echo Enter Name:\c
    read name
```

Shell scripts do this often, and as a result are not portable. POSIX requires neither interpretation, but instead supplies a new `printf` command that accepts `%c` codes and `\c` codes.

There is no easy solution, since neither system supports the other's syntax. The issue is further clouded by the presence of some older versions of the Korn shell, where the `echo` command is built into the shell, with the System V syntax, even on 4BSD systems. Recent `ksh` releases use the local conventions. The only simple portable solution is to prompt on a separate line.

```
echo Enter Name:
read name
```

More complex solutions involve a test to see which syntax is used locally, or provision of a C program of your own to be called by your shell script.

ed [-p *string*] [-] [-s] *file_name*   line editor   *****

This command is part of the POSIX mandatory execution environment, and so it is portable among POSIX P1003.2 conforming systems. Editing files larger than 50K bytes should be considered unportable.

The − option has been marked deprecated by POSIX to be replaced with the new −s option. In practice, the older − option will be more portable until P1003.2 is widespread.

Although all conforming systems have ed, many commands are specific to one version of ed. PWB added a large number of extensions, such as variable tab stops, that were not present in earlier releases. These features are not available in the V7 or 4BSD editors.

Since the ex editor is derived from the V6 ed command, a safe rule is that any command available in ed that is not present in ex is not as portable, and should be avoided for the best portability. It is common to use ex to process an ed script. For example, if the ability to match whole words using \< and \> is needed, or improved error messages are needed to debug a script, it is common to substitute ex for ed. Use of unportable ed features can make such moves difficult. Since POSIX does not require ex, however, it is much safer to restrict yourself to the intersection of ed and ex.

egrep [-cilnv] [-e *expression*]   find patterns in files   ****
[-f *string_file*] [*expression*] [*file_name*] ...

This command is part of the POSIX mandatory execution environment, and so it is portable among POSIX P1003.2 conforming systems. The command has been marked deprecated by POSIX in favor of the new −E option to the grep command.

Some UNIX systems have been released without an egrep command, and others have been released with an egrep command that functioned as if it were grep. Although these systems are few in number, it is more portable to use grep. The egrep command is often faster than grep, however, so if speed is critical, it may be worth the slight portability loss to use egrep.

env [-] [-i] [*name=value*] ...   show environment   **
[*command*]

This command is part of the POSIX mandatory execution environment, and so it is portable among POSIX P1003.2 conforming systems. It came from System III and System V.

4BSD has a similar command called `printenv`, which supports only the printing functionality, not the ability to alter the environment and call a program.

The traditional − option to clear the environment was changed in POSIX to −i, and − was marked deprecated. Until P1003.2 becomes widespread, it will be more portable to use −.

eval [*expression* . . .]   shell command evaluation   ****

This shell built-in command is part of the POSIX P1003.2 standard. It is present in all Bourne shell implementations. It can be considered portable.

ex [−] [−lrvR] [+*command*] [*file* . . .]   line editor   ***

This command is not part of the POSIX standard. It was not present in V7, but since it is a link to `vi`, it is available on nearly any system with `vi`. System III, V7, and earlier distributions did not have `vi`, but it was the first ''Berkeley enhancement'' offered by most commercial derivatives of the UNIX system. System V and 4BSD come with `ex` and `vi` as part of the basic system. It is rare to find a UNIX system that does not provide these commands.

The `ex` command is useful for enhanced editor scripts called from shell scripts and makefiles. In particular, `ex` is useful from makefiles because of the \< and \> ''whole word'' brackets, that search for and replace whole words. On many systems, `ex` can edit larger files than `ed`. The `vi` command is useful to invoke an interactive editor, so the user of your application can edit text files.

exec [*command* [*argument*]]   replace shell with command   ****

This shell built-in command is part of the POSIX P1003.2 standard. It is present in all Bourne shell implementations on UNIX systems. It may not make sense on MS DOS systems.

exit [*value*]   exit from shell   ****

This shell built-in command is part of the POSIX P1003.2 standard. It is present in all Bourne shell implementations on UNIX systems. It can be considered portable.

export [*variable* . . .]   export environment value   ****

This shell built-in command is part of the POSIX P1003.2 standard. It is present in all Bourne shell implementations on UNIX systems. It can be considered portable.

The form `export` *name=value* is new in the Korn shell and P1003.2, but not in the older Bourne shells. It is more portable to set variables and export them separately. Exporting a function with −f is new with P1003.2.

`expr` *expression* ...   calculate expression   ****

This command is part of the POSIX mandatory execution environment, and so it is portable among POSIX P1003.2 conforming systems.

`false`   always false   ****

This command is part of the POSIX mandatory execution environment, and so it is portable among POSIX P1003.2 conforming systems.

`fg` [*job*]   foreground job   *

This shell built-in command was part of an early draft of the POSIX P1003.2 standard, but it was removed later. It was required *only* on systems supporting job control. Systems derived from 4.0BSD or System V release 4 support job control. This command is terminal-oriented, and is generally not useful from a shell script.

`fgrep` [`-cilnvx`]   find text in files   ****
    [`-f` *string_file*] [*strings*] [*file_name*...]

This command is part of the POSIX mandatory execution environment, and so it is portable among POSIX P1003.2 conforming systems.

Draft 7 of P1003.2 indicates that the committee is considering removing the `fgrep` command and adding its functionality to `grep`. This command has been present in all UNIX systems since V7. The command has been marked deprecated by POSIX in favor of the new `-F` option to the `grep` command.

Although it is commonly believed that `fgrep` is a fast and simple version of `grep`, the traditional implementation of `fgrep` is actually *slower* than `grep`. Further, the traditional `egrep` implementation is faster than either. As a result, efforts to use `fgrep` for improved speed are not recommended. The `fgrep` command is appropriate only when the strings might contain regular expression metacharacters that could interfere with the search.

`file` *file_name* ...   determine file type   *****

This command is not part of POSIX P1003.2. It is usually not useful in a portable application.

Although every version of the UNIX system comes with a `file` command, the exact set of formats recognized is not standardized. Formats typically not recognized include `tar` and `cpio`.

find *path* ... *expression*   walk file tree   *****

This command is part of the POSIX mandatory execution environment, and so it is portable among POSIX P1003.2 conforming systems. Some of the options refer to file types present only on some systems, and these options are only as portable as the file types. For example, many systems do not have fifos or symbolic links.

Certain options to find are not portable. The −cpio option is specific to System V, and is not in 4BSD or P1003.2. P1003.2 added new options called −nouser, −nogroup, −xdev, and −prune. (The −xdev option is similar to the System V −mount option.)

P1003.2 specifies an implied −print if no other output is produced. This is new behavior and should not be assumed. Similarly, the −a option was deleted by the P1003.2 committee, so portable programs should use the equivalent concatenation construct (e.g., omit the −a).

fold [-bs] [-w *width*] [*file_name* ...]   fold long lines   *••

This command is part of the POSIX mandatory execution environment, and so it is portable among POSIX P1003.2 conforming systems.

The fold command comes from 4BSD systems. The P1003.2 version of fold has enhanced options, and has changed the syntax for the width in a way that is not upward compatible. There is no fold command in System V release 3. As a result, this command cannot be considered portable until POSIX compatibility can be assumed.

for *name* in *word* ...   control structure   ****
do
    commands
done

This shell built-in command is part of the POSIX P1003.2 standard. It is present in all Bourne shell implementations, and can be considered portable.

fort77 [-cONVw]   FORTRAN compiler   *••
    [-o *outfile*] [-L *dir*] *object* ...
f77 [-cgwpuCFm] [-E*x*] [-R*x*]   FORTRAN compiler   ***
    [-o *outfile*] *object* ...

This command is part of the POSIX Fortran Development Utilities environment. It is a new invention of the P1003.2 committee. Previous UNIX systems often had a Fortran compiler, called f77, with similar options. Many systems are distributed with no Fortran compiler. The quality of the specific Fortran compiler may vary considerably from system to system.

`function` *identifier* { *compound_list* } function declaration   **●

Shell functions are new with System V release 3, POSIX P1003.2, and the Korn shell. The syntax using the `function` keyword is specific to the Korn shell, and is not portable. The syntax using the *function_name*() near the beginning of this chapter is more portable.

A portable shell script should not use shell functions unless it is absolutely necessary, because their use will restrict the portability of the script.

function_name() *compound_command*   function definition   **

The function definition is required by POSIX P1003.2. It is present in the System V Bourne shell with the same syntax. The Korn shell supports a different syntax. Releases of System V prior to release 3 did not support shell functions. In general, external shell scripts are far more portable than shell functions.

`getconf` *parameter_name* [*pathname*]   find configuration   *●●

This command is new with POSIX P1003.2. It was not present in any previous UNIX system version. This command was called `posixconf` in an earlier draft of P1003.2.

`getopts` *optstring name* [*arg ...*]   get options   **●

This command is part of the POSIX mandatory execution environment, and so it is portable among POSIX P1003.2 conforming systems.

The `getopts` command was new in System V release 3. It replaced the older `getopt` command. Although not very widely available at first, it is expected that this command will become more common as POSIX P1003.2 develops.

`grep [-cilnsvEF]`   find text in files   *****
expression [*file_name ...*]

This command is part of the POSIX mandatory execution environment, and so it is portable among POSIX P1003.2 conforming systems.

Although the `grep` command is widely available, the related commands `egrep` and `fgrep` are not quite so widely available. (In practice, they are on nearly all UNIX systems.) The `-E` and `-F` options, providing the functionality of `egrep` and `fgrep`, respectively, are inventions of the POSIX committee.

Some options to `grep` are not universally available. The `-i` or `-y` options to ignore case vary from system to system; some versions, such as V7, provided `-y`, but did not document it. Portable options to `grep` include `-v`, `-c`, `-l`, `-n`, and `-s`. The `-w` option to match whole words and the use of `\<` and `\>` to match the beginning and end of a word are specific to 4BSD. The use of the `\{`*m,n*`\}` syntax is specific to System V and POSIX systems.

`hexdump [-vc] [-b[dox]] [-[hl]i[doux]] hex dump`   *••
`[-[l]f] [-p[dox]] [-o offset[bkm]] [file_name ...]`

This command is part of the POSIX P1003.2 mandatory execution environment, and so it is portable among POSIX P1003.2 conforming systems.

The `hexdump` command is an invention of the POSIX committee. It does not exist on System V release 3 or 4.3BSD. A similar command, `od`, is available on most systems with similar capabilities. The `hexdump` command dumps in hexadecimal, but `od` dumps in octal.

`head [-cl] [-n number] [file ...]`   top of file   **•
`head [-number] [file ...]`

This command is part of the POSIX P1003.2 mandatory execution environment, and so it is portable among POSIX P1003.2 conforming systems. The command is from Berkeley, dating back to 2BSD. It first appeared in System V in release 4.0. The second form, using *-number*, is more portable, but has been marked as deprecated by POSIX. An even more portable, if limited, alternative is `sed 10q`.

`id [-gnru] [user]`   show user id   **•

This command is part of the POSIX P1003.2 mandatory execution environment, and so it is portable among POSIX P1003.2 conforming systems.

This command is specific to System III and System V. 4BSD provides a similar (but incompatible) command called `whoami`.

All options to `id` were invented by P1003.2, and should be considered less portable until P1003.2 is widespread.

`if` *commands* `then` *commands*   control structure   ****
`[elif` *commands* `then` *commands* `...]`
`[else` *commands*`] fi`

This shell built-in command is part of the POSIX P1003.2 mandatory execution environment, and so it is portable among POSIX P1003.2 conforming systems. It is present in all Bourne shell implementations.

`join` *options file_name1 file_name2*   join database   ****

This command is part of the POSIX mandatory execution environment, and so it is portable among POSIX P1003.2 conforming systems.

The `-v`, `-1`, and `-2` options are inventions of the P1003.2 committee, and should be considered less portable until P1003.2 conformance is widespread.

kill [-*signal_number*]   send signal   *****
    [-l] [-*signal_name*] *pid* ...

This command is part of the POSIX mandatory execution environment, and so it is portable among POSIX P1003.2 conforming systems.

This command is built into many shells in order to take advantage of job control. The job control features are not portable. The -*signal_number* option came from the 4.0BSD csh and was first added to sh by P1003.2, which also marked the numeric version deprecated. The -l option was also added to P1003.2 from csh.

The feature allowing process trees to be killed using %i syntax is specific to systems supporting job control, including 4BSD csh and ksh. The use of negative process id numbers to send signals to a group of processes is not required by POSIX. See also considerations of the kill system call.

ld [-rs] [-e entry_point] [-l*library*]   link editor   **
    [-o *outfile*] [-u *symname*] *file_name* ...

This command is not part of the POSIX P1003.2 standard, so it should be considered less portable. It is present in all UNIX releases, but its use is very low level. Some shell scripts use ld -x -r to build stripped object files; this will usually work, but is not really portable.

A truly portable program will not normally use the ld command. The preferred interface is to invoke the C compiler and let it invoke ld with the appropriate options. The set of appropriate options may vary from system to system.

lex [-cntv] [*filename* ...]   scanner generator   *****

This command is part of the POSIX C Development Environment, and so is portable among POSIX conforming systems as part of a C compilation tool, makefile, or shell script. It may not be present on systems with no compiler, so it is not portable from system.

line   read one line   *

This command is not part of the POSIX P1003.2 standard. It is specific to System III and System V.

The line command offers functionality similar to the read command built into the Bourne shell. The read command is far more portable.

lint [-abhnpuvx] *file* . . .   find portability problems   ****

This command is not part of the POSIX P1003.2 standard, so it should be considered less portable.

The lint command is present on all UNIX systems released since V7. The details of the workings of the command differ slightly from system to system. In particular, many systems have a lint whose top level is written in Bourne shell, beginning with # comments. Users whose shell is the C shell on systems that do not recognize the #! convention for shell scripts, may be unsuccessful in running lint. This is a minor concern, most easily fixed by changing the user's SHELL environment variable, and need not be a concern to the software developer exporting a makefile.

The procedures for creating, compiling, and installing a lint library may vary from system to system. System V uses -o *lib* and stores the resulting file in /usr/lib. 4BSD uses -C*lib* and stores the resulting file in /usr/lib/lint.

ln [-fi] *source_file* . . . *target*   link files   *****

This command is part of the POSIX mandatory execution environment, and so it is portable among POSIX P1003.2 conforming systems. It is present in nearly the same form in all UNIX systems.

The *symbolic link* functionality is not present in all systems. It first appeared in 4.2BSD, and in System V release 4. The -s option is not required by POSIX. The -i option is new with P1003.2.

local [*name*[=*word*] . . .]   create local variables   *●●

This shell built-in command is part of the POSIX P1003.2 mandatory environment. It is an invention of the POSIX committee, so it should be considered unportable until POSIX conformance is widespread. In general, the additional functionality of this command is useful mainly for large modular applications written in shell, so most applications can safely avoid it.

locale [-ackv] [-l *locale*]   print locale information   *●●
    [-f *charmap*] [*name*. . .]
locale [-s] [-l *locale*] [-f *charmap*] [*name*. . .]

This command is part of the POSIX P1003.2 mandatory environment. It is an invention of the POSIX committee, so it should be considered unportable until POSIX and ANSI C conformance is widespread.

Since the entire concept of locales is new, there is no similar command in older systems. One possible approach is to avoid querying the implementation for locale-specific information. Another is to write a simple shell command called locale containing several echo commands to be used on a specific older system.

`localedef [-f` *charmap*`]` *name*   define locale environment   *••

This command is part of the POSIX P1003.2 mandatory environment. It is an invention of the POSIX committee, so it should be considered unportable until POSIX and ANSI C conformance is widespread.

This command will be needed by only a few very sophisticated applications. To run such applications in older environments using a dummy `locale` command, the `localedef` command can also be a dummy that silently accepts its input. Another possibility is to implement full locale functionality in both commands and carry it with the application source code.

`logger` *string* `...`   log messages   *••

This command is new with POSIX P1003.2. It was not present in any previous UNIX system version. It should be considered unportable unless you assume POSIX conformance. The 4.3BSD system also has a compatible `logger` command. This command was called `posixlog` in an earlier draft of P1003.2.

An application requiring this functionality in an older implementation can supply its own `logger` command that appends the arguments to a log file.

`logname`   show login name   **•

This command is part of the POSIX mandatory execution environment, and so it is portable among POSIX P1003.2 conforming systems. It is, however, specific to System III and System V, and is not present in 4BSD. The `logname` command takes no arguments.

In System V, this command prints the value in `/etc/passwd` corresponding to the real user id. In 4.2BSD, it is equivalent to `whoami`. There is nothing in either the POSIX standard or the SVID to require this interpretation. Implementations that key on `LOGNAME` or `USER` in the environment, or the owner of the controlling terminal, or the name in `/etc/utmp` corresponding to the controlling terminal are all possible.

`lorder` *file* `...`   logical order   *
`tsort [`*file*`]`   topological sort   *

These commands are not part of the POSIX P1003.2 standard, so they should be considered unportable.

These commands were used in early releases of the UNIX system to sort a library into the proper order for a library. They were part of the standard makefile installation procedure for a library:

```
ar cr libfoo.a `lorder $(OBJS) | tsort`
```

V7 introduced a new command `ranlib` that could be run on a library to create a table of contents. This eliminated the need for `lorder` and `tsort` on systems descended from V7.

```
ar cr libfoo.a $(OBJS)
ranlib libfoo.a
```

To ensure that the table of contents was up to date, the linker only used the table of contents if the write date of the library file was the same as the date on the table of contents in the archive. This meant that `ranlib` had to be run twice: once in the compilation directory for testing, and once again when the library was copied into `/usr/lib`.

```
cp libfoo.a /usr/lib/libfoo.a
ranlib /usr/lib/libfoo.a
```

System V addressed the problem differently. The `ar` command was modified to automatically update the table of contents whenever a new object file was added. This eliminated the need to run `ranlib`, and the `ranlib` command never appeared on System V.

```
ar cr libfoo.a $(OBJS)
```

This change came with the new COFF format, which first appeared in the first System V release. Some older systems claiming System V compatibility do not use COFF, and require `ranlib` instead.

As a result, a portable makefile rarely uses `lorder` or `tsort`. It is best to call `ranlib`, and on a System V machine, the calls to `ranlib` can be removed from the makefile or an empty shell script called `ranlib` can be created in the current directory.

lp [−c] [−d *dest*] [−n *copies*] [*file* . . .] send to printer   **●
lpr [−rm] [*file* . . .]   send to printer   *

The `lp` command is required by the POSIX P1003.2 standard and the SVID. The `lpr` command is not required.

The command to print a file on the local line printer has changed in name from version to version of the UNIX system. The V6 and PWB releases provided a command called `opr` that printed on an ''off-line printer,'' such as the printer on a nearby mainframe. V7 and System III used the `lpr` command to print a file.

The printer spooling system was rewritten in System V, adding features such as printer status requests, aborting a queued printer job, and support for multiple printers on the same system, and the command became `lp`. Berkeley also rewrote the printer spooling system for 3BSD, adding features such as printer-status requests, aborting a queued printer job, and in 4.2BSD, support for multiple printers on a network of machines, but the command name remained `lpr`.

As a result, the two systems offer similar functionality, but with incompatible commands. Since a distributed script is likely to print a file on any ordinary printer or to
typeset a document on any `troff`-capable printer, it is best to make the command name
a macro in a makefile for example:

```
LPR=      lp
TROFF=    qtroff
PR=       pr
FILES=    hdr.h main.c subr.c
MAN=      main.1

print:
          $(LPR) makefile
          $(PR) $(FILES) | $(LPR)

doc:
          $(TROFF) -man $(MAN)
```

In this particular makefile, the `lp` command is used to print text files, and the local
`qtroff` command is a shell script that calls `troff` and other filters for the appropriate
local laser printer. This approach allows a user to easily change the makefile for a different installation.

Shell scripts or applications needing to send a file to the printer should be prepared for
either `lp` or `lpr` commands. One possible method is to use the shell `||` operator: this
will generate a harmless error message on systems not supporting the first alternative.
Unfortunately, this method may be vulnerable to Trojan horse security attacks, so it is not
recommended.

```
pr $files | (lp || lpr)
```

ls [-CFRacdilqrstu1] [*file_name* ...]   list files   *****

This command is part of the POSIX mandatory execution environment, and so it is
portable among POSIX P1003.2 conforming systems.

Although the command is available on all UNIX systems, the options and default
behavior are not always the same. The options -a, -c, -d, -i, -l, -r, -s, -t, and -u
options are universally available. The -f and -g options were present in V6 and are
widely supported, but are not required by POSIX. The -C, -F, and -R options were
added by Berkeley in 3BSD and in System V release 2. The -1 option is also from
Berkeley, and was added to System V in release 4.

The default format varies from system to system. In V7 and System V, the files are
listed, one per line, down the left margin. In Berkeley releases and in System V release 4,
the default is to list in a multi-column format (the -C option) if the standard output is a
terminal and in single-column format otherwise, for upward compatibility with shell
scripts. Berkeley also provides the -1 option (digit one) to force a single-column format.
The -1 option was added to System V release 4.

The output format from the −1 option (letter L) also varies across systems. V7 and Berkeley systems print the modes, the link count, the owner, the length, the modification date, and the file name. System III and its descendents also print the group name after the owner. POSIX requires the System III interpretation.

m4 [*file* ...]   m4 preprocessor   ****

This command is not part of the POSIX P1003.2 standard, so it should be considered less portable. The m4 command is present in most UNIX system variants, including V7, System III, and their descendents.

/bin/mail *person* ...   send electronic mail   *****
/bin/mail [-f *file*]

This command is not part of the POSIX P1003.2 standard, so it should be considered less portable.

The mail command is present on every UNIX system release. It is sometimes called /bin/mail or ''bin mail,'' to distinguish it from the Mail command, which is often found installed as /usr/ucb/mail on Berkeley systems or systems with Berkeley enhancements. (This command is similar to the System V mailx command.) Its capabilities vary considerably, but it is the one common entry point into the mail system.

The POSIX P1003.2 standard created a new command called sendto. This command is intended as a common entry point. It also provides a standard way to specify a subject, carbon copy recipient, and blind-carbon-copy recipient. It does not require support for any particular mailing address syntax, such as the *route*!*host*!*user* bang syntax or the *user@domain* domain format. It does also not require support of any particular addressing semantics, such as routing, domain resolution, or X.400/X.500 attributes. The addresses are assumed to be character strings, and the message body, on standard input, is assumed to be text.

It is rare for a program to start up a mail program to read mail, but it is common for a program to send mail. As long as the destination of the mail is local to the sending machine, /bin/mail or sendto can be counted on to deliver the mail.

In most cases, for the simple delivery of mail, it does not matter if mailx is invoked (from /usr/ucb/mail) from an application. If this is unacceptable, it is more portable to call /bin/mail and if that fails (on some older Xenix systems), try /usr/bin/mail. Another approach, most useful through the shell, is to temporarily alter the PATH environment variable, being secure by avoiding extra directories:

        PATH=/bin:/usr/bin mail *person*

The format that the mail command will deliver the mail into a mailbox varies from system to system. Among UNIX systems, it is fairly safe to assume that the mailbox file may contain more than one message. Each message begins with a line beginning ''From '' and ends with a blank line. No other lines beginning ''From '' can appear in the middle of a message; any such line will have a > inserted to ensure that it is not mistaken for the beginning of a message. Some systems insert additional header lines after the From line.

The mailbox is in the directory /usr/spool/mail on V7-derived systems, and /usr/mail on System III derived systems. In each case, the name of the mailbox file is the same as the name of the user whose mailbox it is. The file is owned, readable, and writable by the owning user. The directory is not necessarily writable by the user, so it may require special permissions to delete the mailbox. Truncation to zero length is usually equivalent to deleting it.

The details of group permissions vary among systems. The V7 mail program is suid to user root to allow it to change the owner of the mailbox to the proper user. The System V /bin/mail program is sgid to group mail, with the spool directory permissions set to allow write permission to group mail, giving a similar effect.

`mailx [eFHinN]  [-f [`*filename*`]]`   electronic mail   ***
`    [-h `*hopcount*`]  [-r `*sender*`]  [-s `*subject*`]`
`    [-u `*user*`]  [`*person* `...]`

This command is not part of the POSIX P1003.2 standard, so it should be considered less portable.

This command is called mailx on System V release 2, /usr/ucb/mail on 4BSD, and Mail on many older systems with "Berkeley enhancements." It may not be available at all on some older systems.

Since this command is a user interface and some users will choose other user interfaces, use of this command from a shell script or the system command is not generally recommended, except as part of a command typed by the user. One possible exception is for an application to send mail with a subject.

```
MAILER=mailx
df | $MAILER -s "Disk Usage" root
```

This technique is convenient and allows setting MAILER=sendto on POSIX systems or MAILER=Mail on Berkeley systems. A slightly more portable alternative is to include the subject on standard input.

```
(echo "Subject: Disk Usage" ; echo "" ; df) | /bin/mail root
```

`make  [-f `*makefile*`]`   compile selectively   ****
`    [-eiknpqrSst]  [`*macro=name* `...]  [`*target_name* `...]`

This command is part of the POSIX Software Development Environment, and so is portable among POSIX conforming systems as part of a compilation tool, makefile, or shell script. It may not be present on systems with no compiler, so it is not portable from system.

The `make` command first appeared in V7, and revolutionized program development on the UNIX system. Any nontrivial UNIX program usually comes with a makefile.

Because `make` is so heavily used, many enhanced versions have been created. System V added extensions such as handling of SCCS files. The ''Fourth Generation Make'' added features that allow the `make` program to deduce many dependencies that must be explicitly spelled out with other versions.

Since there are so many versions of `make` in different UNIX systems, a portable makefile will use only the most basic features. Any feature present in the V7 make can be safely assumed to be present in all systems. These features include explicit commands and dependencies, the use of macros to define commands and lists of files, and the default rules for translating files with extensions `.c`, `.l`, `.y`, `.f`, and `.r` into object files ending in `.o`. It is not safe to assume any rule for translation of object files into an executable.

`mkdir [-p] [-m` *mode*`]`   make directory   *****
`[`*directory_name*`] ...`

This command is part of the POSIX mandatory execution environment, and so it is portable among POSIX P1003.2 conforming systems.

The −p and −m options were new in System V release 3 and P1003.2. They should be considered unportable until POSIX conformance is widespread.

The `mkdir` command appears in every UNIX system release, with essentially the same capabilities. There are, however, two different implementations, with a minor difference in their performance.

The traditional implementation of the `mkdir` command uses a suid `mkdir` program, calling the super-user restricted `mknod` system call. Checking for permissions and legal names is done in the program. Since the program is `suid`, the effective uid is lost, and permission decisions are based on the real uid. If called from a program or shell script running suid, this results in the directory being owned by the real uid.

A newer implementation uses an ordinary program and the new `mkdir` system call. All permissions and checks are carried out by the system call, and the program becomes merely an interface to the system call. Since the system call is not restricted to the super user, there is no need for the command to be suid. As a result, checking can be done with the effective uid.

System V gives the newly created directory the same group as the effective gid, as did Berkeley releases prior to 4.2BSD. 4.2BSD gives the new directory the same group as its parent directory. The merged System V release 4 uses the parent directory's group if the SGID bit is set on the directory, otherwise the gid of the process. POSIX allows either interpretation and provides the new feature `_POSIX_GROUP_PARENT` to allow a C application to determine what the current implementation will do. The FIPS standard requires the Berkeley behavior, so future implementations may migrate toward using the parent's group.

Because of this, it is not portable to depend on the owner or group of the newly created directory. 4.2BSD and its descendents use the system call, and the resulting directory is owned by the effective uid. System V release 3 and its descendents use the system call, but the newly created directory is owned by the real uid, for upward compatibility with the previous version. Earlier releases of both systems use the suid-program implementation and create directories owned by the real uid.

If your program creates a directory and intends to create files in it, be sure to take the umask into account. Some production systems have tighter security than some development systems, and this tighter umask may prevent your program from working.

It is sometimes useful to create a directory and then `chown` it to the desired owner and group. The `chown` may fail on some systems if not running as root.

`mkfifo [-p] [-m` *mode]* *file_name* `...`   make fifo   *●●

This command is part of the POSIX mandatory execution environment, and so it is portable among POSIX P1003.2 conforming systems.

The command is new to POSIX P1003.2, and is not present in 4.3BSD or System V release 3. Its use should be considered unportable until conformance to P1003.2 becomes widespread.

`/etc/mknod` *name* `[c]` `[b]` *major minor*   make inode   *
`/etc/mknod` *name* `p`

The `mknod` command is not part of the POSIX P1003.2 standard, so it should be considered less portable. It is present in all UNIX releases, but the meanings of the particular fields are very low level, and generally device-dependent. This command is normally typed by a person or is part of the installation script for a specific device. Use of `mknod` to create a FIFO is portable within System V, but will not work on V7 or 4BSD.

`mv [-f]` *source_file* `...` *target*   move files   *****

This command is part of the POSIX mandatory execution environment, and so it is portable among POSIX P1003.2 conforming systems.

This command is part of all UNIX systems. The command is highly portable when ordinary files are involved. Special considerations apply when directories are moved or when the target file is an executable file that is currently active.

Renaming directories is subject to special considerations. It is possible to create improper directory structures, such as disconnected and unreachable parts of the filesystem, infinite loops, and hidden directories, with unrestricted use of the `unlink` and `link` system calls by the super user. Commands such as `mv` contain special checks to prevent this.

V7 only allowed the mv command to rename a directory within the current directory. System V has a similar restriction, but provides the program mvdir with a different syntax for the super user to move directories to other locations. 4.2BSD allows the mv command to be used by any user for appropriate directory moves. Since shell scripts, installation scripts, and programs rarely automatically rearrange the directory tree, this should not affect program portability very much.

If the target filename already exists, is executable, and a currently running process started from that file, most UNIX systems will prevent copying a new file onto the same file, since it would affect the running program. (This is not true of some older UNIX systems, which did not swap or page the program image directly from the executable file.) This also affects the mv command.

When a file is moved to an active target file, mv first checks for write permission. If the write check fails, mv will print the mode and double check with the user. If the user says to proceed, it will attempt to unlink the file. On V7 and System V, this will fail, and an error message will be printed. (A workaround is to move the target file somewhere else. Unfortunately, due to cleanup considerations and the possibility of multiple installations during the lifetime of an active process, this workaround is not suitable for a shell script or makefile.) On 4.2BSD, the unlink succeeds, but the file is treated as an open file and continues to exist on the filesystem until the last process using it exits.

If your installation script copies the program into a location that might contain an old version of the program and if the program might already be running, there may be a conflict when copying the new version in. Removing it may not be enough; it may be necessary to move it out of the way. For the above reasons, this workaround is inadequate as well.

A simpler solution may be to require that the installation occur when the programs are not active. For example, when installing a network that contains server programs that are always active, the procedure might involve shutting down the network before installing a new version.

nl [-p] [-h*type*] [-b*type*]   number lines   *
    [-f*type*] [-v*start#*] [-i*incr*] [-l*num*] [-s*sep*]
    [-w*width*] [-n*format*] [-d*delim*] [*file*]

This command is not part of the POSIX P1003.2 standard, so it should be considered less portable. A more portable method uses the -n and -t options to pr.

nm [-u] *object_file* . . .   show symbol table   *

This command is not part of the POSIX P1003.2 standard, so it should be considered less portable.

This command is found on all UNIX systems. The format of the output differs considerably among the systems, making it unportable to use the command from a shell script or makefile.

nohup *command*   run job after disconnect   **

This command is part of the POSIX mandatory execution environment, and so it is portable among POSIX P1003.2 conforming systems. It is rare for a program to use the nohup command directly. It is more common for a user to type nohup at the terminal.

The utility of this command has lessened over time. The command ignores and has no effect on other signals, such as SIGTERM and SIGKILL, which are generated by some network servers. Some shells automatically make arrangements to ignore all appropriate signals, rendering this command unnecessary.

The C shell has a built-in nohup command that behaves slightly differently.

od [-bcdox] [*file*] [[+]*offset*[.][b]]   octal dump   *****

This command is not part of the POSIX P1003.2 standard, so it should be considered less portable. POSIX requires a new command, hd, which dumps in hexadecimal instead of octal. The hd command takes different options from the od command. In practice, the od command was present in V6 and all its descendents.

pack [-] *clear_file* . . .   compress file   *
pcat *packed_file* . . .   *
unpack *packed_file* . . .   *

This command is not part of the POSIX P1003.2 standard, so it should be considered unportable. The pack commands are present in System III and System V, but not in V7 or its descendents.

These commands are seldom needed by a distribution, unless distribution of software or data in a packed format is contemplated. Since there are many different compressed formats in widespread use, each defined by the implementing software, it is unsafe to assume that the recipient has the proper unpacking program. It may still be possible to take advantage of compression, however, by including an unpacking program, which is itself not packed, with the distribution.

One program, called compress, is based on a modified Lempel-Ziv algorithm,[3] It achieves about 50% compression with a typical text file, and is in the public domain. This program, along with the related uncompress and zcat programs, is present on SunOS and System V release 4. It is also available on bulletin boards such as Usenet.

---

[3] Terry A. Welch, ''A Technique for High Performance Data Compression,'' *IEEE Computer*, Vol. 17, No. 6 (June 1984), pp. 8-19.

`passwd` [*name*]   change password   ***

This command is not part of the POSIX P1003.2 standard, so it should be considered less portable.

It is rare for a program, makefile, or shell script to invoke this command. If it is called from a program, the user will normally have to key in the old and new passwords from the keyboard. There is no portable way to supply them from a program.

`paste` [-d*list*] [-s] *file_name* . . .   join columns   **•

This command is part of the POSIX P1003.2 standard, but it is specific to System V. This command, and the related `cut` command, is not present in V7-derived systems. It should be considered unportable unless you assume POSIX conformance.

`pax` [-cimopuvy] [-f *archive*]   portable archiver   *••
          [-s *replstr*] [-t *device*] [*pattern* . . .]
`pax` -r [-cimopuvy] [-f *archive*] [-s *replstr*]
          [-t *device*] [*pattern* . . .]
`pax` -w [-adimuvy] [-b *blocking*] [-f *archive*]
          [-s *replstr*] [-t *device*] [-x *format*] [*pathname* . . .]
`pax` -r -w [-ilmopuvy] [-s *replstr*] [*pathname* . . .] *dir*

This command was created by POSIX. It was not present in any previous UNIX system variants. It should be considered unportable unless you assume POSIX conformance.

The previous commands to get this same functionality were `cpio` and `tar`. The `pax` command can read or write any of these formats. The default format is a new format created by POSIX.

`pg` [-cefns] [-*lines*] [-p *prompt*]   screen pager   *
        [+*startline*] [+/*pattern*] [*file* . . .]
`more` [-cdflsu] [-*lines*] [+*startline*]   **
        [+/*pattern*] [*file* . . .]
`page` [-cdflsu] [-*lines*] [+*startline*]   **
        [+/*pattern*] [*file* . . .]

These commands are not part of the POSIX P1003.2 standard, so they should be considered less portable. While no single paging command is portable to all systems, it is fairly portable (***) to assume that some paging command is available on any given UNIX system. In practice, the `more` and `page` commands are available as a Berkeley enhancement on most UNIX systems except AT&T releases prior to System V release 4.

V7 did not include a paging command, but many subsequent distributions included some paging program. The name and exact semantics of the command vary from system to system.

3BSD and its descendents provide a command called `more`. This command also appears as a "Berkeley enhancement" in many systems based on System III and System V.

System V release 2 and its descendents provide the `pg` command. When used with the following Korn shell alias:

```
alias more='pg -nsp "More? "'
```

the command is similar to the `more` command. In its default configuration, the `pg` command functions much the same, but has a different user interface. System V release 4 provides all three commands.

A few systems have a capability called *page mode* built directly into the terminal driver. On these systems, by setting the appropriate modes, no program need be invoked; output automatically stops after a screen full of output with no input from the user.

One convention often used is to use the environment variable `$PAGER`. If set, this variable is the name of a program to be used as a paging filter. If set to the null string, or to `/bin/cat`, the terminal driver is assumed to provide any necessary paging with no special action on the part of the program. If not set, local system conventions (either `more` or `pg`) apply.

`pr` [–adfmprt] [+*page*] [–*column*] format for printing   ******
    [–e *char*] [*gap*] [–h *header*] [–i *char*] [*gap*] [–l*lines*]
    [–n *char*] [*width*] [–o *offset*] [–s*char*] [–w*width*]
    [*file_name* ...]

This command is part of the POSIX mandatory execution environment, and so it is portable among POSIX P1003.2 conforming systems.

Not all options to `pr` are portable. V7 had the following options: –*column*, +*page*, –h, –w*n*, –l*n*, –t, –s*c*, and –m. Berkeley and System V have both added the –f option to generate form feeds. System V and P1003.2 have added the –a, –d, –e*ck*, –i*ck*, –n*ck*, –o*k*, –p, and –r options.

`prof` [–z] [*program*]   execution profiler   ****

This command is not part of the POSIX P1003.2 standard, so it should be considered less portable.

This command and the –p option to `cc` are generally available on all systems with a C compiler. The hierarchical `gprof` tool is specific to 4BSD.

ps [-al]   show processes   *

This command is not part of the POSIX P1003.2 standard, so it should be considered less portable.

This command is generally present, but the syntax and output format are quite different on different systems. V7 and its descendents use a `tar`-like syntax with option letters as part of the first argument:

```
ps axl
ps lt22
```

System III and their descendents use the `getopt` syntax:

```
ps -ael
ps -l -t tty22
```

System III added options to add a new −f "full" format and to restrict the printout to a particular process list, terminal, user, or group. In System III, the V7 x option was changed to −e.

The only options that are equivalent between the current popular versions of `ps` are the a and l options. Since the V7 and 4BSD `ps` command will ignore a leading −, commands such as

```
ps -al
```

will behave the same on both systems, although the output format is slightly different.

pwd   print working directory   *****

This command is part of the POSIX mandatory execution environment, and so it is portable among POSIX P1003.2 conforming systems. It takes no arguments.

The traditional, and portable, way for a UNIX program to discover its current directory is to call the `pwd` command in a subprocess. The `getcwd` function, where supported, often does this. Although accurate, this method is very slow.

Another method is to look in the environment for a CWD variable. Some shells pass this variable to their children. However, it is not safe to depend on its presence or its correctness if present. A call to the `chdir` system call does not alter this variable, and it is possible for the user to alter it to an incorrect value.

A portable program that wishes to determine its current directory should first consider using the string ".", since that string will work for many applications, even under some other operating systems such as MS DOS. If that is inappropriate, `getcwd` should be called. If `getcwd` is not available, the application can conditionally include an implementation of `getcwd` that calls `pwd`. It is better to use `fork`, `exec`, `pipe`, and `dup` than `popen` or `system`, because the latter two calls go through a shell, causing additional overhead and a possible security problem from casual invocation of the shell.

Older versions of uux called pwd just in case the user gave a command with a file-name argument relative to the current directory. Since uux is suid, it sometimes failed when called from beneath a user's protected home directory. Since uux is mainly called by the mail or inews commands, which pass information on their standard input and arguments, the failure did not matter. Yet a check in the uux command caused an error message to be printed rather than delivery of the mail. The overhead of calling pwd unnecessarily for every piece of mail was also significant.

read [-r] *name* . . .   read one line   ****

This shell built-in command is part of the POSIX P1003.2 standard. It is also present in all Bourne shell implementations. It can be considered portable.

The -r option is an invention of the POSIX committee. It provides functionality similar to the line command present in many systems. In the rare situation where it matters, a portable technique is to call line and provide a one-line shell script or alias, or a short C program called line, in the event that it is not present on system in question.

readonly *name*[=*value*] . . .   mark variable unchangeable   **●

This command is part of the POSIX P1003.2 standard. It is also present in all Bourne shell implementations. It can be considered portable.

The =*value* syntax is an invention of the POSIX committee. It is more portable to simply initialize the value and then execute the readonly command.

return [*n*]   return function value   **●

This command is part of the POSIX P1003.2 standard. It is also present in all Bourne shell implementations supporting functions. It can be considered as portable as the function itself.

rm [-firR] *file_name* . . .   remove files   *****

This command is part of the POSIX mandatory execution environment, and so it is portable among POSIX P1003.2 conforming systems. The -R option is an invention of the POSIX committee, and should be considered unportable until POSIX conformance is widespread. The equivalent -r option is so widely implemented and used that it was not marked deprecated. The -r option is far more portable than -R.

rmdir [-p] *directory_name* ...   remove directories   *****

This command is part of the POSIX mandatory execution environment, and so it is portable among POSIX P1003.2 conforming systems. The -p option is an invention of the POSIX committee, and should be considered unportable until POSIX conformance is widespread.

This command might be implemented either with the rmdir system call or by a series of checks followed by unlink. Since unlink on a directory requires super-user status, the unlink implementation must be suid, although the newer system call based program need not be. Some of the caveats for the mkdir command also apply to rmdir.

rsh [-eiknrstuvx]   restricted shell   *
   [-c *string*] [*argument* ...]
rsh *host* [-l *username*] [-n] *command*   remote shell   **

This command is not part of the POSIX P1003.2 standard, so it should be considered less portable.

While both System V and 4.2BSD have commands called rsh, they were in fact totally different commands. The System V rsh is a restricted version of the shell used for logins without full access to the system. The 4.2BSD rsh is a remote shell client used to run a program (or other shell command) on another machine on a network.

This conflict causes problems when the 4.2BSD networking package is ported to System V environments. The ad hoc solution was to rename the remote shell command as remsh or sometimes rmtsh. In System V release 4, the conflict was solved by calling the restricted shell /usr/lib/rsh and the remote shell /usr/bin/rsh.

The restricted shell and editor are generally considered to be not very secure. Depending on them to make restricted login accounts is not recommended.

SCCS: admin, delta, get,   source code control   *
   prs, rmdel, sact, unget, what, val

These commands are not part of the POSIX P1003.2 standard, so they should be considered less portable. SCCS is specific to PWB, System III, and System V. Also, they may not be present on systems with no compiler.

The implementation of these commands is a major effort, and they are generally not found on systems not supported by a PWB, System III, or System V UNIX license. 4BSD, which comes with a UNIX/32V license, does not include them, but instead includes a package called RCS, developed at Purdue University. This package is not compatible with SCCS, but offers similar functionality.

`sdb` [*object_file* [*core_file* [*directory*]]]   symbolic debugger   **

This command is not part of the POSIX P1003.2 standard, so it should be considered less portable. It is rare for a program, makefile, or shell script to require a debugger.

There are three commonly available debuggers on UNIX systems. V7 supplied an assembly-language debugger `adb`, which replaced the V6 `db` and `cdb` programs. UNIX/32V also supplied the new symbolic debugger `sdb`. `sdb` quickly became popular, and was incorporated into System III and V7 ports, although `adb` remained popular for its speed, simplicity, and because no special compilation options were needed. 4.2BSD added a third debugger `dbx` and made it their preferred debugger. System V dropped support of `adb` and made `sdb` the standard debugger. Berkeley dropped support of `sdb` and made `dbx` the preferred debugger, retaining support for `adb`.

As a result of all this, the most widely available debugger is `sdb`. There is no universally available debugger. There are slight variations with `sdb`, due to separate evolutions. For example, System V requires the `-g` compilation option for use of `sdb`, but under 4.2BSD, `-g` prepares tables for `dbx`, and `-go` prepares for `sdb`.

`sed` [`-n`] *script* [*file* . . .]   stream editor   ***
`sed` [`-n`] [`-e` *script*] [`-f` *scriptfile*] [*file* . . .]

This command is part of the POSIX mandatory execution environment, and so it is portable among POSIX P1003.2 conforming systems.

`sendto` [`-s` *subject*] *address* . . .   send mail   *••

The `sendto` command was a new creation of the POSIX P1003.2 standard. It should be considered unportable unless you assume POSIX P1003.2 conformance.

This command is intended as a common entry point. It provides a standard way to specify a subject. It does not require support for any particular mailing address syntax, such as the *route*!*host*!*user* bang syntax or the *user@domain* domain format. It also does not require support of any particular addressing semantics, such as routing, domain resolution, or X.400/X.500 attributes. The addresses are assumed to be character strings, and the message body, on standard input, is assumed to be text.

In general, it is best to only assume that login names on the system are acceptable addresses or to make all addresses user or configuration parameters to allow an address that makes sense in the local environment to be used.

```
set [aefnuvx] argument ...]      set options/parameters        ****
set - [argument ...]
set -- [argument ...]
set +
```

This shell built-in command is part of the POSIX P1003.2 mandatory execution environment. It was present in all releases of the Bourne shell. It can be considered portable.

Only the -e, -k, -n, -t, -u, -v, and -x options are present in both 4BSD and System V. Of these, the -k and -t options were deleted from POSIX. All other options and the last three forms are less portable.

The primary use of the set command in a shell script is to use the argument parser to break apart a command, such as date, into separate fields and extract one field. For example, the sequence

```
set `date`
day=$3
```

will assign the day of the month (the third field of the output of the date command) to the variable day and will also destroy any input arguments. This practice is in practice quite portable, and for commands with a single line of output, can effectively replace the use of the cut command. Other uses should be limited to the -e, -n, -u, -v, and -x options.

```
sh [-aefinsuvx] [-c string] [argument ...]    shell      ****
```

This command is part of the POSIX mandatory execution environment, and so it is portable among POSIX P1003.2 conforming systems. The -a and -f options are inventions of the POSIX committee and are less portable.

All UNIX systems have a shell called /bin/sh, and on all systems since V7, that shell has been either the Bourne shell or a superset such as the Korn shell. V6 had a different and considerably less powerful shell, and PWB had the Mashey shell, which was similar to the V6 shell but more powerful.

Berkeley has a shell called the C shell, which is usually installed as /bin/csh. This shell comes with 4BSD and SVr4, and a subset version is provided as a Berkeley enhancement on some other UNIX versions based on V7, System III, or System V. (The major feature missing in the subset is job control, which requires some operating system features present in 4BSD and SVr4.) The C shell is similar in many ways to the V6 shell, but with many enhancements comparable to, and in many ways similar to, the Bourne shell. It also provides enhancements not present in the Bourne shell, such as a history list and aliasing.

The Korn shell is a more recent development from AT&T. It first appeared in SVr4. It is usually installed as /bin/ksh, although some systems install it as /bin/sh. (Many systems install it as an add-on in a local directory.) The Korn shell is almost completely compatible with the Bourne shell. It also provides a history and alias mechanism, comparable in power to the C shell, but done differently. Additional features include shell functions (which can be more complex than aliases) and access to the history mechanism using either the `vi` or `emacs` command sets. The Korn shell also supports job control where supported by the operating system.

When writing a shell script, it should be written in Bourne shell. The Bourne shell can be almost universally assumed, but many systems do not have the C shell or Korn shell. The advantages to these shells are primarily for interactive users, and there is little benefit for scripts.

`shar` *archive_name file* ...   shell archiver   *

This command is not required by POSIX P1003.2. It is not present in System V or 4BSD. It should be considered unportable.

It is rare for an application to invoke `shar`. The command is a convenient way for users to bundle files in a portable format. Because the archive format is a shell script, the resulting bundle will be extremely portable, unless one of the files contains a string used to mark the end of the file.

The POSIX committee was considering the possible inclusion of this command in P1003.2a as an interactive application, under the name `pshar`. Since the implementation of `shar` is a simple shell script (see Chapter 4), there is no need to assume that it is present. It suffices to create the command on any system where it is needed.

`shift` [*n*]   shift arguments   *****

This shell built-in command is required by the POSIX P1003.2 mandatory execution environment. The command has been present in all shells since V6. It can be considered extremely portable.

The optional argument *n* is not supported in 4BSD shells and is less portable. The ability to shift by more than one argument is rarely needed, and when multiple argument shifts are needed, it is more portable to invoke `shift` more than once. Since this command is built into the shell, the performance impact of a sequence such as `shift; shift` will usually be minor.

`size` [*object_file* ...]   show executable size   ****

This command is not part of the POSIX P1003.2 standard, so it should be considered less portable.

Although the `size` command is available on all UNIX systems, the format of the output varies considerably from system to system. It is unportable to write a shell script that extracts a part of the output of the `size` command and uses it as an argument to another command.

`sleep` *time*   pause   *******

This command is part of the POSIX mandatory execution environment, and so it is portable among POSIX P1003.2 conforming systems.

`sort` `[-bdfinrmu]` `[-o` *output*`]`   *******
    `[-t` *char*`]` `[-k` *keydef*`]` `[`*file_name* `...]`
`sort` `-c` `[-bdfinru]`
    `[-t`*char*`]` `[+`*pos1* `[`*pos2*`]]` `[`*file_name* `...]`

This command is part of the POSIX mandatory execution environment, and so it is portable among POSIX P1003.2 conforming systems.

The `-k` option is an invention of the POSIX committee. Previous implementations used the syntax `[+`*pos1* `[`*pos2*`]]` to indicate starting and ending columns for the key. The older syntax has been marked deprecated by POSIX. The older syntax will be more portable than the `-i` option until POSIX conformance is widespread.

`spell` `[-bvx]` `[`*file* `...]`   spell checker   ******

This command is not part of the POSIX P1003.2 standard, so it should be considered less portable. It is present in all versions of the UNIX system, but it is rarely needed from a shell script or application.

It is not portable to assume the presence of an on-line dictionary. The text file `/usr/dict/words` is specific to V7 and its descendents. The `/usr/lib/w2006` and `/usr/lib/spell/hlista` files are specific to certain releases of System V. Many systems have unbundled the `spell` program and the dictionary with the document-formatting utilities. As a result, many systems will not have a dictionary on-line. If there is an on-line dictionary, the name of the file and its format are unpredictable.

`split` `[-`*lines*`]` `[`*file* `[`*name*`]]`   split files   *******

This command is not part of the POSIX P1003.2 standard, so it should be considered less portable. It is present in all versions of the UNIX system.

`strip` *objfile* `...`   remove symbol table   *******

This command is not part of the POSIX P1003.2 standard, so it should be considered less portable. It is present in all versions of the UNIX system and is often used in makefiles. It and the `-s` option to the `cc` command are equally portable.

stty [-ag] [[-]echo] [*speed*]   terminal mode settings   **
[erase *c*] [kill *c*] [intr *c*]

This command is part of the POSIX mandatory execution environment, and so it is portable among POSIX P1003.2 conforming systems. The options listed above are the only ones that are portable to V7-derived systems such as 4BSD.

In practice, although every version of the UNIX system has the stty command, there are two major variants corresponding to the two major terminal drivers. POSIX specifies a terminal driver similar to System III and System V. Some other systems use the V7 terminal driver or its extension, the 4BSD terminal driver.

The two terminal drivers are very different at the C program interface level. At the shell level, there are some compatible options. The speed selections (up to 9600 BPS) and the echo, erase, kill, and intr options are generally portable. The raw and cooked options are present in 4BSD and System V, but not quite equivalent, due to side effects from turning off the ICANON mode in System V. Use of stty 0 to hang up the connection is also portable across systems, although not across all hardware. An stty command using only these options can be portable as long as the terminal being set is the one issuing the command.

The (undocumented) conventions for changing the modes of another terminal are different. On V7 and 4BSD, the modes of the standard output are affected, so the normal usage is

        stty echo > /dev/tty12

On System III and System V, the modes of the standard input are affected, so the normal usage is

        stty echo < /dev/tty12

On either system, the modes can be printed by giving no options. On V7 and 4.2BSD, the printout occurs on the standard error, allowing the modes of another terminal to be queried. The System V stty command prints its output on standard out.

Since write permission to other users is sometimes allowed, but read permission is not, only the super user can query and set other terminals on System V. (Besides, it's not nice for an ordinary user to change the modes of another user's terminal. This feature is usually needed for serial communication applications, such as sending data to printers or resetting a terminal after an application aborts in raw mode.)

su [-] [*username*]   substitute userid   ***

This command is not part of the POSIX P1003.2 standard, so it should be considered less portable.

The su command is present in all UNIX systems, but the details of usage are different. In particular, the options most likely to be used in a distributed program are different.

The default usage of su, with no arguments, is similar on each system. A single argument with the name of the desired user may be given, and if omitted, will default to root. Some systems alter environment variables such as HOME to more closely resemble an actual login as the new user.

System III and V allow the −c *command* option to be given, which causes the single command given to be run by the super-user shell, followed by an immediate exit. On V7 and 4BSD systems, this is accomplished by redirecting the standard input of the su command to a shell script containing one or more commands.

sum [*file_name* . . .]   show checksum   **

This command is not part of the POSIX mandatory execution environment, and so it is not portable among POSIX P1003.2 conforming systems. POSIX requires a similar, but incompatible, command named cksum.

Although this command is present in all UNIX systems, the numbers cannot necessarily be compared between different systems. The checksum algorithms are also not consistent. V7 and 4BSD use one algorithm, and System V uses another. The System V −r option uses the V7 algorithm.

The second number is measured in different units. On some systems, including System V, the units are usually 512-byte blocks. (Some mainframe System V implementations use 4096-byte blocks.) On 4BSD, they are BUFSIZ, which is generally 1024.

tabs   set tabs   ****

This command is not part of the POSIX P1003.2 standard, so it should be considered less portable. Although the tabs command does have options, none of the options are portable.

tail [−cfl] [−n *number*] [*file*]   show end of file   *****
tail [±[*lines*] [lcf]] [*file*]

This command is part of the POSIX P1003.2 standard. It is present on 4BSD, System V, and other major releases of the UNIX system. The −n option is an invention of the POSIX committee. The second form is universally supported and in practice quite portable. The −b option is widely implemented, but the interpretation of a *block* varies from system to system. In practice, the −b option is not usually needed.

The tail command is present on all UNIX systems. The −f option to watch a file grow was new with System III and 4BSD; it may be missing on some V7 and older systems.

`tar [bcflmrtuvwx]` *[blocking_factor]*   tape archiver   **
   [archive_file] *[file ...]*

This command is not part of the POSIX P1003.2 standard, so it should be considered
less portable. The position and presence of the *blocking_factor* and *archive_file* arguments depend on the position and presence of the b and options. There is no leading
hyphen for options, although most implementations will ignore one if present.

In general, almost any UNIX system can read a `tar` image, as long as the physical
medium can be read. Even on systems with no tape drive, it is common to transfer `tar`
images with network copy commands such as `uucp`. Only a few UNIX system distributions had no `tar` command.

Some older UNIX systems have a less capable `tar` command. Features such as large
block sizes and writing directories onto the tape are new. The POSIX standard added
new features to `tar` images that will not be supported by older programs. These include
symbolic links and multiple-volume archives.

For text files in a single directory, an even more portable format is the shell archive
described in Chapter 4. Shell archives can be easily shipped to other systems, even using
electronic mail or Netnews.

`tee [-ai]` *[file_name ...]*   tee fittings   *****

This command is part of the POSIX mandatory execution environment, and so it is
portable among POSIX P1003.2 conforming systems.

`test` *expression*   test conditions   ****
`[` *expression* `]`   ***

This command is part of the POSIX mandatory execution environment, and so it is
portable among POSIX P1003.2 conforming systems.

This command is built into the System V and Korn shells, but an ordinary program
also exists on all UNIX systems. Most UNIX systems have an alias [for `test` (actually, a filesystem link) that allows the Bourne shell syntax:

```
if [ -z string ]
then
     echo yes
fi
```

This syntax is also supported by the Korn shell, and by POSIX P1003.2, but a small
number of systems are not distributed with the [link, making `test` a bit more portable.
Note also that there must be blanks around the brackets.

The System V options −h, −k, and −l are not required by POSIX and are less portable. The only options universally available are −d, −f, −n, −r, −s, −t, −w, and −z
options, and the −a, −o, =, !=, −eq, and ! operators .

The −f option is interpreted slightly differently in 4BSD and System V. System V and POSIX use "true if *file* exists and is a regular file", but 4BSD uses "true if *file* exists and is not a directory". The only difference is if the file is a special entity, such as a device, fifo, or a symbolic link.

`time` *command*   time command   ∗∗

This command is not part of the POSIX P1003.2 standard, so it should be considered less portable.

Although this command is available in all UNIX versions, the format and precision of the output varies. This command is intended to time a single process and its descendents. Pipelines are not necessarily descended from the program being timed. Indeed, the command

```
time cat a b c | sort | uniq -c | lp
```

will only time the `cat` command! Timing pipelines is best done with the shell:

```
time sh -c "cat a b c | sort | uniq -c | lp"
```

`time` is a built-in command to the C shell, which prints a single line. The system program prints several lines.

`touch [-acm] [-r` *ref_file*`]`   set write date   ∗∗∗∗∗
`     [-t` *time*`]` *file_name* `...`

This command is part of the POSIX mandatory execution environment, and so it is portable among POSIX P1003.2 conforming systems. Only the −c option is universally available.

`tr [-cds]` *string1* `[`*string2*`]`   transliterate characters   ∗∗∗∗∗

This command is part of the POSIX mandatory execution environment, and so it is portable among POSIX P1003.2 conforming systems.

While all UNIX systems have a `tr` command, the details of the syntax are, in practice, not portable. V7 and its descendents use a range syntax like this:

```
tr A-Z a-z
```

System III and its descendents use brackets (that must be quoted) for the same effect:

```
tr '[A-Z]' '[a-z]'
```

The POSIX P1003.2 standard uses the System III syntax. The System V option [$a*n$] (originally in System III) is not supported in V7-derived systems nor is it part of P1003.2. The −n option to avoid deleting null characters was added in P1003.2, and should be considered unportable unless you assume P1003.2 conformance.

A portable shell script can safely translate a few fixed characters with the `tr` command. If you want to do upper/lower-case conversion, a reasonably portable way is to use the form

```
tr ABCDEFGHIJKLMNOPQRSTUVWXYZ abcdefghijklmnopqrstuvwxyz
```

Even this method has problems, since it assumes the American alphabet. In general, foreign alphabets have many complexities, so it is best to isolate case conversion in a single place, so it can be fixed locally. A C program written to use locales is better suited to do case translation.

`trap` [*action*] [*condition* ...]   catch signals   ****

This shell built-in command is a part of the POSIX P1003.2 standard, so it is portable. In practice, all Bourne shell implementations support the `trap` command. The use of symbolic names such as `INT` for the condition is an invention of POSIX. It is more portable to use signal numbers 0 (exit), 1 (hangup), 2 (interrupt), 3 (quit), 9 (kill), and 15 (terminate). Other signal numbers may not be as portable.

`true`   true constant   ****

This command is part of the POSIX mandatory execution environment, and so it is portable among POSIX P1003.2 conforming systems. The `true` command takes no arguments.

`tty` [-s]   show terminal port   ****

This command is part of the POSIX mandatory execution environment, and so it is portable among POSIX P1003.2 conforming systems.

`umask` [*symbolic_mode*]   set permission defaults   ****

This command is part of the POSIX mandatory execution environment, and so it is portable among POSIX P1003.2 conforming systems.

The `umask` command is, of necessity, built into the shell. Since it affects any files created by the shell or the programs subsequently called by the shell, care must be taken in makefiles and calls to `system`. In practice, the `umask` system call is preferable to the `system` function, so the only necessary care is in makefiles. `umask` is rarely used even in makefiles, with `chmod` preferred.

The *symbolic_mode* can, according to the POSIX standard, be either an octal-integer or an encoded name string. The octal integer format is portable; even the particular bits are specified by POSIX. The name format is new with POSIX and is not portable unless you assume POSIX conformance.

unalias *name* ...   *●●

This shell built-in command is a part of the POSIX P1003.2 standard. This command was an invention of POSIX. It is not portable unless you assume P1003.2 conformance. The Korn shell also supports an `unalias` command.

uname [-amnrsv]   show system name   **●

This command is part of the POSIX mandatory execution environment, and so it is portable among POSIX P1003.2 conforming systems.

The `uname -n` command and the `uname` system call are specific to System III and System V. They are not present in V7 or 4.2BSD. 4.2BSD instead uses the `hostname` command to get the local host name.

In practice, from a shell script or makefile, the `uname -n` command is most often used to determine the name of the local machine. It is important to always specify the `-n` option to `uname`. Some systems print the nodename by default, and others print the system name if no options are specified. Some systems administratively cause both names to be the same, but others use a string such as `unix` for the system name.

A more portable command for determining this name is

```
uuname -l
```

which works in V7, 4BSD, System III, and System V. The `uuname` command is not entirely portable, however. It is not required by P1003.2, and is sometimes unbundled with the UUCP package under names such as Basic Network Utilities. In practice, however, most systems support `uuname`.

The conventions for determining the local host name vary among systems. System III and System V compile it into the operating system for access by the `uname` system call. (Some recent System V releases allow the name to be changed at boot time with the `-S` option to `uname`.) The `uname` system call often restricts the system name to eight characters, causing truncation of longer names.

4.2BSD stores the name in the operating system for access by the `gethostname` system call and `hostname` command. This is normally set at boot time by the `hostname` command.

V7 stored the host name only in the include file `<whoami.h>`, which contained a line such as

```
#define MYNAME "attunix"
```

The UUCP and `mail` commands were recompiled to change the name. Commands that needed to determine the name at run time would open that file and read it, looking for an appropriate line.

Some other systems use other conventions. For example, the name of the system has been stored in the file `/etc/systemid` or `/usr/include/whoami`.

uniq [-cdu] [-f *fields*]   group identical lines   *****
   [-s *chars*] [*input_file* [*output_file*]]
uniq [-cdu] [-n] [+m] [*input_file* [*output_file*]]

This command is part of the POSIX mandatory execution environment, and so it is
portable among POSIX P1003.2 conforming systems.

The second syntax is universally supported, but has been marked deprecated by
POSIX in favor of the first form, which conforms to the standard option guidelines. The
second form will be more portable than the first until POSIX conformance is widespread.

unset [-f] *name* ...   *

This shell built-in command is a part of the POSIX P1003.2 standard. It was new in
System V release 2. It is not present in 4.2BSD. It should be considered unportable
unless you assume POSIX or System V release 2 compatibility.

until *command_list*   control structure   ****
do
   command_list
done

This shell built-in is part of POSIX P1003.2, so it is portable. All Bourne shell implementations support this control structure.

uucp [-cdmr] *source_file* ...   network file copy   ****
   destination_file
uulog [-s *system*]   ****
uuname   ****
uustat [-k *jobid*] [-s *system*] [-u *user*]   ****
uuto [-pm] *source_files* *system*!*user*   ****
uux [-] *command_string*   ****

The uucp, uulog, uuname, uustat, uuto, and uux commands are not part of
P1003.2, so they should be considered less portable. Some commands were present until
draft 8, at which time they were removed. The uustat and uuto commands are
specific to System III and System V, so they are less portable.

In practice, all UNIX systems have the uucp, uulog, uuname, and uux commands.
Some distributions unbundle them onto a separate diskette, making their installation
optional. This is useful for systems that have no modems and no other links to the outside world. It is also useful for systems whose only links to the world are through other
types of networks.

It is common to use dial-up telephone lines and modems to create UUCP links with
other computers running the UNIX system and other operating systems such as MS DOS.

It is also common to establish UUCP links over other similar kinds of circuits, including hard-wired RS232 connections, terminal port switches, and circuit-switched communications networks such as Datakit, X.25, and TCP/IP.

Many people believe that UUCP represents the least common denominator, available on all UNIX systems, over all kinds of media. In addition, many believe that electronic mail addressed using the UUCP "bang path" syntax host1!host2!...!hostn!user will always be passed by all UNIX systems, regardless of their local configuration and networking facilities.

This is not strictly true, as there are many UNIX systems that are connected only to local area networks using other conventions or not connected to any form of outside link at all. (Systems conforming to the ARPANET standards such as RFC822 will interpret *host*!*user@domain* as an address *host*!*user*, which is local to *domain*.)

In the area of networking, there are many standards, some formal, some de facto and undocumented, and some very formal standards adopted by the International Standards Organization. It is seldom safe to make assumptions about networking without first determining local options and configurations.

vi [-rRl] [-t *tag*] [-w*window_size*]   screen editor   ***
    [+*ex_command*] [*file* ...]

This command is not part of the POSIX P1003.2 standard, so it should be considered less portable.

In practice, the vi command is quite portable. It was developed at Berkeley as a descendent of the ex editor, which in turn descended from ed. Berkeley originally released it as an addition to V6, then distributed it as part of 3BSD and 4BSD. vi was not part of the V7 or System III distributions, but most distributors quickly added it as a Berkeley enhancement. In System V, AT&T adopted vi as part of the standard system. POSIX does not require the presence of the vi or ex editors.

The UNIX implementation of these two commands uses two links to the same file, and allows the user to switch between vi and ex editing modes during an editing session. It is likely that most implementations will supply both commands.

In a shell script or makefile, it is sometimes useful to call an editing script. If the editing is to be done from a script, an editor that is not screen-oriented, such as sed, ed, or ex, is usually more appropriate. Screen editors such as vi become useful when a script or program needs to allow a person to interactively edit a file. For example, when composing an electronic mail message, the user may wish to compose the message in an editor.

Although the presence of vi can be almost universally assumed, it is not always appropriate for a shell script, makefile, or program to invoke it. The choice of a text editor is a personal decision, and different users on the same system often prefer different editors. Other screen editors, such as EMACS, are popular. Some prefer the line-oriented editor ex or its faster, less powerful predecessor ed.

By convention, the environment variable EDITOR is used to indicate such a prefer-
ence. If this variable is present, it contains the path name, such as /usr/bin/vi,
/usr/ucb/vi, or sometimes just the command name, such as vi, of the user's preferred text editor. If not set, some local default should apply. Often this default is set to
vi, but it is best to make this an installation parameter, since some organizations have
strong local support for other editors.

wait [*process_id*]   wait for child termination   *****

This command is part of the POSIX P1003.2 standard, so it can be considered portable. The *process_id* argument was added by POSIX, and should be considered unportable unless you assume POSIX conformance.

This command is, of necessity, implemented in the shell. In practice, it is probably
not useful from system or in a makefile, and of very limited use in a shell script.

/etc/wall   write to all users   ***

The wall command is not part of the POSIX P1003.2 standard, so it should be considered less portable. In practice, it is available in most UNIX systems.

The wall command, which is normally delivered in the /etc directory, is intended
primarily for system administrative use. It takes no arguments.

wc [-clw] [*file_name* ...]   word count   *****

This command is part of the POSIX mandatory execution environment, and so it is
portable among POSIX P1003.2 conforming systems.

while *command_list*   control structure   ****
do
command_list
done

This shell built-in command is part of the POSIX P1003.2 standard. It is present in
all Bourne shell implementations. It can be considered portable.

who [*utmp_file*]   show logged in users   *****
who am i

This command is not part of the POSIX P1003.2 standard, so it should be considered
less portable.

The who command is present on all UNIX versions. The format of the output varies
slightly from system to system, as do the options available. If this command is needed in

a shell script, it is best to merely print or store the output without attempting to interpret it.

write *user* [*terminal*]   talk to other user   ******

This command is not part of the POSIX P1003.2 standard, so it should be considered less portable.

In practice, the write command is present in nearly identical form on all UNIX systems. It is portable to redirect the standard input from an echo command or a script. It is not, in general, safe to assume that any particular user will be logged on, or that the particular terminal port found by write will be the currently active port. Indeed, the user might have been idle for several hours. This makes use of write from a script unportable. From a C program, if it has already been determined which user is to be written to and which terminal they are logged into, it is just as easy to directly open the terminal and write to it, unless you want to make use of the built-in header and trailer printed by write.

xargs [-t] [-n *number*]   expand shell arguments   **••*
[-s *size*] [*utility_name*] [*argument* ...]

This command is part of the POSIX mandatory execution environment, and so it is portable among POSIX P1003.2 conforming systems.

This command originally appeared in PWB in conjunction with the Mashey shell. It has survived into System III and System V, but in practice has been supplanted by the `command` construction in the Bourne, C, and Korn shells. One situation when xargs can be preferable to `command` is when the size of the argument list exceeds the maximum number of characters allowed to a command, often 5120. Since xargs can allow multiple invocations of the same command, the list of names is passed on the standard input rather than as an argument list, and is not subject to this limit. The xargs command does not appear in V7 or 4BSD.

yacc [-dltv] [-b *prefix*] *grammar*   parser generator   ******

This command is part of the POSIX C Development Environment, and so is portable among POSIX conforming systems as part of a compilation tool, makefile, or shell script. It may not be present on systems with no compiler, so it is not portable from system.

Only the -d and -v options are universally available. The -b option is an invention of the POSIX committee.

APPENDICES

ANSI X3J11 C LANGUAGE: PORTABILITY ISSUES

This appendix lists some areas of the C language that are left not completely defined by the ANSI C standard. All of these areas should be considered sources of unportability. Any program making use of any unspecified, undefined, or implementation-defined property is not portable.

A.1 Unspecified Behavior

The behavior in some circumstances is unspecified. This means that, although these constructs are correct, there are no requirements on the behavior of a program using such a construct.

— The manner and timing of static initialization are unspecified. The implementation is free to initialize at load time, when the main function is called, or through some special hardware mechanism. In a dynamic linking environment, initialization might not happen until the appropriate function is called.

— If a printable character is written when the cursor is at the final position of a line, the behavior is unspecified. This will depend on the terminal, printer, or display. Some devices go to the next line, some stay at the end of the current line, and some restart the same line. Some terminals may remain at the last column, but start the next line if an additional character is displayed.

— If a backspace character is written when the cursor is at the beginning of a line, the behavior is unspecified. This will depend on the terminal, printer, or display. Some devices remain at the beginning of the line, but others go back to the end of the previous line.

— If a horizontal tab character is written when the cursor is at or past the last defined tab stop, the behavior is unspecified. This will depend on the device. Some devices start the next line, but others ignore the tab.

— If a vertical tab character is written when the cursor is at or past the last defined vertical tab stop, the behavior is unspecified. This will depend on the device. Many devices do not support vertical tabs. Those that do may ignore extra vertical tabs or start the next page.

— The representations of floating-types are unspecified. The IEEE format is popular, but many machines use other floating point formats.

— The order in which expressions are evaluated is unspecified. They may be evaluated in any order conforming to the precedence rules, even in the presence of parentheses.

— The order in which side effects take place is unspecified. Side effects can include function calls, input and output, and autoincremented variables. If a program depends on one side effect being used by another part of an expression, such as `a[i] = i++;` the program is not portable.

— The order of evaluation of the function designator and of the arguments in a function call is unspecified. A function call such as `(*(funfun(a, b)))(c, fun(&a));` is not portable if, for example, `fun` has a side effect that alters `a`.

— The layout of storage for formal parameters is unspecified. It is not safe to assume that formal parameters are sequential in memory or are in a particular order. Some systems pass the first few formal parameters in registers.

— The value of the file-position indicator is unspecified after a successful call to the `ungetc` function, until all pushed-back characters are read or discarded. The `ungetc` function may be implemented by saving the character in a local variable, or by actually pushing it back onto the input stream, or by changing buffer pointers. Some of these methods have limits.

— The details of the value stored by the `fgetpos` function are unspecified. This value might be a byte offset into the file or it might be a structure involving record and byte numbers. The value might take into account mapping newlines into CRLF sequences.

— The details of the value returned by the `ftell` function are unspecified. Although this value is constrained to fit into a long integer, it is still possible to encode block and offset numbers into the value.

— The order and contiguity of storage allocated by the `calloc`, `malloc`, and `realloc` functions are unspecified. Assumptions about the contents of adjoining memory may be wrong with other implementations of these functions.

— For the `bsearch` function, if two members compare equal, it is unspecified which member will be returned. The implementation could return either member.

— For the `qsort` function, the resulting order of two members that compare as equal is unspecified. If the comparison function only looks at part of each record, the remaining parts may appear in any order once the array is sorted.

— The encoding of the calendar time returned by the `time` function is unspecified. The traditional "seconds since 1970" encoding has limitations, and other encodings are consistent with the standard.

A.2 Undefined Behavior

Undefined behavior means that there are no requirements on the behavior when one of these nonportable or erroneous constructs is used.

— Behavior is undefined if a character not in the required character set is encountered in a source program, except within a preprocessing token, a character constant, a string literal, or a comment. This probably represents a syntax error. A compiler may choose to ignore unusual characters or may print an error message.

— The results of attempting to modify a string literal are undefined. An implementation might put literals in read-only memory. It is also allowed to share a string table among several identical or similar literals, and changing one literal would also change other literals sharing the same memory.

— If identifiers that are intended to denote the same entity differ in any character, the behavior is undefined. Some implementations only check the first several characters of identifiers and ignore the rest. Some implementations may ignore upper-case/lower-case differences. It is possible that errors of this sort may not be detected by some compilers.

— If an unspecified escape sequence is encountered in a character constant or a string literal, the behavior is undefined. The compiler may choose to take the literal characters of the escape sequence or to print an error message.

— If an arithmetic conversion produces a result that cannot be represented in the space provided, the behavior is undefined. Some machines may produce a hardware trap. Other machines may produce an incorrect result and continue without detecting an error.

— If an arithmetic operation is invalid (such as division by 0) or produces a result that cannot be represented in the space provided (such as overflow or underflow), the behavior is undefined. An error trap may occur or the program might continue with an incorrect result.

— For a function call with no function prototype declarator in scope, if the number of arguments does not agree with the number of formal parameters, the behavior is undefined. Compilers are not required to detect such errors, and the behavior at run time will depend on implementation details that are not defined by the standard.

— For a function call with no function prototype declarator in scope, if at the function definition there is also no function prototype declarator in scope, and if the types of the arguments after promotion do not agree with those of the formal parameters after promotion, the behavior is undefined. This is the behavior of the K&R C language. If the function call parameters don't match the function declaration, garbage may result.

— The behavior is undefined if a function prototype declarator is in scope when a function is defined, a formal parameter is declared with a type that is affected by the default argument promotions, and a function is called with no semantically equivalent prototype in scope. The compiler would have to promote the argument at the function call, and it doesn't have any way to know that a promotion is necessary.

— If a function that accepts a variable number of arguments is called, but no prototype declarator with the ellipsis notation is in scope, the results are undefined. The compiler may handle variable argument functions specially, so it has to know, at the function call, whether the function takes fixed or variable arguments.

— An invalid array reference, null-pointer reference, or reference to an automatic object in a terminated block will have undefined behavior. Such references point to undefined portions of memory and may result in a trap or a garbage value.

— If a pointer to a function is converted to point to a function of a different type and used to call a function of a type other than the original type, the behavior is undefined. Functions may return different types with different mechanisms. For example, small values may be returned in a register, but large values may be returned in space allocated by the caller, or by the function.

— Adding to or subtracting from a pointer that is not to a member of an array object is undefined. Pointer addition and subtraction are intended for use within an array.

— Pointer subtraction between pointers that are not to the same array object is undefined. The result would necessarily involve memory between them.

— Assigning an object to an overlapping object is undefined. The overlapped region would be destroyed.

— An attempt to modify a `const` object by means of a pointer to a type without the `const` attribute is undefined. Constants may be in read-only memory or their unchanging property may be counted on by another part of the program.

— Referring to a `volatile` object by means of a pointer to a type without the `volatile` attribute is undefined. This would defeat the hint to the compiler that the object might change unpredictably, and an optimization might turn out to be wrong.

— Two external declarations of the same identifier, specifying different types, with external linkage in two source files or in disjoint scopes within one source file have undefined behavior. The declarations would refer to the same memory possibly with different sizes or formats.

— The value of an uninitialized automatic variable, used before a value is assigned, is undefined. The initial value may be garbage. The compiler might detect the error or might return garbage.

— If the value of a function is used, but no value was returned, the behavior is undefined. Depending on the function return mechanism, the error might be caught, garbage might be returned, or a trap could occur.

— The behavior is undefined if a function that accepts a variable number of arguments is defined without a parameter type list ending with an ellipsis. Other mechanisms to use variable arguments, such as the V7 `varargs.h` mechanism, are not supported by ANSI C, but are supported in many implementations.

— If the token `defined` is generated expanding a `#if` or `#elif` directive, the results are undefined. It could interfere with the `#if  defined` construct. Defining `defined` is also undefined.

— A `#include` line with invalid syntax is undefined. Some systems might have additional forms for special file names.

— An empty macro argument (no preprocessing tokens) causes undefined behavior. Macro arguments are intended to look like expressions. Optional arguments are not supported by the language.

— Sequences of preprocessing tokens within the list of macro arguments that would otherwise act as preprocessing directive lines are undefined. These could interfere with the operation of the preprocessor.

— Behavior is undefined if the result of the preprocessing concatenation operator `##` is not a valid preprocessing token. The preprocessor might or might not catch the error.

— Behavior is undefined if the parameter *identifier* of an `offsetof` macro names a bit-field member of a structure. Offsets are intended to be integer byte offsets, not references to bits in the middle of a byte.

— If a library function argument has an invalid value, the results are undefined, unless the behavior is specified explicitly. Some implementations may catch the error, some may return garbage, and some may trap.

— If a library function that accepts a variable number of arguments is not declared, the results are undefined. The compiler is not expected to know about the standard C library; that information is supposed to be in the header files.

— It is undefined if a `#undef  assert` directive is used to obtain access to a real function. The compiler is allowed to handle `assert` specially.

— Behavior is undefined if the argument to a character-handling function is out of the domain. The compiler might or might not detect the error.

— The value of an automatic variable that is not `volatile` is undefined if it has been changed between a `setjmp` and `longjmp` call. The implementation might restore the old value or leave the new one.

— Invoking the `longjmp` function from a nested signal routine is undefined. There may be special cleanup actions associated with signal routines that could be bypassed by a double `longjmp`.

— Behavior is undefined if a signal occurs other than as the result of calling the `abort` or `raise` function, and if the signal handler calls any function in the standard library other than the `signal` function itself, or if it refers to any global object (other than by assigning a value to a volatile static variable of type `sig_atomic_t`). Compilers sometimes make code optimizations when they are convinced that a particular block of code will execute as in sequence. Signal handlers can be called at unpredictable times. If a signal handler were called in the middle of such a block and it had side effects on variables that affect the block, the optimizations could be defeated.

— Behavior is undefined if the parameter *parmN* of a `va_start` macro is declared with the `register` storage class. The implementation of `va_start` is likely to take a pointer to this parameter, and pointers to registers are not allowed.

— If the type of the actual next argument in a variable argument list disagrees with the type specified by the `va_arg` macro, the behavior is undefined. The assignment is likely to be a simple memory copy or pointer reference, and if the types don't match, garbage can result.

— Behavior is undefined if a return occurs from a function with a variable argument list, and the `va_start` macro is called, but the `va_end` function is never called. The implementation may require `va_end` to be called to clean up memory.

— It is undefined if the format for the `fprintf` or `fscanf` function does not match the argument list. The assignment may be done with a simple pointer reference, and any needed conversions may not be done.

— An invalid conversion specification is undefined in the format for the `fprintf` or `fscanf` function. The function may or may not detect the error.

— An aggregate or a pointer is an undefined argument to the `fprintf` function, except for `%s` or `%p` conversion, respectively. These are the only predefined output conversions for structures, unions, and pointer types.

— A single conversion by the `fprintf` function producing more than 509 characters of output is undefined. It is reasonable for an implementation to use a 512-byte buffer.

— If a pointer value printed by `%p` conversion by the `fprintf` function during a previous program execution is the argument for `%p` conversion by the `fscanf` function, the results are undefined. The pointer may not make make sense in the subsequent program.

— If the result of converting a string to a number by the `atof`, `atoi`, or `atol` function cannot be represented, the behavior is undefined. The implementation may trap or may return an incorrect number.

— Behavior is undefined if the pointer argument to the `free` or `realloc` function does not match a pointer earlier returned by `calloc`, `malloc`, or `realloc`, or the object pointed to has been deallocated by a call to `free` or `realloc`. Memory cannot be freed unless it has been allocated in a standard way, and free memory cannot be freed again.

— Space deallocated by a call to the `free` or `realloc` function is undefined. The implementation is free to change it during the call to `free`, for example, to link free blocks together.

— When called by the `exit` function, it is undefined if a function registered by the `atexit` function accesses an automatic object created during program execution. The `atexit` function can be called after `main` has returned, and such automatic variables may already be deallocated.

— Behavior is undefined if the result of an integer arithmetic function (`abs`, `div`, `labs`, or `ldiv`) cannot be represented. Division by zero and the absolute value of the smallest possible negative number (on a two's complement machine) cannot be represented. The implementation may return garbage or detect the error.

— A too small array written to by a copying or concatenation function causes undefined behavior. The function may not know how large the array is and so is likely to overflow the array and destroy other memory.

— Copying to an overlapping object with the `memcpy`, `strcpy`, or `strncpy` function is undefined. Some implementations may go into a loop with such calls, and the implementation is not required to catch this.

— An invalid conversion specification found in the format for the `strftime` function is undefined. The implementation may or may not detect the error.

A.3 Implementation-Defined Behavior

Each implementation will document its behavior in each of these areas. These constructs are correct, but their behavior depends on the characteristics of the implementation.

A.3.1 Environment

— The semantics of the arguments to main are not defined by the language. These represent user arguments to the program and will vary from application to application.

A.3.2 Identifiers

— The number of significant initial characters (beyond 31) in an identifier without external linkage is implementation-defined. Some systems may treat as many as 255 (or more) characters as significant, and others may implement the bare minimum 31. Many older implementations supported only 8 or 16.

— The number of significant initial characters (beyond 6) in an identifier with external linkage is implementation-defined. Some linkers on older operating systems permit only 6 characters in external names. Many older UNIX systems allowed 8, but since the C compiler usually prepends an underscore to names, only 7 were usually available. Recent systems usually consider at least 31 characters significant.

— The implementation will define whether case distinctions are significant in an identifier with external linkage. Some linkers support only upper-case and will consider `putchar` and `Putchar` to be the same function. Others support both upper- and lower-case.

A.3.3 Characters

— The characters in the source and execution character set are implementation-defined, except as explicitly specified in the standard. Some implementations will use ASCII, others will use various national or international character sets, and some will use proprietary character sets such as EBCDIC.

— The mapping of characters in the source character set (in character constants and string literals) to characters in the execution character set is implementation-defined. Normally, these character sets will be the same, but in the case of a cross-compiler, it is possible that some mapping will be required if the target machine uses a different character set.

— The value of a character constant that contains a character or escape sequence not represented in the execution character set is implementation-defined. This only applies in the case of a cross-compiler to a different character set.

— The number and order of `chars` in an `int` is implementation-defined. Generally, 16-bit machines will have 2 characters in an integer and 32-bit machines will have 4 characters in an integer. Other sizes are possible. These differences are invisible to isolated programs that do not indulge in type punning (for example, by converting a pointer to `int` to a pointer to `char` and inspecting the pointed-to storage), but must be accounted for when conforming to externally imposed storage layouts.

— The number and order of bits in a character in the execution character set is implementation-defined. Although most machines will have 8 bits in a byte, some implementations have 7, or 9, or other numbers. It is possible for bytes to have either big-endian or little-endian bit ordering.

— The value of a character constant that contains more than one character is implementation-defined. Multicharacter constants are discouraged because the compiler may choose to pack them into integers in any order. They are in the language primarily as a holdover from assembly language.

— The implementation defines whether a ''plain'' `char` is treated as signed or unsigned. Generally, the representation that is most natural for the hardware will be used.

A.3.4 Integers

— The representations and sets of values of the various types of integers are implementation-defined. These will normally match what the hardware provides. There are many variations in widespread use.

— The result of converting an integer to a shorter signed integer or the result of converting an unsigned integer to a signed integer of equal length is implementation-defined if the value cannot be represented. The implementation may truncate the high-level bits, do some other correction, or trap. Often the hardware will determine what the implementation does.

— The results of bitwise operations are implementation-defined on signed integers. One's complement machines will use a different representation for negative numbers than two's complement machines.

— After integer division, the sign of the remainder is implementation-defined. This will usually match what the hardware provides.

— It is implementation-defined whether a right shift of a signed integral type is logical or arithmetic. This will usually match what the hardware provides.

A.3.5 Floating Point

— The representations and sets of values of the various types of floating-point numbers are implementation-defined. These will usually match what the hardware provides.

— The direction of truncation is implementation-defined when a floating-point number is converted to a narrower floating-point number. This will usually match what the hardware provides.

— The properties of floating-point arithmetic are implementation-defined. These will usually match what the hardware provides.

A.3.6 Arrays and Pointers

— The implementation defines the type of integer required to hold the maximum size of an array, that is, the type of the `sizeof` operator, `size_t`. This is likely to be either `unsigned short` or `unsigned long`, although it could be another type.

— The result of casting a pointer to an integer or vice versa is implementation-defined. The details of the representations, especially of pointers, can vary from system to system.

— The type of integer required to hold the difference between two pointers to members of the same array, `ptrdiff_t`, is implementation-defined. Although this could be a `long` or `short`, the implementation is free to define another type.

A.3.7 Registers

— The number of `register` objects that can actually be placed in registers and the set of valid types are implementation-defined. Although this number is often 3 or 4 per function, it could be any number, depending on the register set of the machine and how the compiler uses the registers.

A.3.8 Structures, Unions, and Bit-Fields

— The behavior is implementation-defined when accessing a member of a union object using a member of a different type. The hardware details may cause different results on different processors.

— The padding and alignment of members of structures are implementation-defined. Different implementations may leave different sized holes in memory between structure members. This can cause programs to fail when reading a structure on a different processor than it was written, and affect network protocol portability. A good solution is to take care in laying out the structure fields to ensure that memory is allocated in exactly the same way as specified by the protocol.

— Implementations will define whether a ''plain'' `int` bit-field is treated as a `signed int` bit-field or as an `unsigned int` bit-field. Although bit-fields are often unsigned, the implementation is free to set the default either way.

— The order of allocation of bit-fields within an `int` is implementation-defined. Compilers might, for example, allocate bits from either end of the word.

— It is implementation-defined whether a bit-field can cross a byte or word boundary. Some implementations can cross word boundaries with bit-fields, and others will pad with extra bits.

A.3.9 Declarators

— The maximum number of declarators (lists of names, etc.) that may follow an arithmetic, structure, or union type is implementation-defined. Compilers will often keep the full list on a stack while processing a declaration, and use of unusually long lists of names (typically in the hundreds or more) can sometimes overflow this stack.

A.3.10 Statements

— The maximum number of `case` values in a `switch` statement is implementation-defined. Many compilers implement `switch` statements using a table, and there may be a maximum size to this table. (128 and 256 are common maximum values.)

A.3.11 Preprocessing Directives

— The implementation will define whether a character constant in an `#if` may have a negative value.

— The method for locating `#include` source files is implementation-defined. The set of directories searched and their order may vary between different operating systems and compilers.

— An implementation need not support quoted names for includable source files. Only the <> form is completely portable. Technically, this means there is no portable way to distribute application-specific #include header files in the same directory as the source program. In practice, this feature is so widely used that it can be safely treated as if it were universal.

— The implementation will define the set of #pragma directives it supports.

A.3.12 Library Functions

— The implementation will define the null-pointer constant to which the macro NULL expands. Although it is traditional to use the value 0, some architectures may have a special built-in illegal pointer or may treat 0 as a legal value.

— The implementation will define the diagnostic printed by the assert function and its termination behavior. These will vary from system to system.

— The implementation will define the sets of characters tested for by the isalnum, isalpha, iscntrl, islower, isprint, and isupper functions. These will vary according to the character set and locale.

— The implementation will define the values returned by the mathematics functions on domain errors. Some systems support special values such as infinity or NotANumber.

— The implementation will define whether the mathematics functions set the integer expression errno to the value of the macro ERANGE on underflow range errors. Underflow may be an error or may be considered normal and ignored.

— The implementation will define the set of signals for the signal function. These will depend on the hardware and the operating system.

— The implementation will define the default handling for each signal and the handling at program startup. This will depend on the operating system and on the environment from which the program was run.

— The implementation will define whether the default handling is reset if SIGILL is received by a signal handler. This will depend on the hardware and operating system.

— The implementation will define whether the last line of a text stream requires a terminating newline character. This will depend on the operating system. Some systems store files as sequences of records, with an implied newline at the end of each record.

— A text line containing only a single-space character and a terminating newline character (i.e., a line containing only a blank) may be converted on input to a line consisting only of the terminating newline character (i.e., an empty line.) This is defined by the implementation.

— The implementation will define the number of NUL characters, if any, that may be appended to data written to a binary stream. Some filesystems keep only a word count or a block count and may leave extra characters after the last valid data character in a file.

— The implementation will define the characteristics of file buffering. It may support full buffering, no buffering, line buffering, or any combination of the three. There are details, such as when to flush a buffer, left for the implementation to define. Some older systems allow a few bytes of garbage, or specific "end-of-file" characters such as control Z to pad the end of a file.

— The implementation will define whether a zero-length file actually exists. It may choose not to create it until data is written to it.

— The implementation will define the rules for composing valid file names. These will depend on the operating system.

— The implementation will define whether the same file can be open multiple times. Some operating systems may not permit this.

— The effect of the `remove` function on an open file is implementation-defined. Some operating systems may still allow the file to be accessed until it is closed, but others will delete it immediately.

— If a file with the new name exists prior to a call to the `rename` function, the effect is implementation-defined. The existing file could be deleted or the call could fail.

— The output for `%p` conversion in the `fprintf` function is implementation-defined. This will depend on the machine representation of a pointer and on the radix most commonly used to represent pointers.

— The input for `%p` conversion in the `fscanf` function is similarly implementation-defined.

— The interpretation of a – character that is neither the first nor the last character in the scanlist for `%[` conversion in the `fscanf` function is implementation-defined. This will generally match a range of characters, inclusive, between the two characters surrounding the –. This is not portable because "inclusive" must be interpreted in the native character set, possibly affected by the current locale.

— The implementation is allowed to choose the `errno` value set by the `fgetpos` or `ftell` function on failure.

— The exact messages generated by the `perror` function are implementation-defined.

— The behavior of the `abort` function with regard to open and temporary files is implementation-defined.

— The implementation will define the set of environment names and the method for altering the environment list used by the `getenv` function. This will depend on the operating system and the calling environment.

— The contents and method of execution of the string by the `system` function are implementation-defined. These will depend on the operating system and the calling environment.

— When calling a comparison function (`memcmp`, `strcmp`, or `strncmp`) and one of the first pair of characters that differ has its high-order bit set, the sign of the value returned is implementation-defined. This may depend on whether the hardware treats bytes as signed or unsigned numbers.

— The contents of the error-message strings returned by the `strerror` function are implementation-defined.

— The local time zone and Daylight Savings Time are implementation-defined, and in fact may be different for different installations of the same implementation.

— The era (that is, the meaning of the value 0) for the `clock` function is implementation-defined. Some implementations may use the time of the first call to `clock`, others the time the program started, others the time the system was rebooted, and others may be based on the time-of-day clock.

A.4 Locale-Specific Behavior

Certain characteristics of a hosted environment are locale-specific. The behavior depends on local conventions of nationality, culture, and language.

— The content of the execution character set is locale-specific, although the required characters must always be present. Different languages have different letters in their alphabets.

— The direction of printing is locale-specific. Some languages write from right to left.

— The decimal-point character is locale-specific. Some languages use a . (period) but others use a , (comma.)

— The implementation-defined aspects of character-testing and case-mapping functions are locale-specific. Different languages may not have upper- and lower-case, or may have special mapping or sorting rules for certain letters.

— Similarly, the collation sequence of the execution character set is implementation-defined.

— The formats for time and date are implementation-defined. These vary widely from country to country.

A.5 Common Extensions

The following extensions are widely used in many systems, but are *not portable*. Examples of such extensions are new keywords, predefined macros, and library functions with names not beginning with an underscore.

A.5.1 Environment Arguments

The `main` function receives a third argument, `char *envp[]`, pointing to a null-terminated array of character strings, each of which provides information about the environment for this execution of the process.

A.5.2 Specialized Identifiers

Characters other than the standard underscore _, letters, and digits, and not part of the required source character set (such as the dollar sign $ or characters in national character sets), may be allowed in identifiers.

A.5.3 Lengths and Cases of Identifiers

All characters in identifiers (either internal or external, separately) may be significant. The standard only requires 31 characters for internal identifiers and 6 for external identifiers, and some older implementations support as few as 8 for internals.

Upper- and lower-case may be considered distinct in external identifiers. The standard allows `Putchar` and `putchar` to be considered identical.

A.5.4 Scopes of Identifiers A function identifier, or the identifier of an object whose declaration contains the keyword `extern`, has file scope. Information about external identifiers must be consistent throughout a program, and some compilers will remember the declaration for the duration of the translation instead of deleting it at the end of the block.

A.5.5 Writable String Literals

String literals may be modified by the application. Normally, in order to permit identical literals to be shared, they are considered read-only.

A.5.6 Other Arithmetic Types

Other arithmetic types, such as `long long int`, may be defined. This could be useful on a machine with 64-bit capabilities, for example.

A.5.7 Function-Pointer Casts

An object pointer may be cast into a function pointer, allowing data to be invoked as a function. This allows a program to generate machine-language code dynamically and then execute the code. (Clearly, such a technique is very unportable.)

A.5.8 Non-i

Types oth [...] signed int may be declared as bit-fields. Chara [...]

A.5.9 The

The for [...] in a function declaration to indicate that function lin [...] be generated. This allows C programs to call FORTR [...]

A.5.10 The

The as [...] sembly-language code directly. The most common in [...] he form asm (*string-literal*);. This is very unpor [...] formance reasons at the expense of portability.

A.5.11 M

There [...] al definition for the identifier of an object, with or v [...] ord extern. Most UNIX systems accept this exter [...]

A.5.12 F

A m [...] ns.) This won't bother some preprocessors.

A.5.13

Mac [...] nderscore may be defined by the implementation [...] ple, this covers predefined macros such as unix [...] em or processor type.

A.5.14 [...] lers

Ha [...] alled with extra arguments in addition to the signal [...] the handler repair the cause of a trap, but are usuall [...]

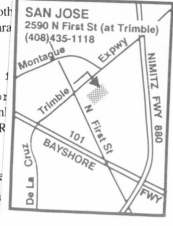

A.5.15 Additional Stream Types and File-Opening Modes

Additional mappings from files to streams may be supported, and additional file-opening modes may be specified by characters appended to the mode argument of the open function. These will usually be specific to the operating system.

A.5.16 Defined File-Position Indicator

The file-position indicator may be decremented by each successful call to the ungetc function for a text stream, except if its value was zero before a call. This implies a different implementation of the standard I/O system. The traditional one can push back a character or two into a buffer for look-ahead purposes, but cannot back up arbitrarily far, and will not affect the actual file.

APPENDIX B: IEEE P1003.1-1988 POSIX SYSTEM

In the 1980s, /usr/group, the UNIX trade organization, set out to define a ''standard'' version of the UNIX system that vendors could conform to, providing a higher degree of portability among UNIX systems. As they began, UNIX System III had been recently released and was adopted as a starting point. In 1984, /usr/group released a document defining their proposed standard.

This document was, of necessity, a compromise. It provided a standard way to accomplish many functions where the existing systems had diverged, such as the function called `index` in V7 and Berkeley systems, but called `strchr` in System III and System V.

In areas where existing systems differed greatly, the standard did not always resolve the conflict. For example, V7 and Berkeley use the `stty` set of ioctl's to change terminal modes, but System III and System V use the `termio` set.

After the 1984 document was published, the committee was adopted by the IEEE, which formed the P1003 committee to draft a formal IEEE standard. This standard became known as POSIX, since UNIX is a registered trademark of AT&T. In 1986, the committee released a book called *IEEE Trial Use Standard Portable Operating System for Computer Environments*. This book was released for public comment and as a Draft American National Standard. In 1988, the final standard was published as *IEEE Std 1003.1-1988*, more commonly called *POSIX*, or the *IEEE Standard Portable Operating System Interface for Computer Environments*.

All of these issues were resolved later by the 1003 committee. Work progressed rapidly after the draft book was released. The full use standard was approved in 1988.

In 1987, another subcommittee was formed to create IEEE 1003.2, a standard set of required shell commands useful for calling by `system`. Chapter 15 of this book is based on draft 9 of this standard from 1989.

Although POSIX is compatible with ANSI C, which requires the support of function prototypes, it is not necessary for an implementation that conforms to POSIX to support full ANSI C. The standard is written to make sense with an older C compiler. A prudent implementor will keep an eye on all three standards when writing an application intended to support or use these standards.

New POSIX Features

POSIX has added some new features that were generally not present before. This section lists the new features provided.

There is a new header file `<limits.h>` that defines various implementation constants. ANSI C also requires `<limits.h>`, but POSIX has included many additional values that are specific to the UNIX and POSIX systems.

There is another new header file `<unistd.h>` that includes several miscellaneous constants that were not present in other header files.

A terminal driver, called `termios`, is defined. This driver is similar to the System III driver.

A job control option, similar to that provided in 4BSD, is defined. It is not necessary for an implementation to support job control to conform to P1003.2, but AT&T chose to include it in System V release 4.

The Berkeley `getgroups` system call is adopted, but made optional.

The Berkeley directory routines `opendir`, `readdir`, `rewinddir`, and `closedir` are adopted. The `telldir` and `seekdir` routines are not included. Some conventions are incompatibly changed from the Berkeley method; in particular, the header file to include is changed from `<sys/dir.h>` to `<dirent.h>` and the structure name is changed from `direct` to `dirent`.

The `O_NONBLOCK` option is used instead of the System V `O_NDELAY` option to `open` and `fcntl`, with a small change in semantics.

The Berkeley `mkdir` and `rmdir` system calls are added.

A system call to make a fifo, `mkfifo`, is added, eliminating the need for a user application to call `mknod`.

The Berkeley and ANSI C `rename` function is added.

The header file `<sys/stat.h>` provides symbolic constants for all mode bits.

The V7 `dup2` system call is added.

Advisory file and record locking is added with the `lockf` system call.

A reliable signal mechanism, similar to the one in 4.3BSD, is provided.

The interchange formats of both `tar` and `cpio` are adopted as standard data-interchange formats.

SYSTEM V INTERFACE DEFINITION

The System V Interface Definition (SVID) is a series of volumes published by AT&T. It is used as a standards document to define what it means to be *System V Compatible* for system builders, and as a reference for application developers who wish to ensure their application will run in all UNIX System V environments.

There have been multiple issues of the SVID, and there are multiple volumes. The original SVID Issue 1, Volume 1, was released in 1985. In 1986, Issue 2 was released, consisting of Volumes 1 and 2. In 1987, Issue 2, Volume 3, was released.

Issues of the SVID do not correspond to a release of System V. Issue 1 documented the language interface of System V release 2.0 (SVr2.) Issue 2 corrected many minor problems with Issue 1, and added a second volume describing shell commands and extensions. The third volume describes features added by System V release 3.0 (SVr3.)

Many vendors claim they are compatible with the SVID. In practice, this often means they support all features present in the base system of Issue 1, Volume 1. Since this definition of SVID compliance is currently in widespread use in the marketplace, it is used in this book. Application developers wishing their software to run on any machine claiming SVID compliance are advised to use this same definition and not to assume the presence of features added to the SVID at a later date. If at some future date the marketplace shifts, and it becomes safe to assume that a claim of SVID compliance means a higher level of conformance, it will become reasonable to use such new features in programs that are portable among SVID-compliant systems.

Features Not Present in the Base System SVID

Some commonly used features are not present in the SVID. This section lists many of them.

The `assert` macro is not required by the SVID. It is, however, required by POSIX and ANSI C. This macro can be considered portable.

The `brk` and `sbrk` system calls are not required by the SVID or POSIX. They should be avoided, since they may be difficult to emulate in some environments.

The `cuserid` function is not required by the SVID. It is, however, required by POSIX. Since it is not present in Berkeley or V7, it should be considered unportable.

The `ecvt`, `fcvt`, and `gcvt` functions are not required by the SVID. Although they are not required by other standards documents, they are widely implemented among UNIX and MS DOS systems.

The `/etc/group` routines `getgrent`, `getgrgid`, `getgrnam`, `setgrent`, and `endgrent` are not required by the SVID, although they are required by POSIX. These routines can be considered portable and are the preferred methods of accessing the group file.

The `/etc/passwd` routines `getpwent`, `getpwgid`, `getpwnam`, `setpwent`, and `endpwent` are not required by the SVID, although they are required by POSIX. These routines can be considered portable and are the preferred methods of accessing the password file. Note that, for security reasons, the encrypted password may be stored in a protected auxiliary file, such as `/etc/shadow` in System V release 3.2. There is no portable way to verify passwords.

The include files `<grp.h>` and `<pwd.h>` are not required by the SVID.

The `getpass` function, which prompts for and reads a password from the terminal, is not required by the SVID. This function is required by POSIX, and in practice can be considered portable.

The SVID does not require the `getpw` function, which returns the raw tax of a line from `/etc/passwd`. It is considered obsolete, to be replaced with `getpwnam`.

The `monitor` and `profil` functions are not required by the SVID. Since these are low-level routines used by the profiler, application programs should not use them.

The `nice` system call, which reduces or increases the priority of a running process, is not required by the base-level SVID, but considered an extension. In practice, this function is present in all major UNIX systems, and can be emulated with a dummy subroutine on systems where it is not available.

The `nlist` function is not required by the SVID, because its use often implies unportable assumptions about the internals of other programs. In practice, code that uses `nlist` is seldom portable.

The `ptrace` function is not required by the SVID. Since this is a low-level function used by debuggers, and since debuggers are generally not very portable, portability of `ptrace` doesn't matter very much. Ordinary user applications should avoid `ptrace`.

The `ttyslot` function is not required by the SVID. This is a low-level function not intended for portable applications.

The `<a.out.h>` header file is not required by the SVID. Its use should be considered unportable.

The `<ar.h>` header file is not required by the SVID. Its use should be considered to be not very portable, since it is compatible only among relatively recent UNIX system releases, those since System V release 2, V8, and 4.0BSD.

The curses package is not required by the base-level SVID. Use of the full package should be considered only portable among AT&T releases of the UNIX system. Many third-party products claiming SVID compatibility offer the Berkeley curses instead. Chapters 11 and 13 describe the common subset of curses that can be considered to be very portable.

Some of the `errno` error conditions present on System V are not required by the SVID. These include ECHRNG, EIDRM, EL2HLT, EL2NSYNC, EL3HLT, EL3RST, ELNRNG, ENOCSI, ENOMSG, and EUNATCH.

The structure `mallinfo` present in `<malloc.h>` in System V release 2 is not required by the SVID. This structure is specific to the optional -lmalloc version of the memory allocator, and its use should be considered unportable.

Many of the constants defined in `<math.h>` in System V are not required by the SVID. Required macros include DOMAIN, HUGE, OVERFLOW, PLOSS, SING, TLOSS, and UNDERFLOW.

The header file `<sgtty.h>` and the related system calls `stty` and `gtty`, and the related `ioctl` codes TIOCGETP and TIOCSETP are not documented or required by the SVID, even though they are present in releases of the UNIX system through System V release 3.0.

Several values from `<signal.h>` are not required by the SVID. These include NSIG and the signals SIGBUS, SIGCLD, SIGEMT, SIGIOT, SIGPWR, and SIGSEGV In practice, it is acceptable to substitute 31 for NSIG if not defined:

```
#ifndef NSIG
# define NSIG 31
#endif
```

SIGBUS, SIGEMT, SIGIOT, and SIGSEGV are universally implemented signals that are also required by POSIX. Their semantics may be somewhat hardware-specific, but a program that catches them, in order to be bulletproof, is reasonably portable among UNIX systems. As a rule, SIGSEGV occurs when a program refers to memory outside the valid range, as when a pointer contains garbage. SIGBUS usually occurs when a 16- or 32-bit value is accessed with an odd address, another indication of likely garbage in a pointer.

Some constants from `<stdio.h>` are not required by the SVID. These include L_ctermid and L_cuserid.

The include file `<sys/stat.h>` is required by the SVID, but the constants such as S_IEXEC are not required. The SVID defines (in the `mknod` description) the values of the st_mode field numerically.

In the include file `<sys/types.h>`, several types are not required by the SVID. These include caddr_t, cnt_t, daddr_t, key_t, label_t, paddr_t, physaddr, and uint.

The include file `<utmp.h>` is not required by the SVID.

APPENDIX D: **MS DOS**

Most UNIX systems either come with a standard C compiler or offer such a compiler as an option. In a few cases, a third-party compiler may be offered as an option. But the language and library calls accepted on the system are generally determined by the system itself.

Other operating systems may not be written in C, and if they are, the C compiler may not be from the vendor of the other operating system. As a result, users of many popular operating systems have a choice of which compiler to buy.

Nowhere is this choice wider than with the MS DOS operating system. Several different vendors sell MS DOS C compilers. Many of these vendors have two or more C products. It is common to offer a subset version for casual programmers to learn about the system, and a full version for serious programmers. The casual version might support only the small model, for example, limiting programs and data to 64K bytes, and the full version offers several memory models.

The size and scope of these MS DOS compilers vary considerably. Some C implementations support only the most widely used functions from the standard I/O package; others emulate a large portion of the UNIX system. Since it is not the purpose of this book to provide a comparison shopping guide for MS DOS C compilers, one or two widely used implementations have been selected as representative of the operating system for the sections that compare systems.

A typical C implementation on another computer system makes an effort to emulate the UNIX system, since C originated on UNIX, and it's difficult to totally separate C from UNIX. Although all implementations will support `fopen` and `fread`, the UNIX system specific functions `open` and `read` are often supported on other systems as well.

Since the underlying operating system is not the UNIX system, it has its own interface and system calls. Where these are different from the UNIX system, it is necessary for the C implementor to invent a C language binding for the system calls. In the absence of documented standards, each vendor is free to make up their own binding. This can cause a portability problem among different C implementations for operating systems such as MS DOS.

In recent years, the MS DOS interface specified by Microsoft in their Microsoft C product has become somewhat of a de facto standard. This may be because Microsoft also controls the MS DOS system. Other implementations are gradually supporting the Microsoft DOS interface. Programs that use this interface will be more portable among MS DOS compilers than those that use other methods.

The set of system calls making up this interface consists of `bdos`, `cgets`, `cprintf`, `cputs`, `inp`, `int86`, `int86x`, `intdosx`, `kbhit`, `movedata`, `outp`, and `segread`.

APPENDIX E: **MACINTOSH, AMIGA, AND ATARI ST**

The trend of the 1980s was toward personal computers and workstations with powerful 32-bit processors, bitmapped screens, mice, and windowing environments. These computers often are priced low enough to be used as home computers, so there are many of them in the marketplace. Examples of these computers are the Apple Macintosh, the Commodore Amiga, and the Atari ST series. This appendix also applies to similar workstations with windowing environments, including 8086 family PCs running window managers such as OS/2, GEM, TopView, or Microsoft Windows, and UNIX workstations such as the AT&T 6386, Sun, Apollo, and so on.

The implementation languages for these computers vary. Usually, BASIC is available on 68K home computers and PCs, but serious software isn't usually written in BASIC. The Macintosh originally used Pascal as its implementation language, but a number of C compilers are available. The Amiga and ST use the C language for most applications. In general, any workstation or PC of this variety can be expected to support C.

Programmers writing applications for windowing environments generally would like their application to run on as many different computers as possible. Since there are no widely used standards for application interfaces in this kind of environment, it is generally not possible to take a program written for one PC and run it on another.

The environment that C was originally designed for was a very different environment from a window-oriented workstation. The most portable features of C involve printing text on the standard output, and reading text from the keyboard. A conversational program, running in scroll mode on a hard-copy terminal, is likely to be portable. Few applications for a windowing environment will be satisfied with such a simple interface when such sophisticated hardware is available.

There are additional complicating factors. C programs are typically called from a command-line environment, passing text-string arguments that were typed on the command line. Window-oriented programs are invoked from a menu or an icon, and have no opportunity to be passed arguments before the program starts. Some systems have both a window environment and a command-line environment, requiring a truly portable program to be callable from either. Other systems have *only* the windowing environment. Assumptions such as "This program must be run from the command line" are not practical for this class of computer.

The C libraries for bitmapped computers are often heavily modified. They may include some core standard I/O routines, some proprietary window-handling functions, and a system-call interface to the underlying proprietary operating system.

Some of the filesystems are not built around the idea of a stream of bytes, but rather have several parts, including a program, data, icon, and the like. Some computers include a library of handy functions, such as the Macintosh *textedit,* which you are encouraged to use to keep the user interface consistent with other applications.

Since this class of computer is relatively new, C implementations tend to be new as well, and it is not uncommon to find rough edges or outright bugs. For example, these operating systems store text files with CR and LF at the ends of each line, and C uses newline internally for this purpose. Most C implementations for this type of filesystem map between newline and CRLF when doing input or output. This mapping can introduce subtle bugs. One widespread bug is that there may be no facility to turn off the mapping, which would allow programs to manipulate binary files. (ANSI C requires a binary b option to the `fopen` function, but this is not yet widely implemented.)

How then is a programmer to write a program that works well on several different computers of this class? It's not an easy task. This appendix provides some advice.

It is important to realize that all things change over time. In the 1980s, there were no standards for windows. There were no widely used methodologies for development of programs that are portable to this class of computer. The general feeling among programmers was that such computers are very difficult for software development, and that you had to change the way you approached the entire program, but that it was worth it since it resulted in a better user interface.

The X windows and NeWS libraries have gathered support on UNIX workstations. There is no clear complete programming-interface standard yet. These libraries were not widely available on the 68K home computers or PCs.

The most important consideration is to carefully design the program to be portable from the start. Survey the range of environments you wish to support. Consider which environments you might add later, both those that exist currently and those that might be introduced later. Decide what features you really must have for your program to be useful.

Develop a paradigm. What will the input to your program be like? How will you display output? What files will you access on disk? Will you need any other special hardware? Do you require a certain degree of performance or a certain response time?

Set up your main loop carefully. Possible loop structures may be based on characters, on commands, or on events. The event structure is the most general, and the most likely to easily port to the Macintosh.

Code your high-level routines in terms of primitives that make sense for your application. If you need a certain kind of menu routine, define one and use it. If you need a pointing device, decide what coordinate system you need, whether you need any buttons and how many, and code in terms of this ideal device. Use windowing functions that describe what you need. Design these primitives in such a way that you are confident they can be implemented on all machines that matter to you.

Implement your primitives in terms of whatever system routines are actually provided. If there is a menu package that meets your needs, use it. If not, write your own in terms of the lower-level features. It is possible to write compatible menu libraries for character-oriented screens without much difficulty, using arrow keys or labels to select from the menu.

For each computer, a certain degree of customization will be necessary. It may be expected that you use *textedit* for all text input or editing on a Macintosh, for example. Option specification, if not done using arguments, may have different local conventions on different machines. Plan this ahead of time, so you won't have to make major design changes later.

Group common code together whenever possible. If you support six different computers and have implemented five different text input libraries, you will probably find yourself with a large amount of duplicated code. Duplicated code is difficult to maintain, since fixes and enhancements must be made in several places. If the libraries are similar, write them once and use `#ifdef` or even a run time `if` in places where differences are necessary. If you keep the number of differences to a minimum, your program will be easier to maintain.

This appendix contains the source code for the version of the getopt subroutine that AT&T has released into the public domain. This will help authors to write software that uses getopt without worrying about whether the target system supports it. When porting to a system that does not support getopt, this subroutine can be typed in as part of the application.

```
/*LINTLIBRARY*/
#define NULL      0
#define EOF (-1)
#define ERR(s, c) if(opterr){\
      extern int strlen(), _write();\
      char errbuf[2];\
      errbuf[0] = c; errbuf[1] = '\n';\
      (void) _write(2, argv[0], (unsigned)strlen(argv[0]));\
      (void) _write(2, s, (unsigned)strlen(s));\
      (void) _write(2, errbuf, 2);}

extern int strcmp();
extern char *strchr();
/*
 * If building the regular library, pick up the definitions
 * from this file.  If building the shared library, pick up
 * definitions from opt_data.c
 */

extern int opterr, optind, optopt;
extern char *optarg;

static char error1[] = ": option requires an argument -- "
static char error2[] = ": illegal option -- ";
```

```
int
getopt(argc, argv, opts)
int   argc;
char  **argv, *opts;
{
      static int sp = 1;
      register char c;
      register char *cp;

      if(sp == 1)
            if(optind >= argc ||
                argv[optind][0] != '-' || argv[optind][1] == '\0')
                    return(EOF);
            else if(strcmp(argv[optind], "--") == NULL) {
                    optind++;
                    return(EOF);
            }
      optopt = c = (unsigned char)argv[optind][sp];
      if(c == ':' || (cp=strchr(opts, c)) == NULL) {
            ERR(error2,c);
            if(argv[optind][++sp] == '\0') {
                    optind++;
                    sp = 1;
            }
            return('?');
      }
      if(*++cp == ':') {
            if(argv[optind][sp+1] != '\0')
                    optarg = &argv[optind++][sp+1];
            else if(++optind >= argc) {
                    ERR(error1,c);
                    sp = 1;
                    return('?');
            } else
                    optarg = argv[optind++];
            sp = 1;
      } else {
            if(argv[optind][++sp] == '\0') {
                    sp = 1;
                    optind++;
            }
            optarg = NULL;
      }
      return(c);
}
```

APPENDIX G: **PORTABILITY OF C LIBRARY FUNCTIONS**

This appendix consists of a table of C library functions. These functions represent Chapters 10 and 11 of this book. The table shows several implementations of the C language and which implementations support which functions.

These tables *are not* a rating of specific products or releases of products. It is recognized that newer releases will often support more features. The purpose of this table is to indicate the *portability of the feature*. Older releases have been deliberately used to better show the degree to which any given feature has historically been in the mainstream. A representative sampling of major compilers for major machines was chosen. There are many other implementations available for many of these and other machines.

Each table entry can be one of:

Y   (yes) – the function is present and is consistent with the standard;
–   (no) – the function is not present;
2   (1003.2) – the function is required by POSIX 1003.2, but not 1003.1;
NS   (nonstandard) – the function is present but differs somehow from the standard version; or
J   (job control) – the function is part of the POSIX job control option.

In general, when two or more different versions of a function are available, the one defined by X3J11, POSIX, or the SVID is taken to be the standard version. Some functions, such as `getw`, are inherently nonstandard because of their nonportable definition.

Columns for GCOS, TSO, K&R, and Stdio were included, since these represent some very old implementations and documents. Any function present in these systems and documents as well as most other systems can be considered at the core of the C language and extremely portable. Other functions present in only the most modern implementations may not be as portable, because some systems are based on older documents, such as K&R, or older libraries, such as V7.

This table was generated by listing functions supported in each implementation, running a shell script to generate the table, and removing all functions that appeared in only one system. (Approximately half the functions from the various manuals are specific to one system and hence unportable.)

A few unusual functions, such as `strlwr` and `intss`, appear in this table because they are present in more than one implementation. This does not mean that they are portable; only functions appearing in most of the columns are portable. The larger the number in the rightmost column, the more portable the function.

The systems referenced here are as follows:

GCOS   *Standard C Library for GCOS*, N-P. Nelson and L. Rosler, Bell Laboratories, Murray Hill, NJ, October 1978.

MVS   *A Programmer's Guide to C/370*, James F. Gimpel, Bell Laboratories, Holmdel, NJ, February 1979.

Amiga   *Aztec C68K, Version 3.20a for the Amiga*, Manx Software Systems, Inc., P.O. Box 55, Shrewsbury, NJ 07701, March 1986.

DOS/MS *Microsoft C Compiler for the MS-DOS Operating System*, Release 4.0, Microsoft Corporation, Box 97107, Redmond, WA 98073, April 1986.

DOS/Lat *Lattice C Compiler for 8086/8088 Series Microprocessor*, Version 2.15, Lattice Inc., P.O. Box 3148, Glen Ellyn, IL 60138, 1985.

V7   *UNIX Programmer's Manual*, Seventh Edition, VAX-11 Version, Bell Telephone Laboratories, Holmdel, NJ, December 1978.

4.2   *UNIX Programmer's Manual, Reference Guide*, 4.2 Berkeley Software Distribution, Virtual VAX-11 Version, Computer Science Division, Department of Electrical Engineering and Computer Science, University of California, Berkeley, CA 94720, March 1984.

SVr3   *UNIX System V Release 3, Programmer's Reference Manual*, Select Code 307-226, Issue 1, AT&T Customer Information Center, P.O. Box 19901, Indianapolis, IN 46219, 1986.

SVID   *System V Interface Definition, Issue 2*, ISBN 0-932764-10-X, Select Code No. 320-012, AT&T Customer Information Center, P.O. Box 19901, Indianapolis, IN 46219, 1986.

1003.1 *Portable Operating System Interface for Computer Environments*, (POSIX, IEEE Std 1003.1-1988.) IEEE Computer Society, 345 East 47th Street, New York, NY 10017, 1988.

X3J11   *Draft Proposed American National Standard for Information Systems – Programming Language C* X3J11/88-159, X3 Secretariat: CBEMA, 311 First St., NW, Suite 500, Washington, DC 20001, December 1988.

Stdio   *A New Input-Output Package*, D. M. Ritchie, Bell Laboratories, Murray Hill, NJ 07974, 1976.

K&R   *The C Programming Language*, Brian W. Kernighan and Dennis M. Ritchie, Prentice-Hall, Englewood Cliffs, NJ, 1978.

n   The number (out of 13) of columns in this table supporting the function.

Portability of C Library Functions

FUNCT	GCOS HW	MVS IBM	Amiga Manx	DOS MS	DOS Lat	V7 BTL	4.2 UCB	SVr3 AT&T	SVID AT&T	POSIX IEEE	X3J11 ANSI	Stdio BTL	K&R BTL	n/ 13
_abort	Y	Y	–	–	–	–	–	–	–	–	–	Y	Y	2
_exit	Y	Y	Y	Y	Y	Y	Y	Y	Y	Y	–	Y	Y	12
_longjmp	–	–	–	–	–	–	–	–	–	Y	–	–	–	1
_setjmp	–	–	–	–	–	–	–	–	–	Y	–	–	–	1
_tolower	–	–	Y	Y	–	–	–	Y	Y	–	–	–	–	4
_toupper	–	–	Y	Y	–	–	–	Y	Y	–	–	–	–	4
abort	Y	NS	–	NS	–	Y	Y	Y	Y	Y	Y	–	–	7
abs	Y	–	–	Y	–	Y	Y	Y	Y	Y	Y	–	–	8
access	–	–	NS	NS	–	Y	Y	Y	Y	Y	–	–	–	5
acct	–	–	–	–	–	Y	Y	Y	–	–	–	–	–	3
acos	Y	–	Y	Y	Y	Y	Y	Y	Y	Y	Y	–	–	10
alarm	–	–	–	–	–	Y	Y	Y	Y	Y	–	–	–	5
asctime	Y	–	–	Y	–	Y	Y	Y	Y	Y	Y	–	–	8
asin	Y	–	Y	Y	Y	Y	Y	Y	Y	Y	Y	–	–	10
assert	Y	–	Y	Y	–	Y	Y	Y	–	Y	Y	–	–	8
atan	Y	–	Y	Y	Y	Y	Y	Y	Y	Y	Y	–	–	10
atan2	Y	–	Y	Y	Y	Y	Y	Y	Y	Y	Y	–	–	10
atof	Y	Y	Y	Y	Y	Y	Y	Y	Y	Y	Y	–	Y	12
atoi	Y	–	Y	Y	Y	Y	Y	Y	Y	Y	Y	–	Y	11
atol	Y	–	Y	Y	Y	Y	Y	Y	Y	Y	–	–	–	9
bdos	–	–	–	Y	Y	–	–	–	–	–	–	–	–	2
brk	–	–	–	–	–	Y	Y	Y	–	–	–	–	–	3
bsearch	–	–	–	Y	–	–	–	Y	Y	Y	Y	–	–	5
cabs	–	–	–	Y	–	Y	Y	–	–	–	–	–	–	3
calloc	Y	Y	Y	Y	Y	Y	Y	Y	Y	Y	Y	Y	Y	13
ceil	Y	–	Y	Y	Y	Y	Y	Y	Y	Y	Y	–	–	10
cerror	Y	Y	–	–	–	–	–	–	–	–	–	–	–	2
cf_getispeed	–	–	–	–	–	–	–	–	–	Y	–	–	–	1
cf_getospeed	–	–	–	–	–	–	–	–	–	Y	–	–	–	1
cf_setispeed	–	–	–	–	–	–	–	–	–	Y	–	–	–	1
cf_setospeed	–	–	–	–	–	–	–	–	–	Y	–	–	–	1
cfree	Y	–	–	–	–	–	–	–	–	–	–	Y	Y	3
cgets	–	–	–	Y	Y	–	–	–	–	–	–	–	–	2
chdir	–	–	–	Y	–	Y	Y	Y	Y	Y	–	–	–	6
chmod	–	–	–	NS	–	Y	Y	Y	Y	Y	–	–	–	5
chown	–	–	–	–	–	NS	NS	Y	Y	Y	–	–	–	2
clearerr	–	–	Y	Y	Y	Y	Y	Y	Y	Y	Y	–	–	9
clock	Y	Y	–	–	–	–	–	Y	Y	–	Y	–	–	5
close	–	–	Y	Y	Y	Y	Y	Y	Y	Y	–	–	Y	9
closedir	–	–	–	–	–	–	Y	Y	–	Y	–	–	–	3
compile	–	–	–	–	–	–	–	–	–	Y	–	–	–	1
cos	Y	–	Y	Y	Y	Y	Y	Y	Y	Y	Y	–	–	10
cosh	Y	–	Y	Y	Y	Y	Y	Y	Y	Y	Y	–	–	10
cprintf	–	–	–	Y	Y	–	–	–	–	–	–	–	–	2
cputs	–	–	–	Y	Y	–	–	–	–	–	–	–	–	2
creat	–	–	Y	Y	Y	Y	Y	Y	Y	Y	–	–	Y	9
crypt	–	–	–	–	–	Y	Y	Y	Y	–	–	–	–	5
cscanf	–	–	–	Y	Y	–	–	–	–	–	–	–	–	2

Portability of C Library Functions

FUNCT	GCOS HW	MVS IBM	Amiga Manx	DOS MS	DOS Lat	V7 BTL	4.2 UCB	SVr3 AT&T	SVID AT&T	POSIX IEEE	X3J11 ANSI	Stdio BTL	K&R BTL	n/ 13
ctermid	–	–	–	–	–	–	–	Y	Y	Y	–	–	–	3
ctime	Y	–	–	Y	–	Y	Y	Y	Y	Y	Y	–	–	8
cuserid	Y	Y	–	–	–	–	–	Y	–	Y	–	–	–	4
dbminit	–	–	–	–	–	Y	Y	–	–	–	–	–	–	2
delete	–	–	–	–	–	Y	Y	–	–	–	–	–	–	2
difftime	–	–	–	–	–	–	–	–	–	–	Y	–	–	1
div	–	–	–	–	–	–	–	–	–	–	Y	–	–	1
drand48	–	–	–	–	Y	–	–	Y	Y	–	–	–	–	3
dup	–	–	–	Y	–	Y	Y	Y	Y	Y	–	–	–	6
dup2	–	–	–	Y	–	Y	Y	Y	–	Y	–	–	–	5
eaccess	–	–	–	–	–	–	–	–	–	Y	–	–	–	1
ecvt	–	–	–	Y	Y	Y	Y	Y	–	–	–	–	–	5
encrypt	–	–	–	–	–	Y	Y	Y	Y	–	–	–	–	4
endgrent	–	–	–	–	–	Y	Y	Y	–	Y	–	–	–	4
endpwent	–	–	–	–	–	Y	Y	Y	–	Y	–	–	–	4
erand48	–	–	–	–	Y	–	–	Y	Y	–	–	–	–	3
erf	–	–	–	–	–	–	–	Y	Y	–	–	–	–	2
erfc	–	–	–	–	–	–	–	Y	Y	–	–	–	–	2
execl	–	–	Y	NS	–	Y	Y	Y	Y	Y	–	–	–	6
execle	–	–	–	NS	–	Y	Y	Y	Y	Y	–	–	–	5
execlp	–	–	Y	NS	–	–	Y	Y	Y	Y	–	–	–	5
execv	Y	–	Y	NS	–	Y	Y	Y	Y	Y	–	–	–	6
execve	–	–	–	NS	–	Y	Y	Y	Y	Y	–	–	–	5
execvp	–	–	Y	NS	–	–	Y	Y	Y	Y	–	–	–	5
exit	Y	Y	Y	Y	Y	Y	Y	Y	Y	Y	Y	Y	Y	13
exp	Y	–	Y	Y	Y	Y	Y	Y	Y	Y	Y	–	–	10
fabs	Y	–	Y	Y	Y	Y	Y	Y	Y	Y	Y	–	–	10
fclose	Y	Y	Y	Y	Y	Y	Y	Y	Y	Y	Y	Y	Y	13
fcntl	–	–	–	–	–	–	NS	Y	Y	Y	–	–	–	3
fcvt	–	–	–	Y	–	Y	Y	Y	–	–	–	–	–	4
fdopen	–	–	Y	Y	–	Y	Y	Y	Y	Y	–	–	–	7
feof	Y	Y	Y	Y	Y	Y	Y	Y	Y	Y	Y	Y	–	12
ferror	Y	Y	Y	Y	Y	Y	Y	Y	Y	Y	Y	Y	–	12
fetch	–	–	–	–	–	Y	Y	–	–	–	–	–	–	2
fflush	Y	Y	Y	Y	Y	Y	Y	Y	Y	Y	Y	Y	–	12
fgetc	Y	–	–	Y	Y	Y	Y	Y	Y	Y	Y	Y	–	10
fgetr	Y	Y	–	–	–	–	–	–	–	–	–	–	–	2
fgets	Y	Y	Y	Y	Y	Y	Y	Y	Y	Y	Y	Y	Y	13
fileno	Y	Y	Y	Y	Y	Y	Y	Y	Y	Y	–	Y	–	11
fionread	–	–	–	–	–	–	–	–	–	Y	–	–	–	1
firstkey	–	–	–	–	–	Y	Y	–	–	–	–	–	–	2
floor	Y	–	Y	Y	Y	Y	Y	Y	Y	Y	Y	–	–	10
fmod	Y	–	–	Y	Y	–	–	Y	Y	Y	Y	–	–	7
fopen	Y	NS	Y	NS	Y	Y	Y	Y	Y	Y	Y	Y	Y	11
fork	–	–	–	–	–	Y	Y	Y	Y	Y	–	–	–	5
fprintf	Y	Y	Y	Y	Y	NS	NS	Y	Y	Y	Y	Y	Y	11
fprompt	Y	Y	–	–	–	–	–	–	–	–	–	–	–	2
fputc	Y	–	–	Y	Y	Y	Y	Y	Y	Y	Y	Y	–	10

Portability of C Library Functions

FUNCT	GCOS HW	MVS IBM	Amiga Manx	DOS MS	DOS Lat	V7 BTL	4.2 UCB	SVr3 AT&T	SVID AT&T	POSIX IEEE	X3J11 ANSI	Stdio BTL	K&R BTL	n/ 13
fputr	Y	Y	–	–	–	–	–	–	–	–	–	–	–	2
fputs	Y	Y	Y	Y	Y	Y	Y	Y	Y	Y	Y	Y	Y	13
fread	Y	Y	Y	Y	Y	Y	Y	Y	Y	Y	Y	Y	–	12
free	Y	Y	Y	Y	Y	Y	Y	Y	Y	Y	Y	–	Y	12
freopen	Y	Y	Y	Y	Y	Y	Y	Y	Y	Y	Y	Y	–	12
frexp	–	–	Y	Y	Y	Y	Y	Y	Y	Y	Y	–	–	9
fscanf	Y	Y	Y	Y	Y	Y	Y	Y	Y	Y	Y	Y	Y	13
fseek	Y	Y	Y	Y	Y	Y	Y	Y	Y	Y	Y	Y	–	12
fstat	–	–	–	NS	–	Y	NS	Y	Y	Y	–	–	–	4
ftell	Y	Y	Y	Y	Y	Y	Y	Y	Y	Y	Y	Y	–	12
ftime	–	–	–	Y	–	Y	Y	–	–	–	–	–	–	3
ftw	–	–	–	–	–	–	–	Y	Y	–	–	–	–	2
fwrite	Y	Y	Y	Y	Y	Y	Y	Y	Y	Y	Y	Y	–	12
gamma	–	–	–	–	–	Y	Y	Y	Y	–	–	–	–	4
gcvt	–	–	–	Y	–	Y	Y	Y	–	–	–	–	–	4
getc	Y	Y	Y	Y	Y	Y	Y	Y	Y	Y	Y	Y	Y	13
getchar	Y	Y	Y	Y	Y	Y	Y	Y	Y	Y	Y	Y	Y	13
getche	–	–	–	Y	Y	–	–	–	–	–	–	–	–	2
getcwd	–	–	–	Y	–	–	–	Y	Y	Y	–	–	–	4
getegid	–	–	–	–	–	Y	Y	Y	Y	Y	–	–	–	5
getenv	–	–	Y	Y	Y	Y	Y	Y	Y	Y	Y	–	–	9
geteuid	–	–	–	–	–	Y	Y	Y	Y	Y	–	–	–	5
getgid	–	–	–	–	–	Y	Y	Y	Y	Y	–	–	–	5
getgrent	–	–	–	–	–	Y	Y	Y	–	Y	–	–	–	4
getgrgid	–	–	–	–	–	Y	Y	Y	–	Y	–	–	–	4
getgrnam	–	–	–	–	–	Y	Y	Y	–	Y	–	–	–	4
getgroups	–	–	–	–	–	–	Y	–	–	Y	–	–	–	2
getlogin	–	–	–	–	–	Y	Y	Y	–	Y	–	–	–	4
getopt	–	–	–	–	–	–	–	Y	Y	2	–	–	–	3
getpass	–	–	–	–	–	Y	Y	Y	–	Y	–	–	–	4
getpgrp	–	–	–	–	–	–	Y	Y	Y	Y	–	–	–	4
getpid	–	–	–	Y	–	Y	Y	Y	Y	Y	–	–	–	6
getppid	–	–	–	–	–	–	Y	Y	Y	Y	–	–	–	4
getpw	–	–	–	–	–	Y	Y	Y	–	–	–	Y	–	4
getpwent	–	–	–	–	–	Y	Y	Y	–	Y	–	–	–	4
getpwnam	–	–	–	–	–	Y	Y	Y	–	Y	–	–	–	4
getpwuid	–	–	–	–	–	Y	Y	Y	–	Y	–	–	–	4
gets	Y	–	Y	Y	Y	Y	Y	Y	Y	Y	Y	Y	–	11
getuid	–	–	–	–	–	Y	Y	Y	Y	Y	–	–	–	5
gmtime	Y	–	–	Y	–	Y	Y	Y	Y	Y	Y	–	–	8
gsignal	Y	–	–	–	–	–	–	Y	–	–	–	–	–	2
glob	–	–	–	–	–	–	–	–	–	2	–	–	–	1
globfree	–	–	–	–	–	–	–	–	–	2	–	–	–	1
gtty	–	–	–	–	–	Y	Y	–	–	–	–	–	–	2
hcreate	–	–	–	–	–	–	–	–	Y	–	–	–	–	1
hdestroy	–	–	–	–	–	–	–	–	Y	–	–	–	–	1
hsearch	–	–	–	–	–	–	–	Y	Y	–	–	–	–	2
hypot	Y	–	–	Y	–	Y	Y	Y	Y	–	–	–	–	6

Portability of C Library Functions

FUNCT	GCOS HW	MVS IBM	Amiga Manx	DOS MS	DOS Lat	V7 BTL	4.2 UCB	SVr3 AT&T	SVID AT&T	POSIX IEEE	X3J11 ANSI	Stdio BTL	K&R BTL	n/13
index	–	Y	Y	–	–	Y	Y	–	–	–	–	–	Y	5
inp	–	–	–	Y	Y	–	–	–	–	–	–	–	–	2
inquire	Y	Y	–	–	–	–	–	–	–	–	–	–	–	2
int86	–	–	–	Y	Y	–	–	–	–	–	–	–	–	2
int86x	–	–	–	Y	Y	–	–	–	–	–	–	–	–	2
intdos	–	–	–	Y	Y	–	–	–	–	–	–	–	–	2
intdosx	–	–	–	Y	Y	–	–	–	–	–	–	–	–	2
intss	Y	Y	–	–	–	–	–	–	–	–	–	–	–	2
isalnum	Y	Y	Y	Y	Y	Y	Y	Y	Y	Y	Y	–	–	11
isalpha	Y	Y	Y	Y	Y	Y	Y	Y	Y	Y	Y	Y	Y	13
isascii	Y	–	Y	Y	Y	Y	Y	Y	Y	–	–	–	–	8
isatty	–	–	Y	NS	–	Y	Y	Y	Y	Y	–	–	–	6
iscntrl	Y	–	Y	Y	Y	Y	Y	Y	Y	Y	Y	–	–	10
isdigit	Y	Y	Y	Y	Y	Y	Y	Y	Y	Y	Y	Y	Y	13
isgraph	Y	–	–	Y	Y	–	–	Y	Y	Y	Y	–	–	7
islower	Y	Y	Y	Y	Y	Y	Y	Y	Y	Y	Y	Y	Y	13
isprint	Y	Y	Y	Y	Y	Y	Y	Y	Y	Y	Y	–	–	11
ispunct	Y	–	Y	Y	Y	Y	Y	Y	Y	Y	Y	–	–	10
isspace	Y	Y	Y	Y	Y	Y	Y	Y	Y	Y	Y	Y	Y	13
isupper	Y	Y	Y	Y	Y	Y	Y	Y	Y	Y	Y	Y	Y	13
isxdigit	–	–	–	Y	Y	–	–	Y	Y	Y	Y	–	–	6
itoa	–	–	–	Y	–	–	–	–	–	–	–	–	Y	2
j0	–	–	–	Y	–	Y	Y	Y	Y	–	–	–	–	5
j1	--	–	–	Y	–	Y	Y	Y	Y	–	–	–	–	5
jcsetpgrp	–	–	–	–	–	–	–	–	–	J	–	–	–	1
jn	–	–	–	Y	–	Y	Y	Y	Y	–	–	–	–	5
jrand48	–	–	–	–	Y	–	–	Y	Y	–	–	–	–	3
kbhit	–	–	–	Y	Y	–	–	–	–	–	–	–	–	2
kill	–	–	–	–	–	Y	Y	Y	Y	Y	–	–	–	5
labs	–	–	–	Y	–	–	–	–	–	–	Y	–	–	2
lcong48	–	–	–	–	Y	–	–	Y	Y	–	–	–	–	3
ldexp	–	–	Y	Y	Y	Y	Y	Y	Y	Y	Y	–	–	9
ldiv	–	–	–	–	–	–	–	–	–	–	Y	–	–	1
lfind	–	–	–	–	–	–	–	Y	Y	–	–	–	–	2
link	–	–	–	–	–	Y	Y	Y	Y	Y	–	–	–	5
localtime	Y	–	–	NS	–	Y	Y	Y	Y	Y	Y	–	–	7
lockf	–	–	–	–	–	–	–	Y	Y	Y	–	–	–	3
log	Y	–	Y	Y	Y	Y	Y	Y	Y	Y	Y	–	–	10
log10	–	–	Y	Y	Y	–	Y	Y	Y	Y	Y	–	–	8
longjmp	Y	–	Y	Y	Y	Y	Y	Y	Y	Y	Y	–	–	10
lrand48	–	–	–	–	Y	–	–	Y	Y	–	–	–	–	3
lsearch	–	–	–	–	–	–	–	Y	Y	–	–	–	–	2
lseek	–	–	Y	Y	Y	Y	Y	Y	Y	Y	–	–	Y	9
mallinfo	–	–	–	–	–	–	–	Y	Y	–	–	–	–	2
malloc	Y	Y	Y	Y	Y	Y	Y	Y	Y	Y	Y	–	–	11
mallopt	–	–	–	–	–	–	–	Y	Y	–	–	–	–	2
matherr	–	–	–	Y	Y	–	–	Y	Y	–	–	–	–	4
mblen	–	–	–	–	–	–	–	–	–	–	Y	–	–	1

Portability of C Library Functions

FUNCT	GCOS HW	MVS IBM	Amiga Manx	DOS MS	DOS Lat	V7 BTL	4.2 UCB	SVr3 AT&T	SVID AT&T	POSIX IEEE	X3J11 ANSI	Stdio BTL	K&R BTL	n/ 13
mbstowcw	–	–	–	–	–	–	–	–	–	–	Y	–	–	1
mbtowc	–	–	–	–	–	–	–	–	–	–	Y	–	–	1
memccpy	–	–	–	Y	–	–	–	Y	Y	–	–	–	–	3
memchr	Y	–	–	Y	–	–	–	Y	Y	–	Y	–	–	5
memcmp	Y	Y	–	Y	–	–	–	Y	Y	–	Y	–	–	6
memcpy	Y	Y	–	Y	–	–	–	Y	Y	–	Y	–	–	6
memmove	–	–	–	–	–	–	–	–	–	–	Y	–	–	1
memset	Y	Y	–	Y	–	–	–	Y	Y	–	Y	–	–	6
mkdir	–	–	–	Y	–	–	Y	Y	–	Y	–	–	–	4
mkfifo	–	–	–	–	–	–	–	–	–	Y	–	–	–	1
mknod	–	–	–	–	–	Y	Y	Y	Y	–	–	–	–	4
mktemp	–	–	NS	Y	–	Y	Y	Y	Y	–	–	–	–	5
mktime	–	–	–	–	–	–	–	–	–	–	Y	–	–	1
modf	–	–	Y	Y	Y	Y	Y	Y	Y	Y	Y	–	–	9
monitor	–	–	–	–	–	Y	Y	Y	–	–	–	–	–	3
mount	–	–	–	–	–	Y	Y	Y	Y	–	–	–	–	4
movedata	–	–	–	Y	Y	–	–	–	–	–	–	–	–	2
movmem	–	–	Y	–	Y	–	–	–	–	–	–	–	–	2
mrand48	–	–	–	–	Y	–	–	Y	Y	–	–	–	–	3
nargs	Y	Y	–	–	–	–	–	–	–	–	–	–	–	2
nextkey	–	–	–	–	–	Y	Y	–	–	–	–	–	–	2
nice	–	–	–	–	–	Y	Y	Y	–	–	–	–	–	3
nlist	–	–	–	–	–	Y	Y	Y	–	–	–	–	–	3
nrand48	–	–	–	–	Y	–	–	Y	Y	–	–	–	–	3
onexit	–	–	–	–	–	–	–	–	–	–	Y	–	–	1
open	–	–	Y	Y	Y	Y	NS	Y	Y	Y	–	Y	–	8
opendir	–	–	–	–	–	–	Y	Y	–	Y	–	–	–	3
outp	–	–	–	Y	Y	–	–	–	–	–	–	–	–	2
pause	–	–	–	–	–	Y	Y	Y	Y	Y	–	–	–	5
pclose	–	–	–	–	–	Y	Y	Y	Y	Y	–	–	–	5
perror	–	Y	Y	Y	–	Y	Y	Y	Y	Y	Y	–	–	9
pipe	–	–	–	–	–	Y	Y	Y	Y	Y	–	–	–	5
popen	–	–	–	–	–	Y	Y	Y	Y	Y	–	–	–	5
posixconf	–	–	–	–	–	–	–	–	–	Y	–	–	–	1
pow	Y	–	Y	Y	Y	Y	Y	Y	Y	Y	Y	–	–	10
printf	Y	Y	Y	Y	Y	NS	NS	Y	Y	Y	Y	Y	Y	11
profil	–	–	–	–	–	Y	Y	Y	–	–	–	–	–	3
ptrace	–	–	–	–	–	Y	Y	Y	–	–	–	–	–	3
putc	Y	Y	Y	Y	Y	Y	Y	Y	Y	Y	Y	Y	Y	13
putch	–	–	–	Y	Y	–	–	–	–	–	–	–	–	2
putchar	Y	Y	Y	Y	Y	Y	Y	Y	Y	Y	Y	Y	Y	13
putenv	–	–	–	Y	–	–	–	Y	Y	–	–	–	–	3
puts	Y	–	Y	Y	Y	Y	Y	Y	Y	Y	Y	Y	–	11
qsort	–	–	Y	Y	–	Y	Y	Y	Y	Y	Y	–	–	8
raise	–	–	–	–	–	–	–	–	–	–	Y	–	–	1
rand	Y	–	–	Y	Y	NS	NS	Y	Y	Y	Y	–	–	7
read	–	–	Y	Y	Y	Y	Y	Y	Y	Y	–	–	Y	9
readdir	–	–	–	–	–	–	Y	Y	–	Y	–	–	–	3

Portability of C Library Functions

FUNCT	GCOS HW	MVS IBM	Amiga Manx	DOS MS	DOS Lat	V7 BTL	4.2 UCB	SVr3 AT&T	SVID AT&T	POSIX IEEE	X3J11 ANSI	Stdio BTL	K&R BTL	n/13
realloc	Y	NS	Y	Y	–	Y	Y	Y	Y	Y	Y	–	–	9
regcomp	–	–	–	–	–	–	–	–	–	2	–	–	–	1
regexec	–	–	–	–	–	–	–	–	–	2	–	–	–	1
regfree	–	–	–	–	–	–	–	–	–	2	–	–	–	1
remove	–	–	–	–	Y	–	–	–	–	Y	Y	–	–	3
rename	–	–	Y	Y	Y	–	Y	–	–	Y	Y	–	–	6
rewind	Y	Y	–	Y	Y	Y	Y	Y	Y	Y	Y	Y	–	11
rewinddir	–	–	–	–	–	–	Y	Y	–	Y	–	–	–	3
rindex	–	–	Y	–	–	Y	Y	–	–	–	–	–	–	3
rmdir	–	–	–	Y	–	–	Y	Y	–	Y	–	–	–	4
sbrk	–	–	Y	Y	Y	Y	Y	Y	–	–	–	–	Y	7
scanf	Y	Y	Y	Y	Y	Y	Y	Y	Y	Y	Y	Y	Y	13
seed48	–	–	–	–	Y	–	–	Y	Y	–	–	–	–	3
seekdir	–	–	–	–	–	–	Y	Y	–	–	–	–	–	2
segread	–	–	–	Y	Y	–	–	–	–	–	–	–	–	2
setbuf	Y	Y	Y	Y	Y	Y	Y	Y	Y	Y	Y	Y	–	12
setgid	–	–	–	–	–	Y	Y	Y	Y	Y	–	–	–	5
setgrent	–	–	–	–	–	Y	Y	Y	–	Y	–	–	–	4
setjmp	Y	–	Y	Y	Y	Y	Y	Y	Y	Y	Y	–	–	10
setkey	–	–	–	–	–	Y	Y	Y	–	–	–	–	–	3
setmem	–	–	Y	–	Y	–	–	–	–	–	–	–	–	2
setpgrp	–	–	–	–	–	–	NS	Y	NS	Y	–	–	–	2
setpwent	–	–	–	–	–	Y	Y	Y	–	Y	–	–	–	4
setuid	–	–	–	–	–	Y	Y	Y	Y	Y	–	–	–	5
setvbuf	–	–	–	–	–	–	–	Y	Y	–	Y	–	–	3
sigaction	–	–	–	–	–	–	–	–	–	Y	–	–	–	1
sigismember	–	–	–	–	–	–	–	–	–	Y	–	–	–	1
siglongjmp	–	–	–	–	–	–	–	–	Y	–	–	–	–	1
signal	Y	NS	–	NS	–	Y	NS	Y	Y	Y	Y	–	–	6
sigpending	–	–	–	–	–	–	–	–	–	Y	–	–	–	1
sigprocmask	–	–	–	–	–	–	–	–	–	Y	–	–	–	1
sigsetadd	–	–	–	–	–	–	–	–	–	Y	–	–	–	1
sigsetdel	–	–	–	–	–	–	–	–	–	Y	–	–	–	1
sigsetempty	–	–	–	–	–	–	–	–	–	Y	–	–	–	1
sigsetfull	–	–	–	–	–	–	–	–	–	Y	–	–	–	1
sigsetinit	–	–	–	–	–	–	–	–	–	Y	–	–	–	1
sigsetjmp	–	–	–	–	–	–	–	–	Y	–	–	–	–	1
sigsuspend	–	–	–	–	–	–	–	–	–	Y	–	–	–	1
sin	Y	–	Y	Y	Y	Y	Y	Y	Y	Y	Y	–	–	10
sinh	Y	–	Y	Y	Y	Y	Y	Y	Y	Y	Y	–	–	10
sleep	–	–	–	–	–	Y	Y	Y	Y	Y	–	–	–	5
sprintf	Y	Y	Y	Y	Y	NS	NS	Y	Y	Y	Y	Y	Y	11
sqrt	Y	–	Y	Y	Y	Y	Y	Y	Y	Y	Y	–	–	10
srand	Y	–	–	Y	Y	Y	Y	Y	Y	Y	Y	–	–	9
srand48	–	–	–	–	Y	–	–	Y	Y	–	–	–	–	3
sscanf	Y	Y	Y	Y	Y	Y	Y	Y	Y	Y	Y	Y	Y	13
ssignal	Y	–	–	–	–	–	–	Y	–	–	–	–	–	2
stat	–	–	–	NS	–	Y	NS	Y	Y	Y	–	–	Y	5

Portability of C Library Functions

FUNCT	GCOS HW	MVS IBM	Amiga Manx	DOS MS	DOS Lat	V7 BTL	4.2 UCB	SVr3 AT&T	SVID AT&T	POSIX IEEE	X3J11 ANSI	Stdio BTL	K&R BTL	n/13
step	–	–	–	–	–	–	–	–	Y	–	–	–	–	1
stime	–	–	–	–	–	Y	–	Y	Y	–	–	–	–	3
store	–	–	–	–	–	Y	Y	–	–	–	–	–	–	2
strbrk	Y	Y	–	–	–	–	–	–	–	–	–	–	–	2
strcat	Y	Y	Y	Y	Y	Y	Y	Y	Y	Y	Y	–	Y	12
strchr	Y	Y	–	Y	Y	–	–	Y	Y	Y	Y	–	–	8
strcmp	Y	Y	Y	Y	Y	Y	Y	Y	Y	Y	Y	–	Y	12
strcpy	Y	Y	Y	Y	Y	Y	Y	Y	Y	Y	Y	–	Y	12
strcspn	–	–	–	Y	Y	–	–	Y	Y	Y	Y	–	–	6
strdup	Y	–	–	Y	–	–	–	Y	–	–	–	–	–	3
strerror	–	–	–	–	–	–	–	–	–	–	Y	–	–	1
strlen	Y	Y	Y	Y	Y	Y	Y	Y	Y	Y	Y	–	Y	12
strlwr	Y	–	–	Y	–	–	–	–	–	–	–	–	–	2
strncat	Y	–	Y	Y	Y	Y	Y	Y	Y	Y	Y	–	–	10
strncmp	Y	–	Y	Y	Y	Y	Y	Y	Y	–	Y	–	–	9
strncpy	Y	Y	Y	Y	Y	Y	Y	Y	Y	Y	Y	–	–	11
strpbrk	–	–	–	Y	Y	–	–	Y	Y	Y	Y	–	–	6
strrchr	Y	–	–	Y	Y	–	–	Y	Y	Y	Y	–	–	7
strspn	Y	Y	–	Y	Y	–	–	Y	Y	Y	Y	–	–	8
strstr	Y	–	–	–	–	–	–	–	–	Y	Y	–	–	3
strtod	Y	Y	–	–	–	–	–	Y	Y	–	Y	–	–	5
strtok	–	–	–	Y	–	–	–	Y	Y	Y	Y	–	–	5
strtol	Y	Y	–	–	Y	–	–	Y	Y	–	Y	–	–	6
strtoul	–	–	–	–	–	–	–	–	–	–	Y	–	–	1
strtrm	Y	Y	–	–	–	–	–	–	–	–	–	–	–	2
strupr	Y	–	–	Y	–	–	–	–	–	–	–	–	–	2
stty	–	–	–	–	–	Y	Y	–	–	–	–	–	–	2
swab	–	–	–	Y	–	Y	Y	Y	Y	–	–	–	–	5
sync	–	–	–	–	–	Y	Y	Y	Y	–	–	–	–	4
system	Y	NS	–	Y	Y	Y	Y	Y	Y	Y	Y	Y	Y	11
sysconf	–	–	–	–	–	–	–	–	–	Y	–	–	–	1
tan	Y	–	Y	Y	Y	Y	Y	Y	Y	Y	Y	–	–	10
tanh	Y	–	Y	Y	Y	Y	Y	Y	Y	Y	Y	–	–	10
tcdrain	–	–	–	–	–	–	–	–	–	Y	–	–	–	1
tcflow	–	–	–	–	–	–	–	–	–	Y	–	–	–	1
tcflush	–	–	–	–	–	–	–	–	–	Y	–	–	–	1
tcgetattr	–	–	–	–	–	–	–	–	–	Y	–	–	–	1
tcgetpgrp	–	–	–	–	–	–	–	–	–	J	–	–	–	1
tcsendbreak	–	–	–	–	–	–	–	–	–	Y	–	–	–	1
tcsetattr	–	–	–	–	–	–	–	–	–	Y	–	–	–	1
tcsetpgrp	–	–	–	–	–	–	–	–	–	J	–	–	–	1
tdelete	–	–	–	–	–	–	–	Y	Y	–	–	–	–	2
tell	–	–	–	Y	–	Y	–	–	–	–	–	–	–	2
telldir	–	–	–	–	–	–	Y	Y	–	–	–	–	–	2
tempnam	–	–	–	–	–	–	–	Y	Y	–	–	¬	–	2
tfind	–	–	–	–	–	–	–	Y	Y	–	–	–	–	2
time	Y	Y	–	Y	–	Y	Y	Y	Y	Y	Y	–	–	9
times	–	–	–	–	–	Y	Y	Y	Y	–	–	–	–	4

Portability of C Library Functions

FUNCT	GCOS HW	MVS IBM	Amiga Manx	DOS MS	DOS Lat	V7 BTL	4.2 UCB	SVr3 AT&T	SVID AT&T	POSIX IEEE	X3J11 ANSI	Stdio BTL	K&R BTL	n/13
timezone	–	–	–	–	–	Y	Y	–	–	–	–	–	–	2
tmpfile	–	–	Y	Y	–	–	–	Y	Y	Y	Y	–	–	6
tmpnam	Y	Y	Y	Y	–	–	–	Y	Y	Y	Y	–	–	8
toascii	Y	NS	–	Y	–	–	–	Y	Y	–	–	–	–	4
tolower	Y	Y	Y	Y	Y	–	–	Y	Y	Y	Y	Y	Y	11
toupper	Y	Y	Y	Y	Y	–	–	Y	Y	Y	Y	Y	Y	11
tsearch	–	–	–	–	–	–	–	Y	Y	–	–	–	–	2
ttyname	–	–	–	–	–	Y	Y	Y	Y	Y	–	–	–	5
ttyslot	–	–	–	–	–	Y	Y	Y	–	–	–	–	–	3
twalk	–	–	–	–	–	–	–	Y	Y	–	–	–	–	2
tzset	–	–	–	Y	–	–	–	Y	Y	–	–	–	–	3
ulimit	–	–	–	–	–	–	–	Y	Y	–	–	–	–	2
umask	–	–	–	NS	–	Y	Y	Y	Y	Y	–	–	–	5
umount	–	–	–	–	–	Y	Y	Y	Y	–	–	–	–	4
uname	–	–	–	–	–	–	–	Y	Y	Y	–	–	–	3
ungetc	Y	Y	Y	Y	Y	Y	Y	Y	Y	Y	Y	Y	Y	13
ungetch	–	–	–	Y	Y	–	–	–	–	–	–	–	–	2
unlink	Y	–	Y	Y	Y	Y	Y	Y	Y	Y	–	–	Y	10
ustat	–	–	–	–	–	–	–	Y	Y	–	–	–	–	2
utime	–	–	–	NS	–	Y	Y	Y	Y	Y	–	–	–	5
vfprintf	–	–	–	–	–	–	–	Y	Y	–	Y	–	–	3
vprintf	–	–	–	–	–	–	–	Y	Y	–	Y	–	–	3
vsprintf	–	–	–	–	–	–	–	Y	Y	–	Y	–	–	3
wait	–	–	–	–	Y	Y	Y	Y	Y	Y	–	–	–	6
waitpid	–	–	–	–	–	–	–	–	–	Y	–	–	–	1
wcstombs	–	–	–	–	–	–	–	–	–	–	Y	–	–	1
wctomb	–	–	–	–	–	–	–	–	–	–	Y	–	–	1
wdleng	Y	Y	–	–	–	–	–	–	–	–	–	–	–	2
write	–	–	Y	Y	Y	Y	Y	Y	Y	Y	–	–	Y	9
y0	–	–	–	Y	–	Y	Y	Y	Y	–	–	–	–	5
y1	–	–	–	Y	–	Y	Y	Y	Y	–	–	–	–	5
yn	–	–	–	Y	–	Y	Y	Y	Y	–	–	–	–	5

PORTABILITY OF SHELL COMMANDS

This appendix consists of a table of UNIX system shell commands. These commands represent Chapter 15 of this book. The table shows several implementations supporting shell commands and which implementations support which commands.

These tables *are not* a rating of specific products or releases of products. It is recognized that newer releases will often support more features. The purpose of this table is to indicate the *portability of the feature*. Older releases have been deliberately used to better show the degree to which any given feature has historically been in the mainstream. A representative sampling of major systems was chosen.

Each table entry can be one of:

Y   (yes) – the command is present.

BI   (built-in) – the command is present and is a shell built-in command.

Dir   (nonstandard directory) – the command is present but is not in one of the default PATH directories such as /bin and /usr/bin. These commands are often found in /etc or /usr/lib.

Opt   (optional) – the command is offered by the system, but is part of an optional package, so it may not be present on all systems. Note: if a command is both optional and installed in a directory not in the default PATH, it is shown as Opt.

csh   (C shell) – the command, a shell built-in, is present in the C shell but not in the Bourne shell.

cmd   (name of a command) – the command is present with a different name, and the name of that command is shown in the table.

–   (no) – the command is not present.

This table was generated by listing commands supported in each implementation, running a shell script to generate the table, and removing all commands that appeared in only one system. (Approximately half the commands from the various manuals are specific to one system and hence unportable.)

The systems referenced here are as follows:

V7   *UNIX Programmer's Manual*, Seventh Edition, VAX-11 Version, Bell Tele-phone Laboratories, Holmdel, NJ, December 1978.

4.2   *UNIX Programmer's Manual, Reference Guide*, 4.2 Berkeley Software Distri-bution, Virtual VAX-11 Version. Computer Science Division, Department of Electrical Engineering and Computer Science, University of California, Berke-ley, CA 94720, March 1984.

SIII   *UNIX User's Manual* (System III), AT&T Bell Laboratories, Murray Hill, NJ, June 1980.

SVR3   *UNIX System V Release 3, User's and System Administrator's Reference Manual*, Select Code 305-646, Issue 1, AT&T Customer Information Center, P.O. Box 19901, Indianapolis, IN 46219, 1988.

SVID   *System V Interface Definition, Issue 2*, ISBN 0-932764-10-X, Select Code No. 320-012, AT&T Customer Information Center, P.O. Box 19901, Indianapolis, IN 46219, 1986.

P.1003   *Draft Shell and Utility Application Interface for Portable Operating System Environments* (POSIX, P.1003.2, draft 9 8/29/89.) Institute of Electrical and Electronics Engineers, 345 East 47th Street, New York, NY 10017, 1989.

MKS   **MKS Toolkit**, 1988, Mortice Kern Systems Inc., 35 King St. N., Waterloo, ON, Canada N2J 2W9.

n   The number (out of 7) of columns in this table supporting the command.

Portability of UNIX System Shell Commands

CMD	P1003.2	SVID	SVR3	SIII	V7	4.2	MKS	COUNT
#	BI	BI	BI	BI	–	–	BI	5
.	BI	BI	BI	BI	BI	Y	Y	7
300	–	–	Y	Y	–	–	–	2
300s	–	–	Y	Y	–	–	–	2
4014	–	–	Y	Y	–	–	–	2
450	–	–	Y	Y	–	–	–	2
:	BI	BI	BI	BI	BI	BI	BI	7
[	Y	Opt	Y	Y	Y	Y	–	6
ac	–	–	–	–	Y	Dir	–	2
acctcms	–	Opt	–	Y	–	–	–	2
acctcom	–	Opt	–	Y	–	–	–	2
acctcon1	–	Opt	–	Y	–	–	–	2
acctcon2	–	Opt	–	Y	–	–	–	2
accton	–	Opt	–	Y	Dir	Dir	–	4
acctprc1	–	Opt	–	Y	–	–	–	2
acctprc2	–	Opt	–	Y	–	–	–	2
acctwtmp	–	Opt	–	Y	–	–	–	2
adb	–	–	–	Y	Y	Y	–	3
admin	–	Opt	Opt	Y	–	–	–	3
adv	–	Opt	Y	–	–	–	–	2
ar	Opt	Y	Y	Y	Y	Y	–	6
arcv	–	–	–	Y	Y	Dir	–	3
as	–	Opt	Opt	Y	Y	Y	–	5
asa	Opt	–	–	–	–	–	–	1
at	–	Opt	Y	–	Y	Y	–	4
awk	Y	Y	Y	Y	Y	Y	Y	7
banner	–	Y	Y	Y	–	–	Y	4
basename	Y	Y	Y	Y	Y	Y	Y	7
batch	–	Opt	Y	–	–	–	–	2
bc	Y	–	Y	Y	Y	Y	–	5
bdiff	–	–	Y	Y	–	–	–	2
bfs	–	–	Y	Y	–	–	–	2
break	BI	BI	BI	BI	BI	BI	BI	7
bs	–	–	–	Y	Y	–	–	2
c89	Opt	–	–	–	–	–	–	1
cal	–	Y	Y	Y	Y	Y	Y	6
calendar	–	Y	Y	Y	–	Y	–	4
cancel	–	Opt	Y	–	–	–	–	2
case	BI	BI	BI	BI	BI	BI	BI	7
cat	Y	Y	Y	Y	Y	Y	Y	7
cb	–	–	Opt	Y	Y	Y	–	4
cc	–	Opt	Opt	Y	Y	Y	–	5
cd	Y	BI	BI	BI	BI	BI	BI	7
cdc	–	–	Opt	Y	–	–	–	2
cflow	–	Opt	Opt	–	–	–	–	2
checkeq	–	–	–	Y	–	Y	–	2
chgrp	Y	Opt	Y	Y	Y	Y	–	6
chmod	Y	Y	Y	Y	Y	Y	Y	7
chown	Y	Opt	Y	Y	Y	Dir	–	6

Portability of UNIX System Shell Commands

CMD	P1003.2	SVID	SVR3	SIII	V7	4.2	MKS	COUNT
chroot	–	Opt	Dir	Y	–	–	–	3
cksum	Y	–	–	–	–	–	–	1
clri	–	Opt	Dir	Y	Y	Dir	–	5
cmp	Y	Y	Y	Y	Y	Y	Y	7
col	–	Y	Y	Y	Y	Y	–	5
comb	–	–	Opt	Y	–	–	–	2
comm	Y	Y	Y	Y	Y	Y	Y	7
command	Y	–	–	–	–	–	–	1
continue	BI	BI	BI	BI	BI	BI	BI	7
cp	Y	Y	Y	Y	Y	Y	Y	7
cpio	–	Y	Y	Y	–	–	Y	4
cpp	–	Opt	Opt	–	–	–	–	2
crash	–	–	Dir	Dir	–	–	–	2
create	Y	–	–	–	–	–	–	1
cref	–	–	–	Y	Y	–	–	2
cron	–	Opt	Dir	Dir	Y	Dir	–	5
crontab	–	Opt	Y	–	–	–	–	2
crypt	–	–	Y	Y	Y	Y	Y	5
csplit	–	Opt	Y	Y	–	–	–	3
ct	–	–	Y	Y	–	–	–	2
ctags	–	–	–	–	–	Y	Y	2
cu	–	Opt	Y	Y	Y	Y	–	5
cut	Y	Y	Y	Y	–	–	Y	5
cxref	–	Opt	Opt	–	–	–	–	2
date	Y	Y	Y	Y	Y	Y	Y	7
dc	–	–	Y	Y	Y	Y	–	4
dcheck	–	–	–	–	Y	Dir	–	2
dd	Y	Opt	Y	Y	Y	Y	Y	7
delta	–	Opt	Opt	Y	–	–	–	3
deroff	–	–	Y	Y	Y	Y	Y	5
devnm	–	Opt	Dir	Y	–	–	–	3
df	–	Y	Y	Y	Y	Y	Y	6
diff	Y	Y	Y	Y	Y	Y	Y	7
diff3	–	–	Y	Y	Y	Y	Y	5
dircmp	–	Opt	Y	Y	–	–	–	3
dirname	Y	Y	Y	Y	–	–	Y	5
dis	–	Opt	Opt	–	–	–	–	2
dname	–	Opt	Y	–	–	–	–	2
dtoc	–	–	Y	Y	–	–	–	2
du	–	Y	Y	Y	Y	Y	Y	6
dump	–	–	–	Y	Y	Dir	–	3
echo	Y	BI	BI	Y	Y	Y	BI	7
ed	Y	Y	Y	Y	Y	Y	Y	7
edit	–	–	Y	–	–	Y	–	2
efl	–	–	–	Y	–	Y	–	2
egrep	–	Opt	Y	Y	Y	Y	Y	6
env	Y	Opt	Y	Y	–	–	Y	5
eqn	–	–	Opt	Y	Y	Y	–	4
eval	BI	BI	BI	BI	BI	BI	BI	7

Portability of UNIX System Shell Commands

CMD	P1003.2	SVID	SVR3	SIII	V7	4.2	MKS	COUNT
ex	–	Opt	Y	–	–	Y	–	3
exec	BI	BI	BI	BI	BI	BI	BI	7
exit	BI	BI	BI	BI	BI	BI	BI	7
expand	–	–	–	–	–	Y	Y	2
export	BI	BI	BI	BI	BI	BI	BI	7
expr	Y	Y	Y	Y	Y	Y	Y	7
f77	–	–	Opt	Y	Y	Y	–	4
factor	–	–	Y	Y	–	–	–	2
false	Y	Y	Y	Y	Y	Y	BI	7
fg	–	–	–	–	–	Opt	Y	2
fgrep	–	Opt	Y	Y	Y	Y	Y	6
file	–	Y	Y	Y	Y	Y	Y	6
find	Y	Y	Y	Y	Y	Y	Y	7
fmt	–	–	–	–	–	Y	Y	2
fold	Y	–	–	–	–	Y	Y	3
for	BI	BI	BI	BI	BI	BI	BI	7
fort77	Opt	–	–	–	–	–	–	1
fsck	–	Opt	Dir	Dir	–	Dir	–	4
fsdb	–	Opt	Dir	Dir	–	–	–	3
fumount	–	Opt	Y	–	–	–	–	2
function	BI	–	–	–	–	–	BI	2
fusage	–	Opt	Y	–	–	–	–	2
fuser	–	Opt	Dir	–	–	–	–	2
fwtmp	–	Opt	–	Y	–	–	–	2
ged	–	–	Y	Y	–	–	–	2
get	–	Opt	Opt	Y	–	–	–	3
getconf	Y	–	–	–	–	–	–	1
getopt	–	–	Y	Y	–	–	Y	3
getopts	Y	–	BI	–	–	–	–	2
getty	–	Opt	Dir	Dir	Dir	Dir	–	5
graph	–	–	Y	Y	Y	Y	–	4
graphics	–	–	Y	Y	–	–	–	2
greek	–	–	Y	Y	–	–	–	2
grep	Y	Y	Y	Y	Y	Y	–	6
grpck	–	Opt	Dir	Y	–	–	–	3
gutil	–	–	Y	Y	–	–	–	2
hash	–	BI	BI	–	–	–	–	2
head	Y	–	–	–	–	Y	Y	3
help	–	–	–	Y	–	–	Y	2
hexdump	Y	–	–	–	–	–	–	1
hp	–	–	Y	Y	–	–	–	2
icheck	–	–	–	–	Y	Dir	–	2
id	Y	Opt	Y	Y	–	–	–	4
idload	–	Opt	Y	–	–	–	–	2
if	BI	BI	BI	BI	BI	BI	BI	7
init	–	Opt	Dir	Dir	Dir	Dir	Y	6
install	–	–	Dir	Y	–	–	–	2
iostat	–	–	–	–	Y	Y	–	2
ipcrm	–	Opt	Y	–	–	–	–	2

Portability of UNIX System Shell Commands

CMD	P1003.2	SVID	SVR3	SIII	V7	4.2	MKS	COUNT
ipcs	–	Opt	Y	–	–	–	–	2
join	Y	Opt	Y	Y	Y	Y	Y	7
kill	Y	Y	Y	Y	Y	Y	Y	7
killall	–	Opt	Dir	–	–	–	–	2
labelit	–	Opt	Dir	Dir	–	–	–	3
ld	–	Opt	Opt	Y	Y	Y	–	5
lex	Opt	Opt	Opt	Y	Y	Y	–	6
line	–	Y	Y	Y	–	–	Y	4
link	–	Opt	Dir	Dir	–	–	–	3
lint	–	Opt	Opt	Y	Y	Y	–	5
ln	Y	Y	Y	Y	Y	Y	–	6
local	BI	–	–	–	–	–	–	1
locale	Y	–	–	–	–	–	–	1
localedef	Y	–	–	–	–	–	–	1
logger	Y	–	–	–	–	–	–	1
login	–	Opt	Y	Y	BI	BI	Y	6
logname	Y	Opt	Y	Y	–	–	–	4
look	–	–	–	–	Y	Y	–	2
lorder	–	Opt	Opt	Y	Y	Y	–	5
lp	Y	Opt	Y	–	–	–	–	3
lpd	–	–	–	Dir	Dir	Dir	–	3
lpr	–	–	–	Y	Y	Y	–	3
lpstat	–	–	Y	–	–	–	–	1
ls	Y	Y	Y	Y	Y	Y	Y	7
m4	–	Opt	Opt	Y	Y	Y	–	5
mail	–	Y	Y	Y	Y	Y	–	5
mailx	–	Opt	Y	–	–	mail	–	2
make	Opt	Opt	Opt	Y	Y	Y	–	6
makekey	–	–	Dir	Dir	Dir	Dir	–	4
man	–	–	–	Y	Y	Y	–	3
mesg	–	Opt	Y	Y	Y	Y	–	5
mkdir	Y	Y	Y	Y	Y	Y	Y	7
mkfifo	Y	–	–	–	–	–	–	1
mkfs	–	Opt	Dir	Dir	Dir	Dir	–	5
mknod	–	Opt	Dir	Dir	Dir	Dir	–	5
mount	–	Opt	Dir	Dir	Dir	Dir	–	5
mv	Y	Y	Y	Y	Y	Y	Y	7
mvdir	–	Opt	Dir	Dir	–	–	–	3
ncheck	–	Opt	Dir	Y	Y	Dir	–	5
neqn	–	–	Opt	Y	–	–	–	2
newgrp	–	Opt	BI	BI	BI	–	–	4
news	–	Opt	Y	Y	–	–	–	3
nice	–	Opt	Y	Y	Y	Y	–	5
nl	–	Y	Y	Y	–	–	Y	4
nm	–	Opt	Opt	Y	Y	Y	Y	6
nohup	Y	Y	Y	Y	Y	Y	BI	7
nroff	–	–	Opt	Y	Y	Y	–	4
nsquery	–	Opt	Y	–	–	–	–	2
od	–	Opt	Y	Y	Y	Y	Y	6

Portability of UNIX System Shell Commands

CMD	P1003.2	SVID	SVR3	SIII	V7	4.2	MKS	COUNT
pack	–	Y	Y	Y	–	–	Y	4
passwd	–	Opt	Y	Y	Y	Y	Y	6
paste	Y	Y	Y	Y	–	–	Y	5
pax	Y	–	–	–	–	–	–	1
pcat	–	Y	Y	Y	–	–	Y	4
pcc	–	–	–	Y	Y	–	–	2
pg	–	Opt	Y	–	–	–	Y	3
plot	–	–	–	–	Y	Y	–	2
pr	Y	Y	Y	Y	Y	Y	Y	7
prfdc	–	–	Dir	Dir	–	–	–	2
prfld	–	–	Dir	Dir	–	–	–	2
prfpr	–	–	Dir	Dir	–	–	–	2
prfsnap	–	–	Dir	Dir	–	–	–	2
prfstat	–	–	Dir	Dir	–	–	–	2
printf	Y	–	–	–	–	–	–	1
prof	–	Opt	Opt	Y	Y	Y	Y	6
prs	–	Opt	Opt	Y	–	–	–	3
ps	–	Y	Y	Y	Y	Y	Y	6
pstat	–	–	–	–	Y	Dir	–	2
ptx	–	–	–	Y	Y	Y	–	3
pwck	–	Opt	Dir	Y	–	–	–	3
pwd	Y	BI	BI	Y	Y	Y	BI	7
quot	–	–	–	–	Y	Dir	–	2
ratfor	–	–	–	Y	Y	Y	–	3
read	Y	BI	BI	BI	BI	BI	–	6
readonly	BI	BI	BI	BI	BI	BI	–	6
red	–	Y	Y	–	–	–	–	2
refer	–	–	–	–	Y	Y	–	2
regcmp	–	–	Opt	Y	–	–	–	2
restor	–	–	–	Y	Y	restore	–	2
return	BI	BI	BI	–	–	–	–	3
rev	–	–	–	–	Y	Y	Y	3
rfadmin	–	Opt	Y	–	–	–	–	2
rfpasswd	–	Opt	Y	–	–	–	–	2
rfstart	–	Opt	Y	–	–	–	–	2
rfstop	–	Opt	Y	–	–	–	–	2
rm	Y	Y	Y	Y	Y	Y	Y	7
rmail	–	Y	Y	Y	Y	Y	–	5
rmdel	–	Opt	Opt	Y	–	–	–	3
rmdir	Y	Y	Y	Y	Y	Y	Y	7
rmntstat	–	Opt	Y	–	–	–	–	2
rsh (net)	–	–	–	–	–	Y	–	1
rsh (sec)	–	Y	Y	Y	–	–	–	3
runacct	–	Opt	–	Y	–	–	–	2
sa	–	–	–	–	Y	Dir	–	2
sa1	–	Opt	Dir	–	–	–	–	2
sa2	–	Opt	Dir	–	–	–	–	2
sact	–	Opt	Opt	Y	–	–	–	3
sadc	–	Opt	Dir	–	–	–	–	2

Portability of UNIX System Shell Commands

CMD	P1003.2	SVID	SVR3	SIII	V7	4.2	MKS	COUNT
sadp	–	Opt	Y	–	–	–	–	2
sag	–	–	Y	Y	–	–	–	2
sar	–	Opt	Y	–	–	–	–	2
sccsdiff	–	–	Opt	Y	–	–	–	2
sdb	–	Opt	Opt	Y	Y	Y	–	5
sdiff	–	–	Y	Y	–	–	–	2
sed	Y	Y	Y	Y	Y	Y	Y	7
sendto	Y	–	–	–	–	–	–	1
set	BI	BI	BI	BI	BI	BI	BI	7
setmnt	–	Opt	Dir	Dir	–	–	–	3
sh	Y	Y	Y	Y	Y	Y	Y	7
shift	BI	BI	BI	BI	BI	BI	BI	7
shl	–	Opt	Y	–	–	–	–	2
shutdown	–	–	Dir	Dir	–	Dir	–	3
size	–	Opt	Opt	Y	Y	Y	Y	6
sleep	Y	Y	Y	Y	Y	Y	Y	7
sno	–	–	–	Y	Y	–	–	2
sort	Y	Y	Y	Y	Y	Y	Y	7
spell	–	Y	Y	Y	Y	Y	Y	6
spellin	–	–	Dir	Dir	Dir	Y	–	4
spellout	–	–	–	Dir	Dir	Y	–	3
spline	–	–	Y	Y	Y	Y	–	4
split	–	Y	Y	Y	Y	Y	Y	6
stat	–	–	Y	Y	–	–	–	2
strings	–	–	–	–	–	Y	Y	2
strip	Opt	Opt	Opt	Y	Y	Y	Y	7
struct	–	–	–	–	Y	Y	–	2
stty	Y	Opt	Y	Y	Y	Y	–	6
su	–	Opt	Y	Y	Y	Y	–	5
sum	–	Y	Y	Y	Y	Y	Y	6
sync	–	Opt	Y	Y	Y	Dir	Y	6
sysdef	–	Opt	Dir	Dir	–	–	–	3
tabs	–	Opt	Y	Y	Y	Y	–	5
tail	Y	Y	Y	Y	Y	Y	Y	7
tar	–	Opt	Dir	Y	Y	Y	–	5
tbl	–	–	Opt	Y	Y	Y	–	4
tc	–	–	–	Y	Y	Y	–	3
tee	Y	Y	Y	Y	Y	Y	Y	7
test	Y	BI	BI	BI	Y	Y	Y	7
tic	–	Opt	Y	–	–	–	–	2
time	–	Opt	Y	Y	Y	Y	Y	6
times	–	BI	BI	BI	BI	BI	–	5
timex	–	Opt	Y	Y	–	–	–	3
tk	–	–	–	–	Y	Y	–	2
touch	Y	Y	Y	Y	Y	Y	Y	7
tp	–	–	–	Y	Y	Y	–	3
tplot	–	–	Y	Y	–	–	–	2
tput	–	Opt	Y	–	–	–	–	2
tr	Y	Y	Y	Y	Y	Y	Y	7

Portability of UNIX System Shell Commands

CMD	P1003.2	SVID	SVR3	SIII	V7	4.2	MKS	COUNT
trap	BI	BI	BI	BI	BI	BI	–	6
troff	–	–	Opt	Y	Y	Y	–	4
true	Y	Y	Y	Y	Y	Y	BI	7
tsort	–	Opt	Opt	Y	Y	Y	–	5
ttoc	–	–	Y	Y	–	–	–	2
tty	Y	Opt	Y	Y	Y	Y	Y	7
type	–	BI	BI	–	–	–	BI	3
typo	–	–	–	Y	Y	–	–	2
ulimit	–	BI	BI	–	–	–	–	2
umask	Y	BI	BI	BI	BI	BI	–	6
umount	–	Opt	Dir	Dir	Dir	Dir	–	5
unadv	–	Opt	Y	–	–	–	–	2
uname	Y	Y	Y	Y	–	–	Y	5
unexpand	–	–	–	–	–	Y	Y	2
unget	–	Opt	Opt	Y	–	–	–	3
uniq	Y	Y	Y	Y	Y	Y	Y	7
units	–	–	Y	Y	Y	Y	–	4
unlink	–	Opt	Dir	Dir	–	–	–	3
unpack	–	Y	Y	Y	–	–	Y	4
unset	BI	BI	BI	–	–	–	BI	4
until	BI	BI	BI	BI	BI	BI	BI	7
update	–	–	–	–	Dir	Dir	–	2
uuclean	–	–	–	Y	–	Y	–	2
uucp	–	Opt	Y	Y	Y	Y	–	5
uulog	–	Opt	Y	Y	Y	Y	–	5
uuname	–	Opt	Y	Y	–	Y	–	4
uupick	–	Opt	Y	Y	–	–	–	3
uustat	–	Opt	Y	Y	–	–	–	3
uuto	–	Opt	Y	Y	–	–	–	3
uux	–	Opt	Y	Y	Y	Y	–	5
val	–	Opt	Opt	Y	–	–	–	3
vc	–	–	Opt	Y	–	–	–	2
vi	–	Opt	Y	–	–	Y	Y	4
volcopy	–	Opt	Dir	Dir	–	–	–	3
vpr	–	–	–	Y	Y	Y	–	3
vtoc	–	–	Y	Y	–	–	–	2
wait	Y	BI	BI	BI	BI	BI	–	6
wall	–	Opt	Dir	Dir	Y	Y	–	5
wc	Y	Y	Y	Y	Y	Y	Y	7
what	–	Opt	Opt	Y	–	Y	–	4
which	–	–	–	–	–	Y	Y	2
while	BI	BI	BI	BI	BI	BI	BI	7
who	–	Opt	Y	Y	Y	Y	Y	6
whodo	–	Opt	Dir	Dir	–	–	–	3
write	–	Opt	Y	Y	Y	Y	–	5
wtmpfix	–	Opt	–	Y	–	–	–	2
xargs	Y	Opt	Y	Y	–	–	–	4
yacc	Opt	Opt	Opt	Y	Y	Y	Y	7

INDEX